EARLY CHILDHOOD STUDIES

EARLY CHILDHOOD STUDIES

A MULTIDISCIPLINARY APPROACH

JENNY WILLAN

First published 2017 by
PALGRAVE

Palgrave in the UK is an imprint of Macmillan Publishers Limited, registered in England, company number 785998, of 4 Crinan Street, London, N1 9XW.

Palgrave® and Macmillan® are registered trademarks in the United States, the United Kingdom, Europe and other countries.

ISBN 978–1–137–27401–4 paperback

This book is printed on paper suitable for recycling and made from fully managed and sustained forest sources. Logging, pulping and manufacturing processes are expected to conform to the environmental regulations of the country of origin.

A catalogue record for this book is available from the British Library.

A catalog record for this book is available from the Library of Congress.

For Emma Gardner (1982–2016) and Mike, and their daughters Annabelle (b. 8/7/2012) and Alice (b. 22/4/2015)

Brief contents

Contents

List of Illustrations

Tables

Acknowledgements

I would like to thank former colleagues and students from Plymouth University and Somerset College of Arts and Technology for all the challenging and lively discussions about early childhood. Also Prossie Maraka and her children Brian, Josh and Patricia for allowing me to reproduce photographs (on p. 10 and 362). Thanks also to editor Lauren Zimmerman, and copyeditor Ryan Dunlop, and the team at Palgrave who provided astute criticism and advice, and to my children, Julia and Richard, for all they taught me about early childhood. Finally, I would like to thank my husband, Brian, for his unfailing support throughout the writing of this book.

Introduction

These are exciting times for Early Childhood Studies (ECS). Working with young children is enjoyable and rewarding - even more so when you have an insight into some of the history and theories that lie behind the practices that exist today. Over the past three decades, Early Childhood Studies has become a significant area of scholarship around the world as educationalists, health professionals, social scientists and policy makers have turned their attention to the lives of children in the years from birth to 8. They have concluded that early childhood really matters. There is a renewed focus on the ways in which we can support children and families in the present to lay the foundations for them to have fulfilling lives in the future.

ECS is made up of an eclectic mix of disciplines. We can think of it as being at the centre of a Venn diagram, crossing the boundaries into history, literature, art, philosophy, sociology, psychology, cultural studies and politics and it is for this reason that the book is sub-titled 'a multidisciplinary approach'. ECS will introduce you to ideas that explain how and why, at different times and in different places, adults choose very different ways to initiate and integrate their children into their particular community. In some societies boys and girls are prepared for different roles, in others gender is less deterministic; in some traditions children with disabilities are considered impossible to educate, in others they are supported to achieve and participate as far as they can; in some societies children may be seen but not heard, in others their opinions are actively sought and respected. ECS presents competing beliefs about children and childhood and challenges us to ask why these differences exist. Above all, it asks us to consider whether or not present early childhood practice is appropriate for a changing world.

Child study can trace its modern origins to the late nineteenth century. It began with the study of physical, intellectual and emotional development through investigations into patterns of growth from which norms could be established. Deviations from the norm were a cause for concern. Children were 'done unto' by adults, guided and moulded according to adult beliefs about what was best for particular groups of children. The Declaration of the Rights of the Child (1924 and 1959) which set out the legal requirements for the protection of children was replaced in 1989 by the United Nations Convention on the Rights of the Child which proposed that children should have the right to participate in society and to have their opinions taken seriously. Towards the end of the twentieth century, in the turmoil of civil rights movements that lobbied for equal treatment of all people regardless of gender, ethnicity, sexual orientation or ability, scholars began to realise that younger children were still being marginalised and silenced. By the dawn of the twenty-first century, early childhood had become recognised as an important area for investment amongst national and international policy makers in the belief that 'starting strong' is essential for every child. Money was allocated to meet the needs of pre-school children and with the money came calls for accountability, tighter controls and regulation.

Gradually, as the case for high quality education and care for pre-school children was made, there came a demand for the establishment of early learning goals which, in many countries, resulted in programmes designed to prepare children to be 'school-ready'. Alongside this development came a call for the professionalization of the children's workforce and the study of children and childhood was established in higher education courses, accompanied by a burgeoning of academic journals and research programmes in early education and care.

Although we may think that working with children is an essentially practical undertaking, the kinds of practical work we engage in is underpinned by our twenty-first century beliefs. Even within our own experience, we know that dominant beliefs about childcare and learning can change rapidly – grandmothers often have very different views on childcare practices and are not necessarily reticent in their criticism of modern practices! What adults believe is 'in the best interests of the child' changes with each generation and we are just part of that changing landscape – as practitioners our role is to develop our own philosophy of childhood and to reflect on everything we learn and to relate it to our direct interactions with children.

As Early Years practitioners, you will meet a wide and diverse community of children, parents and professionals but it is important to remember that your own way of viewing the world is only one amongst many. Cultivating a habit of reflection within an overall personal philosophy of care and respect for others is central to your work. The habit of reflection keeps us open to changing our own beliefs and to critically challenging and appraising the theories put forward by others. It allows us to cultivate empathy - to stand in other people's shoes and to see the world as they see it. We need to be able to look at our practice and to question it, not to merely follow what is already laid down. We might ask ourselves 'What does it feel like to hand over a child to a stranger on the first day of term? How do children feel about sitting on the floor while their teacher sits on a chair during carpet time? How would I feel if an adult spoke to me in the way that child was just addressed? How would my practice look to a visitor from overseas?' Asking questions and not being satisfied with easy answers is part of any academic study and this book seeks to reveal some of the areas of contention that abound in Early Childhood Studies.

Who is this book for?

The book is aimed primarily at students on degree courses in ECS at university or in further education. It will also be useful for students specialising in education in early years settings and primary schools or professionals already working in early childcare and education. It is designed to help tutors providing courses in ECS to give their students an overview of the field. Parents and general readers who want to know more about current trends in the early years Foundation Stage and Key Stage 1 classrooms will also will also find much of interest.

The book aims to increase knowledge and understanding of children and childhood while at the same time encouraging readers to take a critical stance towards the ideas presented – in other words to help students and practitioners to shed light on what they do and why they do it. Throughout is the belief that the child's voice, ignored for centuries, should be listened to. Adult society has a duty to support children's development in such a way as to maximise their chances of being happy, safe, respected and respectful, well-rounded individuals who can enjoy their childhoods positively and can, as they grow, contribute to their communities and to pass on their positivity to their own children.

Primarily, the book is intended to provide knowledge about children and childhood for people working with children and to inspire readers to find out more by following up questions posed in the text. The boxes, questions and suggestions for further study are designed to challenge pre-conceived ideas, to extend learning or to encourage critical evaluation of what is represented as relevant or effective amongst competing theories. The aim is to foster a reflective mind-set to prevent uncritical acceptance of every fad and fashion in Early Childhood Studies and to prompt thoughtful and confident practices based on respectful interaction with the people we call children.

The structure of the book

As ECS develops, contested areas emerge which echo the arguments going on in other academic disciplines. The book aims to explore the significant themes in Early Childhood Studies and to provide an overview of the current concerns occupying scholars in the subject.

There are seventeen chapters organised within six Parts:

1 Understanding Early Childhood Studies
2 Understanding Child Development: Supporting the Unique Child
3 In the Best Interests of the Child: Shaping Children's Lives
4 Children in Society: Every Child Matters
5 The Children's Workforce: Professional Practice
6 Research in Early Childhood: Seeing Children Differently

Part I, 'Understanding Early Childhood Studies', is concerned with the emergence of Early Childhood Studies as a conceptual and theoretical area of study around the world. It discusses how the significance of care and education of young children from 0-8 has emerged as an important area of concern for the twenty-first century.

Chapter 1, 'What is Early Childhood Studies?' considers why early childhood represents a special and important stage in the life-cycle and shows how different cultures and traditions embody different views of children and how these views shape the practice of parents and professionals. One area of twenty-first century debate is about how far children should have the right to participate in discussions about things that affect them and how far adults should decide what is best for them. Chapter 2, 'Early childhood in a global context', looks at how children, just like adults, are caught up in a culture of globalisation that has real implications for the way they live their lives. It explores the ways in which children are both beneficiaries and victims of global forces in economics, politics and communication. Chapter 3, 'Some theories of child development', takes an overview of the theories associated with the study of children that feed into our present-day understanding of how we think about children in terms of nature and nurture. The arguments about how we can best serve the needs of children to promote their present and future well-being is contested by each generation as new understandings develop.

Part II, 'Understanding Child Development: Supporting the Unique Child', recognises that children develop holistically. Although the traditional division between bodies and minds is artificial it is nonetheless convenient, for ease of reference, to organise the chapters under the headings of physical, intellectual, social and linguistic and emotional and moral development.

Chapter 4, 'Physical development—the interplay of body and brain', looks at the importance of good physical health before and after birth. It emphasises the importance of physical movement in the development of thinking skills and considers how parents and professionals can engage with children to promote learning through physical challenge. Chapter 5, 'Cognitive development', looks more closely at how children develop understanding and discusses some of the theories that have influenced the ways in which we conceptualise the process of learning. Chapter 6, 'Socialisation, language and play', considers how language grows out of physical social interactions from the earliest moments after birth. For young children play is an important part of socialising and learning language as they develop an increasingly sophisticated understanding of the social roles and rules governing their culture.

Chapter 7, 'Emotional and moral development', covers the ways in which love and attachment to others provides a secure foundation for individual emotional health and a growing understanding of the emotional needs of others. The chapter discusses how children learn to regulate their own emotions and to empathise with other people. It examines the ways in which adults can provide an ethos to promote self-regulation rather than relying on authoritarian interventions that take responsibility for behaviour away from the individual child.

Part III, 'In the Best Interests of the Child: Shaping Children's Lives', shows how the social context of children's worlds influences the way they develop. Chapter 8, 'Children and families in context', discusses the changing nature of modern families and the plurality of family forms in which children may live. Although the family remains the site for early socialisation, the wider world of peer groups, neighbourhoods, school and the media - including the internet - can challenge or reinforce family values while the wider worlds of politics, economics and culture can affect and change the way children live. The chapter examines how a new sociology of childhood has emerged to explore what it means to be a child today. Chapter 9, 'Representations of childhood' traces the way in which the history of childhood has often been a history of adults imposing their beliefs on children without stopping to ask what it feels like to be on the receiving end of their intentions. Poets, artists, philosophers and writers of every sort have left a treasure trove of evidence to show how at different times and in different places adults have sometimes glorified, sometimes vilified and sometimes sanctified the notion of childhood. This long history feeds our own understanding of childhood and shapes the way we treat children today. Chapter 10, 'Early education' provides a sketch of the main themes in current practice for early education. It covers the significant milestones in the development of a suitable curriculum over the past century and some of the programmes used in other countries. It looks at the development of parent partnerships, the role of the Key Person in professional settings, the importance of play and the transition from Foundation Stage to Key Stage 1 in the UK. Chapter 11, 'Early childhood social policy', looks broadly at the development of support systems for families and children from the Poor Laws to the welfare state. The philosophy of social support for vulnerable members of society divides between those who believe families should rely on their own efforts and resources and those who think society should help those in difficult circumstances. In countries where taxation is high, welfare provision tends to be high too. The belief that spending on welfare, health, protection and education for babies and infants and primary age children is the best guarantor of future individual and national prosperity and well-being is supported by evidence that children receiving high quality care and education build better relationships as adults, are more likely to be employed and less likely to be involved in crime when they grow up.

Part IV, 'Children in Society: Every Child Matters', considers the unique experiences of children as they navigate through a world of diversity – gender, income, ability, ethnicity and health. Chapter 12, 'Diversity and inclusion', focuses on how professionals can provide opportunities for respect and equality and can model the virtues themselves with children, parents and other professionals. It considers the delicate balance required in order to maintain respect for others' cultural traditions and beliefs while at the same time observing the tenets set out in human rights legislation. Chapter 13, 'Health and well-being' looks at how professionals can help families to provide the best start for children by encouraging healthy living. Disease prevention and health promotion are twin prongs in the battle to keep children healthy but even in a Welfare State there is still a social gradient of health outcomes, with the poorest and most deprived experiencing higher incidences of physical and mental ill-health. Fostering resilience by providing love and respect for each individual child can help to ameliorate the disadvantages of a poor or disrupted background and with the right support no child needs to be left behind.

Part V, 'The children's workforce: professional practice', looks at working in and managing children's sector settings. Chapter 14 'Professional practice for early childhood', considers the attributes required to become an effective professional in the early childcare and education sector and indicates some of the career paths and qualifications available. It provides case studies of various routes taken by students in early years. The role of a professional is complex and requires particular expertise in observation, assessment and planning and, because the sector is multi-professional, learning to work together with people from different disciplines and to communicate meaningfully across different agencies is an important part of the job. Chapter 15, 'Taking the lead in early years professional practice', looks at theories and models of leadership and considers which may be suitable in early years settings. Good communication, respect and a willingness to preserve confidentiality are important attributes but clear objectives, good planning, systematic monitoring of outcomes and a readiness to review practice are also pre-requisites for effective leadership. Delegating, cultivating assertiveness, managing conflict and maintaining a healthy work–life balance makes the role of leader more manageable.

Part VI, 'Research in Early Childhood: Seeing Children Differently' offers suggestions for delving into the child's own experience and seeing the world as they see it. Cultivating empathy is one way into understanding what it means to be a child in a given situation. Chapter 16, 'Understanding young children through observation and assessment' describes some of the techniques commonly used in gathering information about children in order to optimise their opportunities to make the most of their experience. The importance of listening cannot be over-emphasised – respecting and valuing children, observing the ethics of confidentiality and avoiding judgmental pronouncements underpin the best assessments and observations. Chapter 17, 'Doing early childhood research', sets out to give students a recipe for undertaking an extended project exploring some aspect of early childhood. It supplies a summary of the main types of research used in early years and alerts readers to some of the pitfalls. It also introduces the extensive literature available in this area.

The key message throughout the book is that, as someone working alongside children, you should be ethical in all your dealings with children, parents and colleagues by maintaining respect for their values while at the same time not compromising your own. The importance of early education and care in society has never been greater. The challenge for students and professionals in Early Childhood Studies is to remember this in the face of the economic, social and political realities that may take sudden and unforeseen turns in the future.

UNDERSTANDING EARLY CHILDHOOD STUDIES

What is Early Childhood Studies? 1

Introduction

Working with young children is great fun and very rewarding – every day can bring unexpected delights and unexpected challenges. Sometimes young children seem just like us; at other times they seem to live in their own different world. There are so many questions. When a newborn baby fixes his gaze on his mother's eyes, what does he see? When a one-year old offers a toy to a crying companion, is she showing empathy? Why do some children crawl and others shuffle? When a two-year-old hops around on all fours, declaring he is Peter Rabbit, does he really believe it? And how do children learn language so fast? Why do they have imaginary friends? What is the point of play? Should seven-year-olds still be playing make-believe? Are computer games bad for young children? Besides these questions about individual children, there are wider ones which ask how children fit into society. Where do parents' and children's rights begin and end? How far can the state intervene in family life? Who is responsible for safeguarding children at risk of harm? Should parents bear the full financial responsibility for their off-spring, or should the state provide support? These are just some of the questions you will address in this book. You will discover that, far from being straightforward, ideas and values about children and childhood are continually contested and differ according to contexts of time, place and culture.

Why study 'early' childhood?

When we talk about early childhood, we are generally referring to children from birth to age eight. Early Childhood Studies (ECS) is concerned with early childhood education and care (ECEC). There is a strong tradition that *early* childhood, as opposed to childhood generally, is a precious and special time in the lifecycle of a human being. We can see it in the Jesuit saying 'Give me the child until he is seven, and I will give you the man'. Influential European Enlightenment thinkers from the seventeenth and eighteenth centuries, like Comenius, Locke, Rousseau and Pestalozzi (you will meet them later in this book) all emphasised the importance of early experiences in the development of the adult. Early childhood was a common theme for the Romantic poets of the eighteenth century and early nineteenth century who believed that early influences provided the wellspring for creativity – Wordsworth famously wrote in his *Intimations of Immortality from Recollections of Early Childhood* 'The Child is Father of the Man'. Similarly, later in the nineteenth century, Dickens explored the effects of early childhood experiences in his novels *David Copperfield*, *Oliver Twist* and *Dombey and Son*. Contemporary autobiographies provide an insight into current attitudes to early childhood; 'misery memoirs' like *A Child Called It* and *Angela's Ashes* recall the crushing effects of deprivation and neglect, while autobiographies like *This Boy* and *I Know Why the Caged Bird Sings* celebrate childhood resilience in the face of adversity.

Even from our own personal observations, most of us would probably argue that there are valid reasons for defining the years from birth to eight as distinct from later childhood. Young children are *biologically* weaker and more dependent on adults for food, warmth and shelter; they are *socially* and *emotionally* immature and still need the reassurance of a carer; and they are *intellectually* challenged by things that adults take for granted. It is the stage when children are busy with the hard work of controlling their bodies and emotions, building relationships and discovering how the world works through their play and imagination.

Figure 1.1 The Maraka family enjoying a day out in Kampala, Uganda. Early childhood is a time for learning to control bodies and emotions, for building relationships and for play and imagination.
Source: Photo taken by Prossie Maraka, the children's mother.

Alison Gopnik, an influential psychologist and author of *The Philosophical Baby* (2009), provides a different kind of perspective on why the first eight years of a child's life are so important. She argues that a child is not a miniature, primitive adult but is a different form of *Homo sapiens*, just as the caterpillar is a different form of the adult butterfly. She suggests that children metamorphose from one stage to the other. In early childhood their complex minds, brains and consciousness are organised differently, more flexibly, in a way which is perfectly suited to their evolutionary phase of rapid learning and adaptation. The long period of infancy is essential to give the brain time to adapt to the infinitely different worlds that each individual is born into; a shorter period would reduce the development time for the brain and limit the possibilities for developing language and creativity. She points out that young children's behaviour is specially tailored to elicit love, warmth and protection from adults. Freed from the need to fend for themselves, they have the time and energy to devote to learning and imagining and creating. In the first three years, they need to learn so much: to communicate, to investigate, to crawl, to walk, to talk. All this learning takes a huge amount of time and effort, and the development of imagination and creativity requires space, tranquillity and freedom from want and worry if children are to realise their potential as human beings.

Time to reflect

How far do you think that early childhood is a special time in the life cycle?
Do you think adults and children (from birth to age eight) think in qualitatively different ways?

Studying early childhood

In Britain, childhood studies has its origins in the nineteenth century social reform movements and early twentieth century child study movements, which drew on medical science, welfare studies, psychology and psychiatry. For much of the second half of the twentieth century, the study of childhood became the domain of sociologists. Currently, childhood has come under the scrutiny of new disciplines, such as neuroscience (study of the brain) and epigenetics (how genes and environment interact).

In Britain, the first scientific studies of children began in Victorian times prompted by alarm about the poor condition of young men enlisting in the army, particularly at the time of the Anglo-Boer War of 1899–1902. The Childhood Society (1896–1907) carried out large-scale surveys of schoolchildren and found widespread evidence of stunted growth and limited mental capacity (Wooldridge, 1994). In the early twentieth century 1907 the Child Study Society carried out studies with individual children in an effort to find ways to improve matters. At the same time, various experimental schools sprang up in Europe and the United States to study children's 'natural' development in settings with constant access to the outdoors where they were given freedom to play and learn as they chose.

Early Childhood Studies, as a separate university level subject, is relatively new. Traditionally, it was a subsidiary subject within education or health and social care, but by the end of the twentieth century it had become a discrete subject in universities around the world, and a huge body of research now gives the subject a distinctive academic profile. Instead of being an add-on, it has now developed its own degree structure, leading to work in many sectors:

- the health sector (health visitors, dieticians, occupational therapists, physiotherapists, speech therapists, mental health workers, paediatricians);
- the education sector (nursery workers, teachers, educational psychologists, educational welfare officers);
- social services (social workers, care workers, childminders, foster carers, portage workers, early years staff);
- justice teams (support workers for the families of prisoners and those suffering domestic violence, police officers, probation teams, community support officers);
- housing, community and environment teams (housing officers, benefits staff, community workers, sport and leisure staff, faith-based workers);
- policy development (early years advisers, civil servants, managers in local education authorities, managers of early years settings and services);
- associated third-sector voluntary and charity work.

With such a variety of job opportunities, ECS typically draws on a whole range of academic disciplines to explore the multi-faceted worlds of children.

A multidisciplinary subject

Young children are a complex mixture of individual histories, abilities and inclinations, who are shaped and moulded by the social conditions and cultural norms of their environments. To understand what it means to be a child today, we need to take a multidisciplinary approach that allows us to study individual development in context, much as an ecologist studies a particular plant in relation to its whole ecosystem. In this book you will come across work by psychologists, sociologists, political scientists, lawyers, historians, cultural theorists and others, all working in different areas of early childhood.

Woodhead (in Qvortrup et al., 2011: p. 56) suggests rather mischievously that childhood studies curricula are characterised by a '*pick and mix*' quality. However, we can safely identify the following components as common to all ECS courses:

- history and philosophy of early childhood
- early years development
- early childhoods in context
- working with children
- policy and provision in the early years
- leading and managing in early childhood professions
- research with young children.

As well as drawing upon different disciplines, early childhood courses often identify broad themes like 'being a child today', 'early interventions' or 'inclusive practice'. Here you could expect to examine concepts from different theoretical perspectives and make judgements about the practical implications of each. For example, you might examine 'inclusive practice' and discover that in the past a hearing-impaired child would have been placed in a 'special school for the deaf' to take advantage of specialist help and expertise; today this child is more likely to be found in a mainstream school. Why has the change come about? The arguments are drawn from the disciplines of psychology, sociology, economics and law.

You will find that in many of the debates, there are no universally correct answers. However, a multidisciplinary analysis (which includes listening to the child's own views) can help professionals to understand the issues and in order to make more informed decisions.

'Early childhood' as a social construct

At the beginning of the chapter, we noted that early childhood generally refers to children from birth to age eight and that when we use the term *early childhood*, we assume that we are all talking about the same thing. However, notions of childhood are culturally subjective and vary according to contexts of time and place and belief. At various times children have been seen as both uncorrupted innocents in need of gentle nurturing or as wilful sinners in need of constant correction – 'spare the rod and spoil the child' was once a popular justification for corrective physical punishment. Sociologists Prout and James (1997: p. 8) point out that childhood is a social construction that is in constant flux – although children are seen as *biologically* immature in all societies, expectations about their roles and capabilities differ according to their culture. For example, in nomadic societies a seven-year-old may have a responsible, economic role as a productive worker tending sheep, but in Western cultures most seven-year-olds are financially dependent and expected to be in school under the close supervision of adults.

There are an infinite number of childhoods variously constructed through gender, class, ethnicity, family, status, language, wealth, location and social and political environments. Think, for example, about the different childhoods of a child born under the 'one child' policy in China and a child born into a large family in a *favela* (slum) in Brazil. Or look at paintings or old photographs, to see how boys and girls, wealthy and poor, country child and city child were differently understood in the past. In our own times, Western childhoods have become more private, and we no longer see groups of children playing outside in the streets because traffic, fears of 'stranger danger' and the lure of electronic games have driven childhood indoors so that for the most part children live under the constant surveillance of adults. These changes have reconstructed childhood and altered our understanding of what a 'normal' childhood looks like today.

> ### *Focus on* Preschool in three cultures – different cultural traditions
>
> Given the assumption that all three- and four-year-olds have similar needs, abilities and interests, we might expect that pre-schools around the world would be rather similar. But in a famous extended study comparing three pre-schools in Japan, China and the US, James Tobin and his colleagues (1989), uncovered some surprising cultural differences.
>
> Tobin et al. filmed activities in preschool classrooms across all three countries and then showed the recordings to preschool staff, parents and child development experts asking them to comment on their own and each other's pre-schools. This led to discussions about different adult expectations about children's freedom of choice, conformity, creativity and discipline in the three countries. Some of the most interesting differences of opinion arose when video sequences showed behaviour that violated traditional cultural norms.

For example, Americans were uncomfortable when they saw Japanese children squabbling violently while their teachers chose to ignore the behaviour. The Americans argued that teachers had a responsibility to maintain order and discipline and should have intervened so no one got hurt. But the Japanese teachers expressed surprise – they argued that children should police themselves because group peer pressure is a more sensitive tool for discipline than adult intervention. In addition, they believed they had a duty to protect children from the greater shame and humiliation of being singled out for reprimand by an adult. They explained that Japanese children are given every opportunity to remain in the group, even when their behaviour is disruptive, because it is thought that isolation from the social group causes psychological harm. This belief that children should be spared shame is deeply embedded in Japanese culture.

In another example, both American and Japanese observers were uncomfortable when they watched a Chinese child telling a story to his class and then being subjected to intense criticism from classmates. The teacher encouraged the other children to point out errors and weaknesses in the narrative and in the child's performance. At the end of the session, the class was asked to vote on whether the storyteller deserved the accolade 'Story Teller King'. The children voted 24 for and 18 against! American and Japanese observers worried that such criticism could undermine the self-esteem of the storyteller but the Chinese preschool teachers explained that collective criticism was a traditional part of learning to be a storyteller and was an essential component of helping children to improve their skills.

Preschool in three cultures demonstrates different attitudes towards teaching and learning in different cultures. Tobin repeated the study 20 years later (*Preschool in Three Cultures Revisited*, 2009) to find out whether globalisation had had any impact on traditional cultural expectations about children, education and care since the first study. The answer seemed to be 'no'; the authors concluded that cultural differences are remarkably persistent even when ideas and practices from other countries are shared and incorporated.

How far should non-Western early years practitioners be concerned about cultural homogenisation through the spread of Western ideas about raising children?

A child-centred model of ECEC

As you work through this book, you will find that even within the same culture there are tensions between conflicting adult beliefs about how best to raise children.

One particularly Western twenty-first-century debate concerns 'child-centred practice'. Child-centred practice generally refers to contexts where children are encouraged to make their own democratic choices and to voice their preferences without undue adult intrusion and direction. For example, in family casework, health and social care professionals are advised to consult children directly about the particular problem rather than relying solely on parents' accounts. In schools and nurseries, this debate about child-centred practice often crystallises around the provision of self-directed and play-based learning as opposed to teacher-directed formal learning.

In the early twentieth century, educationalists like Maria Montessori in Italy, John Dewey in the United States and Susan Isaacs in Britain argued that *play is the work of childhood* and the driving force for learning, socialisation and creativity. They placed more importance on child-led learning than on adult-led teaching in the belief that young children should be free to choose for themselves the manner and pace of their play and learning. This child-centred philosophy was tested in *experimental schools* like Susan Isaacs' Malting House School, A.S. Neill's Summerhill School and Bertrand Russell's Beacon Hill School, in all of which children were encouraged to develop 'naturally' through play and to learn through their own discoveries and awakening interests (Selleck, 1972). Current practice in early childhood education treads a fine line between demands for teacher-led learning regimes and demands for exploration and discovery through self-directed play.

Focus on *Child-centred practice at the Malting House School*

In the early part of the twentieth century, experimental schools were set up in reaction to the harsh discipline, rote learning and sedentary style of instruction available in traditional schools. One of these experimental schools, The Malting House School in Cambridge (1924–1927), was run by Susan Isaacs, who later became director of the first University Department of Child Development in Britain. Her aim was to study, through observation, the natural development of children.

The Malting House School catered for children aged around three to seven. It consisted of a large house with extensive gardens, and there were no formal classrooms. Children had small plots for gardening and free access to climbing frames, scientific apparatus, dressing-up clothes, books, art and craft materials, a typewriter, a gramophone and a piano. There were small animals in hutches and dogs and cats wandering freely. Adults were on hand to answer questions and to help when required. At the same time, the adults observed the children closely and made notes on how they played, how they coped with emotional upsets and social relations, how they grappled with intellectual problems and how they dealt with moral and spiritual questions.

Isaacs was influenced by the work of the educationalists Froebel, Dewey and Montessori, who all advocated active, play-based, child-centred learning built on children's natural curiosity and their desire to engage physically with the world around them. To this she added opportunities for fantasy play and role play. In fantasy, children could act out their own fears and aspirations; in role play they could transcend the boundaries of time and space and try out situations not available to them in the real world.

The children were free to choose their activities and to play in their own way. Isaacs famously wrote that 'Play is indeed the child's work, and the means whereby he grows and develops' (1929: p. 9). Children were encouraged to have lots of physical exercise, to practise physical skills, to dance and to sing. Stories, dramatic play and spontaneous make-believe took up much of their time. They did handwork and drawing and painting. They spent time in the garden tending their plants and caring for the animals. Their scientific interests grew out of their curiosity about everyday events in the natural world around them – including, on one occasion, dissecting Mrs Isaacs' dead cat. They played with sharp knives and carpentry tools and used matches to make fires. Children were also offered reading and writing materials and number and geometry activities. The emphasis was on providing opportunities for creative activity and learning by doing.

The days were spent in active social companionship with other children. Verbal and physical disputes were discouraged, but there was none of the harsh discipline commonly meted out in traditional schools; instead, children were asked to think about the effects of their behaviour on others. Children were treated affectionately and given a sense of security by relating to a key member of staff who was under instruction to apply only mild, steady control through positive alternatives rather than negative injunctions.

Isaacs wanted her staff, and later her students, to have a wide and deep general knowledge of young children's mental, physical, social, emotional and spiritual development so that they could learn to adapt to the particular needs of each child in their care. This knowledge, she believed, came most directly and memorably through observing and reflecting on children at play. The observational methods she devised, with strict rules about writing down only what is seen and heard and avoiding all judgemental language, provide the templates for the observations practitioners carry out today.

Think about your own experiences of early years settings. How far would you describe them as child centred?

This debate about child-centred and adult-led practice is very much alive today among health, welfare and education professionals. When, for instance, should young children be given a say in their own medical care pathways? When are they competent enough to express their wishes in cases of family breakdown? Who should decide when they are 'ready' to move from play-based learning to formal instruction? The debate is a global one; in early education circles around the world, more and more countries are adopting Western-style national policy frameworks with core curricula for educating young children. The structured curriculum goals set out in the policies seem to go against the spirit of a 'child-centred' philosophy of free choice and play, and many professionals are concerned that children have fewer opportunities to pursue their own interests, at their own pace.

Studying early childhood

Sociologist Mary Jane Kehily (2004) offers three broad approaches to the study of children and childhood:

- *Historical perspectives* examine past childhoods in order to illuminate our present understandings of, for example, child labour, children's literature, children and advertising, media images of children, institutional care, gender, ethnicity and (dis)ability. These perspectives help us to uncover the contingent nature of our socially constructed definitions of childhood.
- *Sociocultural perspectives* unpick the language (or *discourse*) we use in relation to children and childhood to reveal the realities and distortions, habitual beliefs and dominant values we hold unconsciously about adult/child roles and relationships,.
- *Policy perspectives* unravel government policies that impact on children to discover what might be the intended and unintended outcomes.

These three approaches provide a framework for examining how children and childhood are understood.

Historical approaches

We can get an insight into children today by looking at children from the past – what is different, what remains the same? We could start our history of childhood by asking parents and grandparents about their lives, or by visiting a museum of childhood. Toys and books and pictures can tell us a great deal about children's lives; for example, in Brueghel's famous painting *Children's Games* (1560) it is difficult to see whether the playmates are adults or children. Why might that be? Or we might look at the emigrant family in the painting *The Last of England* (1852) by Ford Maddox Brown and ask how it compares with contemporary images of migrants or refugees on our television screens today. Do we feel the same sympathy for the families in both?

Literature provides another good source. For example, we might compare *Tom and Lucy* by Shirley Hughes with *The History of the Fairchild Family* by Mary Martha Sherwood and ask ourselves why stories for children have changed so much. Or we might look at the social conditions in Victorian Britain through the works of Elizabeth Gaskell or Charles Dickens or George Eliot. Or compare the lives of the industrial poor in William Blake's poems *Songs of Innocence and Experience* with the Romantic ideal of childhood presented by the poets Wordsworth and Coleridge.

Sociohistorical documents like *London Labour and the London Poor* by Henry Mayhew (1862) are rich in detail – we might reflect on his description of the life of a child crossing sweeper in Industrial England and compare it with the life of a child scavenger in present day Bangladesh. What issues are raised about the morality and economics of child labour? Or we might look at some surveys of infant mortality, past and present. Are rates rising or falling around the world? What seem to be the greatest risks to infants and babies now, are they different from the risks of the past?

Sociocultural approaches

Sociocultural theories offer explanations about the way in which wider social and environmental factors like family values, media, language, culture and power relations affect our understanding of children.

We can get a feel for sociocultural theories by analysing the language and pictures in newspaper reports involving children. Are the children seen as 'little angels' or 'little devils'? Are they described as 'victims' or as resilient 'captains of their fate'? Or you could compare the attitudes in parenting books past and present. For example, Dr Truby King (1858–1938), a leading New Zealand child 'expert' during the inter-war years, instructed parents to go by the

Figure 1.2 The Malting House School building in Cambridge

Source: Keith Edkins and licensed for reuse under this Creative Commons Licence: http://creativecommons.org/licenses/by-sa/2.0/

clock, offering strict four hourly feeds to babies, enforcing routines and training for toddlers, setting a daily limit of ten minutes for cuddles, and applying strict discipline for misdemeanours. Later, Benjamin Spock (1903–1998), an American child expert popular in the sixties, advocated a relaxed approach to childcare and told parents to go with the flow, adapting their child-rearing to suit the individual characters of their children and, most importantly, to provide love, security and understanding. In the 1970s and 1980s, Penelope Leach, a British child expert, advised parents to be child centred: to put their own needs on hold and to focus on bringing up baby.

Time to reflect

Review the child-rearing advice currently offered by television and newspaper child 'experts'.
What advice is given?
What sort of language is used?
Can you discover any underlying sociocultural beliefs about the nature of children and child-hood today?

Policy approaches

Policies, in a general sense, are plans of action – they might be developed by individuals, groups, businesses or governments. They arise out of the recognition that there is an issue to be addressed, 'something needs to be done'. Policies set out *intentions*, providing a framework for making and monitoring 'improvements'. At a local level these may take the form of guidelines for practitioners, parents and children; at a national level they may provide the basis for legislation. By looking at the way policy and legislation is framed (*the language of discourse*), we can glean a great deal about how children are perceived and valued in society. Policy analysis can provide a useful method for researching the underlying themes and trends in early education and care.

We can illustrate this by thinking about the evolution of children's rights legislation and thinking about the discourses framing it at different points in its development. Look, for example, at *The Geneva Declaration of the Rights of the Child*, issued by the League of Nations in 1924, the earliest of its kind. Children were primarily regarded as being their parents' 'possessions' and what went on in the privacy of the home went unaddressed. After the Second World War, a different discourse about children emerged, one that recognised that not all parents acted in the best interests of their children. In 1959, the United Nations extended the Declaration to include a right of protection from parents and neglectful circumstances. But the emphasis was still on protection. It would be another 30 years before children across the world had the same rights to self-realisation as other human beings. In 1989, the United Nations Convention on the Rights of the Child (UN, 1989) included the right for children to participate, placing an obligation on adults to consult them on issues directly affecting them.

Case study: What makes a good foster carer?

This case study is about a couple who wanted to foster a child. Changing discourses about a parent's right to use physical punishment put them on a collision course with their social work team.

In 2008 the couple's biological daughter Emma, aged eight, denied writing rude words in a note that her mother found in her bedroom. Two young boys had been visiting Emma and she put the blame on them. When her lie was exposed, she was given a light smack on the leg. This was an infrequent form of punishment for Emma and she cried. Later mother, father and child had a loving cuddle.

Asked whether she had been badly treated, Emma later said, 'No, I told a lie, and it was a fair punishment'. 'It's such a rare event to have to smack Emma', said her mother, 47, a special needs adviser who had just been offered a job as a primary school teacher. 'We would only smack her as a very last resort or perhaps in haste if she was doing something that put her in immediate danger. And we know she understands that chastising her in that way is done within the context of a loving relationship.' Asked if they would ever smack anyone else's child, the parents said, 'Definitely, definitely not.'

Emma's parents wanted to be foster parents following the stillbirth of their baby three years before. It was unlikely that they could conceive again. They had completed exhaustive observations and interviews with social service personnel and had the backing of their caseworker. The local council's guidelines for prospective foster parents state that parents should not 'administer corporal punishment to any child or young person placed with you'.

When their application to be foster parents was assessed, the smacking incident was discussed. The parents agreed that they would not administer physical punishment to a foster child but argued strongly that they should retain the right to smack their *own* child occasionally. When the panel asked them to reconsider, they refused.

The couple were turned down with the following explanation: 'Although the panel felt you are experienced parents with a lot of competence and skills, they feel your approach to behaviour management could have an impact on foster children placed. And they have concerns around your ability to work with the department.'

The father said, 'We have been portrayed as bad parents, made to feel as though we are criminals. Yet the law in this country is on our side. Corporal punishment, as long as it is mild, and causes no injury, is perfectly legal'.

(Adapted from a newspaper report in *The Telegraph*, 13 April 2008)

Discussion questions

Do you think the fostering panel was right to turn the couple down?
Is the father right to say that mild corporal punishment is legal?
Can you tease out the underlying rights discourses behind the two positions taken by social services and the parents?

The voice of the child

One of the notable changes in twenty-first-century attitudes to young children in the West is the emphasis now put on listening to their concerns and enabling them to participate in decisions. In the past, professionals were advocates for children, making decisions on their behalf and conferring with parents about them rather than talking directly to the children themselves. The concern with 'voice' and 'participation' has arisen out of two changes in the way we understand childhood.

The first change comes out of a commitment to human rights. Respect for the dignity of the child is at the very heart of the UNCRC (United Nations Convention on the Rights of the Child) (1989) and all signatory states undertake to respect children and to protect their rights irrespective of 'race, colour, sex, language, religion, political or other opinion, national, ethnic or social origin, property, disability or other status' (Article 2, paragraph 1). This ethic has been incorporated into UK policy in documents such as *Every Child Matters* (DfES: 2003) and the Children Act 2004, which underpin work with children.

Secondly, change has grown out of debates in the sociology of childhood, where the sophistication of children's capacity to understand and engage with the world provides evidence that even very young children are capable of independent thought and can make insightful contributions. Qvortrup (1994: p. 4) argues that children should not be regarded as 'deficit' adults or incomplete '*human becomings*' but rather as '*human beings*'. This conviction shifts the paradigm such that rather than thinking of children as passive recipients, we come to see them as active agents, people with a point of view which may be different from our own but which has its own validity.

The reality of participation for children under eight isn't always evident and many people still think that consulting children is misguided and undermines the authority of adults (Alderson: 2001).

Time to reflect

What is the difference between seeing children as *human becomings* and *human beings*? How might these different ways of seeing affect the way professionals work with children?

Children as participants

David Kennedy (2006) argues that, in the past, children were viewed from an adult perspective and that this perspective skewed the way in which people conducted research related to children. He argues that the objectifying gaze of the research scientist, peering down from on high, provides only an adult view of children's worlds. He suggests that we should do studies *with* children, not *on* them. Involving children and really listening to what they have to say provides a richer, more textured account which may overturn adults' preconceived notions about what children are capable of doing and thinking.

Currently, researchers in childhood studies are exploring different ways of involving children in consultations with adults (Fraser et al., 2004; Mukherji & Albon, 2010; MacNaughton et al., 2011; Clark & Moss, 2011). It requires high levels of skill and creativity to engage in meaningful research with young children, and the ethical guidelines for participation are strict. When children directly participate in, and comment on, research that involves them, their engagement changes the way adults see them. When we listen to children, we recognise them as human beings with rights, as individuals who have a valid point of view. Consider the life of Malala Yousafzai, who voiced the feelings of her generation. From early childhood, she knew that, as a girl, she was privileged to receive an education in her home country of Pakistan. Aged 11, she produced an anonymous diary piece for BBC Urdu, explaining how it felt to go to school in a country where girls' education is considered a dangerous threat to the traditional view that girls and women should remain silent and hidden from view. The broadcast of her diary struck at the heart of the patriarchal and religious ideology of local Taliban conservatives.

Four years later, in an attempt to bring her campaign for girls' education to an end, a Taliban gunman shot her as she travelled home on the school bus. She was brought to Britain with her family and slowly recovered. Now, she travels the world, carrying her message for girls' education to a global audience. Her face and ideas are familiar to millions of people. Malala was an older child, and this is a dramatic example of a child exerting her right to participate in her country's debate.

Less dramatically, my own town council wanted to make a piece of derelict land into a playground for children under eight. They asked children to provide drawings and photographs of things they would like to feature and invited them along to a meeting to discuss the architect's draft plans. The adults had in mind a green space dotted with play equipment, picnic tables and shrubs. The younger children asked for a tarmac path around the perimeter where they could ride their tricycles and scooters. A group of older boys wanted dirt humps that they could use for mountain biking. The planners incorporated their ideas, and the space is now well used and offers a range of activities for families with children of different ages.

These ideas about 'voice' and participation – listening, respecting and responding to children – are central to the ethical practices of childcare professionals, and finding ways to facilitate it is a major question in Early Childhood Studies.

The future of ECEC

Reviews of scientific research worldwide provide strong evidence that good-quality support in the early years helps to raise health, education and welfare standards across the board and in particular for children suffering the worst effects of poverty and deprivation (Field, 2010; Allen, 2011; Tickell, 2011; ILO, 2012). The reviews cite recent work in neuroscience that show that the development of the brain is most rapid during the period of conception to three years old and also refer to evidence from epigenetics suggesting that physical, emotional, social and intellectual deprivation during these critical years produces long-lasting negative physical and mental feedback effects in young children.

A commitment to early years care and education is now a major part of government policy in Britain and elsewhere as nations try to improve the health and wealth of their citizens. In 1990 UNESCO (the United Nations Education, Scientific and Culture Organization) declared that 'Learning begins at birth' and that early childhood education and care is the right of every child on the planet (World Declaration on Education For All (EFA) UNESCO, 1990). This cultural shift, called 'the childcare transition' by the UN agencies (UNICEF, 2008), has been characterised among wealthier nations by increasing provision of preschool care so that many young children are now spending more of their time in some form of professional care. But in poorer countries, the introduction of ECEC has been much slower (UNESCO, 2007) because high infant mortality, poor infant and child health, poverty, lack of safe childminding environments and competing demands for basic primary education are more urgent.

As you can see, it is an exciting time to be studying ECEC! New research is expanding our understanding of what young children can do while the human rights agenda is altering the relationships between children and adults in new and unexpected ways. You, of course, are an important part of the process of the education and care of the next generations of young children.

Summary

- Early childhood covers the age range of birth to eight years old.
- Early childhood is a relatively new area of study as a specialist subject.
- It is a multidisciplinary subject that provides a foundation for professional work with children in health, social care and education; it draws on academic studies in child development, psychology, sociology, policy studies, law, medicine, history, art and literature; the history of ECEC over the past 300 years is one of increasing children's rights.
- Childhood is not a fixed entity; it is a 'social construction' which is continually reconstructed by adults and children according to time, place and culture.
- Children are *human beings* rather than *human becomings*: their own concerns in the here and now are just as important as adults' concerns to prepare them for their futures.
- Under the UNCRC, there is a recognition that children have a right to have their say; children have a right to be heard and to participate in matters that directly concern them; learning to listen to children is a central part of every early childhood professional's role.

Topics for further discussion

1 Consider some popular television programmes for young children. What can they tell you about current beliefs about children and childhood? Were any children consulted during the making of the programmes?
2 Think about your own beliefs about children's learning. What do you understand by 'child-centred, play-based learning'?
3 Is there any place for bricks, sandpits and dolls for children growing up in an electronic age?

Assignments

1 Watch the *Secret Life of Babies* (ITV, 2013 and 2014). What does it tell you about the first three years of life?
2 Find out what journals are available in the area of early childhood and childhood. Look at some recent issues. Make a list of current 'hot topics'.
3 Spend ten minutes observing the behaviour of adults with young children in public spaces. Share your observations with colleagues. What can you learn from your observations about the range of contemporary attitudes towards children?
4 Find out about the current children's minister and the children's commissioner. What are their key policy objectives in relation to early years?

Further reading

Cunningham, H. (2006) *The Invention of Childhood*. London: BBC Books. This provides a good introduction to the history of childhood. It also has some lovely pictures and is accompanied by a CD.

Faulkner, D. and Coates, E. (2013) Early Childhood policy and practice in England: twenty years of change. *International Journal of Early Years Education* 21(2–3): 244–263. http://dx.doi.org/10.1080/09669760.2013.832945. This will give you an overview of recent changes.

Qvortrup, J., Corsaro.W. and Honig, M.S. (eds) (2011) *The Palgrave Handbook of Childhood Studies*. Basingstoke: Palgrave Macmillan. This provides scholarly articles on all aspects of twenty-first-century childhood studies.

Useful websites

The Effective Provision of Pre-school Education (EPPE) provides systematic reviews of international child research drawn from papers in health, education and social care that can be accessed at the EPPI-Centre Evidence Library (http://eppi.ioe.ac.uk/) based at the Institute of Education in London.

UNESCO (United Nations Educational, Scientific and Cultural Organisation) produces annual *Global Monitoring Reports* (http://unesdoc.unesco.org.) about the state of early childhood care and education around the globe.

OECD (Organisation for Economic Co-operation and Development) provides information on Early Childhood Education and Care around the world through its *Starting Strong* series.

References

Alderson, P. (2001) *Young Children's Rights: Exploring Beliefs, Principles and Practice*. London: Save the Children

Allen, G. (2011) 'Early Intervention: The Next Steps', in *The Allen Report*. London: The Cabinet Office

Child Poverty Review (2004). London: HM Treasury

Children Act (2004) http://www.legislation.gov.uk/ukpga/2004/31/contents

Clark, A. and Moss, P. (2011) *Listening to Young Children: The Mosaic approach* (2nd edn). London: National Children's Bureau

DfES (Department for Education and Skills) (2003) *Every Child Matters*. London: DfES

Field, F. (2010) 'The Foundation Years: Preventing Poor Children Becoming Poor Adults', *The Field Report*. London: Cabinet Office

Fraser, S., Lewis, V., Ding, S., Kellert, M. and Robinson, C. (2004) *Doing Research with Children and Young People*. London: Sage Publications

Gopnik, A. (2009) *The Philosophical Baby*. London: Bodley Head

Hadow Committee (1933) Board of Education Report of the Consultative Committee on Infant and Nursery Schools (The Hadow Report). London: HMSO

ILO (International Labor Organization) (2012) *Right Beginnings: Early Childhood Education and Educators*. Global Dialogue Forum on Conditions of Personnel in Early Childhood Education, Geneva, 22–23 February 2012, International Labour Office, Sectoral Activities Department: Geneva. http://www.fruehe-chancen.de/fileadmin/PDF/Archiv/ilo_2012_right_beginnings_ecec.pdf

Kehily, M.J. (ed.) (2004) *An Introduction To Childhood Studies*. Maidenhead: Open University Press

Kennedy, D. (2006) *The Well of Being: Childhood, Subjectivity, and Education*. Albany, NY: SUNY Press

MacNaughton, G., Rolfe, S.A. and Siraj-Blatchford (eds) (2010) *Doing Early Childhood Research: International Perspectives on Theory and Practice* (2nd edn). Maidenhead: Open University Press

Mayhew, H. (2010 edn) *London Labour and the London Poor*. Oxford: Oxford University Press

Mukherji, P. and Albon, D. (2010) *Research Methods in Early Childhood: An Introductory Guide*. London: Sage

Pascal, C. and Bertram, T. (2000) OECD Country Note: Early Childhood Education and Care Policy in the United Kingdom. http://www.oecd.org/unitedkingdom/2535034.pdf. Accessed 24 June 2014

Prout, A. and James, A. (1997) 'A New Paradigm for the Sociology of Childhood? Provenance, Promise and Problems', in A. James and A. Prout (eds) *Constructing and Re-constructing Childhood* (2nd edn) (pp. 7–34). London: Routledge Falmer

Qvortrup, J., Bardy, M., Sgritta, G.B and Wintersberger, H. (eds) (1994) *Childhood Matters: Social Theory, Practice and Politics*. Aldershot: Avebury

Qvortrup, J., Corsaro, W. and Honig, M.S. (2011) 'Introduction: Why Social Studies of Childhood? An Introduction to the Handbook', in *The Palgrave Handbook of Childhood Studies* (pp. 1–18). Basingstoke: Palgrave Macmillan

Selleck, R.J.W. (1972) *English Primary Schools and the Progressives 1914–1939*. London: Routledge

Tickell, C. (2011) The Early Years: Foundations for Life, Health and Learning. *The Tickell Review*. www.education.gov.uk/tickellreview

Tobin, J., Hsueh, Y., Karasawa, M. (2009) *Pre-school in Three Cultures Re-visited*. Chicago, IL: University of Chicago Press

Tobin, J., Wu, D.Y.H. and Davidson, D.H. (1989) *Pre-school in Three Cultures: Japan, China and the United States*. Newhaven, CT: Yale University Press

UN (1989) *UN Convention on the Rights of the Child*. http://www.unicef.org.uk/Documents/Publication-pdfs/UNCRC_PRESS200910web.pdf

UNESCO (1990) 'World Declaration on Education For All' (EFA). *Jomtien Declaration*. http://unesdoc.unesco.org/images/0012/001275/127583e.pdf. Accessed 26 December 2016

UNESCO (2007) *Strong Foundations: Early childhood care and education* (Education For All, Global Monitoring Report 2007). Paris: UNESCO Publishing

UNICEF (2008) *The State of the World's Children 2008: Child Survival*. http://www.unicef.org/sowc08/. Accessed 26 December 2016

Woodhead, M. (2011) 'Child Development and the Development of Childhood' in J.W. Corsaro and M.-S. Honig (eds) (2011) *The Palgrave Handbook of Childhood Studies* (pp. 46–61). Basingstoke: Palgrave Macmillan

Wooldridge, A. (1994) *Measuring the Mind: Education and psychology in England, c. 1860-c.1990*. Cambridge: Cambridge University Press

Early childhood in a global context

Introduction

Early childhood education and care does not take place in isolation; it is part of a larger movement concerned with improving the lives of all young children around the globe. One of the pleasures and challenges of working in ECEC is meeting families and children from a wide variety of backgrounds and ethnicities; this is a sign of the 'global' times we live in. Previous generations grew up in largely monocultural nation states, but since the 1960s the world has witnessed complicated migration patterns prompted by economic, social and political pressures. You may become part of this migration yourself, perhaps working abroad in the future, or perhaps you already are; but even if you stay in the country of your birth, you will meet children from many different cultures, part of a modern 'global' movement of people. The movement is both physical and cultural; products, processes and ideas all spread rapidly around the world through electronic media, and no adult or child on the planet is unaffected. These global trends provide the macro-context for Early Childhood Studies, and their effects filter down to local workplaces, raising all sorts of issues for early childhood specialists.

Time to reflect

Inward and outward migration has become a global phenomenon over the past half century as people follow jobs or flee from war or persecution. Migration brings together different cultural attitudes and beliefs, sometimes in challenging ways. One visible difference lies in the clothes people choose to wear.

Think about dress codes in a professional early childhood setting.
How comfortable would you feel working alongside someone who

a) reveals her cleavage,
b) keeps her face hidden behind a veil,
c) displays his underwear above low slung trousers?

Discuss this with colleagues. Is there any consensus about appropriate dress for ECEC professionals? How far should professional settings respect individual choice? Would it be helpful to have a clear dress code for everyone? What would be the underlying principles of such a dress code?
How should we accommodate different dress codes in a multicultural society?

Note that when we talk about global issues, there is some debate about the best way to distinguish between the prosperous world and the less prosperous world. Some people prefer to use the terms Global North and Global South; others use developed and less developed; others use the West and Third World; and yet others refer to minority world (rich) and majority world (poor). Since the balance of power and prosperity is continually shifting from one part of the globe to another, I have elected to use whatever fits most naturally in the context.

A global village

Marshall McLuhan, a Canadian sociologist and philosopher, coined the term 'global village' in the 1960s to describe how the world was shrinking as news and information spread rapidly to even the remotest regions through radio, film and television (McLuhan, 1964). Globalisation is the term

Figure 2.1 The world is shrinking: news and information now spreads rapidly to even the remotest regions through radio, film and television. We term this 'globalisation'.
Source: PhotoDisc/Getty Images

we now use to refer to all those aspects of modern life that link us into an increasingly connected world – instant communication, rapid dissemination of ideas and information, fast transport of goods and people, instant transfers of money, the spread of multinational companies and international governance and the wide availability of technological networks that makes it all possible.

Anthony Giddens, a British sociologist, writes that one effect of globalisation is that 'local happenings are shaped by events occurring many miles away and *vice versa*' (Giddens, 1990: p. 64). Globalisation has positive benefits – it spreads the protection of human rights and labour laws and has improved health, welfare and education provision for children. But it also brings challenges when cultures clash, when people sense that borders are dissolving around them and when they feel personally threatened by distant events, such as acts of terrorism or infringements of human rights. Ulrich Beck, a German sociologist, argued that this global connectedness has heightened people's perception of risk and made them more suspicious and more cautious. He wrote about '*risk society*' where rapid technological innovation brings unpredictable social change, such as shifting employment patterns, migration, challenges to traditions and customs and changes to relationships between citizen and government, parents and children (Beck, 1992).

ECEC is itself part of this globalisation of ideas and cultures. Around the world, the education and care of children from birth to eight is high on the international agenda as evidence (mainly drawn from the Western world) shows how support for early childhood health, welfare and education improves individual lives and brings brighter prospects for nations. The dominance of the English language as the lingua franca (international language) of science, commerce and international relations means that Western models of early childhood provision and Western ideas about education and care are more likely to be taken up even where political and social conditions are very different. This Western dominance makes people uneasy and sometimes provokes accusations of 'cultural imperialism', especially when demands to do things in a Western way are linked to aid or business contracts.

As early childhood specialists, you will be faced with dilemmas around this global interchange, either as a member of the 'host' country or as a professional in someone else's country. In either situation, you may find yourselves facing challenges to your own values and beliefs and experience the feelings of heightened risk that Beck describes. Children are directly and personally affected by these changes as they filter down to families; in Western countries parents have become increasingly fearful about danger and respond by keeping their children close and putting restrictions on their freedom, so that children are less likely to play outside and are more likely to be confined to the home than are children in less developed countries. Some commentators argue that this makes modern Western childhoods 'toxic' because children's opportunities for outdoor play and independent decision making are reduced and because they are less likely to learn resilience and resourcefulness (Palmer, 2007).

The 'mobile' child

Travel is a feature of modern life; it is likely that you will have travelled more extensively than your grandparents' generation. Countless numbers of children are involved in every sort of journey each year – in family holidays and tourism, in cross-border migrations for work, asylum or refuge and in international adoptions. This mobility brings exposure to different cultural values and beliefs, challenging everything from dress codes to parenting practices, gender relations, social structures and legislation. Children growing up in such diverse communities in such rapidly changing global conditions are 'natives' in a world that would have been unimaginable 50 years ago.

Some children are mobile because they are escaping conflict or persecution to seek *refugee* or *asylum* status; often they flee without identity papers. In Britain, undocumented new arrivals are taken to reception centres, where they are confined sometimes for many months while their claims are investigated. They are particularly vulnerable in this situation. The uncertainty, fear and anxiety associated with leaving their home country is compounded by the fear and uncertainties associated with being locked up with no immediate prospect of release in a foreign country where the language and the judicial system are unfamiliar.

Other children may be mobile because their parents work for international companies with all the disruption that that entails. Others may be mobile within their home country, as their parents move for a new job or to a new home. Others may be fleeing domestic violence, or debts, spending distressing weeks and months in hostels and temporary accommodation.

Bailey (2011) argues that global mobility is responsible for a '*trans-nationalisation of society*', which has particular implications for children. He points to several pressures common to all 'mobile' children who suffer any form of dislocation. These may include, in varying degrees, the following:

- *Tensions about who will care for them*, such as for orphans from war-torn regions, may arise from the bewildering requirements of a host nation state couched in an unfamiliar language and based on incomprehensible cultural assumptions; for left-behind children whose parents are economic migrants sending home 'remittance money', it may come from being left in the unreliable care of an extended family.
- *Impaired well-being* may arise when past traumas, challenges to expectations, language difficulties and uncertainties about the duration of separation contribute to a loss of identity and feelings of intense sadness.
- *Generational pressures* concern mobile children who are living on the borders of two cultures and often play a powerful role in the adaptations and accommodations between the 'old' group and the 'new'. For instance, some migrant children will embrace the 'new' culture and may risk alienation from the old ways maintained by their parents while others may become fiercely loyal to the 'old' culture and may risk alienation from the new. Migrant children may act as interpreters for their family when they become proficient in the host language, taking on a 'parenting' role at an early age. In the case of separated families, children may try to substitute themselves for the absent parent and take on adult roles. For children in care, being looked after by strangers will exacerbate their confusions.

Constantly shifting patterns of migration around the globe engender new forms of social interaction, which bring changes to families, societies and cultures (Bryceson & Vuorela, 2002). Young children brought up in multicultural communities are likely to have very different perceptions about race, gender, diversity and inclusion when compared to previous generations.

The 'international child' of consumer capitalism

Heinz Hengst (2011) suggests that another new kind of child is emerging in the twenty-first century – the *international child*. The international child is a participant in the global exchange of brands and goods. This child can be found just about anywhere on the planet. Thanks to the Internet, international business and the inward and outward migration of

Figure 2.2 Hallowe'en. Village children in Devon, England, celebrate American-style with trick or treating. Their grandparents would have marked the day by carving a turnip lantern to place on the doorstep.
Source: Author's own.

peoples, he or she is born in a borderless world of cultural mobility. Hengst argues that this child and similar children share a global consumer culture where distinctions between generations are blurred, where race and nationality are of little importance and where, from infancy onwards, identity and self-image are mediated through (mostly Western) images, brands and attitudes.

Children of the twenty-first century cannot avoid consumer culture. Cook (2011) points out that they do not *become* consumers but grow up *as* consumers – their sense of themselves and their place in society is embedded in a hyper-commercialised world manipulated by corporate power. Everything around them is branded and labelled – toys, stories, clothes, films, TV programmes, even food – and given significance beyond mere usefulness or pleasure. Through these commercial brands and objects of desire, the Global North spreads its ideology outwards to the Global South. Cook argues that consumerist ideology elevates the *individual* above the community by emphasising private ownership as a kind of moral value – '*because you're worth it!*', as one advertising slogan has it. Traditional values of giving, sharing and reciprocating are replaced by competitive values of buying, having and owning which lead to tensions between young and old, rich and poor.

Western consumerist values become embedded in popular culture, and from the cradle onwards, children are routinely targeted by advertisers. For example, in developing countries, young children are exposed to ubiquitous posters encouraging them to take up smoking as sales of tobacco decline in the West. In richer countries, free downloads of 'advergames' are targeted at young children to get round the restrictions imposed on television advertising. In advergames, branded cartoon characters introduce children subliminally to the manufacturers' products – clothes, food and toys. The games are designed to be addictive and to capture children's interest, to encourage them to use 'pester-power', to persuade parents to buy into the latest 'fads'.

Time to reflect

In many Western countries, advertisers are no longer allowed to advertise harmful or unhealthy products directly to children. Instead, they offer free games for children to download. In these games, the advertisers' brands are presented subliminally or through narrative to encourage 'pester-power' purchases.

Do you think children under eight can see through these advertising campaigns? Should advergames be regulated, or should parents be responsible for policing the games their children access?

The globalisation of consumer capitalism has had the effect of increasing the gap between rich and poor – between rich and poor countries, between rich and poor families, between individual 'haves' and 'have-nots'. These inequalities can have local and global effects. For example, children from low-income families in Britain may feel humiliated when their parents can't afford to send them to school in the latest brand of trainers. In poorer countries, however, some families may reject the Western culture of consumerism and individualism, while others may see it as an enticing dream feeding their aspirations for a better life in Europe, Australia or North America.

A global charter for children's rights – the UNCRC

In 1979, the long process began to get a legally binding United Nations Convention on the Rights of the Child (UNCRC, 1989) agreed by all members of the United Nations. The moral force behind the UNCRC is a belief that civilisation is measured in terms of how states treat their most vulnerable – and some of the most vulnerable are children (Burr and Montgomery, 2003). The charter expresses the belief that children's rights are *human rights*. These rights are internationally recognised and are binding on the signatories to the UNCRC – they are part of the new order of global governance where nation states have agreed to accept international regulation on human rights issues.

After ten years of intense negotiation, a form of words was agreed and ratified by most countries (not Somalia, because there was no government, and not the United States, because they argued that their 1969 American Convention on Human Rights includes children's rights). Today the UNCRC provides a basis for legislation for children around the world and is at the heart of Britain's Children Acts (1989, 2004).

Focus on *The United Nations Convention on the Rights of the Child*

The UNCRC (1989) covers what are sometimes known as the 4 Ps – *Protection, Provision, Participation and Prevention of harm*:

- *Protection* deals with problems such as violence against children, child neglect and the plight of street children. However, it fails to deal with issues such as coercion in the provision of protection: What if the child chooses not to be protected?
- *Provision* refers to the provision of education and welfare, by the state or through private means. The intention is that every child has a right to these provisions. In reality, however, poverty and social exclusion present great challenges for families and states and to their ability to ensure that all children can take up this right.
- *Participation* is linked with democratic principles of representation. Ironically, no children were asked to participate in designing the UNCRC. For children, participation is still dependent upon adults' providing opportunities for their voices to be heard.
- *Prevention of harm* places a duty on adults and societies to keep children's environments safe and free from hazards (like pollution, toxic waste, dangerous work practices). Sadly, war and economic necessity leaves many children in the world dangerously exposed to harm and takes away any possibility of healthcare and education.

Enforcement of the UNCRC at an international level is about maintaining a balance between the internationally agreed rules and the desire of individuals, states or leaders to behave differently. The UN enforces international standards by monitoring compliance through reports required at five yearly intervals from each country. Supporters of the UNCRC (see Kaufman & Rizzini, 2011) argue that since the Convention was worked on over many years in an international forum and was ratified by 193 member countries, it represents our best opportunity to establish the interests and rights of all children, regardless of nationality or cultural background.

Multiculturalism

The monocultural nation states of the eighteenth and nineteenth centuries have now largely been replaced by multicultural societies where ethnic diversity is the norm. *Multiculturalism* is an ideology or belief system that encourages the promotion of diversity on the grounds that all cultures and identities deserve equal respect. 'Multiculturalism' is often contrasted with 'integration theory' – multiculturalism celebrates pluralism, a mosaic of cultures existing side by side, while 'integration theory' celebrates assimilation, a 'melting pot' where diverse cultures accept the core values of the majority.

During the 1970s and 1980s, 'multiculturalism' was the dominant ideology for promoting harmony in multi-ethnic communities. Schools, health professionals and social workers were encouraged to celebrate and respect cultural diversity so that all children could enjoy their heritage with dignity. In early childhood education, for example, great emphasis was put on giving equal value to children's different religious festivals and foods, while professionals in children's health and welfare services often accepted a wide variety of 'traditional' practices (including female circumcision and child betrothals) on the grounds of respecting cultural differences. However, the 1989 UNCRC, ratified and adopted by most countries, set up a *common code of accepted principles* of human behaviour, a universal set of values that all children everywhere could expect to apply to them.

As nation states have become more ethnically diverse – Latinx arriving in large numbers in the United States, Asians arriving in Australia, Africans and East Europeans settling in Western Europe – commentators have expressed increasing unease with 'multiculturalism', arguing that it leads to cultural segregation, community isolation, religious fundamentalism and a growing intolerance between host nations and migrants. Fears about community cohesion have surfaced, and the discourse has begun to shift away from a multicultural position of '*celebrating difference*' to a more 'integrative' position of '*highlighting common values*'. Indeed, the UK government has recently introduced the *Prevent duty guidance* (Home Office, 2015) to counter radicalisation and to introduce *British values* into the curriculum for all nurseries, child minding settings and schools.

Cultural relativism

Some argue that 'multiculturalism' embodies a form of *cultural relativism* which encourages an acceptance of a variety of practices that are customary or traditional among certain groups but which run counter to universal values about human dignity. Freeman (2011) argues that this *cultural relativism* puts children at risk when their community traditions come into conflict with their rights under the UNCRC. He points out that the UNCRC was hammered out over ten years of intense international negotiation before agreement was reached between signatories. He argues that enforcing children's rights is already very difficult and suggests that children's rights could be undermined if cultural traditions are allowed to take precedence over universal rights. But others argue that a global imposition of 'common values' is a new form of Western colonialism which leads to homogenisation and ignores the rights of groups to practise their traditional customs.

Focus on *Cultural relativism*

Cultural relativism is the belief that different societies have different but equal value systems. Respecting cultural differences can be difficult in practice because people often want to defend their own ways of doing things. We are naturally inclined to be ethnocentric – to think our art is the most beautiful, our values the most worthy, our beliefs the most venerable.

Cultural relativism poses questions for every generation when one set of cultural beliefs comes into contact with a different set. In classical times, the Greek historian Herodotus observed tribal funeral practices and noted that people preferred the customs and values of their own culture. During the Enlightenment, empiricists and rationalists argued about how best to discover the objective truth between opposing beliefs – empiricists believed that true knowledge came through our senses and could be revealed through careful scientific observation; rationalists believed that knowledge came from within and could be discovered through hard thinking, logic and rational argument. Immanuel Kant (1724–1804) pointed out that neither empiricists nor rationalists could discover objective truth because everyone wears the 'irremovable goggles' of their own culture and any 'true knowledge' is necessarily subjective.

Modern arguments about cultural relativism grew out of a reaction against the widespread belief in the 'superiority' of Europeans over 'native' races common during colonial times. Anthropologists of the late nineteenth and twentieth centuries gradually came to reject the idea that the West had a monopoly on truth and value. They undertook comparative studies of different cultures to show how other groups viewed the world differently – not 'wrongly' or 'primitively'. Linguistic anthropologists like Sapir and Whorf argued that language shapes thinking and binds each culture to particular ways of seeing; ethnologists like Ruth Benedict compared and contrasted different cultures (ethnology) to argue that 'moral principles' are just expressions of social customs in particular societies; ethnographers like Margaret Mead, who embedded themselves in 'native' communities (ethnography) to study culture from the inside, showed that the way concepts were 'framed' in different societies changed the way people behaved. In her book, *Coming of Age in Samoa* (1928), she explored the experience of motherhood and childhood and found that child-rearing practices in Samoa were very different from those in North America. These anthropologists argued that cultural practices were *different but equally valid* and that we should resist the urge to judge between them.

'Cultural relativism' caused particular problems in the drafting of children's rights under the UNCRC (Freeman, 2011) when different countries, coming from different cultural perspectives, tried to agree on universal rights for children. The following are some examples.

- Some Islamic signatories objected to the idea of *freedom of thought, conscience and religion* because they were opposed to the idea that people could convert to other religions.
- Venezuelan delegates objected to *inter-country adoption* clauses, arguing that children should be cared for only by families who shared their race and culture.
- Some Catholic signatories argued that the *rights of the unborn child* began at conception and that abortion should never be permitted.
- Some African countries objected to the banning of *traditional practices* such as female 'circumcision' (female genital mutilation, or FGM), arguing that it was an important ritual with significance for girls' marriage prospects.

■ Some Western countries found it hard to accept the idea that every child had an *obligation to respect and care for parents*, which many African and Asian countries insisted on.

The arguments continue. Some people believe that taking a culturally relative point of view encourages tolerance and provides a buttress against racism; they point out that an unquestioning belief in one's own cultural values can lead to a denial of other people's rights. Others warn that cultural relativism can lead to excessive tolerance because it fails to recognise core principles of human behaviour enshrined in beliefs about human rights; they argue that excessive tolerance may lead inadvertently to injustice, inequality and abuse. There are no easy answers.

As governments introduce new policies to maintain national stability among their increasingly multicultural populations, ECEC professionals have the delicate task of managing the practicalities in the community and may feel nervous and insecure about 'doing the wrong thing'. There are no simple solutions; there is a fine line between advocating children's rights as laid out in the UNCRC and at the same time respecting cultural diversity.

Case study: What are the limits of tolerance?

A health visitor liaising with a Somali family after the birth of a baby girl discovered that the couple's five-year old daughter was incontinent and suffering recurrent urinary infections. The health visitor suspected that the girl had been 'cut', but the family refused to let her be examined. She wanted to protect the child and her baby sister, but she didn't want to offend the family.

Female 'circumcision' (the 'cut', FGM or female genital mutilation) is practised in more than 20 countries throughout Africa, the Middle East and Asia, and within immigrant populations throughout the world, with prevalence rates ranging from 5 per cent to 99 per cent. Its practice can be found among many different religious, ethnic and cultural groups and across all socioeconomic classes. It is carried out for what people believe to be reasons of hygiene and in order to safeguard marriage prospects. It is estimated that up to 130 million women and girls have already been subjected to some form of FGM and 2 million more are expected to experience it each year (ednahospital, 2012).

The practice of FGM has been condemned by international organisations and huge efforts are ongoing under UNCRC to eradicate it on the grounds that it infringes children's right to be kept safe from harm. But at a community level, the right to practise this traditional custom is strongly supported. In the United Kingdom, FGM is against the law, although there have been very few prosecutions.

Discussion questions

What course of action might the health visitor take?
What would be the effect of taking a position of 'cultural relativism' on this issue?

International aid and ECEC

You may find yourself working abroad at some stage in your career. If you come to your new job with preconceived notions about childcare and education, you may experience severe culture shock when faced with the reality of children's lives in poorer countries. You will need to be circumspect and to tread lightly. International development work is about more than transferring knowledge, money or expertise from the developed world to the developing world; it is about listening and helping to build *capacity* for long-term growth so that when you leave, others can take on the work.

Sustainability is the keyword in discussions about international development in the twenty-first century – that is, providing the kind of help that will encourage people to take on the development tasks for themselves: training local people to become trainers, helping them to adapt local knowledge and expertise, offering language skills, working alongside local education and healthcare providers, learning from them and sharing your skills.

In September 2000 world leaders adopted eight *Millennium Development Goals* designed to raise the quality of life for future generations:

- Goal 1 – eradicate extreme hunger and poverty.
- Goal 2 – achieve universal primary education.
- Goal 3 – promote gender equality and empower women.
- Goal 4 – reduce child mortality.
- Goal 5 – improve maternal health.
- Goal 6 – combat HIV/AIDS, malaria and other diseases.
- Goal 7 – ensure environmental sustainability.
- Goal 8 – develop a global partnership for development.

Progress is being made, but it is slow. Although the number of children living in poverty is reducing (UNICEF, 2012), it is still a major cause of infant mortality and malnutrition. It is estimated that 25 per cent of children in the world (i.e. 170 million) are stunted in brain and body due to the effects of malnourishment (Save the Children, 2012). A further 2.6 million children (mostly in Africa and Asia) die from malnutrition each year. A child stunted by malnutrition will have only 20 per cent of the productive capacity of their peers in adulthood, and failure to tackle poverty and malnutrition in infancy and early childhood can have lifelong consequences for individuals and society. Children suffer most under harsh economic conditions – through maternal ill health, from disease, from malnutrition, from poor sanitation and from poor housing. Young children are disproportionately vulnerable to these adverse environmental effects – in the womb, as infants and as children.

Finding the mechanisms to eradicate poverty and its associated problems is politically difficult. Heywood (2011) points out that while international aid is designed to alleviate poverty and that many children have benefited from it and will do so in the future, some recipients regard it with suspicion; some accuse donor organisations of *paternalism*, imposing their views from above and taking little account of local sensibilities; some argue that aid does little to restore the dignity and economic independence of the recipients; others say it is *exploitative* because it creates dependency and traps recipients in a downward spiral of poverty (Burman, 2010). Institutions like the World Bank and the International Monetary Fund choose to *lend* money to fund aid programmes, rather than to give charitably – they do not like the idea of state support or 'hand-outs' because they believe it creates dependency and stifles creativity. They believe that employment and wealth are created through the pursuit of business, growth and profit and that only free markets and entrepreneurship bring higher living standards.

However, some political economists think that poverty is a direct result of free market forces because money and markets and growth have become more important than the well-being of communities and the quality of the environment. Others argue that consumerism breeds poverty by reinforcing competition rather than cooperation, imposing individualism on societies that have traditionally relied on communal reciprocity to maintain a balance between the 'haves' and 'have-nots'. *Environmentalists* argue that the gap between rich and poor will increase unless we learn to live in a sustainable way within the finite resources of our natural world. *Feminists* argue that better standards of living can be achieved through growing 'human capital' rather than growing 'financial capital', particularly by educating and empowering women and girls. Marmot (2010) argues that poor children have poorer health and that we need to relieve poverty to improve health. He believes that health equity for all children should be at the heart of global economic policy and that any economic policies which damage children's health and well-being should be outlawed.

In response to these criticisms about the unfettered growth of 'financial capital', international organisations have increasingly adopted a 'human capital' approach, directing money towards programmes that *invest in people* to improve health, skills and literacy. International aid agencies working with the Millennium Development Goals are increasingly focused on providing *sustainable* improvements so that they can eventually hand over power for self-determination to local people. ECEC is a very important part of this 'human capital' approach in the war on poverty and is a high priority for national and international funding because investing in children leads to sustainable improvement for society as a whole.

However, it would be wrong to assume that poverty is construed by children themselves as a major disadvantage. Poverty is not the same thing as misery! Poor children express pride in their *resourcefulness*, their *competence* and their *relationships* rather than focusing on their material deprivations (Crivello et al., 2010). The UN recognises this by measuring quality of life more broadly than in purely economic terms – its Human Development Index regards other factors as equally significant:

- life expectancy and health
- educational literacy
- access to resources to keep warm and dry
- sustainability for future generations
- security for individuals
- equality of opportunity in jobs, voting rights, education for men and women.

On these measures, the ranking of 'poor' and 'rich' might easily change because *material* wealth is not necessarily a determinant of well-being (though it helps).

Time to reflect

How do global factors shape the lives of children in your local community?

Models of ECEC around the world

According to UNESCO, ECEC is a basic human right (2007).

But how can we provide it for every child?

Who pays?

Should parents fund it directly?

Should the state provide it free of charge for every child?

Should parents and the state share the burden?

Where children are seen as *primarily the responsibility of parents* and not the state, ECEC tends to be provided through the private sector and to be bought by parents who can afford it; this is the case in many parts of India and Africa and among wealthier groups in North America and Western Europe where parents pay for private provision. Where children are regarded as the responsibility of the *whole society*, ECEC is provided free by the state and paid for through taxes – as in Nordic countries like Denmark, Sweden and Finland. In most Western countries, there is a mixture of both state and private funding; typically, there is a limited supply of free provision for every child, alongside extra 'targeted' provision for the most disadvantaged children, any extra childcare over and above the free hours is paid for by parents.

In the United Kingdom, this *mixed economy* gives all three- and four-year-olds in Britain 15 hours of ECEC per week (there are plans to raise this to 30 hours to help working parents in the near future) – anything beyond this is funded personally by parents. In addition, disadvantaged pre-school children, including the most disadvantaged two-year-olds, receive extra funding to access programmes like Sure Start to help to raise them to a similar level of 'school readiness' as their peers. However, in many Western countries this mixed economy is rapidly becoming unsustainable for many families because costs have risen so much, and so fast, that the extra childcare hours parents need to stay in employment are unaffordable. At the moment many low-earning parents (generally mothers but increasingly fathers) with pre-school children find it difficult to pay childcare fees, and paid employment is unviable. This can deprive children of education and social play at a critical time in their development, and it also deprives their parents of the opportunity to pursue employment opportunities (Polakow, in Yelland, 2010). On the other hand, there is the view, held by many, that children get a better start if one parent is able to stay at home to look after them rather than going out to work.

In 2006, the Organisation for Economic Co-operation and Development (OECD) reviewed ECEC in 20 countries and concluded that equal access and quality can best be ensured by *direct state funding* to providers. This finding suggests that the Nordic model of state provision is the most likely to bring benefits to *all* children worldwide. However, the ECEC model that is most often adopted in poorer countries is the mixed economy model where the private sector supplies most pre-school care and the state limits its support to those children on the poorest margins of society. Penn (2010) argues that a Nordic European model is more appropriate for countries in the Global South because it is paid for by the state and freely available to *all* children. She argues that when the services are provided through a mixed economy where parents have to make a contribution, families and young children on the margins of society cannot afford healthcare or education and are destined to be excluded in the future. For this reason, poorer countries should be encouraged to spend donor money on *universal* provision of ECEC wherever this is practicable.

Time to reflect

ECEC funding – private versus state

Think about the different economic models of ECEC above (state provision, private provision, mixed provision).
What are the advantages and disadvantages of each?
When childcare is unaffordable, what are the implications for children's rights, for mother's rights and for father's rights?

The central importance of ECEC is recognised internationally – both for children themselves and for the future health and well-being of the global society. For many countries where primary education and basic healthcare are the first priorities, it is still a distant dream, an unaffordable luxury for parents to access ECEC. Nevertheless, by making ECEC a priority on the international agenda, we may gradually improve the life chances of more and more children around the world.

Summary

- Globalisation 'shrinks' the world so that distant events have a local impact on children's lives.
- Rapid spread of news and information may heighten perceptions of risk and increase fears about children's safety.
- Migration poses direct and indirect threats to children's well-being.
- Cross-cultural connections challenge cultural beliefs and traditions.
- Worldwide markets and the rapid shift of money may destabilise local economies and increase poverty among vulnerable families with young children.
- The spread of Western goods and attitudes encourages individualism rather than cooperation.
- Western efforts to improve children's lives may be seen as 'cultural imperialism'.
- Consumerism and economic 'growth' leave children's futures in the balance.
- Affordability is a key factor in making ECEC sustainable both locally and globally.

Topics for further discussion

1 How do you feel about celebrities (or anyone) in the West adopting children from Third World countries?
2 Westerners are encouraged by some charities to 'sponsor a child' from the Third World. What might be the benefits and disadvantages of overseas sponsorship of an individual child's education?

Assignments

1 Find out about Mrs Jellyby, a character in *Bleak House*. What point was Dickens making about her charity work for children in Africa?
2 Watch the film *Rabbit Proof Fence*. How did the Australian government justify the forcible removal of mixed race children from their Aboriginal families?
3 Find out about the arrangements made by border agencies in the United Kingdom for newly arrived asylum-seeker children and the children of refugees.
4 Read *Toxic Childhood* by Sue Palmer. How much do you agree or disagree with her analysis of contemporary childhoods in Western societies?

Further reading

Heywood, A. (2011) *Global Politics*. Basingstoke: Palgrave Macmillan. This provides an excellent introduction to general globalisation theories and issues.

For articles on ECEC and global questions, *The Palgrave Handbook of Childhood Studies* (Qvortrup et al., 2011). This has some very challenging scholarly articles by key figures in the academic field.

For an interesting approach to the (inappropriate) domination of Western medicine and mental health practices, see Timimi S. (2005) 'The effect of globalisation on children's mental health', *British Medical Journal*, 331(7507), 37–39.

Useful websites

OECD (Organisation for Economic Co-operation and Development): http://www.oecd.org/
United Nations organisations:
UNESCO: https://en.unesco.org/
UNICEF: http://cwg.unicef.org.uk
WHO (World Health Organisation) and for the NGOs (non-government organisations):
http://www.who.int
OXFAM: http://www.oxfam.org.uk/
Greenpeace: http://www.greenpeace.org.uk/
In the United Kingdom, information on migrant labour, refugees and asylum seekers is held by the Home Office: www. homeoffice.gov.uk.

References

Bailey, A. (2011) 'Transnational Mobilities and Childhoods' in J. Qvortrup, W.A. Corsaro and M.-S. Honig (eds) *The Palgrave Handbook of Childhood Studies* (pp. 408–421). Basingstoke: Palgrave Macmillan

Beck, U. (1999) *World Risk Society.* Malden, MA: Polity

Bryceson, D. and Vuorela, U. (eds) (2002) *The Transnational Family* in Bailey, 2011, 'Transnational Mobilities and Childhoods' in J. Qvortrup, W.A. Corsaro and M.-S. Honig (eds) *The Palgrave Handbook of Childhood Studies* (p. 411). Basingstoke: Palgrave Macmillan

Burman, E. (2010) 'Between two debts: child and (inter)national development' in N. Yelland (ed.), *Contemporary Perspectives on Early Childhood Education.* Maidenhead: Open University Press/McGraw-Hill Education

Burr, R. and Montgomery, H. (2003) 'Children's Rights' in M. Woodhead and H. Montgomery (eds) *Understanding Childhood: an interdisciplinary approach.* Chichester: John Wiley/Open University Press

Cook, D. T. (2011) 'Children as Consumers' in J. Qvortrup, W.A. Corsaro and M.-S. Honig (eds) *The Palgrave Handbook of Childhood Studies* (p. 332). Basingstoke: Palgrave Macmillan

Crivello et al. (2010) *Young Lives; An International Study of Childhood Poverty.* www.younglives.org.uk.

Crivello, G., Camfield, L. and Porter C. (eds) (2010) Editorial: Researching Children's Understandings of Poverty and Risk in Diverse Contexts, *Children and Society,* 24: 255–260

ednahospital (2012) www.ednahospital.org. Accessed 7 March 2012

Freeman, M. (2011) 'Children's Rights as Human Rights: Reading the UNCRC' in J. Qvortrup, W.A. Corsaro and M.-S. Honig (eds) *The Palgrave Handbook of Childhood Studies* (pp. 377–393). Basingstoke: Palgrave Macmillan

Giddens, A. (1990) *The Consequences of Modernity.* Cambridge: Polity

Hengst, H. (2011) '*Collective Identities*' in J. Qvortrup, W.A. Corsaro and M.-S. Honig (eds) *The Palgrave Handbook of Childhood Studies* (p. 213). Basingstoke: Palgrave Macmillan

Heywood, A., (2011) *Global Politics.* Basingstoke: Palgrave Macmillan

Home Office (2015) *Prevent duty guidance.* www.gov.uk/government/uploads/system/uploads/attachment_data/file/439598/prevent-duty-departmental-advice-v6.pdf. Accessed 20 June 2016

Home Office Statistics https://www.gov.uk/government/organisations/home-office/about/statistics. Accessed 26 December 2016

Kaufman, N. H. and Rizzinin, I. (2011) 'Closing the Gap Between Rights and the Realities of Children's Lives' in J. Qvortrup, W.A. Corsaro and M.-S. Honig (eds) *The Palgrave Handbook of Childhood Studies* (pp. 422–434). Basingstoke: Palgrave Macmillan

Marmot, M. (2010) *Fair Society, Healthy Lives.* London: Marmot Review

McLuhan, M. (1964) *Understanding Media: the extensions of man.* New York: Mentor

OECD (2006) *Starting Strong II: Early Childhood Education and Care.* Paris: OECD

Palmer, S. (2007) *Toxic Childhood: How the modern world is damaging our children and what we can do about it.* London: Orion

Penn, H. (2010) 'Shaping the future: how capital arguments about investment in early childhood are being (mis)used in poor countries' in N. Yelland (ed.) *Contemporary Perspectives on Early Childhood Education.* Maidenhead: Open University Press/McGraw-Hill Education

Polakow, V. (2010) 'Reframing rights: poverty discourse and children's lives in the United States' in Yelland (ed.) *Contemporary Perspectives on Early Childhood Education*. Maidenhead: Open University Press/McGraw-Hill Education

Save the Children (2012) *A life free from hunger: tackling child malnutrition* http://www.savethechildren.org.uk/resources/online-library/life-free-hunger-tackling-child-malnutrition. Accessed 26 December 2016

UNCRC (1989) United Nations Convention on the Rights of the Child

UNESCO (2007) *Education for All Global Monitoring Report 2007*

UNICEF (2012) *Measuring Child Poverty: New league tables of child poverty in rich countries*, Innocenti Report Card 10, UNICEF Innocenti Research Centre, Florence https://www.unicef-irc.org/publications/pdf/rc10_eng.pdf. Accessed 26 December 2016

Some theories of child development

Introduction

Every generation asks the question, 'How can we best promote the physical and mental health of our children so that they can lead satisfying and fulfilling lives?'

For most of us, theories of child development are embedded implicitly in an oral culture passed from generation to generation, as parents seek advice from grandparents, families and friends about how to raise children – how to get babies to sleep through, when to wean, how to discipline, how to support, the role of praise and punishment in socialisation, and so on. Underpinning this collective advice are beliefs and theories about child development which may differ across history and culture. Over the past century, Western theories of child development have come to dominate the academic and popular literature.

Theories about child development often divide into those which hold that inherited genes (*nature*) largely determine physical and mental well-being and those which hold that environment (*nurture*) is largely responsible. However, most theories recognise that both are implicated, and philosophers and scientists argue over the relative influence of nature and nurture on individuals and societies. Every generation revisits the debate with a fresh eye – one way or another most of us believe that 'the child is father of the man', but we are less certain whether it is the hand that rocks the cradle or the character children are stamped with at birth that makes the most difference to the way lives turn out.

As early childhood practitioners, you will find yourselves making decisions about children's health, welfare and education based on underlying theories that you have absorbed through your family, your culture and your studies. Through your reading, you will discover that different nature and nurture theories have their moments of ascendancy and decline depending on the prevailing political, economic, social and scientific climate of the times, but like the wheel, they come round and round. In this chapter, we will look at some of the theories that have been put forward at different times to explain why children develop as they do and where your own beliefs about early childhood practices fit in.

Thinking about theories

Some people are impatient with 'theory' because they think it gets in the way of doing the job. But for early childhood practitioners, theory is at the centre of everything we do – it determines how we relate to children and what we provide for them. Theories are mental models, the nearest we can get to describing how we think things work, and these theories underpin the actions we carry out and the policies we design.

Time to reflect

Think about your own theories of child development.

Do you think your own development has been influenced more by the 'nature' you were *born with*, or by the 'nurture' you were *born into*?

Think about the American Dream. Is it based primarily on nature or nurture? How realistic is it to believe that any child, from any background, can become whatever they aspire to?

A theory is a story we tell ourselves to explain how the world works. Like a story, it may echo the world as we know it, but it is not the 'real' thing – it is just a working model in our heads. Like a story, a theory can be convincing when it is consistent with our experience, but we need to remember that it is only one interpretation among many. Theories are always open to debate – and theories about child development are no exception. Sometimes theories challenge the status quo – for instance, theories about autism were once linked to cold and unresponsive parenting until advances in neuroscience demonstrated that autistic children showed differences at a cellular level (Frith, 1989). Sometimes theories confirm existing prejudices or political positions – for instance, theories about links between gender and intelligence were once widely held, and people believed that because, on average, women have smaller brains than men, they must have less thinking capacity than men. This led to generations of girls being guided towards 'soft' or 'female' studies in the arts and humanities while boys were guided towards the 'hard' or 'male' subjects like science, technology, engineering and maths.

Theories arise in different ways. Sometimes we theorise on the basis of what we already have in our minds. This is called the *cognitive* or *rational* or *ideational* approach; in this case, we *reflect* on our own experience, using examples and precedents to test our theory through argument. At other times we construct a theory around the evidence we gather through our observations. This is called the *empirical* or *scientific* approach; in this case, we build our theory through *systematic inquiry*, carefully collecting and recording data and building a hypothesis which can be tested again and again to establish its veracity. However, in both cases, a good deal of imaginative interpretation is required because even 'scientific facts' are liable to revision as new evidence and new viewpoints emerge.

The earliest advice manuals on child development were written by physicians who took a medical approach; in England these manuals included William Cadogan's *Essay on Nursing* (1749) and William Buchan's *Advice to Mothers* (1804), in which the authors covered sleeping, feeding, weaning, toilet training and the character implications of controlling anger and fostering independence (Cunningham, 2006).

Modern Early Childhood Studies is multidisciplinary and belongs to the *social sciences*, which deal with the totality of human behaviour. Theories in the social sciences combine both cognitive and empirical approaches and involve the interpretation of evidence drawn from a wide range of different sources, such as statistical data, scientific studies, interviews and observations. The resulting models or theories may challenge or support commonly held beliefs, and part of your job as practitioners is to consider the competing claims carefully in order to construct your own philosophy of child development.

Changing views of child development

Where written records exist, we can get a fascinating insight into the theories that held sway in other times and cultures. For instance, the earliest Greeks believed that the gods mapped out the Fate of each person at birth and that nothing could be done to change it – a fatalistic view still held by some people today. But the philosopher **Socrates** (469–399 BCE) challenged this fatalism and argued that humans have a degree of control over their own destinies and that it is possible for parents and teachers to *shape* the children in their care for good or ill. **Plato** (427–347 BCE), a pupil of Socrates, took this idea further and argued that to ensure that children *developed* a sound mind in a healthy body, it was necessary to surround them with harmony, balance, beauty and virtuous people; he thought the basic requirements were play, gymnastics, dance, music, uplifting stories and 'good', morally upright role models. **Aristotle** (384–322 BCE), a pupil of Plato, extended these ideas and advised adults to shape children's characters by insisting on strict *discipline and training* in the virtues of cleanliness, obedience, duty, honesty, courage, unselfishness and industry. Later, Judaco-Christian traditions replaced the classical theories of the Greeks and Romans and dominated Western culture until the sixteenth century. The strictest religious parents viewed child development as a matter of leading an inherently sinful child towards a god-fearing adulthood. The driving philosophy behind child-rearing at this time was to instil children with the fear of an all-seeing God in order to guarantee them a place in Heaven in the hereafter. The use of physical punishment to shape children's social behaviour and moral character was widely accepted as necessary.

All these ideas survive today. For instance, Steiner nurseries espouse Platonic ideas about art and music and harmony; public schools like Gordonstoun famously base their philosophies on ancient Greek ideas about building character through disciplining the body and training the mind; and some religious foundation schools reinforce the moral teachings of sacred texts with threats of a hellish afterlife for those straying from the straight and narrow.

The emergence of scientific theories

At the end of the late Middle Ages in Europe (from 1500 onwards), new scientific ideas began to challenge religious thinking in Europe and with it beliefs about child rearing. Old certainties about 'truth' shifted, and **Descartes** (1596–1650), a French philosopher, risked being branded a heretic when he argued that people could know things only through the scientific evidence provided through observation and experience rather than by *divining* God's purpose from Scripture. It was no longer enough to rely on biblical texts to guide understanding; instead, philosophers turned to studying the natural world to find out how things worked – and from then on, child development became a proper subject for study by natural scientists of the new age of Enlightenment.

Nature and nurture

In Britain, the Enlightenment philosopher **John Locke** (1632–1704) followed up Descartes' ideas and published *An Essay Concerning Human Understanding* (1690), where he put forward the theory that every child's mind is a *tabula rasa* (a blank slate) waiting to be inscribed by the experiences (nurture) he or she received.

He argued that coercion and physical punishment promoted by religious institutions could be harmful and advocated a child-rearing regime based on nurturing children's natural powers of reasoning. He believed that developing children's rational, logical thinking through carefully planned instruction was an important part of helping them to develop into good citizens.

> ### Time to reflect
>
> What are the implications of regarding a newborn baby as a *blank slate*?
> Are babies and young children capable of logical thought?

In France, **Jean-Jacques Rousseau** (1712–1778) took exception to some of Locke's 'rationalist' theories of development, especially the idea that adults should lead children's development through instruction and reasoning (see also Chapter 9). In his book, *Emile: Or, On Education* (1762), he put forward the idea that childhood is a special time, a time of innocence and imagination when children are close to God and Nature; he advised adults to allow children to develop in their own way without too much interference and to encourage them to exercise their bodies and limbs and senses but to keep their minds idle for as long as possible and not force them into formal education too early. He argued that *boys* up to the age of 12 (at least upper- and middle-class boys) should be allowed to grow undisturbed, roaming freely in Nature like *noble savages*. Girls, on the other hand, required strong guidance and lots of religious instruction to rein in their unreasonable passions.

In England, **Mary Wollstonecraft** (1759–1797), took particular exception to Rousseau's attitude towards girls. In her book, *A Vindication of the Rights of Women* (1792), she argued that women and girls were by *nature* equally capable but were handicapped by the *nurture* they received in a society that did not value them enough to give them an education. Later, her daughter, Mary Shelley, put this nature/nurture debate into the heart of her novel *Frankenstein* (1818).

Theories into practice

The ideas of Locke and Rousseau spawned heated debates about child-rearing among educators, which led to a gradual softening of attitudes towards children and an increasing belief in concerned guidance rather than harsh coercion. **Maria Edgeworth** (1767–1827), an influential English writer and teacher, watched her father put Rousseau's *noble savage* idea into practice with one of her brothers (her brother went off the rails…). She came from a family of 20 children, and as she grew older, she helped her father educate her younger siblings and began to develop her own theories. Later, she wrote *Practical Education* (1798), where she brought together her own experience and her readings of Rousseau and Locke. *Practical Education* encouraged adults to *listen* to children and to be guided by the child's individual needs. She believed all children could benefit from education because 'justice, truth and humanity are confined to no particular rank' (in Benziman, 2012: p. 66). She wanted children to have time and space for play and exercise, nature study and music and art. She disapproved of harsh discipline, believing that 'whenever we can use reason, we should never use force' (in Benziman, 2012: pp. 275–276).

In Switzerland, **Johann Pestalozzi** (1746–1827) noted the stunted physical and spiritual condition of poor children, and in 1794, he published a series of letters called *How Gertrude Teaches Her Children* to show parents and teachers how they could best support their children's development. He took a holistic approach to child development, arguing that children developed equally through *head, heart and hand* and should have every opportunity to use their body, brain and imagination. He believed that with the right conditions for health and welfare, even the poorest children could benefit from education (Pestalozzi, 1774, in Parker-Rees and Willan, 2006).

At about the same time, **Friedrich Froebel** (1782–1852) set up his first *kindergarten* for young children in Germany. Unusually, he employed women. He believed that children should be 'cultivated' like plants and offered warmth, nourishment and sunlight to grow strong and healthy in mind and body. He divided childhood into the 'child centred' period from birth to eight and the 'scholar period' from eight onwards: the younger children spent their days in physical play and outdoor activities; only older children received 'instruction' (Froebel, 1826, in Parker-Rees and Willan, 2011; Giardello, 2014).

Figure 3.1 Maria Edgeworth (1768–1849). In her book *Practical Education*, Edgeworth encouraged adults to listen to children and be guided by the child's individual needs.
Source: By John Downman (1750–1824) [Public domain], via Wikimedia Commons

In Britain, **Robert Owen** (1771–1858), a cotton mill owner and a utopian socialist, developed a revolutionary community nursery and school for the infants and young children of his factory workers.

> ### *Focus on* Robert Owen (1771–1858)
>
> Robert Owen, a radical utopian socialist, set up the first workplace nursery in Britain. Born in 1771, the son of a Welsh saddler and ironmonger, he left school at the age of ten. He was a good scholar and an avid reader, and he was apprenticed to a London draper who shared his enthusiasm for books. At age 18, he set up his first business spinning and weaving cloth in Manchester. At age 21, he was elected to the Manchester Literary and Philosophical Society, where he discussed the ideas of Locke, Rousseau, Wollstonecraft and Pestalozzi. He was appointed to the Manchester Board of Health, which promoted improvements in the health and working conditions of men, women and children in factories.
>
> In 1799 he married the daughter of David Dale, who owned the New Lanark cotton mills in Scotland, a working community of several thousand people set in a beautiful secluded river valley. It included a school for apprentices. Owen took over the business with his partners (one of whom was the philosopher Jeremy Bentham) and set about improving the social conditions of his workforce. He phased out the unpaid employment of young children, set up a Sickness Fund, provided free medical care, built a Village Store, introduced street cleaning, improved sanitation and established an education system for all. He set up a 'School for Children' attended by every child as soon as they could walk (freeing up mothers for work), together with his 'New Institution for the Formation of Character' for older children and adults.
>
> Owen wanted the children to grow up robust and cheerful. He believed in lots of fresh air and outdoor exercise, singing, dancing, good food and a loving atmosphere where 'real affection' existed between pupils and teachers and where teachers worked in cooperation with the *nature* of the child. He believed that the youngest children developed best through lots of physical outdoor and indoor play, and he banished all books from the nursery. From the age of three to seven, children progressed to the infant school, where they still played but where the emphasis was on learning to share and to be kind to one another. There were no rewards or punishment, because Owen believed that children learned best when they were interested and enjoying their lessons. The children played and learned in spacious rooms decorated with pictures and murals; they wore Roman-style dresses that left their limbs free; and they received nutritious meals from the public kitchen. Children washed themselves in state-of-the-art bathing machines, and their school clothes were washed and changed three times a week. Formal schooling began at age seven, and children learned the 3 R's as well as history, geography, natural history, dancing, art and music. Adults and children alike were encouraged to use the well-stocked reading room and to attend evening lectures, concerts and dances.
>
> In 1816 Owen gave an *Address to the Inhabitants of New Lanark* in which he declared that he wanted to build a society 'without poverty, with health greatly improved, with little, if any misery, and with intelligence and happiness increased a hundredfold'. He wanted charity and kindness to prevail and believed that the only obstacle was 'ignorance'. Owen was far ahead of the Factory Acts in limiting the working day for adults and forbidding child labour. His mills received thousands of interested visitors from Europe and America, and Owen himself travelled and lectured widely – on one occasion he visited the prison reformer Elizabeth Fry at her newly introduced prison school, where the small children of incarcerated women were given instruction.

Owen was ultimately disappointed that his programme of health, welfare and education services for their workers and their children was not taken up more widely. In 1826 he emmigrated to America to set up a community called New Harmony. New Harmony housed the first kindergarten and infant school, the first trade school, the first public library and the first women's group in America.

New Lanark and New Harmony are now heritage sites dedicated to the preservation of Owen's revolutionary ideas.

(From *The Story of Robert Owen 1771–1858*, 2012 (4th edn) New Lanark: New Lanark Trust)

Theories of heredity and development

During the eighteenth and nineteenth centuries, there was a great deal of interest in genetic inheritance in an effort to understand breeding lines in plants and animals. In 1859, **Charles Darwin** (1809–1882) published *On the Origin of Species*, his theory of evolution and heredity. The theory suggests that each individual contains random variations or mutations that affect their ability to adapt successfully to their environment and that these variations can be inherited and passed on to subsequent generations. Besides his more famous work on evolution, Darwin also turned his naturalist's eye to the development of his son William. He kept a diary of William's growth, language and thought processes which he published as *A Biographical Sketch of an Infant* (1887). This was the first observational account of a child's development from birth.

Other scientists seized on Darwin's idea of heredity and used it for their own political purposes, to argue that human potential was fixed in the genes and so a person's rank and status in society was naturally and biologically fixed at birth. This became known variously as *Social Darwinism*, *biological determinism* or *eugenics*. In 1869, **Sir James Galton** (1822–1911) wrote *Hereditary Genius*, in which he argued that genes were destiny (Wooldridge,1994) and proposed that the British upper classes were genetically endowed to occupy their superior position in society through generations of inter*marriage* within their class; the lower classes were similarly biologically programmed to occupy an inferior position through generations of inter*breeding*. This theory was widely taken up and, over the next century, fed into beliefs about racial inferiority and racial purity, which led to laws against interracial marriage in a number of different countries and provided the underpinning ideology for genocides in Nazi-occupied Europe. The theory survived in 'incapacity' laws, which held that 'defectives' should be sterilised to prevent further breeding (these 'incapacity' laws were still in place in Sweden as recently as 1976). Notions about natural abilities and inherited characteristics still hold currency in many contemporary debates about how best to allocate resources to support and educate our children.

Case study: Social Darwinism – a contemporary issue?

In 2014 Old Etonian and former science editor on *The New York Times* Nicholas Wade caused a furore when he published *A Troublesome Inheritance: Genes, Race and Human History*, in which he argues that there is indeed a biological basis for cultural success. He writes that natural selection has resulted in marked differences in brain function between racial groups, which are passed down the generations and which influence cultural development. He believes that contemporary theorists choose to ignore the evolutionary and genetic evidence for these differences in *nature* and to attribute cultural success *solely to nurture*.

Nearly 150 leading population geneticists signed a letter denouncing his book. They accused him of providing an incomplete and inaccurate account of research on genetic differences and rejected his ideas as guesswork. They argued that there was no evidence for defining the concept of 'race' biologically because patterns of genetic variation cross ethnic and geographic boundaries. They pointed out that it is the *interaction* between individuals and environment that offer more likely explanations for social and cultural differences. Jerry Coyne, an evolutionary geneticist at the University of Chicago, said '...the idea that genes and natural selection are everything in explaining culture is simply bad science'.

Wade defended himself by saying that his detractors were driven by politics rather than science.

Discussion questions

What do you think Wade means when he says that his critics are driven by politics rather than science?
How might the definition of 'cultural success' affect the way people investigate questions of nature and nurture?
In what ways do you think nature and nurture might interact to affect cultural success?

Social dimensions of development

In the late nineteenth and early twentieth centuries, eugenics was widely debated, and those in power sometimes dismissed the 'poor' as biologically destined to be degenerate, delinquent, innately idle, of limited understanding and incapable of reform (Wooldridge, 1994). But many Victorian social scientists and reformers took issue with this position and instead focused on the *nurturing* factors associated with poverty which they believed impacted on physical and mental health. They collected statistical evidence and first-hand accounts from people bringing up their families on the margins of society to argue that 'poor physical and mental development' was related to poor *nurture* rather than poor *nature*. The studies showed that harsh economic and social conditions stunted children physically, intellectually, linguistically, emotionally and morally (Keating, 1976).

For example, in London, **Henry Mayhew** (1812–1887), compiled a statistical analysis of poverty, *London Labour and the London Poor*. He interviewed people in the poorest parts of London, making extensive lists of living conditions, wages, diet and employment. He studied his subjects as a naturalist would study them, and by analysing the patterns of their lives, he was able to show how social conditions of poverty, poor housing and inadequate food had a direct effect on the learning and development of poor children. In Nottingham, **William Booth** (1829–1919), founder of the Salvation Army, provided further evidence (*In Darkest England and the Way Out*, 1890) showing how education, particularly religious education, good food and shelter could lift children out of ignorance and destitution to live healthy and fulfilling lives.

Another social economist, **Charles Booth** (1840–1916) from Liverpool, explored the statistics of poverty and investigated the human factors involved in destitution, 'moral depravity' and ignorance in *Life and Labour of the People in London* (1889–1903). Later, **B.S. Rowntree** (1871–1954) showed how economic necessity prevented families from valuing education because children's earnings were an essential part of family income, making education an irrelevant luxury. Dickens used many of the earlier reports to expose the plight of poor children and to challenge the entrenched attitudes of those who might regard the poor as a subspecies of humanity, destined always to remain the 'undeserving poor'. Rowntree's work on the effects of poverty on child development, health and well-being continues today through the Joseph Rowntree Foundation, which critiques the impact of social policies on families at risk of poverty and social exclusion.

Women were deeply involved in trying to ameliorate the lives of poor children and to explain their plight to a wider audience. In 1851, **Mary Carpenter** (1807–1877) wrote the splendidly titled *Reformatory Schools for the Children of the Perishing and Dangerous Classes, and for Juvenile Offenders*, in which she argued for three kinds of schools to be set up for education and improvement of the children of the poor – free day schools for the majority, special feeding industrial schools for children in need, and reformatory schools for young criminals.

Mary Higgs (1854–1937) wrote *Three Nights in Women's Lodging Houses*, detailing the precarious lives of prostitutes and their children to show that economic necessity, rather than innately immoral character, was responsible for their poor prospects. **Lady Florence Bell** (1851–1930) wrote *Reading Habits in Middlesborough*, a study of the attitudes and habits of the poor in relation to literacy, an attempt to discover why so many poor children failed to learn to read. She concluded that reading was necessarily low on the list of priorities in families whose existence was marginal and where basic survival was precarious. Most famously, the pioneers of early education and care, the McMillan sisters, Rachel (1859–1917) and Margaret (1860–1931), led the way in providing nursery places for the children of the poor. They opened Night Camps where children could wash and receive clean clothes. Later, they established Open Air Camp schools to provide healthcare, nourishing food and a little education for the most destitute. In 1930, Margaret incorporated these twin concerns of health and education into new training programmes for nurses and teachers at the Rachel McMillan Training College. The Open Air Nursery still survives as the Rachel McMillan Nursery, where the focus is on play and exploration.

Economic and social reports and initiatives like those of the McMillans strengthened the case that children were not *innately* destined to a particular developmental pathway but that poor children were victims of social deprivation and that enlightened *intervention* in the form of financial and social support could improve their physical and mental well-being.

The child study movement and theories of 'normal development'

At the end of the nineteenth century, the nature/nurture debate continued to be widely discussed. Was the condition of the poor down to breeding from poor stock as social Darwinists suggested? Or were the social reformers right to blame the dreadful living conditions? What could be done to improve the general physical and mental health of the nation's children, the adults of the future upon whom the Empire would come to depend?

The child study movement addressed these questions. Started in the United States by Granville Stanley Hall (1844–1924), it was made up of medical doctors, psychologists and laypeople. Members of the movement set about classifying children according to a 'medical model' of 'normal', 'sub-normal' and 'gifted' based on physical and mental measures (Wooldridge, 1994).

In England, **Dr Frederick Warner** (1847–1926) carried out surveys of around 100,000 children and published a *Report on the Scientific Study of the Mental and Physical Conditions of Childhood, with particular reference to children of defective constitution, and with recommendations as to education and training* (1895). Warner believed that the quality of the mind was expressed in physiology – size of cranium, gait, carriage, gesture, clarity of speech and so on. He categorised what was 'normal' across the population and then identified four categories of 'abnormality': the physically handicapped, the nervous (generally female!), the malnourished and the dull (Wooldridge, 1994). Another prominent member of the movement was **James Sully** (1842–1923). Sully believed that the scientific study of children should be conducted by men because women's 'baby worship' and 'sentimental adoration of infant ways' made them incapable of the 'perfectly cool and impartial process of scientific observation' (in Wooldridge, 1994: p. 38). Sully studied *individual* differences rather than differences across entire populations. He argued that 'abnormal' children were '*maladjusted*' to their environment (Wooldridge, 1994: p. 38). Maladjusted children showed *intellectual dullness, emotional instability* and *moral waywardness*. Tests to measure 'intelligence' (later developed as intelligence quotient tests) resulted in several generations of children being labelled as innately *retarded, defective, slow … average … bright, exceptional, gifted*. IQ measures still excite the interest of many – as the numerous online IQ tests demonstrate.

Psychoanalytic theories of development

While the child study movement measured and charted children's mental and physical development across whole populations in order to establish benchmarks and milestones to provide a picture of 'normal' patterns of growth, psychoanalysts were busy looking *inside* individuals to identify the emotional factors that might affect development.

In Vienna, **Sigmund Freud** (1856–1939) developed his theories of psychosexual development, arguing that repressed feelings associated with incomplete maturation through oral, anal and genital phases of development from the age range of birth to six could interfere with mental health and the ability to become a successful learner. He placed particular emphasis on the mother–child relationship, where attachment and responsiveness provide the basis for a confident sense of self. His daughter **Anna Freud** (1895–1982) applied his ideas in her work in her nursery in Hampstead. She insisted on each child's having a consistent carer or '*maternal figure*' in the nursery setting, who, in the absence of the birth mother, could respond on a daily basis to changes in maturation and emotional needs. She advised adults to listen carefully to children in order to be able to provide sensitive support so that the children could develop

Figure 3.2 Sigmund Freud (1856–1939) with his daughter Anna (1895–1982). Anna Freud applied her father's ideas of psychosexual development in her own work with children.

Source: Author unknown [Public domain by age] via Wikipedia Commons

a robust sense of self, which would make them more resilient to physical and mental stresses and would help them to develop their abilities more fully.

Her contemporaries **Melanie Klein** (1882–1960) and **Susan Isaacs** (1885–1948) took up these Freudian ideas (see Klein and Isaacs in Rickman, 1936) and put 'emotional well-being' at the centre of healthy child development. They showed how small children are at the mercy of their internal *fears*, particularly in connection with the conflicting roles of parents, who simultaneously represent care /control and love/threat. They argued that young children developed best when they were encouraged to play naturally with a minimum of adult instruction in an atmosphere of warm and loving concern. They advised parents not to interfere in their children's primal desires – thumb sucking, excretion and masturbation – for fear of humiliating them and damaging their self-esteem. Isaacs pointed out that 'Even with the best parents in the world, the most considerate and the most skilful, the child will have his internal problems, since these arise from the inherent issues of human development' (Isaacs in Rickman, 1936: p. 169).

In the second half of the twentieth century, psychoanalytic theorists began to investigate the role of *family relationships* in healthy development. At the Tavistock Clinic in London, **John Bowlby** (1907–1990) studied the effects of separation on children and developed his *attachment* theory, in which he suggested that warm and intimate bonding between *mother and child* was a key indicator for healthy development. (See Chapter 7)

Time to reflect

Attachment theory developed out of studies of child evacuees separated from their families during the Second World War. In the 1970s as women were beginning to take up professional training and to agitate for equal pay for equal work, 'second wave' feminists objected to Bowlby's attachment theory. They accused Bowlby of making too much of the mother–child relationship and of being politically motivated by a desire to chain women to the kitchen sink. They argued that healthy attachment bonds can form between a child and any 'significant other' without interfering with development.

Richard Bowlby (2004), son of John, argues that children who are insecurely attached within the family are put at extra risk when they receive childcare outside the home if their relationship with a 'secondary attachment' figure is also insecure. In his studies of Romanian adoptees, Rutter showed that poor emotional bonding during the early years has negative effects on emotional development, which persist into adulthood. Belsky's study of children aged between three and 54 months who receive full-time childcare outside the home found that although they were cognitively and linguistically advanced for their age, they also showed more emotional disturbance, aggression and disobedience. Therapists Patricia Crittenden in *Raising Parents* and Steve Biddulph in *Raising Babies* examine the evidence for and against placing children in childcare before the age of three and advise caution on the grounds that at this age, children need one-to-one attention in order to develop healthy emotional bonds.

It seems that for children growing up in societies where both parents are encouraged to work while their children are under three, attachment-focused childcare has an important part to play in fostering healthy emotional development.

Steve Biddulph, in an interview for *The Telegraph* (13 March 2006) characterises British nurseries as 'Babies lying in rows of cots, then milling about in garish rooms through their toddler years, aching for one special adult to love them'. He adds that they are looked after by *underpaid teenagers with minimal qualifications*. How far does this chime with your own experience of day-care for children under three?

Do you think parents and grandparents should be funded to provide childcare in the home for children under three?

Another psychoanalyst, **D.W. Winnicott** (1896–1971), suggested that small children could suffer feelings of abandonment when separated from their main carer and that this could stunt their mental and physical growth. But, like Anna Freud, he thought the ill-effects could be ameliorated if young children could be looked after in an *emotionally* secure environment with a consistent carer and an empathetic ethos. He also suggested they could be helped through their anguish with a '*transitional object*' from home (such as a comfort blanket) and through a physically comforting *holding environment*. These psychoanalytic theories led to gradual changes in care and attitudes towards the emotional needs of all children and brought about changes in the way that adults treated children who were separated from their families – in hospitals and orphanages and in the initial transition from home to school (Nutbrown et al., 2008).

Other psychoanalytic thinkers like **Erik Erikson** (1902–1994) showed that positive relationships and support through the early stages of emotional and social development were crucial for health and balance, and he showed that when these stages of development were interrupted, there were negative effects on children's sense of identity and self-worth which prevented them building trust and independence. **Carl Rogers** (1902–1987) showed that lack of empathy and adverse emotional encounters like neglect and abuse put children at risk of delinquency, mental ill-health and criminality. He developed the idea of '*empathic understanding*', a process in which the adult consciously respects the child through careful, non-judgemental listening in order to help them overcome trauma. As a result of these psychoanalytic insights, the effects of poor nurture, including emotional abuse and physical neglect, were increasingly recognised as critical factors in poor physical and mental development (Nutbrown et al., 2008).

Focus on *The Tavistock Clinic*

The Tavistock Clinic is a famous centre for the study of children's mental health. Established in London in 1920, it initially offered help for shell-shocked soldiers and damaged children in the aftermath of the First World War. After the Second World War, following the traumas suffered by children during evacuation and bombing, it became a centre for paediatric mental health care and research. At the clinic, Esther Blick pioneered training in *close infant observation*; John Bowlby developed his *attachment theory*; and Mary Ainsworth investigated children's responses to separation through her *Strange Situation* observations.

In 1952, James and Joyce Robertson, both researchers at the clinic, were studying the effects of separation on hospitalised infants and children. They made an influential film, *A two year old goes to hospital*, which led to important changes in hospital practice. They found that although children were receiving excellent medical care in hospital, they failed to thrive. At the time, they noted that visiting hours for children in London hospitals were severely restricted:

Guy's Hospital: Sundays 2–4

St Bartholomew's: Wednesdays 2–2.30

St Thomas's: First month no visits; parents can see sleeping children 7–8 p.m.

West London: No visits

London Hospital: No visits for children under three; parents can see older children through partition twice weekly

The Robertsons observed the effects of separation on the children. They identified three consecutive phases of behaviour as the children tried to come to terms with their separation from family – *protest, despair and detachment*. At first the children cried furiously every time their parents left; next time they became quiet and miserable when their parents had visited; finally they withdrew into themselves and when their parents returned, they barely acknowledged them. The Robertsons showed that the lack of empathy shown by nurses and doctors towards children's feelings of terror and abandonment was delaying children's healthy recovery and that the restricted visits were negatively affecting parent–child relationships. In a very obvious way, emotions were interfering with healthy development.

How are children treated in hospitals today?
Could the Robertsons theories be applied to children in nursery settings?
Can you think of your own examples of the effects of separation on children in the world today?

Constructivist theories of development

Perhaps the most influential current theories associated with child development, particularly cognitive development, are those of the constructivists and social constructivists who have mapped the way in which children are constantly engaged in building their own learning through their own exploratory and investigative efforts (Wood, 1998; Pound, 2011). Chief among these are Jean Piaget (1896–1980), Lev Vygotsky (1896–1934), Lawrence Kohlberg (1927–1987) and Jerome Bruner (1915–2016). Piaget believed that children's capacity to learn was dependent upon their stage of maturity such that their understanding followed a set trajectory from concrete thinking in early childhood (an egocentric world view based on their immediate experience) to abstract thinking in later childhood (when they can decentre sufficiently to see other points of view). Vygotsky's work challenged this account by showing how children in mixed age groups, or supported by a more knowledgeable adult, could use other people's ideas and language to make leaps into abstraction even at a young age. Kohlberg's work on moral development supported the idea that children are capable of decentring at a young age to produce sophisticated abstract understanding. Jerome Bruner took up these ideas and applied them to parenting and teaching styles to show how the culture and language in which the child is embedded can facilitate or hinder the development of sophisticated thinking (see also Chapter 5).

Ecological theories of child development

In 1965, President Johnson launched his 'war on poverty' campaign and made early education a cornerstone of his plan to improve the lives of children in the United States through a project called *Head Start*. At the same time, David Weikart (1931–2003) set up the HighScope Perry Preschool Project to study how high quality health, welfare and education interventions for preschoolers from deprived backgrounds worked in practice. Researchers documented the progress of each child in minute detail and followed participants for the next 30 years (Schweinhart et al., 1993, 2005). The results suggested that *every dollar spent* on early intervention represented *seven dollars saved* because children who had been through the Head Start programme were more likely to continue in education, to make stable partnerships, to enter employment and to stay out of prison. Besides influencing governments around the world, Head Start also spawned the television programme *Sesame Street*, which spread the message around the world that the *early years matter*. *Sesame Street* is still broadcast to millions of pre-schoolers and their parents across 120 countries.

Urie Bronfenbrenner (1917–2016), a developmental psychologist associated with Head Start and the HighScope Perry Preschool Project, developed his ecological systems theory to explain how local, national and global factors affect individual development (see Chapter 8). In *The Ecology of Human Development: Experiments by Nature and Design* (1979), he showed how the child is *nested* at the centre of a complex ecology of interacting forces. His theory states that children's development is not fixed at birth but is shaped by the particular ecology of family, institution, culture and politics they are born into. He argued that development could be supported and *enhanced* through enlightened interventions with families and young children.

Bronfenbrenner's ecological approach to child development takes the spotlight off nature and shines it instead on the wider contexts of nurture that promote or limit healthy development. It is this wider perspective which underpins local, national and international efforts to support preschool intervention programmes for the most economically and socially disadvantaged children and their families. However, not everyone accepts the idea that early intervention can enhance children's development: they argue that the nature children are born with is a more potent force than the nurture they receive. For example, **Arthur Jensen** (1923–2012), a proponent of Spearman's *g* theory of general intellectual development (see Ch 5), controversially criticised the Head Start programme and raised the question of inherited intelligence by suggesting that IQ is differentially distributed across populations (and races) making it unlikely that interventions can make any significant improvements for individuals (Jensen, 1969).

Neuroscientific theories of development

At the beginning of the twenty-first century, advances in brain studies brought new neurological and biochemical explanations of development into focus. Neuroscientists observed that development of the brain is most rapid during the years from birth to three when neurones are forming connections. High neurone activity is an important adaptive feature of human development to allow for language learning and the constant updating of information throughout our lives; it appears that the denser the neurological connections the better equipped children will be to adapt to the challenges they meet (Gopnik, 2009).

Any form of deprivation (nutritional, physical, emotional or social) is likely to be detrimental to children's neurological development, and there is evidence to suggest that impoverished environments actually inhibit the development of neural networks. **Michael Rutter**'s work with adopted Romanian orphans shows how this development is arrested in severely deprived infants (Rutter 1998, 2002). He showed how orphaned children who spent their first few years in impoverished institutions – without warmth, affection and stimulation – suffered severe delays in development. However, with intense help in foster families, these children were able to overcome much of their developmental delay. Unfortunately, children who had spent longer in the orphanages and were older when interventions began were less likely to overcome the neurological damage inflicted by early neglect. (see Ch 4 and Ch 13)

Epigenetic theories of development

Most recently, discoveries in the field of epigenetics have provoked a good deal of interest among researchers in child development. Epigenetics is the study of the bio-chemical processes which switch genes on and off at a cellular level (Spector, 2003, 2012). Intriguingly, research shows that environmental stresses like emotional trauma from abuse or war, nutritional deficiencies in childhood, the mother's diet in pregnancy or child neglect can leave 'markers' on genes that can be passed down through the generations.

The idea that the human genome is responsive and not fixed has stirred debate, especially with the added insight that changes can be passed to succeeding generations. These discoveries are rewriting the rules of heredity, health and identity. Put simply, environmental factors can leave a mark on an individual's genes that can affect the developmental pathways of their children and grandchildren positively or negatively. Epigenetic theories seem to suggest that genes can change in response to environmental factors throughout life, which holds out the hope and possibility that wise interventions can promote healthy development at any stage (see also Chapter 5).

This idea has social policy implications for childcare – for example, we know that parent–child bonding is made more difficult by the effects of poverty, dislocation and strife and that 'attachment' is important for the mental and physical health of children – so we need to think carefully about the way we organise our society and our childcare settings to maximise the opportunities for emotional security for our youngest children.

Focus on The nature/nurture debate

In Steven Pinker's (2002) book *The Blank Slate: The Modern Denial of Human Nature*, he challenges his readers to answer the following questions:

- Are boys and girls interchangeable?
- Do all differences in physical and mental development come from the environment?
- Can parents micromanage the personalities of their children?

He suggests that in contemporary accounts of child development, the pendulum has swung too far towards *nurture* because researchers are afraid to acknowledge the effects of *nature*. He claims that nurture theories are based on an assumption that everyone starts with an equal chance in the developmental process and that this leads to a belief that children are like blank slates waiting to be inscribed at will by family and society.

He argues that somehow *nature has to be accommodated* because an exclusive focus on nurture perverts child-rearing into a form of social engineering. He points to new discoveries in neuroscience, epigenetics and evolutionary psychology that suggest that *nature* is a crucial element in shaping development, and he believes that our anxieties about acknowledging this are associated with fears about biological determinism and Social Darwinism.

He concludes that in order to understand human development, we need to take account of the *dynamic and reciprocal interactions* between nature and nurture:

Why might twenty-first century researchers be reluctant to acknowledge the effects of nature in determining child development?
How might findings from epigenetic research be implicated in nurture theories of child development?

Understanding child development

In Maria Robinson's (2011) book, *Understanding Behaviour and Development in the Early Years*, she suggests that child development is like a jigsaw where each piece contributes to the kind of behaviour children display. This jigsaw comes from Robinson (2011: preface) and is made up of

- brain growth and maturation
- the impact of sensory information
- the quality of interactions and relationships
- the broadly time-related emergence of skills, abilities, growth and change
- the impact of the adult's own internal world, their perceptions, attitudes, expectations and interpretations of the child's behavioural cues.

In other words, children do not develop in isolation, their biological development is subject to and modified by the behaviours and responses of the people who care for and educate them. For this reason, practitioners need to know how children perceive and organise their experiences as they grow and how to support them sensitively through each stage of the process. Robinson reminds us that the quality of early relationships and adults' reactions to children's emotional needs have a lasting impact on both brain and sensory development. The child is a unique individual, but the culture in which they exist determines how well they thrive.

At the root of every theory about human development is this basic puzzle about the relative effects of nature and nurture. Most people would agree that children around the world follow some pre-programmed patterns of development: they start off small, and they grow bigger; they cry, and then they talk; they crawl, and then they walk; and they move from emotional dependency to independence. But few believe that developmental patterns are fixed and immutable from birth. The nature/nurture debate is about the relative weights we give to each side of the argument. As early childhood specialists, you will find yourselves constantly balancing these nature/nurture arguments as you work towards *nurturing the unique natures* of the children in your care.

Summary

- Theories of development are often contested on the basis of nature and nurture.
- Theories of children's development are products of historical time and place and should be understood in context.

- The emergence of science during the Enlightenment challenged religious beliefs about good child-rearing practices.
- Theories about heredity led to theories of biological and social determinism.
- Social theories explored the effects of environment on children's development.
- Psychoanalytic theories uncovered emotional factors implicated in development.
- Ecological systems theories show how global, political, social, community and family factors affect children's development differently in different cultures.
- Neuroscientific theories explores how environmental factors alter the body's chemistry to stimulate or limit development.
- Epigenetic theories investigate the reciprocal relationship between nature and nurture at the cellular level and how positive and negative effects can be passed on to future generations.
- Although we need to recognise individual differences (nature), we need not assume that they are fixed; nurture theories offer hope for early interventions to help children develop to their full potential.

Topics for further discussion

1 Why is it important to 'know thyself' when working with young children?
2 What can an understanding of the history of theories of child development bring to the work of an early years specialist?
3 'Physically fit children are brainier than their peers' was a headline reporting research from the journal *Frontiers in Human Neuroscience* in 2014. How does this relate to the nature/nurture debate?

Assignments

1 Imagine Mary Wollstonecraft and her daughter Mary Shelley having a picnic with Jean-Jacques Rousseau. How might the conversation go?
2 Read the novel *Room* by Emma Donoghue. The book deals with the strategies a mother adopts to ensure that her son survives physically and mentally during forced captivity. During the writing of the book, the author consulted paediatricians and early childhood experts. What can you learn about the relative effects of nature and nurture on child development from the book?
3 Choose a modern childcare expert. How far are his or her ideas influenced by their beliefs about the relative influence of nature and nurture? How far are the ideas an expression of the expert's own contemporary cultural beliefs?

Further reading

Pinker, S. (2002) *The Blank Slate: the modern denial of human nature*. London: Allen Lane, The Penguin Press

Pound, L. (2011) *Influencing Early Childhood Education: Key Figures, Philosophies and Ideas*. New York: Open University Press/McGraw-Hill Education

Robinson, M. (2011) *Understanding Behaviour and Development in the Early Years: A Guide to Theory and Practice*. London: Routledge

References

Benziman, G. (2012) *Narratives of Child Neglect in Romantic and Victorian Culture*. Basingstoke: Palgrave Macmillan

Bowlby, R. (2004) *Fifty Years of Attachment Theory: The Donald Winnicott Memorial Lecture Given by Sir Richard Bowlby*. London: Karnac Books

Cunningham, H. (2006) *The Invention of Childhood*. London: BBC Books

Darwin, C. (1877) A Biographical Sketch of an Infant. *Mind* 2(7, July): 285–294

Edgeworth, M. and Edgeworth, R.L. (1798) *Practical Education*. London: J. Johnson

Frith, U. (1989) *Autism: explaining the enigma* (2nd edn, 2003). Oxford: Blackwell

Froebel, F. (1826) 'In childhood' from *On the Education of Man* reprinted in R. Parker-Rees and J. Willan (eds) (2006) *Early Years Education: Major Themes in Education*, Vol. 1 (pp. 66–72). London: Routledge

Giardello, P. (2014) *Pioneers in Early Childhood Education: The roots and legacies of Rachel and Margaret McMillan, Maria Montessori and Susan Isaacs*. Abingdon: Routledge

Gopnik, A. (2009) *The Philosophical Baby: What Children's Minds Tell Us About Truth, Love and the Meaning of Life*. New York: Farrar, Straus and Giroux

Isaacs, S. (1939) 'The Nursery as a Community' in J. Rickman (ed.) *On the Bringing up of Children* (pp. 167–232). London: Routledge

Jensen, A.R. (1969) How Much Can We Boost IQ and Scholastic Achievement? *Harvard Educational Review* 39(1): 1–123

Keating, P. (ed.) (1976) *Into Unknown England: 1866–1913, Selections from the Social Explorers*. Glasgow: Fontana

Klein, M. (1939) 'Weaning' in J. Rickman (ed.) *On the Bringing up of Children* (pp. 31–56). London: Routledge

Kuhn, T. (1962) *The Structure of Scientific Revolutions*. Chicago, IL, and London: University of Chicago Press

Locke, J. (1695) *Some Thoughts Concerning Education* extracts reprinted in R. Parker-Rees and J. Willan (eds) (2006) *Early Years Education: Major Themes in Education*, Vol. 1 (pp. 28–49). London: Routledge

Mayhew, H (2010) *London Labour and the London Poor*, based on original 1861–1862 edition. Oxford: Oxford University Press

Nutbrown, C., Clough, P. and Selbie, P. (2008) *Early Childhood Education: History, Philosophy and Experience*. London: Sage

Parker-Rees, R. and Willan, J. (eds) (2006) 'Extract from Letter 1 by Johann Heinrich Pestalozzi' in in R. Parker-Rees and J. Willan (eds) *Early Years Education: Major Themes in Education*, Vol. 1 (pp. 73–80). London: Routledge

Pinker, S. (2002), *The Blank Slate: the modern denial of human nature*. London: Allen Lane, The Penguin Press

Pound, L. (2011) *Influencing Early Childhood Education: Key Figures, Philosophies and Ideas*. New York: Open University Press/McGraw-Hill Education

Robinson, M. (2011) *Understanding Behaviour and Development in the Early Years: A Guide to Theory and Practice*. London: Routledge

Rousseau, J.J. (1762/1911) *Émile* (trans. by Barbara Foxley). London: DentRutter, M. and the English and Romanian Adoptees (ERA) Study Team (1998) Developmental catch-up, and deficit, following adoption after severe global early privation. *Journal of Child Psychology and Psychiatry* 39(4): 465–476

Rutter, M. (2002) Nature, nurture, and development: From evangelism through science toward policy and practice. *Child Development* 73(1): 1–21

Schweinhart, L.J.,Weikhart, D.P. and Toderan, R. (1993) *High quality Preschool Programmes Found to improve Adult status*. Ypsilante, MI: High/Scope Foundation

Schweinhart, L., Montie, J., Xiang, Z., Barnett, W.S., Belfield, C.R. and Nores, M. (2005) *Lifetime effects: the High/Scope Perry Preschool Study Through Age 40*. Monographs of the High/Scope Educational Research Foundation 14. Ypsilanti, MI: High/Scope Press

Spector, T. (2003) *Your Genes Unzipped*. London: Robson Book Chrysalis Books Group

Spector, T. (2012) *Identically Different: Why You Can Change Your Genes*. London: Weidenfeld and Nicolson

Wollstonecraft, M. (1792) *A Vindication of the Rights of Women*. London: J. Johnson (Penguin edition, 2004)

Wood, D. (1998) *How Children Think and Learn* (2nd edn) Oxford: Blackwell Publishing

Wooldridge, A. (1994) *Measuring the Mind: Education and Psychology in England, c. 1860–1990*. Cambridge: Cambridge University Press

UNDERSTANDING CHILD DEVELOPMENT: SUPPORTING THE UNIQUE CHILD

Physical development – the interplay of body and brain

4

Introduction

Part 2 considers the ways in which bodies and brains develop holistically as children engage physically, cognitively and emotionally with the world around them. Although the process is holistic, it seems easier for the purposes of study to break it into the classical areas of development, covering physical, cognitive, social, linguistic and emotional development.

The human child has a very long period of dependency compared to other mammals, and it takes around eight years to develop from vulnerable baby through mobile toddler to chatty preschooler and independent schoolchild. Parents and carers need to constantly adapt to the growing child in order to provide the right balance of nutrition, exercise, sleep and stimulation to support each developmental phase.

Development is a holistic process of interaction between body and brain, involving reciprocal physical, social, emotional and intellectual responses. It is dependent on the interplay of heredity, character, family, neighbourhood and culture, and no two children will develop in exactly the same way – even identical twins brought up in the same home will be different. Children progress at different speeds, and it is important to remember that the charts included in this chapter showing the 'normal' path of development can provide only a rough guide to what might be expected for a particular child at a given age.

Stages of development

We all know that tiny babies have to be kept warm and safe, fed and clean, but it would be a mistake to think that is all they need in the first year and to assume that their minds begin to grow only when they start talking. There is much more going on in the mind of a baby than most people imagine. Within minutes of birth, the baby is searching for her mother's face, gazing steadily into her eyes as she feeds and making the first connections between herself and the outside world; within a few weeks, she will already be turning her head to get a better view of what's going on. From the very beginning, body and brain grow in tandem – every movement the baby makes, every sensation of taste, touch, sound, sight and smell is mapped onto neural pathways linking to the spinal cord and brain (Gregory, 2004).

Physical maturation and control begin with the head and then proceed to the limbs – new born babies can turn their heads searching for the nipple and within a few months they have the strength and motor control to lift their heads when placed on their tummies. It takes longer to learn to control arms and legs, and babies characteristically flail their limbs in an uncoordinated way, especially when they are excited. The baby gradually learns where her limbs are (*proprio-centrism*) as their position is mapped onto the developing neural pathways in the brain, and very soon she is able to reach out deliberately for whatever she can see (Robinson, 2011). By the end of the first year, most babies have enough control over their larger muscles (*gross motor control*) to shuffle, crawl or even walk towards a desirable object and enough control over fingers and thumbs (*fine motor control*) to feed themselves and handle objects (usually by putting them in their mouths first!). Soon, her control over the muscles in her mouth and tongue will have developed enough to turn experimental babble into distinguishable speech.

By age two, children are entirely mobile and have begun using language with increasing fluency. By this time, they are clearly individual characters with their own preferences and desires, already making a bid for independence. On the cusp between babyhood and childhood, they are still physically clumsy and mentally fragile and are likely to collapse in a tantrum when things take an unexpected turn. They need constant vigilance to protect them from accidents, along with a great deal of cherishing to help them overcome the frustrations involved in the mastery of their bodies and emotions.

By age three, they are more independent: they are generally in control of their bodily functions; they play actively with others; they constantly ask questions; and they endlessly practise their physical skills, delighting in their new-found prowess. But they still need a lot of support and nurturing to keep them safe and happy. There is an enormous amount for them to discover in this third year of life, when their brains are working at maximum capacity. At this age they ask sophisticated questions and seek out physical challenges, both of which develop the dense neural networks necessary for optimal development – any lack of physical and mental stimulation during the first three years can leave them impaired and make it hard to catch up later. For carers it can often be difficult to strike the balance between protecting a three year old and giving them opportunities to expand – one minute they think they can fly like Superman, the next they are cowering in their mother's skirts and sucking anxiously on their fingers. This is the peak time for accidents, and adults have to be extra vigilant.

The four- to five-year-old is more predictable; he moves confidently and has some understanding of his limitations. He may already be riding a bicycle, playing computer games or catching and kicking a ball. He is less reliant on family and takes his cue from other children as he forms friendships and rivalries and establishes his place in the world. He still needs the family for protection and nourishment, but his focus is on the outside world.

The years from six to eight are a time for consolidation; by age six, children have a high degree of control over their limbs and delight in refining their physical skills. By now they can recognise hunger, thirst and fatigue, and by the time they are eight, most will have a clear understanding of what is required to keep them well and healthy so that they can begin to make informed choices about wholesome food, drink, exercise, rest and recreation.

Figure 4.1 By age six, children have a high degree of control over their limbs and delight in refining their physical skills.

Source: Getty Images/Nino H. Photography

Although we are all pre-programmed to develop along a typical path – like caterpillars turning into butterflies – no two children follow exactly the same path, because their experiences inside and outside the womb will make their development uniquely different (Gopnik, 1999).

Typical development is represented in charts that show approximate timings for each developmental milestone, but there will always be developmental variation across any group of children. In a study of conjoined twins, Tim Spector (2012), a leading epigeneticist and neuroscientist, found that even conjoined twins who share the same genes and environment had quite different personalities and abilities. Reaching milestones 'late' is not usually a cause for concern, and reaching them 'early' is not an indicator of incipient genius.

Body and brain

Bodies and brains do not develop separately but interact with one another, responding to macro- and micro-environmental factors in such personal ways that every child develops into a *unique* individual (Shonkoff et al., 2000; Trevarthen, 2004, 2005). The brain is not 'hardwired' but instead changes physically in response to experience.

We can illustrate this neuroplasticity in the dynamic interaction between body, brain and environment by thinking about the neural networks involved in the baby's first smile – that is, the early reflex smile designed to promote bonding between newborn baby and carer. When a baby first produces this smile, most adults respond with extra attention and an answering smile, which provides a positive feedback loop in the baby's neural network. But for babies with unresponsive carers, there may be no feedback, and for babies suffering autism or impaired vision, the carer's response may be missed; these disadvantaged babies may take longer to learn to smile or may never learn without specific, targeted help. These same feedback mechanisms in the nervous system operate across the whole range of children's interactions with their environments.

Neural networks

Imaging technology and neuroscience have brought new insights to our understanding of how the body and brain develop complex neural networks as the child grows from infant to adult:

- The embryo is particularly vulnerable to damage while it develops the neural tube from which the brain and spinal cord arise.
- Once *neurons* (nerve cells) are in place, they extend *axons* (transmitting nerve fibres) and *dendrites* (receiving nerve fibres), ready to form connections across the *synapses* (junctions between the two).
- Synapses allow the nerve cells to communicate with each other, and they continue to proliferate, particularly through the first three years of life, enabling rapid learning.
- Most neurons are already present before birth and the brain develops rapidly in the early years with a blossoming of *synapses* between nerve cells.
- The brain 'prunes' any synapses that are under-used in a *use-it-or-lose-it* process that occurs around the third year of life; this makes the neural pathways more efficient but may make it harder to acquire certain skills later on.
- Children develop the structures that maintain physical, social, emotional and intellectual development in the first few years of childhood, and their capacity to build these structures decreases as they get older; this suggests there may be *critical periods* for maximising the learning of some skills.
- Some stresses inhibit and even damage developing brain structures, such as maternal ill-health or substance abuse during pregnancy; childhood illness; malnutrition; neglect; parental depression; and family trauma.
- Early interactions with people and with stimulating physical environments are crucial for brain development.
- There is some evidence that there are developmental differences associated with gender, heredity and cultural circumstances.
- At birth the brain is 25 per cent of adult size; by age six, it is about 95 per cent of adult size.

In the past, people tended to believe that babies just needed physical care – parents were encouraged to swaddle their babies' limbs to limit movement and not to overtax their brains with too much excitement.

Time to reflect

How might new understandings of early brain development influence the behaviour of modern parents and carers in their interactions with babies and toddlers?

Antenatal environments

All babies in utero are affected by their maternal environment (Robinson, 2011). They may suffer damage from drugs, alcohol, cigarettes, toxic environmental chemicals, diseases like rubella (measles) or the effects of stress hormones (especially in early pregnancy) when harmful substances are transferred directly from the mother's bloodstream to the baby's bloodstream through the placenta. In later pregnancy, these substances may cause detectable foetal distress – this can be seen in scans when, for example, the foetus recoils violently when the mother inhales cigarette smoke. Babies are sometimes born with alcohol and drug dependency and suffer terrible withdrawal symptoms for many weeks after birth. Others may contract HIV or other sexually transmitted diseases as they pass through the birth canal. So even before and during birth, physical development can be compromised by external factors.

The importance of good maternal health

The mother's health is a major factor during in utero development of a baby. Fresh air, sunlight, a nutritious diet, exercise, sleep and a calm atmosphere provide the best environment for an expectant mother and her growing baby. Mothers with poor diets may be unable to provide enough nutrients for themselves and their baby, and across the world, millions of mothers are at risk from deficiencies in folic acid, iodine, vitamin A, iron and vitamin D, which can cause ill-health and birth defects. This has led to controversial public health initiatives to fortify staple foods with micronutrients to redress the balance (WHO & FAO, 2006).

Some problems may be sensitive to cultural differences. For instance, there is concern about vitamin D deficiency among Asian women living in North European countries, which, during pregnancy, may adversely affect the developing foetal brain. The main source of vitamin D (80–90 per cent) comes from the body's reaction to sunlight, while secondary sources are found in fish, fish liver oil, egg yolks, fortified grains and dairy products. Vegetarians are at higher risk of deficiency than meat eaters, and people with darker skins cannot absorb as much vitamin D from the weak sunlight of the northern hemisphere. Many Asian families have a vegetarian diet, which compounds the problem of living in a northern climate. The UK Committee on Medical Aspects of Food Policy advises all Asian parents to give their children vitamin D supplements for the first five years of life to counteract problems that may result from deficiency, such as fits, poor dentition, infantile rickets and cataracts (Shaw & Pal, 2002).

Rigorously monitoring pregnancy and foetal health and providing birthing facilities help to reduce the incidence of neonatal mortality in wealthier countries, but in countries where facilities are poor, where child marriages and early motherhood are common or where girls are subject to FGM, mortality rates for mothers and babies during labour and just after birth remain high. For instance, in 2008, 3.57 million deaths among neonates occurred globally across 192 countries, and of these 49 per cent were recorded in just five countries: India, Nigeria, the Democratic Republic of Congo, Pakistan and China (Black et al., 2010)

Gestation

Prenatal maternity care is an important part of healthy child development. The length of gestation (the period from conception to birth) varies in humans from 34–42 weeks after fertilisation – normal gestational length is shorter in Black and Asian women compared with White European women (Patel et al., 2003). Brain development in the womb is highly vulnerable to hazards such as toxic chemicals, malnutrition, viral infections and stress hormones; it also appears to be markedly modified by the presence of testosterone, which influences the development of male sexual organs and male brains so that some gender differences may be present at birth (Robinson, 2011).

Table 4.1 In utero physical development

From conception	Length	Features
Weeks 0–2		*Germinal* stage from fertilisation to implantation.
Month 1	8 mm	*Embryo* stage (before skeletal development) – organ differentiation; limb buds appear.
Month 2	13 mm	Brain developing, lungs forming, face and ears visible, major organs in place.
Month 3	8 cm	*Foetal* stage – liver active, genitals differentiate, tooth buds present, cartilage for skeletal development begins to form; can make a fist; eyes closed heart beat detectable at 3 months.
Month 4	15 cm	Foetus doubles in length in one month, active movements, lips make sucking motions, pancreas active, muscle and bone evident.
Month 5	20 cm	Eyelashes, eyebrows, finger and toe nails; lanugo, a creamy protective substance, covers body; mother will feel 'quickening'.
Month 6	28 cm	Weighs 725 g, foot and finger prints; eyes develop; lungs have air sacs; evidence of 'startle reflex'; foetal brain scans show gender differences.
Month 7	38 cm	Weighs 1.2 kg; eyes open and close, can distinguish light and dark; auditory bones and canals are already adult size, responds to sounds from inside and outside womb, especially the mother's voice; brain, nervous system and respiratory system grow fast; responsive to pressure, pain, vibrations and temperature; may survive premature birth – but hazardous because respiratory and digestive tracts still immature.
Month 8	43 cm	Weighs 2 kg; skeleton in place but bones soft; a better chance of surviving premature birth.
Month 9	48 cm	Weighs 3 kg; sucking reflex strong, digestive tract matures; can be born safely from 34 weeks.
Month 10	53 cm	*Lanugo* disappears. The most likely time for birth (34–42 weeks, average full term delivery date differs by race). Average weight for boys 3.6 kg, for girls 3.2 kg (again differs by ethnicity). Oxytocin (the 'bonding hormone') released into the blood as the baby passes through the birth canal. Caesarean section may *not* release oxytocin.

Where conditions are stressful (for example, in war zones and areas of famine), the incidence of twins falls markedly and fewer boys than girls are born. It seems that boys are the weaker sex – they are more likely to be miscarried, more likely to be born prematurely and more likely to die during birth and in the first year of life. Various explanations have been put forward: boys may be more adversely affected by the mother's stress hormones; they are bigger at full term and may have more difficulties during birth; they have poorer immune systems; and they are more likely to suffer respiratory problems associated with premature birth. In times of peace and plenty, 105 boys are born for every 100 girls (although selective abortion of girls in some cultures skews this figure globally).

Birth

Although babies have only 25 per cent of their adult brain size at birth (compared to 50 per cent in other primates), they still have relatively large heads in relation to the size of the birth canal. They are born with flexible skulls and rather 'rubbery' bones to make the journey through the birth canal easier. Birth is traumatic, and the transfer to a world of loud noise, bright light, temperature changes and activity can be unsettling, but immediate contact with the mother's skin brings reassurance.

Newborn babies are checked over immediately after birth. In the West, they will be given an Apgar test (Appearance, Pulse, Grimace, Activity, Respiration) to check the following:

- breathing effort
- heart rate
- muscle tone
- reflex irritability
- skin colour.

This first test gives an indication of how well the baby has survived the birthing process. After five minutes, the test is repeated to establish how well the baby is adapting to life outside the womb so that babies with poor scores can be given special care.

Infancy

Bonding

In the womb, babies already have a sucking reflex so that at birth they are ready to latch onto the nipple and feed. Within a very short time, mothers and babies will be staring at one another intently, learning each other's facial features, listening to each other, enjoying skin-to-skin contact and starting to bond. This bonding process is activated in the mother by *oxytocin* released into the bloodstream during birth and is strengthened by her response to the newborn baby's reflexes of grasping and rooting. This early bonding lays the foundation for later attachment behaviour with the person who nurtures, loves and plays with the child and which in turn underpins later well-being and health (Gerhardt, 2004).

Feeding

Babies need a very high protein diet for all the growth and development that happens in the early days – modern formula milk mimics breast milk very closely but it does not contain the antibodies that help develop a robust immune system, so breast feeding with the first milk from the mother is recommended. Breast-fed babies gain weight more slowly than bottle-fed babies, but within 10–20 days all babies should have regained their birth weight. A review of existing studies suggests that breast-fed babies are at lower risk of obesity than bottle-fed babies (Owen et al., 2005).

The first few weeks

Newborn babies usually cry a lot during the first three months; it is their only way of alerting carers to their needs. They may feel pain, discomfort, hunger or thirst, loneliness, fatigue, boredom or frustration, or they may be too hot or too cold (because in the early weeks, they are unable to regulate their own temperature). The carer has to decide which reason is most likely. A common assumption is that the baby wants food, but it may be that they just want cuddling and reassurance, playtime or even some peace and quiet.

Some unlucky babies have colic in the first weeks of life – the reasons for this are unclear, but affected babies pull up their legs as if they have painful abdominal cramp and cry continuously for several hours. The crying bouts often start in the early evening and continue until baby and carer are both exhausted. The condition may present at about two weeks and last until three months, when it magically disappears – much to everyone's relief. Colic can put a severe strain on the bonding relationship when parents and baby become stressed and exhausted, and practitioners need to be very sympathetic.

Smiling

All babies have an instinctive reflex smile. It is rather weak at first, and some people dismiss it as 'wind', but it has an important part to play in fostering the bonding process. By five weeks, it has developed into a deliberate smile, with a lit-up face and twinkling eyes and is bestowed on everyone; later, the smile is used selectively and only beamed onto trusted family members!

Babbling

The random noises made by accidental combinations of lips and breath are the same sounds the world over. To turn babble into words requires the coordination of over 70 muscles, and it takes nearly a year to master the first word. Blowing, bubbling, calling, listening, watching, feeling lips and even crying and screeching are all part of the process of bringing mouth, vocal cords and brain under coordinated control. Talking to babies in high-pitched 'parentese' (simple speech) is a universal phenomenon because this is what they respond to best (particularly their mother's voice, which they already know from the womb).

The importance of touch

There is evidence that close physical contact is particularly important for early development. This was first highlighted in a famous article, called *Family vs. Institution*, by Henry Dwight Chapin (1926). Chapin surveyed American orphanages in the early twentieth century and found that infant mortality among babies in orphanages was 422.5 per thousand as against 87.4 per thousand among babies in families. He noticed that orphaned babies were deprived of touch and human contact in their first few weeks and soon became listless and unresponsive; he concluded that one-to-one contact was an essential part of the developmental process in human infants. More recently, in the English and Romanian Adoptees (ERA) study, Rutter et al. (2007) concluded that a lack of physical human comfort and warmth amounting to 'psychological privation' in the early months was probably the most important contributory factor in slowing children's development. (See ch 13)

Babies in need of special care

Some babies may need special care – and often their parents, siblings and wider family will need special care too. Practitioners should remember that

- every life is of equal value;
- care should be provided on the basis of need;
- parents should be given clear and comprehensive information about care plans in plain and neutral language.

Helping parents meet their child's difficulties smooths the way for the bonding process, which can be disrupted when there is cause for concern. Maternity staff are most likely to rely on a 'medical model', providing facts and figures to explain prognosis; however, after the initial diagnosis, it may be more appropriate for practitioners to work from a 'social model', encouraging parents to focus on the support services that will empower them in the care of their child and giving them information that allows them to see the baby as a small person with rights who will be respected and 'enabled' in and by the wider community.

Focus on *Sir Michael Rutter (1933–)*

Michael Rutter was born in 1933 to English parents in Lebanon, where his father was a doctor. The family returned to England before the outbreak of the Second World War. In 1940 when the threat of a German invasion seemed imminent, he was separated from his parents and sent, with his sister, to North America. He attended school there, before returning to take up a place at Wolverhampton Grammar School. Later, he studied at Birmingham Medical School.

His interests lay in child development, particularly the psychosocial factors affecting attachment and separation. He became the first professor of child psychiatry, and his groundbreaking work in neuropsychiatry and psychiatric epidemiology led to him being dubbed the 'father of child psychology'.

In 1972 his book *Maternal Deprivation Re-assessed* famously challenged John Bowlby's attachment theory. He showed that babies make multiple attachments and that separation from attachment figures was less problematic than the *disruption* to familiar routines and expectations which followed. He argued that different children have different 'vulnerability factors' which make them more or less 'resilient' in coping with the harm of separation and disruption.

In 1974, he published *The Qualities of Mothering* where he discussed the ways in which emotionally deprived environments lead to intellectual retardation and the emergence of anti-social personality disorders.

In 1989, after the end of Ceaucescu's regime in Romania, he led the English and Romanian Adoptees (ERA) study (see ch 13). This longitudinal study followed the lives of Romanian orphanage children adopted into English families to assess their progress across a range of behavioural, emotional, cognitive, academic, social and health measures. Children were assessed at four, six, 11 and 15 years of age and researchers concluded that early adoption offered the best chance of good outcomes for children who had spent the first years of their life in institutions.

In 1994, Rutter set up the Social, Genetic and Developmental Psychiatry Centre and expanded his studies into genetics, neuroimaging and the interaction of biological and social factors in child development. The Michael Rutter Centre for Children and Adolescents, at the Maudsley Hospital in London is named in his honour.

From neonate (newborn) to two-year-old

Human babies are less developed than primate babies when they are born. The *fontanelles* ('soft spots' in the skull) which allowed them to pass through the birth canal gradually harden into a skull plate over the first two years of life, and the soft bones of the skeleton gradually *ossify* (harden through mineralisation) as they grow to provide the rigid structure they need to support their body later. Their *muscles* and *ligaments* develop in tandem with their bones as they become increasingly mobile.

Babies are born with relatively short limbs which grow very fast in the first months and they need lots of opportunities to wave their arms and legs about. These movements are random, but with repetition they become patterned into the brain and neural system. As they encounter new objects, the information they get from touch, sight, sound and taste will be recorded in their internal representation of the world. As they move, the brain maps the position of the limbs (proprio-centrism) until they can accurately predict distance from self to object and the effort required to grasp it. Impaired babies with muscle or skeletal problems may need to have their limbs manipulated to simulate this patterning onto the brain.

Movement is integral to every facet of development – both as a part of physical development itself and as a means of facilitating the development of other skills and abilities – movement helps young children quite literally to get to grips with reality. Between four and nine months

Table 4.2 Pattern of physical developments, from birth to two

Age	Gross motor development	Fine motor and sensory development
Newborn	Lies prone, body floppy. When picked up, shows reflex stepping (plantar motion), flails limbs, shows startle reflex in response to a loud noise. Grasps a proffered finger.	Turns head to light or sound. Controls eyes and blinks. Focal length of 25 cm. Clasps and unclasps hands. Feels heat and cold but cannot regulate own body temperature. Hearing fully functional. Likes sweet tastes – breast milk.
Around 1 month	Begins to hold up head and turns it at will. Presses down with his feet into carer's lap. First 'real' smile.	Can follow a moving object with eyes and head. Distinguishes between black and white and some primary colours. Face shows interest. Preference for images of faces particularly the mother. Opens hand to grasp a proffered finger.
Around 3 months	Beginnings of reaching. Movement smoother and less jerky. Holds head up with straight back if held in sitting position. Holds head and chest up when placed flat on tummy. May roll over. Shows excitement with vigorous motions of limbs and head.	Begins to explore by watching everything, including own hands. May clasp hands together. Likes to bash and kick at hanging objects. May suck thumb or fingers. Seems to recognise that things are separate and tangible.
Around 6 months	Raises arms to be picked up. Rolls over, can lift head and shoulders when lying on back. Sits when propped up.	Reaches and holds things confidently in fist. Can pass things hand to hand. Will hold and suck on finger food. Will test everything by putting it to his mouth.
Around 9 months	Wriggling, crawling and shuffling. Sits up unaided. Pulls herself up to standing position.	Begins to use finger and thumb to pick things up (pincer movement), pokes and points with one finger. Shares gaze to focus on an object of joint interest with another person. Can manage a spoon. Plays clapping games and peekaboo. May self-comfort with thumb sucking or by carrying a comfort blanket.
Around 1 year	Sits well, pulls herself round furniture, may walk holding hands. May climb – a dangerous time.	Can pick up tiny objects (and may put them in his mouth). Will listen to and follow instructions. Begins to imitate and pretend. Plays with stacking toys. First words.
Around 15 months	Staggering walk. Bold physical movements – she will need extra vigilance. Peak age for accidents.	Builds with bricks. Makes marks with crayons, especially on walls! May begin arranging toys in patterns.
Around 18 months	Walks with swinging arms, kneels, squats, climbs and carries things around. Still only has 3 bones in wrist (27 in adult wrist).	May hammer pegs into holes, thread beads, fix bricks like Duplo. May want to help with household jobs.
Around 2 years	Runs, pulls wheeled toys, rides wheeled push-alongs, throws and kicks balls. Manages steps up and down.	Manages a vocabulary of around 300 words, likes wrapping and unwrapping, construction toys and even jigsaws. May be clean and dry (but may not be).

babies learn to sit up, to reach out and grasp objects, to shake them about and to put them to their mouths. Sensitive and responsive parents tune into the baby's changing needs and provide them with optimum support, help and interest (Panksepp, 1998, in Robinson, 2011). This is a good time to introduce baskets of random items (*treasure baskets*) for them to explore with eyes, fingers, mouths and ears as their movements become more deliberate so that the pathways in the neural networks are patterned and strengthened by repetition.

> ### Time to reflect
>
> Many waiting rooms and nurseries have a 'treasure basket' for babies to explore. What would you put in a treasure basket to ensure there was something to stimulate every sense?

Between nine and 12 months babies will show increasing coordination. Their muscle movements become less jerky, and they can reach out confidently. Sequences and patterns in their neural networks make planning possible, and their actions show more deliberation. They will soon start trying to crawl or shuffle or to reach things that are beyond their grasp and they will need more opportunities and space for exercising muscles and strengthening bones.

This is a difficult time for carers and a dangerous time for infants – a time when every electrical flex acts like a magnet, when every animal tail must be grasped, when every step must be climbed – sometimes with disastrous consequences. Toddler proofing the environment is essential, but at the same time, children need opportunities for 'safe accidents' in order to learn to manage risk.

Between 12 and 18 months they begin to walk and talk. They will show more control over the fine muscles in mouth and tongue so that they can reproduce particular sounds from the stream of babble that has characterised their 'language' so far. As they move around, their bones get thicker, their muscles grow stronger and their ligaments get tougher. By age two, the knee caps will have finally set and hardened, but not the

Figure 4.2 Between nine and 12 months is a difficult time for carers and a dangerous time for infants - every animal tail must be grasped, every step must be climbed.

Source: Photodisc/Getty Images

ankle and wrist bones. Their gait will become 'normal' once the ankle bones and associated muscles and ligaments have become fully developed – the pigeon-toed walk of many infants is a result of soft ligaments not yet tough enough to hold the developing bones of the ankle in place.

Young children's brains are highly *plastic* and are more densely connected than adults' brains. These connections sap energy, and the brain continually fine-tunes them, discarding those that are under-used or slow and retaining those which are efficient and fast. This is the brain's *use-it-or-lose-it* facility, mentioned earlier in this chapter, which gradually prunes the thickets of neural connections into fewer, stronger and more reliable branches as the child grows (Santos & Noggle, 2011).

Focus on *'Critical periods' of development*

In the second half of the twentieth century, biologists such as Nikolaas Tinbergen and Konrad Lorenz suggested that there were *'critical'* or *'sensitive'* periods in animal development that offered limited opportunities for learning essential behaviours. Animals that 'missed' these critical periods failed to develop the behaviours later. Other observers noticed similar limitations in human infants: children who had received little or no stimulation in the early years were typically unresponsive; they rarely cried, cooed or babbled and hardly ever exhibited the busy muscle movements that most children display.

The concept of critical or sensitive periods in child development and evidence for their existence in various domains of human cognition and learning – including basic sensory systems; social and emotional development; and language learning and acquisition – has had an impact on early childhood policy and practice (Shonkoff et al., 2000). Early interventions based on 'readiness' and 'developmentally appropriate practice' (DAP) are widely promoted to capitalise on these *critical* periods, when learning is most efficient.

However, other research, including evidence from the English and Romanian Adoptee study, suggests that although the parts of the brain responsible for complex operations like controlling movement and acquiring language are almost complete by the time the child is two, development and maturation can continue through childhood and adolescence and into adulthood. For the most part, it seems that brain plasticity allows humans to learn new skills throughout their lives.

(A collection of articles on 'critical periods' can be found in Bailey et al., 2001).

From three to eight

From age three onwards, children are honing their muscle coordination, focusing on what most interests them and directing their energies outwards. The way they gradually gain control over their bodies – their motor development – is fairly automatic, and there is little that can be done to speed up the process. However, lack of suitable stimulation and opportunity can *slow* the process down. Particular physical skills may develop in fits and starts depending on the child's gender, interests and disposition, but by age eight most children will be physically coordinated to a very high degree and will have the capacity to improve for the rest of their lives.

> **Focus on** *Fine motor skills and gender*
>
> Practitioners sometimes observe that girls develop fine motor skills, such as threading beads or handling Lego, earlier than boys. A medical article entitled 'Automatic bone age assessment for young children from newborn to seven-year-old using carpal bones' (Zhang et al., 2007) describes how babies are born with only 'outline' carpal (wrist) bones made of soft cartilage and these gradually differentiate into the 27 overlapping bones found in adults. This overlapping begins in girls at around five years and in boys at around seven years. The researchers report that *carpal* bone maturation is generally complete in girls by age six but is not complete in boys until age eight.
>
> How might this research affect our understanding of developmental scales designed to assess *typical* fine motor skills?

Children need lots of opportunities to practise their newly learned physical skills. They need spaces and challenges to develop their coordination and to strengthen muscles, to build bone density and toughen cartilage. As they engage physically with the world and the people in it, they develop a sense of risk and adventure, building on experience to keep safe and learning what works socially, emotionally and cognitively.

From age five onwards they may ask to play sports like football, dancing, gymnastics, bat and ball. Gradually they will master fine motor skills like tying shoelaces, using implements and tools, playing games on consoles, using a keyboard, painting, drawing and writing. Soon, usually by age seven, they will be able to grasp rules (although they may not like losing) and be able to play team games, which will improve their predictive skills as they take account of others' actions and intentions.

Table 4.3 Pattern of physical developments, ages three to eight

Age	Gross Motor Development	Fine Motor Development
Around 3 years	Can jump from a low step, climbs, walks backwards and sideways, stands on one leg, walks on tiptoe, throws and kicks a ball. Can carry and manoeuvre large objects. May even be able to pedal.	Can draw simple shapes, and model in dough. Can eat with a fork and spoon, get washed and dry. May be able to dress and undress (with help). Is often dry at night.
Around 4 years	Can walk, run and climb confidently. Hops, bends and swings from his arms on a climbing frame. Is better at throwing and is able to catch sometimes. More boys than girls may actively seek out rough and tumble and hero play.	Can manage a pencil more easily (especially girls), draws and builds from memory. Can copy drawings. Uses toilet unaided (mostly), better at undressing and dressing (although buttons may still be a problem), Helps with tasks. More girls than boys may actively seek out table top play. Computer games attract their interest.

Age	Gross Motor Development	Fine Motor Development
Around 5 years	Confident children will test out their athleticism – somersaulting, trying to do handstands, hanging upside down on climbing frame. They will show rhythm and enjoy dancing. Less confident children may be more cautious and may need to be encouraged to use their bodies more boldly. They can now cope with simple team games.	Will actively seek out 'making' opportunities – construction toys, wood working, cooking, sewing, digging tunnels, making dens and hideaways. All these depend on the services of a helpful adult to demonstrate the associated skills. Show great ease and familiarity with computer games (especially if available at home). Girls may show more fine muscle control than boys at this stage.
Around 6–8	This is a period of consolidation of muscle coordination. Sporty children will begin to be visible among their peers. Strength will increase, and demands for opportunities for independent outside play will also increase. Skipping ropes, roller skates, skateboards and bicycles allow them to show off their improving skills. Able to coordinate successfully in team sports. Enjoy vigorous exercise and difficult physical challenges.	The fine muscles movements will be continually refined. Children will become more adept at writing and more fluent in their hand movements. Girls will have fully developed wrists by age 6. Boys will have fully developed wrists by age 8. Computer may be preferred writing instrument when available.

School-age children still need lots of hands-on experience to grasp abstract concepts, like number and shapes or scientific and artistic principles and need to physically manipulate materials to support their cognitive learning. But it is easy to overlook just how important physical engagement is once formal schooling begins and the emphasis of education shifts towards the intellectual skills that can be measured through tests (Whitebread & Coltman, 2015). This need to manipulate things physically gradually decreases as they acquire an invisible 'symbolic' representation of the world in their heads that they can work on without the need for actual objects.

Developmental delay and impairment

Some children will have special educational needs and disabilities (SEND). Early detection of visual, auditory and perceptual-motor impairment is essential to ensuring that the right early interventions that will maximise the child's capacity to progress are provided. Infants with special needs may need more time, special help and extra resources to achieve the same patterning on the brain as the majority of children. The neural pathways may develop differently, but the end result will be similar (Karmiloff-Smith, 2012).

Hearing impairment

Children who are born deaf can still learn language with great proficiency during their early years, as long as they get the right stimulation and have imaginative and thoughtful people around them who can envisage ways to overcome obstacles. Hearing-impaired children will need to have their attention brought to bear on the speaker perhaps by a touch. For hearing-impaired children, Makaton (a system of picture communication cards) and 'sign language' are important tools to help avoid misunderstanding and frustration. Practitioners should remember these simple points when working with hearing-impaired children:

- Get their attention before you start talking and look at them as you speak.
- Don't talk too quickly or too slowly. Speak clearly as you would to anyone else.
- Lip reading helps, but don't exaggerate your mouth movements or talk too loudly.
- If it is important, write or draw the message or take the child somewhere quiet to explain.
- Explore sign language and Makaton with them.
- Make sure you know how to make the best of any mechanical aids they may be wearing.
- Be patient. It can be frustrating for you both.

Time to reflect

How might you introduce a hearing-impaired child to a new group of children in nursery? What practical steps would you take to help them integrate with their peers?

Visual impairment

Visually impaired children usually have some residual vision (only around 15 per cent suffer total blindness) and they will need extra help from adults and careful monitoring by medical staff and ophthalmologists in order to move around confidently.

Practitioners should bear in mind the following points when working with visually impaired children:

- Keep things tidy – right things in the right places. Unexpected obstacles can be dangerous and can make partially sighted children nervous about moving around.
- Take time to guide children around unfamiliar places. Point out any changes in the environment that they may need to be aware of, describe the territory and indicate distances and potential hazards.
- Explain carefully when you want to draw their attention to particular features – the pointed or sharp ends of tools, for example. Give them lots of opportunities to feel their way around new objects. Supervise and comment, but don't interfere.
- Don't let your anxieties undermine their active exploration – they need the same challenges as other children if they are to successfully learn to negotiate the world.
- Let *them* guide *you* as to the amount of help they require.

Time to reflect

Think about a setting you know well. Are there any potential hazards for a visually impaired toddler?
How might the environment be improved for them so that they could explore independently?
How would you encourage a visually impaired toddler to

- use the climbing frame,
- catch a ball,
- make a picture of a face?

Stress in infants

Trauma and emotional stress can have a major impact on infant brain development by flooding the system with *cortisol* (the fight or flight hormone), which keeps the body and brain on extended 'high alert'. Elevated readings of cortisol are found in young children living in families with warring parents or in neglectful or abusive households. They are also found in babies and young infants who are temporarily separated from their families. Stressed children with persistently raised levels of cortisol may show developmental delay, aggression and poor concentration; even after the immediate threat has passed, the high readings can persist for days and weeks (Dettling et al., 1999; Sims et al., 2006). Children who suffer or witness violence or who feel abandoned can be severely affected and may become unnaturally still and passive or wildly physical and out of control; it is important to remember that these behaviours are the child's way of communicating distress, and the way adults respond to the behaviours may alleviate or exacerbate the child's pain (Crittenden, 2008; Robinson, 2011).

Time to reflect

Evidence of raised cortisol levels in babies and infants attending nurseries have led some commentators to argue that nursery care is harmful for children under age two.
What practical steps might nursery staff take to try to reduce stress for babies and infants in their care?
Aggressive or antisocial behaviour is often categorised as naughty or bad, and adults may react negatively. Is this helpful? How could you go about investigating the reasons behind the behaviour?

Supporting physical development

Physical development is part and parcel of the holistic growth of the child; health, well-being and self-realisation depend on actively engaging with materials, with other people and with the environment. In wealthier parts of the world, maintaining good child health may appear relatively easy – there is clean water, sanitation, medical, welfare and social support, decent housing, education, play space and cultural opportunity. However, even in rich countries, healthy physical development is not necessarily guaranteed. Western-style diets high in fat, salt and sugar raise the incidence of obesity and diabetes; traffic restricts access to outdoor play; electronic media keep children indoors away from sunlight and social interaction and vigorous physical play.

Maintaining and exercising the body also maintains and exercises the brain. It is important that children have opportunities for physical play in both outdoor and indoor spaces to give them the chance to improve their stamina and to strengthen their muscles and bones by meeting the physical challenges of balancing, climbing, running and jumping while building the self-confidence needed to meet emotional and intellectual challenges. Outdoor play equipment with ropes and climbing frames and slides encourage children to compete with one another to take risks and to stretch their capabilities. Organised games which exercise muscles and teach cooperation are a staple part of the preschool curriculum, but children also need plenty of time and space just to run about freely to raise their heartbeat (Edgington & Titchmarsh, 2002: p. 13). From the earliest moments after birth, children are busy honing their perceptual skills and their coordination, gradually achieving greater and greater mastery over their bodies and learning to regulate their relations with the material and social world in order to become confident and engaged members of their community.

In schools, physical activity and hands-on active play have a lower profile than the more intellectual pursuits of literacy and numeracy, but this underestimates the importance of movement and activity in the development of the child's cognitive and emotional development. Dance, gymnastics and ball games, drawing, playing a musical instrument, building and making, all develop the motor skills that are essential for children's learning in all areas of the curriculum – fit, healthy, alert children are likely to be more energetic and enthusiastic than their sedentary peers and to make more of the learning opportunities available to them.

Summary

- Prenatal care is an important part of healthy child development.
- Support for children's healthy development is a societal responsibility as well as an individual responsibility.
- Children are unique and develop at different rates and in a variety of ways.
- Development is holistic and proceeds in tandem in brain and body.
- Movement and physical activities are essential to brain development and continue to be important sources of health and well-being beyond childhood and throughout life.
- Neuroscience shows that the brain grows and develops throughout life.
- The brain retains a high degree of plasticity, and although there may be 'critical' or 'sensitive' periods when children are most receptive to learning particular skills, development is a

lifelong process. Early thinking is grounded in physical sensation and action; in later child-hood, thinking relies more heavily on language and imagination.

■ Extended exposure to stress raises cortisol levels; practitioners need to be sensitive to chil-dren's behavioural displays and to understand that 'behaviour' is a form of communication.

■ Enlightened intervention from responsive and caring adults can help to overcome early dis-advantage.

■ Health and well-being can be undermined by poor nutrition, poverty and stress; in devel-oped societies there is increasing anxiety about the effects of modern lifestyle choices on the physical and mental health of children.

Topics for further discussion

1 Think about working with a group of pregnant teenage mothers in a mother-and-baby unit. What key points would you want them to know about a baby's physical development to prepare them for motherhood?
2 What sort of play activities and equipment would you ideally offer for Key Stage 1 children to maximise opportunities for physical development?
3 In a nursery setting, should outside play be timetabled, or should children have free access to the outdoors?

Assignments

1 Find out more about 'critical' periods of development. What are the core issues in the debate?
2 Read Chapter 2, 'A journey through the brain and the senses', in Maria Robinson's *Under-standing Behaviour and Development in Early Childhood*. What part does movement play in brain development?
3 Make a presentation to your colleagues about working with children who have a visual or hearing impairment.

Further reading

Robinson, M. (2011) *Understanding Behaviour and Development in the Early Year: A Guide to Theory and Practice*. London: Routledge. A comprehensive survey of present knowledge about brain maturation, behaviour and development.

Shonkoff, J.P. and Phillips, D.A. (National Research Council Institute of Medicine) (2000) *From Neurons to Neighbourhoods*. Washington, DC: National Academy Press. A review of the arguments from neurobiology, behavioural and social sciences that support early interven-tion programmes for young children.

Rutter, M. (2002) Nature, nurture and development: from evangelism through science toward policy and practice. *Child Development* 73(3): 1–22. This explores the strengths and weaknesses of research into genetic and environmental effects on development.

4children (2015) *What to expect, when?* http://www.foundationyears.org.uk/what-to-expect-when/. A quick summary guide to development from birth to age five, designed primarily for parents.

Useful websites

What to expect, when? (4children: 2015) Guidance to children's learning and development in the early years foundation stage at **http://www.foundationyears.org.uk/what-to-expect-when/**

Organisation for Economic Cooperation and Development compiles information from around the world about the social, economic and governance challenges that affect childhoods in a globalised economy at **www.oecd.org**

Social Care Institute for Excellence looks at a wide range of issues around poverty and childhood at **www.scie.org.uk**

Department of Health produces a range of documents based on research findings on maternal and child health at **www.dh.gov.uk**

References

Bailey, D.A., Bruer, J.T., Symons, F.J. and Lichtman, J.W. (eds) (2001) *Critical Thinking about Critical Periods*. National Center for Early Development and Learning. Baltimore: Paul H. Brookes Publishing

Black, R.E., Cousens, S., Johnson, H.L., Lawn, J.E., Rudan, I., Bassani, D.G., Jha, P., Campbell, H., Fischer Walker, C., Cibulskis, R., Eisele, T., Liu, L., Mathers, C. (2010) Child Health Epidemiology Reference Group, WHO and UNICEF. Global, regional, and national causes of child mortality in 2008: a systematic analysis. Published Online 12 May 2010. doi:10.1016/S0140-6736(10)60549- http://www.thelancet.com/journals/lancet/article/PIIS0140-6736(10)60549-1/fulltext. Accessed 27 December 2016

Chapin, H.D. (1926) Family vs. Institution. *Survey* 55 (Jan. 15): 485–488

Crittenden, P. (2008) *Raising Parents: Attachment, parenting and child safety*. Cullompton: Willan Publishing

Dettling, A.C., Gunnar, M.R. and Donzella, B. (1999) Cortisol levels of young children in full-day childcare centers: relations with age and temperament. *Psychoendocrinology Journal* 24(5, July): 519–536. http://www.psyneuen-journal.com/article/S0306-4530(00)00028-7/abstract. Accessed 27 December 2016

Edgington, M. and Titchmarsh, A. (2002) *The Great Outdoors: Developing Children's learning Through Outdoor Provision*. London: Early Education

Gerhardt, S. (2004) *Why Love Matters: How affection shapes a baby's brain*. London: Routledge

Gopnik, A., Meltzoff, A. and Kuhl, P. (1999) *How Babies Think*. London: Weidenfeld & Nicholson

Gregory, R.L. (ed.) (2004) *The Oxford Companion to the Mind* (2nd edn). Oxford: Oxford University Press

Karmiloff-Smith, A. (2012) 'From constructivism to neuroconstructivism: the activity-dependent structuring of the human brain', in E. Marti and C. Rodriguez (eds) *After Piaget*. Piscataway, NJ: Transaction Publishers

Owen, C.G., Martin M.R., Whincup P.H., Davey Smith, G. and Cook D. (2005) Effect of Infant Feeding on the Risk of Obesity across the life course: A Quantitative Review of Published Evidence. *Paediatrics* 115(5, May 1): 1367–1377

Patel, R.R, Steer, P., Doyle P., Little, M.P. and Elliot P. (2003) Does gestation vary by ethnic group? A London-based survey of over 122,000 pregnancies with spontaneous onset of labour. *International Journal of Epidemiology* 33: 107–113

Panksepp, J. (1998) 'Affective Neuroscience' in M. Robinson (ed.) (2011) *Understanding Behaviour and Development in the Early Year: A Guide to Theory and Practice*. London: Routledge

Robinson, M. (2011) *Understanding Behaviour and Development in the Early Year: A Guide to Theory and Practice*. London: Routledge

Rutter, M. (1972) *Maternal Deprivation Re-assessed*. London: Methuen

Rutter, M. (2002) Nature, nurture and development: from evangelism through science toward policy and practice. *Child Development* 73(3): 1–22

Rutter, M., Beckett,C., Castle, J., Colvert, E., Kreppner, J., Mehta, M., Stevens, S. and Sonuga Burke, E. (2007) Effects of profound early institutional deprivation: An overview of findings from a UK longitudinal study of Romanian adoptees. *European Journal of Developmental Psychology* 4(3): 332–350

Santos, E. and Noggle, C.A. (2011) Synaptic Pruning, in S. Goldstein and J.A. Naglieri (eds) *Encyclopedia of Child Behaviour and Development* (pp. 1464–1465). New York: Springer Publications

Shaw, N.J. and Pal, B.R. (2002) Vitamin D deficiency in UK Asian families: activating a new concern. *Archives of Disease in Childhood* 86: 147–149. doi: 10.1136/adc.86.3.147

Shonkoff, J.P. and Phillips, D.A. (eds) (National Research Council and Institute of Medicine) (2000) *From Neurons to Neighbourhoods: The Science of Early Child Development*. Washington, DC: National Academy Press

Sims,M., Guilfoyle, A. and Parry, T.S. (2006) Children's cortisol levels and quality of child care provision. *Child: care, health and development* 32(4): 453–466

Spector, T. (2003) *Your Genes Unzipped*. London: Robson Book Chrysalis Books Group

Spector, T. (2012) *Identically Different: Why You Can Change Your Genes*. London: Weidenfeld and Nicolson

Trevarthen, C. (2004) 'Brain development', in R.L. Gregory (ed.) *The Oxford Companion to the Mind* (2nd edn) (pp. 116–127). Oxford: Oxford University Press

Trevarthen, C. (2005) First things first: infants make good use of the sympathetic rhythm of imitation, without reason or language. *Journal of Child Psychotherapy* 31(1): 91–113

Whitebread, D. and Coltman, P. (eds) (2015) *Teaching and Learning in the Early Years* (4th edn). Abingdon: Routledge

WHO and FAO (World Health Organisation and Food and Agriculture Organisation of the United Nations) (2006) *Guidelines on food fortification with micronutrients*

Zhang, A., Arkadiusz, G. and Liu, B.J (2007) Automatic bone age assessment for young children from newborn to 7-year-old using carpal bones. *Journal of Comput Med Imaging Graph* 31(4–5): 299–310

Cognitive development **5**

Introduction

Children demonstrate an awesome capacity to learn from the moment they are born. How do they do it? And how can we help them?

There is no definitive answer, of course – every theory of learning is tied to its social, cultural and historical context. What we call cognitive development in the West is sometimes thought of rather narrowly as an individual mental journey through what is known as 'knowledge', culminating in a particular kind of rational abstract thought that can be measured and tested and delivered through 'schooling'. In other cultures, cognitive development is more widely defined as enculturation, the process through which children gradually learn to take up their social responsibilities in the family and the community.

Over the last century, several grand theories of learning held sway before new theories emerged to challenge them. Some theories postulate that cognitive ability is fixed and determined at birth, others that children can be trained to think and learn. Some suggest that children learn through trial and error like solitary little scientists, others that learning is a social activity. More recently, learning theories have described children as little apprentices gradually progressing from novice to master. Currently, there is great interest in exploring the emotional self-regulation required for children to develop the focus and involvement required for learning new information and skills. All these theories have a place, but none of them provide a complete explanation.

Until about 50 years ago, learning in the formal sense of 'being taught' was only thought appropriate once children started school. But today there is a consensus that the first five years of childhood are a time of enormous growth in language, thinking and learning, and practitioners in preschool settings are under pressure to start formal instruction early. Current research heightens this pressure by showing that children who receive good-quality early education benefit throughout their lives.

But 'learning' is a complex area of study. As professionals we need to understand some of the history and debates around learning theory in order to make decisions about how best to help the individual children in our care. This chapter will look at some of the more influential models of learning that feed into early childhood practice today.

Requirements for successful learning

In a review of cognitive development and learning, Shonkoff and Phillips (2002: p. 124–162) summarise what we know about the general requirements for successful learning:

- *Health and well-being*. Good physical and emotional health aids learning and speeds up cognitive development.
- *Rich environments*. Good-quality dialogue, trust between participants, and fulfilling activities stimulate thinking and learning. Good relationships are more important than the 'right equipment' or 'state of the art facilities'.
- *Healthy social interactions*. Children who can interact well socially and who can ask for help make faster progress in their learning than those who rely simply on their own resources. Some children (with physical impairments or emotional difficulties) may find it harder to participate in social situations and may need extra support.
- *Good communication*. Children who can communicate clearly receive more attention from peers and adults. Being listened to and getting positive feedback builds confidence and improves learning.
- *Emotional regulation*. Children with high levels of *emotional self-regulation* can 'stop, look, listen and think'; this helps them to plan, sequence and organise their learning more effectively. Children harbouring internal fears and frustrations find emotional self-regulation difficult.
- *Motivation*. Motivation is an important factor in learning because wanting to acquire a new skill or to satisfy curiosity is a driving force in cognitive development. Children remain motivated when they encounter a balance of solvable tasks and interesting challenges that they can overcome with some extra effort; success helps them to develop a can-do attitude. Children presented with tasks beyond their powers or those who 'fear failure' are reluctant to engage with new challenges.
- *Attentiveness*. Emotional well-being and involvement scales (see Laevers, 2011) measure how closely children concentrate on tasks. Children who can focus and persevere are more effective learners. Children with attention disorders find attentiveness difficult, although quiet regulation, a predictable timetable, a calm environment and support with social relationships can help.

What do we know about children's minds?

It is now possible, using brain imaging, to observe changes inside children's brains as they perform tasks (Robinson, 2011). Imaging shows brain activity by measuring increased blood supply to local areas that 'light up' when they are being used. Some local areas regulate particular sensory processes like seeing and hearing, while others regulate language production, emotion, social control and so on. When children are carrying out high-level thinking and learning, imaging reveals that widely separated brain areas are activated, suggesting that social and emotional factors are intrinsically implicated in all intellectual activity (National Research Council, 2001).

The infant brain

Behavioural observations of babies show that 'active learning' starts at birth (Gregory, 2004). Studies of 'attentiveness' show that healthy babies give selective attention to new sounds and sights; they show excitement at novelty and lose interest when the novelty wears off. They are active, *sociable* learners from the start, and studies of institutionalised babies show that without social interaction with other people, their learning is delayed (Rutter et al., 2007). In the first few days, they get excited about faces, particularly their mother's face, and about voices, particularly their mother's voice (even perking up when they hear it among recordings of several voices). By the end of the first week, they can mimic the faces gazing down at them – poking out their tongues, yawning, pursing their lips. Within a few weeks, they learn to smile and coo, engaging the attention of everyone around them. Murray (2014) suggests that the quality of *social* engagement at this stage sets up feedback loops in the babies' brains that alter its electro-chemistry, speeding up or slowing down learning from the earliest interactions.

Carolyn Rovee-Collier (in Shaffer, 2002) wanted to find out how good babies' memories are for learning. She studied a group of babies aged two and three months. For each baby, she attached one end of a ribbon to a cot mobile and the other end to their leg. The babies soon learned that their random limb movements set off the mobile, and so they kicked vigorously with great enjoyment. When the experiment was repeated three days later, the babies immediately kicked. But when she untied the ribbon, and their kicking failed to move the mobile, the babies showed distress. She repeated the procedure several times at different intervals. She found that after the initial experiment, two-month-old babies seemed to retain the memory for up to three days; the three-month-old babies retained the memory for up to four weeks. So it seems that babies are already storing information in some form and are basing their actions on predictions drawn from past experiences – already thinking much like everyone else.

Once infants can sit up (around five months), they already know a great deal: they can recognise lots of words, they have a concept of 'more' and 'less', they can share their mother's gaze when she points something out, they can give and take toys and enjoy passing things to other people, they can investigate new things closely (tasting it first); very soon

Figure 5.1 When playing hide and seek with young children, they will sometimes just close or cover their eyes. What does this tell us about the way they think?

Source: BRAND X

they can balance bricks and roll a ball to another person. Between the ages of 10 and 24 months they will be busy learning to crawl, walk and talk, ready to take their first steps into a larger social world. From research collected over the past 30 years (De Loach et al., 1998) we know that by the age of two and a half, they will have developed a 'theory of mind' which will help them to socialise and even enable them to empathise and to understand that different people have different points of view. This cognitive transition around 'viewpoints' is a great help when it comes to playing hide and seek.

Time to reflect

Think about playing hide and seek with young children. A quick search on the Internet will reveal dozens of very funny photographs of children hiding – sometimes with their bodies in full view and their back to the seeker, sometimes with their feet showing, sometimes just with their eyes shut.

What does this funny hiding tell us about the way the children think?
When do children get really good at hiding?
What sort of cognitive development is required to become successful at hiding?

The child's brain

In evolutionary terms, the most primitive part of the brain is the reptilian brain made up of the brainstem at the top of the spine and the cerebellum. This reptilian brain controls autonomous systems like breathing, heart rate and temperature and is involved in coordination of movement. Above the reptilian brain is the mammalian brain, or limbic system, which processes emotions (the four F's of fighting, feeding, fleeing and … mating). Finally, the outer layer of brain, the convoluted cerebral cortex helps us to organise our sensations and experiences so that we can learn, predict and plan. The cortex is divided into two hemispheres, the left and right, which are connected through the corpus callosum, and most processes require simultaneous activity across both hemispheres (McGilchrist, 2009). However, the right hemisphere is more involved in processing multiple forms of information into patterns, while the left hemisphere seems to be more heavily implicated in processing fine details (Claxton, 1994). Claxton compares the right hemisphere to a candle which illuminates areas of potential interest and the left hemisphere to a torch beam that focuses on detail. The benefit of this 'lateralisation' (division into two hemispheres) is that general, intuitive awareness from the right hemisphere can be harnessed to active exploration of significant features by the left hemisphere.

The child's brain is much more densely interconnected than an adult brain because every action and encounter is recorded along multiple pathways; as they grow older, the brain employs a 'use it or lose it' strategy, and the most frequently used or most efficient neural pathways are reinforced into strongly marked routes, whereas less frequented pathways are pruned away as the brain selects the most promising neural connections and allows others to atrophy. But brains are incredibly 'plastic', and if one part is damaged, new connections will arise to provide alternative routes for information received through the senses or muscles.

Brains and bodies work in tandem, and movement, physical engagement and active play provide the main route for learning for all children. All mammals play; the larger the brain, the more they play. This play serves an important function: for example, a wolf or lion cub plays in order to coordinate and refine its muscle movements and then to time and match its movements to others in the pack, an important precursor to perfecting hunting skills in adulthood. Similarly, children engage in physical play to learn the limits of movement and balance and effort, or to regulate emotional, social and linguistic processes as they learn the rules that govern the behaviours and roles they observe around them. In Piaget's (1962) description of the stages of children's play, he first identifies a stage he calls sensorimotor play (patterning movement onto the brain). This is followed by symbolic play when language becomes increasingly important as children learn to manipulate ideas and concepts and act out new roles through pretence and imitation. And this stage is followed at around the age of six or seven by play governed by rules and instructions (any breaches of protocol are fiercely resented at this point!). However, as Vygotsky (1962, 1978) pointed out, the rules governing role play and imitation are just as binding as rules in more formal games, and children are already operating within agreed and negotiated constraints from the moment they begin to play 'pretend'.

Through active play, children explore relationships and connections between things and between people. They establish patterns and expectations as they represent the world to themselves and map those representations onto the brain. Their active, hands-on engagement with materials, ideas and people provides them with the sensory building blocks they need before they can successfully manipulate abstract concepts inside their own heads – and for many children, play in the concrete world of objects and roles continues to play an important part in cognitive development through primary school age and beyond.

Theories of learning

There are many different theories about how children learn; in this chapter, we will cover five main categories:

- **Nativist theories** are based on the idea that learning ability is largely a matter of genes and heredity.
- **Behaviourist theories** put training at the centre of learning.
- **Constructivist theories** suggest learning is an active process of solitary investigation.

Figure 5.2 Through active play, children are exposed to hands-on engagement with materials, ideas and people.
Source: ImageSource

- **Social constructivist theories** suggest that learning is a collaborative activity involving dialogue.
- **Situated theories** suggest that learning grows directly out of the activity, context and culture in which the 'apprentice' learner is embedded.

David Wood (2011) points out that *situated* theories are in the ascendancy at the moment, but he also reminds us that the other theories still have much to contribute. Cognitive theories are not set in stone; they are influenced by time and culture (Wooldridge, 1994). As you read through the following sections, think about the historical, social and political contexts that influenced the various theories presented.

Nativist and neonativist theories – the great intelligence quotient (IQ) debate

Alfred Binet (1857–1911) believed that learning abilities were inborn. His underlying premise was that the capacity to understand is innate and unchangeable. He wanted to identify the 'clever' and the 'dull' so that teachers could tailor their instruction to each child's *natural* abilities. He did not ask questions about physical or emotional health, class, culture or gender; instead, he concentrated on individual mental ability. He devised tests to establish the 'average' child's ability to 'reason'; these tests examined verbal, spatial and mathematical logic. He 'standardised' his tests across a large population to determine at what age most children would be able to complete each test item and subsequently distinguished between children who were *above or below average*. It was widely believed that only those who were above average would benefit from an extended academic education; the rest required only a basic education to fit them for life and labour.

Time to reflect

Intelligence tests measure verbal, spatial and mathematical logic. In the past, they were widely used to assign children to ability groups and to determine whether or not a child was suited to an academic or a technical education. Here are a couple of test items for you to consider, taken from Cyril Burt's *Handbook of Tests 1923* and reproduced by Susan Isaacs in *Intellectual Growth in Young Children* (1930).

1 Test item for seven-year-olds:
   Kate is cleverer than Mary. Mary is cleverer than Jane. Who is the cleverest of Jane, Kate or Mary?

2 Test item for eight-year-olds:
   I started from the church and walked 100 yards. I turned to the right and walked 50 yards. I turned to the right again and walked 100 yards. How far am I from the church?

What are the answers?
How did you arrive at your answers?
How far do you think success or failure on these tasks could be said to be a measure of 'intelligence'?
What other things might the test items measure?

The English psychologist Charles Spearman (1863–1945) also investigated 'natural' intelligence. He developed a theory of IQ. He believed that cognitive performance was linked across different tasks, and children with good memories tended to have good verbal and spatial reasoning skills too. He called this overall description of mental aptitude 'general intelligence', or *g*. But he also noticed that some children with poor IQ scores nevertheless excelled in fields like mathematics or music. He theorised that there must be two kinds of intelligence – general (*g*) and specific (*s*) and that both were present and fixed at birth.

The view that intelligence was fixed and measureable was widely accepted from the beginning; in 1930 Susan Isaacs wrote 'It is now pretty certain, for instance, that nature is all-powerful in fixing the level of intelligence or general mental ability to which any one of us attains' (1930: p. 59). IQ tests are still being developed and used today; one you may come across in early years (ages three to eight) is the *Wechsler Preschool and Primary Scale of Intelligence – Revised (WPPSI-R)*, which has some similar test items to those developed by Binet but also includes nonverbal items related to manipulating shapes, or solving visual puzzles or ordering pictures into narrative sequences.

Contemporary *neo*nativists like Noam Chomsky, Steven Pinker and Howard Gardner still argue that heredity plays some part in learning, although they would not take such an extreme position as earlier nativists. Gardner (1983) in particular has had an impact among educationists with his theory of 'multiple intelligences'. His original theory suggests that individuals are inclined to use one kind of intelligence rather than another. He identifies eight discrete 'intelligences' implicated in children's preferences for learning in particular ways. For instance, he suggests that some children are born with a *bodily/kinaesthetic* bias that makes them want to express themselves through physical action, like making things or dancing, while other children favour a *logical/mathematical* bias that expresses itself through problem solving and a facility with numbers and codes. His ideas have been embraced in a variety of ways by early childhood specialists, most notably by practitioners who adopt a VAK (visual, auditory and kinaesthetic) approach and design 'personalised learning strategies' with teaching activities to match each child's 'preferred learning style'.

Recently, Gardner (2007) has distanced himself from some of the interpretations of his work, particularly that multiple intelligences imply a single learning style or that 'intelligences' can be matched to teaching styles. Instead, he has developed a theory of *minds* rather than *intelligences*, to encapsulate the idea that learning and thinking involve a complex set of interactions that draw on a *variety* of intelligences. He argues that it is the *way the mind organises* and connects intelligent information that determines learning outcomes (see below) and that children with rich and varied learning environments that encourage creative thinking are likely to be more effective learners.

Focus on *Howard Gardner (1943–)*

Professor Howard Gardner is an American developmental and educational psychologist at Harvard University. He was born to German Jewish parents who fled Nazi Germany. As a child, his greatest pleasures were studying and playing piano, pleasures he now shares with his four children and two grandchildren,

Gardner's work focused on countering the standard theory of 'general intelligence', which holds that if a child is good at one thing, he will probably be good at everything. Instead, he developed his theory of 'multiple intelligences', which listed kinds of intelligence:

- linguistic
- logico-mathematical
- musical
- spatial
- bodily/kinaesthetic
- interpersonal, intrapersonal
- naturalistic.

He believed that children showed strong biases towards particular intelligences that made them more likely to excel in one kind of learning than another.

He applied his theories in Project Zero (1972–2000), a programme designed to enhance thinking, learning and creativity among students and children. He focused on 'good work, good play and good collaboration'. His ideas became ubiquitous through *Toolkits*, a commercially published series of guides for teachers and trainers. His ideas became associated with 'learning styles' and 'teaching styles' and were adopted in schools, nurseries and universities.

Gardner objected to his theory of multiple intelligences being interpreted simply as 'learning styles'. In 2007 he wrote *Five Minds for the Future,* in which he described the characteristic organising principles controlling how we think and learn. He suggested five categories of mental organisation:

- *disciplined minds* associated with 'experts' in a limited field;
- *synthesising minds* associated with 'decision makers' who can prioritise and order data;
- *creating minds* associated with 'innovators' who can see new possibilities;
- *respectful minds* associated with 'mediators' who can make social links across disparate groups;
- *ethical minds* associated with 'philosophers and law makers' who can tease out underlying principles of rights and obligations.

Gardner now believes that education should focus on these wider aspects of 'mind development' rather than on the narrower concerns of 'intellectual development' traditionally promoted in nurseries, schools and colleges.

You may have been asked to fill in a 'multiple intelligence' questionnaire. Did you agree with the resulting categorisation of your learning preference?
Do you think multiple intelligence theory helps teachers to work more effectively with children?
How might a focus on 'multiple minds' rather than 'multiple intelligences' change our practice with children?

Measuring intelligence is still a staple of psychology, and in 2003 American theorist Arthur Jensen (1923–2012) was honoured for his work in this area. He argued, controversially, that inherited genetic factors influence IQ; he produced data to show that 'race' influenced scores on measures of reasoning, verbal manipulation and problem solving (in Wooldridge, 1994). However, objectors pointed out that IQ tests measure a very narrow definition of 'intelligence' and in reality test language skills rather than intelligence per se. They also pointed out that individual IQ scores change over a lifetime and that the test items are culturally specific and always favour 'Western' respondents. Indeed, James Flynn (2012) discovered that IQ around the world as measured by standard tests seemed to be rising at the rate of three points every decade for as far back as the tests had been conducted. The Flynn Effect is now recognised and accepted by most psychologists and calls into question the whole notion of measuring intelligence on a simple linear scale.

Contemporary research using neuroscientific brain mapping shows that *at least* three areas of the brain are activated during learning – short-term memory, reasoning and language (Hampshire et al., 2012) – and that 'intelligence' therefore cannot be a single entity. Hampshire and his colleagues suggest that what 'intelligence' tests measure correlate most closely with measures of *well-being*. They conclude that socioeconomic factors (including health, material circumstances, education and culture) have a stronger effect on children's learning ability than biologically inherited factors.

Behavioural theories of learning – 'training' the mind

While Binet and Spearman were developing their theories of 'native' intelligence (Wooldridge, 1994), other researchers were investigating behaviourist explanations of learning.

Behaviourist theories originated in the work of Pavlov (1849–1936), a Russian physiologist, who showed how dogs could be trained to associate a bell with food so that they 'learned' to salivate when they heard the bell, whether food was present or not; this phenomenon became known as classical conditioning. J.B. Watson (1878–1958) applied Pavlov's ideas to children and showed that they too could be 'conditioned' or 'trained' to learn desirable 'habits'. Watson argued that parents could shape learning and behaviour by training their babies from birth and instilling good habits of self-regulation from the outset.

B.F. Skinner (1904–1990) modified these classical conditioning theories into a model he called operant conditioning, based on his observations of rats. He showed how his laboratory rats repeated actions that had positive, pleasurable outcomes (food) and avoided actions that resulted in negative, unpleasant outcomes (electric shocks). At its simplest, operant conditioning is based on a stimulus-response model where 'action + pleasure' or 'action + pain' encourages or discourages learning. This led to a belief that children could be encouraged to learn more effectively through a system of rewards and sanctions; parents who 'bribe' their children to succeed are subscribing to Skinner's theory.

Behaviourist theories dominated the middle years of the twentieth century, and the idea of a well-trained mind in a well-trained body supported children's learning in homes, schools and clubs: mothers potty 'trained' their infants; schools offered PT (physical 'training'); teachers 'trained' children's minds through rote learning of tables and spellings and poems; scout and guide leaders 'trained' children to march, to obey and to lead.

But not everyone was happy with learning theories that extrapolated from laboratory experiments on animals. Psychoanalysts like Bowlby and Winnicott (see Chapter 7) suggested there was much more to learning than a simple stimulus-response mechanism and argued for an 'affective' or emotional dimension to be considered.

One psychologist, Albert Bandura (originally from a behaviourist tradition) wanted to know how children learned their cultural and social beliefs and attitudes. Classical behaviourism presented children as passive recipients of direct adult teaching but he thought this theory was too simple to explain social learning. In a series of experiments, he showed that children are *active* participants drawing on a variety of indirect sources for their learning. He called his model *social cognitive theory* and demonstrated how children learn social behaviour indirectly from exposure to the behaviour of other people – such as their peers or parents or hero figures – and then model their own behaviour to match in an effort to gain social acceptance. (Bandura's work is sometimes cited to justify censorship of screen violence or sexual activity in films for young people in case they are encouraged towards violent or sexual behaviour in their own lives).

Focus on *Albert Bandura (1925–) and the Bobo doll experiment*

Albert Bandura, born in Alberta, Canada, was the youngest of six children and the only son of Ukrainian/Polish parents. He went to a tiny local school where resources were limited. One summer, in his teens, he took a job road building in the Yukon where he encountered a culture of drinking and gambling and fighting that was at odds with his own upbringing and with the behaviour encouraged by Canadian society. He wondered how people learned to behave in ways that were so different from what was generally taught.

As an undergraduate, he first studied biology. But the vagaries of his travel timetable meant that he arrived very early at college before his classes began, so he enrolled in a psychology course to fill in the time. Soon psychology became his main academic interest.

He began by studying behavioural models of learning. Later, for his doctoral thesis, he set up his own experiments to examine how children learned social behaviours. In a series of famous experiments called the Bobo doll experiments (1961–1963), he investigated social modelling. In the experiments, he measured children's play behaviour with a Bobo doll. He then introduced an adult actor who, without a word, came into the room and beat the doll up! He then observed children's play with the doll again. In some experiments, the actor was rewarded for his aggressive behaviour; in others, he was punished; and in yet others, no comment was made, and there were no consequences. In their subsequent play, the children who had seen the actor *rewarded* reproduced the behaviour they had witnessed. This lead Bandura to suggest that children learn not just through direct reward and punishment (behaviourism) but also through seeing someone else rewarded or punished. The experiment was important because it showed that children can be strongly influenced by the indirect, hidden messages they receive from the people around them.

Bandura went on to study how children learn by actively observing and thinking about the world around them. He called this process social cognitive learning (Bandura, 1986), where children take an active part in accepting or rejecting evidence from their environment. He argued that the degree of *self-efficacy* they felt – that is, the strength of their belief in their own ability to take responsibility for their own independent actions – strongly influenced their ability to copy or reject the behaviour they see around them.

How does Bandura's social cognitive theory contradict classical behaviourist theory?

Why do you need to understand 'social modelling' in your role as an early childhood practitioner?

Why is *self-efficacy* an important concept for working with families and children in health, social care and education?

Classical behaviourist theories linger in our collective consciousness and underpin many training programmes for children – 'toddler-taming' and 'brain gym'; sweeties charts for potty training; stars for good behaviour; computer game tokens that encourage players to repeat their play. Contemporary theorists think behaviourism provides a rather primitive account of learning; however, that doesn't stop it being popular with game designers.

Constructivist theories of learning – the little scientist

While scientists like Skinner were extrapolating behaviourist theories of learning from the study of rats, Jean Piaget (1896–1980), a Swiss biologist with a strong interest in psychology, was studying his own children, Laurent and Jacqueline, to track their learning as they developed from infancy into childhood and adolescence. During the course of his studies, he carried out laboratory observations and experiments on groups of babies, infants and young children which were designed to reveal how they understood the world around them as they grew and what kind of thinking they were capable of at various ages and stages. He likened children to little scientists, actively investigating their environment and *constructing* increasingly sophisticated mind maps, cognitive representations which he called *schemata* (singular *schema*). His investigations seemed to suggest that learning or 'cognitive development' progresses through discrete 'ages and stages' as children's minds mature. Piaget's constructivist theory of learning has been (and is) a staple of all child development courses since the 1960s.

Piaget believed that children are active rather than passive learners who construct their own individual representations of the world. They do this by integrating sensory information with motor information through a scientific method of hypotheses and synthesis until they have arrived at a satisfactory theory, or world view. Although he recognised that all children are different, he nevertheless argued that they all progress through the same stages of cognitive development, in the same order and at roughly the same age, in an '*invariant*' developmental sequence (Table 5.1) (Piaget, 1936/1959).

Table 5.1 Piaget's stages of invariant cognitive development

Age	Stage	Features
0–2 years	Sensorimotor	Learning is dominated by sensation (vision, sound, taste, smell and touch) and muscle action. From 0 to 8 months, differentiates self from others. From 8 to 12 months shows intentional, goal-directed actions requiring planning. Develops rudimentary sense of object permanence. From 12 to 18 months experiments with new materials and practices physical actions. From 18 to 24 months evidence of *symbolic* internal representation – the beginnings of imagination. Establishes object permanence (things that are out of sight are still there).
2–7 years	Pre-operational stage	Uses language and represents objects by images and words. Still *egocentric*; has difficulty taking the viewpoint of others. Displays animistic beliefs that everything in the world is conscious. Classifies objects by their most obvious feature (e.g. assumes a tall thin vase holds more than a small fat vase of the same volume).

Age	Stage	Features
7–11 years	Concrete operational stage	Makes a distinction between animate and inanimate objects. Becomes less egocentric and begins to understand different viewpoints (*empathy*). Becomes less perception bound; begins to search for principles rather than relying on superficial appearances. Evidence of logical thought; can classify and quantify along several dimensions and understand causality. Can mentally reverse events and understand the implications of adding and subtracting.
11 onwards	Formal operational stage	Can formulate abstract hypotheses and test them out in imagination. Can think hypothetically about the future; can weigh up other points of view.

Piaget believed that children could proceed only once they had mastered each stage; intervention and 'teaching' by adults was doomed to failure if the child was not cognitively 'ready' to move on to the next stage. This idea (sometimes called stage theory) underpins programmes that are based on 'readiness' or 'developmentally appropriate practice' (Bredekamp & Copple, 1997) where children are measured against 'developmental milestones' and matched with appropriate teaching materials.

Various objections have been raised in relation to stage theory. In 1929, Susan Isaacs provided evidence of children performing many of Piaget's operations at a much earlier age than his theory predicted. In 1978, Margaret Donaldson argued that his findings were based on a highly abstract 'clinical interview' based on adult-oriented questions and that her own work with children demonstrated that they can understand very complex concepts as long as the questions are based on familiar activities in familiar surroundings. Recently, Erica Burman (2008) has argued that Piaget's 'stages and ages' model fails to take account of the different expectations associated with gender, culture and class in different countries.

> ### Time to reflect
>
> Look through the ages for stages information in Table 5.1.
> Can you find examples from your own experience of children's progressive understanding that illustrate Piaget's 'ages for stages' theory of cognitive development?
> Can you think of any examples that contradict his theory?
> Do you think Piaget's stage theory provides a useful broad guide to children's cognitive development?

Besides cataloguing the stages of cognitive development, Piaget also investigated what *drives or motivates* learning. He argued that as long as children are comfortable with the notions they hold, they have no reason to move on to a different level of understanding. It is only when their ideas are challenged, when their *equilibrium* is disturbed and they experience *disequilibrium*, that they feel the need to rethink, or *modify their schema*.

Table 5.2 Piaget's description of learning

Term	Description	Illustration
Equilibrium	The child's experience and his mental map (*schema*) match.	Mother and toddler arrive at a house and walk through the front door.
Assimilation	The child tries to fit new information into existing schema.	In one room there is a doll's house. The toddler tries to walk through the front door.
Disequilibrium	Information is at odds with her expectations.	When she can't get her foot in the door, she cries.
Accommodation	The child modifies his mental map (*schema*) to account for the puzzling experience.	His mother picks up one of the dolls and places it next to the doll's house.
Organisation	She rearranges her existing schema in a new way to reflect the complexity she has just experienced.	She stops crying and puts the doll inside the doll's house. She begins to understand that although the houses may look the same, size is an independent variable.

This constant modification of understanding, as we try to integrate old and new information, is a process that we employ throughout our lives, and sometimes it can be very difficult to jettison beliefs in the light of challenging or conflicting data – for instance, abandoning a belief in Santa Claus and realising that your parents lied. Sometimes the truth is just too painful.

Social constructivism – supporting learning with dialogue

Piaget's *constructivist* account still works well as a description of how we learn to process new information and how our cognitive powers increase. But learning might be rather slow if it relied on *only* a 'scientific' approach, and one of the criticisms levelled at Piaget's theory is that it underestimates the importance of language, dialogue and teaching in speeding up learning.

Lev Vygotsky (1896–1934), a Russian psychologist and cultural historian, was aware of Piaget's work but was not entirely convinced. He provided an alternative *social constructivist* model of children's learning (Vygotsky, 1962). He showed that children learned not just through their own intellectual efforts but through language, dialogue and teaching. He believed that most learning happens during collaboration and discussion rather than during solitary thinking.

He observed that through dialogue children reveal the gaps in their understanding, 'errors' that offer an insight into the workings of their mind which can be picked up by sensitive adults. He called the borderland where children struggle to grasp some concept just beyond their reach the *zone of proximal development* and argued that it is in this *zone* that teaching can be most effective (Wood, 1998). He suggested that peers and adults help children to move to a new zone of development through guided participation (like the mother in Table 5.2 who offers a doll as a reference point for the doll's house). The central feature of guided participation is the dialogue that takes place between learner and 'knowledgeable other' – the 'knowledgeable other' listens closely to the 'learner' and asks a series of guiding questions, demonstrates a different technique or offers alternatives. Learning is thus a social activity.

Jerome Bruner, a developmental psychologist, studied the work of both Piaget and Vygotsky and showed how it could be usefully adapted in teaching and learning situations. He coined the word *scaffolding*, a word that has now passed into the lexicon of early education specialists, to describe how adults support children through the zone of proximal development. Bruner (1996) showed that children give adults clues about what might help them to progress to the next stage of understanding by revealing errors in their thinking as they talk around a problem. A sensitive 'learning partner' can pick up on these 'errors' and tailor their support for the child to help them achieve a deeper understanding. Bruner emphasised the importance of the *social relationship* between teacher and learner; for him, good social relationships encourage the dialogue that drives cognitive development.

Time to reflect

Reread the information in Table 5.2.

Imagine a conversation between mother and toddler during the incident.
What abstract words might the mother use in the conversation?
What learning concept is involved?
Could the child have made the discovery without his mother's help?
How might 'dialogue' help the child's learning?
Can you recall an incident from your own childhood where you were discombobulated by a new learning experience?

Focus on *Jerome Bruner*

Bruner (1915–2016), an American developmental psychologist, synthesised the work of Piaget and Vygotsky and provided a social model of learning that could be useful for teachers. In the 1950s, he set up the Harvard University Center of Cognitive Studies.

He took Piaget's developmental stages and suggested that they could be expressed as three modes of thinking: enactive (action based), iconic (picture based) and symbolic (language based). Bruner said these modes of thinking overlap, they are not developmental stages but coexist in infants and adults alike. When faced with new material, all humans follow a progression of thinking from enactive to iconic to symbolic – first 'handling' new material, then 'getting the picture' and finally 'exploring the possibilities' through language. Very young children rely heavily on enactive and iconic modes in their learning but not exclusively; as they grow older and use language in increasingly sophisticated ways, more and more of their thinking is symbolic, and the enactive and iconic modes take place only inside their heads.

Bruner emphasises the quality of social relations between children and adults and believes that learning grows out of practical activities and dialogue in a socially supportive environment. Recently, he championed the 'Hundred Languages of Children' project developed by Malaguzzi in his nursery in Reggio Emilia, Italy (see Chapter 10). Reggio nurseries promote the idea that anyone, of any age, can learn anything, as long as materials, tools, dialogue and social relations are managed appropriately.

Think about the best teacher you ever had. What made him/her your best teacher? How would you describe the *social relationship* the teacher had with the group? What single learning event do you remember most clearly? Can you draw any conclusions about what makes a good teaching and learning context?

Socially situated learning theory – apprentices in a community of practice

Situated learning theories emphasise 'community activity' above 'individual study'. One of its most famous proponents is Barbara Rogoff. As an anthropologist, Rogoff first studied communities in South America; she was particularly interested in learning and enculturation. Later, she studied learning in Western early childhood settings. She drew on the work of Piaget, Vygotsky, Bruner and Bronfenbrenner to devise a universal model of learning based on the notion of the child as apprentice. Her background in psychology and anthropology led her to postulate that the driving force behind learning is *social*. She points out that every child is born with an innate capacity to socialise and that every child in the world shows social behaviour from the moment of birth. She argues that this social behaviour (rather than 'intelligence') drives learning because children are motivated to become fully participating members of their particular social setting; she suggests that a socially situated or apprenticeship model of cognitive development best explains how children learn. In this apprenticeship model, children develop from novice learner to expert through a reciprocal process of sharing knowledge through a joint focus on a shared activity with someone more knowledgeable than themselves.

In the apprenticeship model, the social relationship between the expert and the apprentice is the key driver for success (Rogoff, 1990). As the apprentice reveals their prior knowledge, their misunderstandings, their strengths and their growing expertise, the 'expert' adjusts his/her language and behaviour to move the apprentice forward. Instead of categorising the learner as 'able' or '*not*-able', Rogoff's apprenticeship model encourages the 'teacher' to think about the *learning environment* and the adaptations of style, materials and activities that provide the most 'enabling' conditions. Instead of asking, 'Is this *child* capable?' practitioners ask, 'Am I providing an enabling learning environment for this child?' The focus shifts from the individual learner to the social interactions between learner and 'knowledgeable other'.

Situated learning theory suggests that individuals are restricted not by their own natural abilities but by their lack of access to supportive learning communities. Social participation is the key to learning, and when children are welcomed into a 'community of practice' as an apprentice (whether that is a sports club, a nursery, a science class, a reading group, a maths group or an orchestra) where sensitive, supportive experts are on hand to guide and respond, they learn quickly and with eager pleasure. But when children are excluded from a community of practice because they are unhappy or unwell; because they are non-native speakers, have poor social skills or poor self-regulation; or because they are the wrong gender, class or race, they are less likely to learn effectively – not because they are less able but because they are *dis*abled. Children's well-being feeds into the level of their involvement in a task; focus and engagement provides practitioners with a good indicator to measure how well children are actually concentrating and learning as they play (Laevers, 2011).

> **Focus on** *Jean Lave and Etienne Wenger, socially situated learning in a community of practice*
>
> In the late 1980s, anthropologists Jean Lave and Etienne Wenger travelled to West Africa to study apprenticeship as a model of situated learning. They observed a group of apprentice tailors progressing from novice to mastery. In their 1991 book *Situated Learning*, they used the term 'community of practice' to describe the cluster of novices and experts working on a common activity. Their research focused on how apprentices learned specific skills and expertise in their particular community of practice, organised around tailoring.
>
> They noted that apprentices were motivated to learn by a desire to share the common values and skills of their colleagues in the social world of the workplace. At first the apprentices watched and observed attentively. When they felt ready, they were given simple tasks, undertaken under the close supervision of their more skilful colleagues, who could talk to them as they worked and help them if required. Their learning was characterised by increasing levels of participation. Gradually, as they got more competent and when they felt confident enough, the apprentices progressed to more complex tasks. They asked questions, shared insights and listened to group discussions about the work. After several years they became fully fledged members of the community of tailors.
>
> Lave and Wenger point out that in order to capture the knowledge and skills for themselves, the apprentices have to *participate*; their motivation to learn is driven by a social desire to become a valued member of the group. They concluded that learning is primarily a social phenomenon, rooted in activity, dialogue and shared experience. Socially situated learning theory has now been taken up around the world in work-based learning programmes for health, social care and education.
>
> Do you think 'social participation' is a key predictor for successful learning?
>
> Do you think socially situated learning theory offers a useful model of how children learn?

Holistic approaches to learning theory

Currently there are efforts to synthesise learning theory across disciplines to provide a unifying account of how children learn. Allan Schore (2003) draws on psychotherapy, biology and neuroscience to examine the ways in which early trauma or disrupted attachment patterns can interrupt the development of a sense of self and bring about fearfulness, aggression or social withdrawal to the detriment of cognitive learning. In an article with the unlikely title of 'Elephant Breakdown', Schore and others show the devastating effects of trauma on young elephants and extrapolate from their behaviour lessons to be learned about human infants (Bradshaw et al., 2005). Socialisation and cognition in the young elephants was severely impaired after they had witnessed an attack on their family group.

Another researcher synthesising learning theory across disciplines is Usha Goswami. She draws on earlier theories of learning to show how they can be incorporated into the present state of knowledge from other disciplines to provide a holistic theory of learning that is useful to practitioners. It is worth quoting the key conclusions from her recent report in full (Goswami, 2015):

- Learning in young children is socially mediated. Families, peers and teachers are all important. Even basic perceptual learning mechanisms such as the statistical learning of linguistic sounds requires direct social interaction to be effective. This limits the benefits of educational approaches such as e-learning in the early years.

- Learning by the brain depends on the development of multi-sensory networks of neurons distributed across the entire brain. For example, a concept in science may depend on neurons being simultaneously active in visual, spatial, memory, deductive and kinaesthetic regions, in both brain hemispheres. Ideas such as left-brain/right-brain learning, or unisensory 'learning styles' (visual, auditory *or* kinaesthetic) are *not* supported by the brain science of learning.

- Children construct explanatory systems to understand their experiences in the biological, physical and psychological realms. These are implicit causal frameworks, for example that explain why other people behave as they are observed to do, or why objects or events follow observed patterns. Knowledge gained through active experience, language, pretend play and teaching are all important for the development of children's causal explanatory systems. Children's causal biases (e.g. the essentialist bias) should be recognised and built upon in primary education.

- Children think and reason largely in the same ways as adults. However, they lack experience, and they are still developing important metacognitive and executive function skills. Learning in classrooms can be enhanced if children are given diverse experiences and are helped to develop self-reflective and self-regulatory skills via teacher modelling, conversation and guidance around social situations like play, sharing and conflict resolutions.

- Language is crucial for development. The ways in which teachers talk to children can influence learning, memory, understanding and the motivation to learn. There are also enormous individual differences in language skills between children in the early years. Interactions around books are one of the best ways of developing more complex language skills.

- Incremental experience is crucial for learning and knowledge construction. The brain learns the statistical structure of 'the input'. It can be important for teachers to assess how much 'input' a child's brain is actually getting when individual differences appear in learning. Differential exposure (for example to spoken or written language) will lead to differential learning. As an example, one of the most important determinants of reading fluency is how much text the child actually reads, including outside the classroom.

- Thinking, reasoning and understanding can be enhanced by imaginative or pretend play contexts. However, scaffolding by the teacher is required if these are to be effective.

- Individual differences in the ability to benefit from instruction (the zone of proximal development) and individual differences between children are large in the primary years; hence, any class of children must be treated as individuals.

(From Usha Goswami (2015) *Children's Cognitive and Developmental Learning* (pp. 25–26). CPRT Research Survey 3, Cambridge Primary Review Trust)

Throughout your career, you will meet practitioners who hold strong views about children's learning: there will be those who believe that some children are naturally gifted and talented; there will be others who believe that given the right support, any child can learn anything. You must decide where on the spectrum your beliefs lie. But mostly, in your day-to-day interactions with children and families, you will probably rely on a pick and mix from several theories: Bandura might help you to find ways to talk to parents about how social attitudes are transferred to children; Piaget can be a useful guide as to what you can expect from a two-year-old or an eight-year-old; Vygotsky and Bruner can help you to argue for more collaborative methods in your interactions with children and adults; Rogoff, Lave and Wenger can help you to rethink your workplace to make it more inclusive and enabling for children and for colleagues. Schore and Goswami will remind you that all children are unique and that their individual social, emotional and family histories will enhance or impede their ability to learn.

Learning is a lifelong process, and part of the process is to develop your own working theories of learning through your own practice. Research shows that sensitive and thoughtful interventions and a rich, supportive environment provide the best conditions for progress.

Summary

- Early twentieth-century nativist learning theories focused on individual intellectual ability; implicit in these is the notion that learning abilities are genetically fixed at birth.
- Behaviourist theories prioritise training through rewards such as material gain or adult approval and through sanctions such as adult disapproval.
- Bandura's social cognitive theory suggests that children can pick up attitudes and beliefs without direct instruction.
- Piaget's constructivist model of learning provides a general guide to cognitive maturation, but it underestimates children's cognitive abilities and downplays the role of dialogue in learning.
- Vygotsky's social constructivist theory of learning prioritises social interaction and dialogue in the learning process.
- Bruner synthesises previous theories of learning and adapts them for classroom use. He suggest that 'ability' changes across a lifetime depending on structural opportunities for intellectual growth.
- Socially situated learning theories explain differences in learning outcomes in terms of socio-cultural contexts; apprenticeship models of learning are the norm in most situations (except in formal education settings).
- Rogoff, Lave and Wenger argue that a desire for *social participation in a community of practice* is a major motivating factor in learning.
- There is no grand unifying theory of learning as yet, but studies from neuroscience, biology, psychobiology and psychology are being incorporated into multidisciplinary meta-analyses to provide a more holistic account than has been available before.

Topics for further discussion

1 Politicians sometimes suggest that we should identify intellectually gifted children at an early age and fast-track them through the educational system. Do you agree or disagree?

2 How do the learning theories in this chapter relate to the current Early Years Foundation Stage guidance?

3 Currently there is a debate about the wisdom of investing heavily in the preschool years. Opponents use the term 'early years determinism' to deride those who hold the view that early education is the most important period for learning in the human life cycle. How could you convince them otherwise?

Assignments

1 John B. Watson conducted a famous experiment called the 'Little Albert Experiment' to support his ideas that young children can be 'conditioned' to learn certain material. Find it on the Internet. Consider the ethics of the experiment. Discuss the findings.

2 Read *Children's cognitive development and learning* by Usha Goswami. How does she synthesise past and present learning theories?

3 Find out about and critique 'developmentally appropriate practice' in early childhood. You might start with the work of Sue Bredekamp and Carol Copple. How useful is this approach for practitioners?

4 Read Virginia Woolf's essay *A Room of One's Own*, first published in 1929. How does she refute the belief (commonly held at the time) that women/girls can never be as 'intelligent' as men/boys?

Further reading

If you are interested in the history of the psychological aspects of understanding learning, *Measuring the Mind* by Peter Wooldridge is a wonderfully scholarly summary of key thinkers from 1860 to 1990.

David Wood provides a detailed analysis of contemporary thinking about learning in *How Children Think and Learn*, 2nd edn (2011), Oxford: Blackwell.

Barbara Rogoff has written several accounts of socially situated learning. You might like to try *Apprenticeship in Thinking* (1990), *Learning together: Children and Adults in a School Community* (2001) and *Developing Destinies: A Mayan Midwife and Town* (2011).

Usha Goswami (2015) provides an up-to-date and concise account of the current state of understanding of children's learning in the CPRT (Cambridge Primary Review Trust) Research Survey 3. *Children's cognitive development and learning*.

Useful websites

Several universities, especially in the United States, offer lecture notes on learning theory which are freely accessible to all. Just enter a keyword and browse!

References

Bandura, A. (1986) *Social Foundations of Thought and Action: A Social Cognitive Theory.* Englewood Cliffs, NJ: Prentice Hall

Bowman, B.T., Donovan, M.S. and Burns, M.S. (eds) (2001) *Eager to Learn: Educating our Pre-schoolers.* Washington, DC: National Academy Press

Bradshaw, G.A., Schore, A.N., Brown, J.L., Poole, J.H. and Moss, C.J. (2005) 'Elephant Breakdown. Social trauma: early disruption of attachment can affect the physiology, behaviour and culture of animals and humans over generations'. *Nature* 433(24, February) at www.nature.com/nature

Bredecamp, S. and Copple, C. (eds) (1997) Developmentally Appropriate Practice in Early Childhood Program: Serving children from birth through 8 (revised edn). Washington, DC: National Association for the Education of Young Children

Bronfenbrenner, U. (1979) *The Ecology of Human Development.* Cambridge, MA: Harvard University Press

Bruner, J. (1996) 'Folk Pedagogy', in *The Culture of Education* (pp. 44–65). Cambridge, MA: Harvard University Press. Reprinted in R. Parker-Rees and J. Willan (eds) (2006) *Early Years Education: Major Themes in Education* (p. 211–228). Abingdon: Routledge

Burman, E. (2008) *Deconstructing Developmental Psychology* (2nd edn). Hove: Routledge

Claxton, G. (1994) *Noises from the Dark Room: The Science and Mystery of the Mind.* London: Aquarian/Harper Collins

De Loach, J.S., Miller, K.F., Pierroutsakos, S.L. (1998) 'Reasoning and problem-solving' in D. Kuhn and R. Siegler (eds) *Handbook of Child Psychology*, Vol. 2 (pp. 801–850). New York: Wiley

Donaldson, M. (1978) *Children's Minds.* London: Collins

Flynn, J.R. (2012) *Are We Getting Smarter? Rising IQ in the Twenty-First Century.* Cambridge: Cambridge University Press

Gardner, H. (1983) *Frames of Mind: the Theory of Multiple Intelligences* (2011 edn) New York: Basic Books

Gardner, H. (2007) *Five Minds for the Future.* Watertown, MA: Harvard Business Review Press

Goswami, U. (2015) *Children's cognitive development and learning.* CPRT Research Survey 3: Cambridge Primary Review Trust at cprtrust.org.uk

Gregory, R.I. (ed.) (2004) *The Oxford Companion to the Mind* (2nd edn). Oxford: Oxford University Press

Hampshire, A., Highfield, R.R., Parkin, B.L. and Owen, A.M. (2012) Fractionating Human Intelligence. *Neuron* 76(6): 1225. doi: 10.1016/j.neuron.2012.06.022

Laevers, F. (2011) Experiential Education: Making Care and Education More Effective Through Well-Being and Involvement, Leuven University/Centre for Experiential Education, Belgium http://downloads.averbode.be/Microsites%20Algemeen%20DOWNLOADS/CEGO/CEGOeng/pdf/EXE%20-%20an%20introduction.pdf. Accessed 27 December 2016

Lave, J. and Wenger, E. (1991) *Situated Learning. Legitimate peripheral participation.* Cambridge: Cambridge University Press

Lave, J. and Wenger, E. (1998) *Communities of Practice: Learning, Meaning, and Identity.* Cambridge: Cambridge University Press

McGilchrist, I. (2009) *The Master and his Emissary: The Divided Brain and the Making of the Western World.* New Haven, CT/London: Yale University Press

Meltzoff, A. (1990) in Shaffer, D.R. (ed.) (2002) *Developmental Psychology: Childhood and Adolescence* (6th end) (p. 325–328). Belmont, CA: Wadsworth Thomson Learning

Murray, L. (2014) *The psychology of babies: how relationships support development from birth to two.* London: Constable & Robinson

National Research Council (2001) *Eager to Learn: Educating our Preschoolers.* In B.T. Bowman, M. Suzanne Donovan and M. Susan Burns (eds) Committee on Early Childhood Pedagogy. Washington, DC: National Academy Press[RD4]

Piaget, J. (1936/1959) *The Origins of Intelligence in Children.* New York: International University Press (first published in French 1936, translated into English 1959)

Rogoff, B., Turkanis, C.G. and Bartlett, L. (eds) (2001) *Learning Together: Children and Adults in a School Community.* New York: Oxford University Press

Schore, A.N. (2003) *Affect Dysregulation and Disorders of the Self.* New York: W.W. Norton

Shonkoff, J.P. and Phillips, D.A. (eds) (2000) *From Neurons to Neighbourhood: The Science of Early Childhood Development.* Washington, DC: National Academy Press[RD5]

Shaffer, D.R. (2002) *Developmental Psychology: Childhood and Adolescence* (6th end). Belmont, CA: Wadsworth Thomson Learning

UNESCO (1998) *Learning: The Treasure Within.* UNESCO Publishing

Vygotsky, L.S. (1962) *Thought and language.* Cambridge, MA: MIT Press

Vygotsky, L.S. (1978) 'The Role of Play in Development' in M. Cole, V. John-Steiner, S. Scribner and E. Souberman (eds) *Mind in Society: The Development of Higher Psychological Processes* (pp. 92–104). Cambridge, MA, and London: Harvard University Press, 1978

Wood, D. (1998) *How Children Think and Learn* (2nd edn). Oxford: Blackwell Publishing

Wooldridge, A. (1994) *Measuring the Mind: Education and Psychology in England, c. 1860–1990.* Cambridge: Cambridge University Press

Socialisation, language and play

Introduction

As we saw in Chapters 4 and 5, the urge to socialise drives both physical and cognitive development. In this chapter we look at how early socialisation also lays the foundations for play and language development. Play, language and socialisation are intricately bound and develop in lockstep with one another; they grow together out of the first interactions between the mother and her newborn baby. Progress is rapid, so that by the age of four, children have the full repertoire of language and communication skills at their disposal and can fit into a range of social situations. By age eight language and social skills are developed enough for children to work in groups and to take on sophisticated leader and follower roles in their play.

Relationships are the key to developing language and social skills; early nurturing environments that provide emotional warmth, interactive social opportunities and stimulating experiences offer the best chances for children to develop language, play and social skills. The task of the practitioner is to work with parents to ensure that they understand the importance of playing and talking and to work with their children to provide enabling environments which offer support for a range of play opportunities which extend language and thinking.

Socialising from the beginning

The first social interaction begins in the delivery room, in those intense mother-and-baby moments just after birth, and they gradually extend over the next few years to include the wider family, friends, child carers and neighbourhood networks that constitute the child's particular cultural milieu.

Imagine an early feeding session. The baby gazes up at the mother; the mother gazes back. The baby nuzzles at the breast or bottle; the mother helps by guiding the nipple into his mouth. He feeds fast at first and then pauses, letting the nipple slide from his mouth, shifting his gaze upwards to his mother's face, the mother smiles and talks before offering to feed again. He returns to his feed, sucking contentedly now with little grunts and sighs of pleasure and delighted kicks and wriggles. The mother is flooded with feelings of warmth and love and responds with delight and affection.

Through these reciprocal interactions, the baby and her mother begin to get to know one another and to learn to adapt to one another's needs; Fogel (1977) calls this process 'co-regulation'. Healthy mothers and babies will rapidly establish a harmonious co-regulation – for example, at a biological level the baby's cry will stimulate the mother's milk to flow and prompt her to pick up the baby for a cuddle and a feed. This co-regulation is the basis of the baby's first active communication and is the foundation for play, language and social participation.

Early social development

Over the first few months, babies experience the world in terms of relationships and social patterns – first the patterns shared with their mothers around feeding and changing, sleeping and playing, then the patterns in the wider world beyond such as arrivals and departures of family members. Very quickly they notice a 'resonance' when others are present, and within weeks of birth, they can already sense

Figure 6.1 The first socialisation is between mother and baby. Gradually, it extends to include the wider family, friends, child-carers and neighbourhood networks.
Source: Emy Kat/Grapheast/Emy Kat

when they are alone (Trevarthen, 1993). They are designed by nature to be social, to captivate the attention of others – they are born with large eyes, a following gaze and a weak smile – and these features conspire to make them fascinating to adults. Babies are adept at building one-to-one relationships in their first months and learn surprisingly early to read quite complex social cues – for instance, they can tell the difference between a happy face and a sad face, and they can distinguish between the soothing tones of harmony and the edgy tones of dispute – and will respond accordingly with coos and smiles or with fear and distress (Gopnik et al., 1999).

Primary intersubjectivity, two to nine months

The period from two to nine months has been called the period of 'primary intersubjectivity' (Trevarthen & Hubley, 1978) when the infant attends directly to another person or another thing in a one-to-one fashion. At first babies focus on the adults caring for them, then they begin to turn their gaze outward, towards objects in the immediate vicinity. By the time they can sit up alone (around five months), they will be actively engaged in exploring whatever is within reach. They will interact with objects, sucking them, bashing them on the floor, bringing them under close examination. But they will *not share the experience with another person yet*. At this stage of primary intersubjectivity, they can relate to only one thing at a time – either directly with an object or directly with another person – they can't interact with a person *and* an object at the same time.

Time to reflect

Think about babies of between two and five months.
Think about 'sharing' toys, objects or mobiles with a baby of this age. What happens?
Compare notes with other students in your group.
Does your experience support Trevarthen and Hubley's theory of *primary intersubjectivity*?

Secondary intersubjectivity, from nine months

At around nine months, babies make a great leap in terms of social interaction. They make the transition from 'primary intersubjectivity' to 'secondary intersubjectivity' – that is, they are able to hold both another person and an object in mind at the same time, showing a *shared* interest in things together (Trevarthen & Hubley, 1978). The transition from primary to secondary subjectivity marks a key moment in the development of language, play and social participation – not just for the baby but for the adult too.

Adults will automatically adopt a high-pitched tone when talking to babies, sometimes called *motherese* or *parentese* and more formally known as *infant-directed speech* (IDS). IDS is characterised by having fewer words per utterance, more repetitions, better articulation and simpler constructions than adult-directed speech. It is also marked by a higher overall pitch, a wider pitch range, more distinctive pitch patterns, a slower tempo with longer pauses and an increased emphatic stress on key words. Adults also adjust their tonal patterns and facial expression to match their words. This simplified high-pitched speech is a universal feature of adult interactions with babies and even at one month old, babies focus more acutely when they are spoken to in IDS (Cooper & Aslin, 1990); it is an efficient way of providing the basic building blocks of the language and its grammar – the musical and rhythmic emphasis marks out the most significant words in a way that alerts babies to key meanings (Mithen, 2005).

During the shift from primary to secondary intersubjectivity, adults notice the change in the baby's orientation to the world and use IDS less often (Trevarthen, 2004). Once infants have transitioned into this new phase of secondary intersubjectivity, they can engage other people in a more direct way – for example, stretching up their arms to be picked up, holding up an interesting object, calling out when they want company or pointing at a cup to show that they want a drink. This sharing of meaning is what characterises 'secondary intersubjectivity'. Changes in maternal responses and patterns of speech in these episodes of shared focus have been documented by Bruner (1983) and Trevarthen (1978).

From about nine months onwards, babies become aware not only that can they convey their own thoughts and intentions to other people but that other people also have thoughts and intentions of their own. This is sometimes called being 'mind-minded'. By ten months 'secondary intersubjectivity' is well established, and infants can share their mother's gaze and her pointing finger to focus with her on some object that is jointly interesting to them both (Tomasello et al., 2005). In this shared focus, adults typically *name* the object and provide a commentary. The infant will move his gaze from adult face to shared object, taking his cue as to how to react from the adult expression or body language. For children with visual or hearing impairments or with autistic spectrum disorders, this 'mind-mindedness' may take longer to establish, and professionals may need to arrange specific strategies to ensure that these children do not suffer developmental delay.

The transition from primary to secondary intersubjectivity

Fogel and DeKoeyer-Laros (2007) describe a study that shows the transition from primary to secondary intersubjectivity in action. A mother and her infant were filmed over several months at the same time each day when the baby was in her high chair (this kind of research into one activity 'frame' as it changes over time is called 'dynamic systems analysis'). The case study below shows how the mother and infant co-regulate their activities in an increasingly sophisticated way from 26 weeks to 40 weeks. Play, social interaction and language develop in an integrated way, and both the mother and baby changed their behaviour throughout the study. After the transition from primary to secondary intersubjectivity, the baby was able to communicate her own needs by shaking her head to show she doesn't want to play anymore, and the mother responded to this new level of communication by changing her language from IDS to a more adult form.

Case study: The transition from primary to secondary intersubjectivity

Observing Susie in her high chair – a longitudinal dynamic systems analysis

26 weeks First action	First observation of Susie randomly banging her highchair tray with her hands. She does not attend to her hands but looks away. Her mother responds with 'Oom! Boom! Boom!', matching the rhythm and intensity of banging with her voice. Susie pauses and looks at her mother. They smile.
28 weeks Primary intersubjectivity	Susie bangs the tray, this time looking at her hands. Mother responds with vocal 'boom!' and then begins to match the rhythm by tapping her fingers in unison *underneath* the tray. Susie pauses, looks at her mother and then bangs again. They repeat the action. Susie leans over to look under the tray. She bangs again looking intently at her own hands.
29–32 weeks Co-orientation	Susie pays attention to her own hands as she bangs the tray but now alternates her gaze between her hands and her mother's face. When her mother joins in and mirrors Susie's actions, Susie stares intently at her hands and then gazes up at her mother and smiles. They repeat the sequence.

▶

33–34 weeks Intentional action and stabilisation of concept of noise making	Susie watches her own hands with focused fascination, banging first one and then the other while vocalising at the same time. She looks intently at her still hands as they rest on the tray and seems to be listening. She resumes the banging but louder and faster and looks up at her mother to watch her reaction. The mother responds with 'Oooo! Bang! Bang!' Susie smiles and lets her jaw drop open.
35–37 weeks Emergence of mutual, coordinated joint action	When Susie bangs, her mother responds. The activity takes on the pattern of turn taking. They repeat each other's actions. Sometimes Susie abruptly ends the action and turns away from her mother's gaze. No amount of prompting gets her to join in again.
37–38 weeks Evidence for gradual stabilisation of mutual coordinated joint action. Transition period for language and intersubjectivity	Susie watches her own hands and then her mother's hands, registering the alternate sounds and rhythms each makes. Both mother and baby show a change in behaviour. Susie initiates the game and watches her mother's face and hands to see if she will join in. Instead of calling 'boom!' her mother says, '*You* made that noise!' and claps her hands. Susie kicks the bottom of her tray in response to her mother's clapping.
39–40 weeks Stable sense of secondary intersubjectivity with a corresponding change in communication pattern of both mother and infant	Susie now joins in when requested or shakes her head to indicate 'no' she will not join in her mother's initiated game. Susie claps for the first time. Sometimes Susie initiates the banging; sometimes she joins in when her mother initiates; sometimes she chooses not to join in and exercises her right to refuse by shaking her head. Her mother responds by vocalising Susie's refusal: 'You're not going to do it, are you?' and shaking her own head in mimicry of Susie. This produces delight and laughter, and her mother says first 'yes' and then, when Susie shakes her head, 'no'. The mother uses adult forms of speech; she speaks faster and lower; she uses less 'motherese'.

(From Fogel, A. and DeKoeyer-Laros, I. (2007) The developmental transition to secondary intersubjectivity in the second half year: a microgenetic case study. *Journal of Developmental Processes* 2(2, Fall))

In this study play, social interaction and language learning proceed together.

Do you think the case study convincingly illustrates the concepts of primary and secondary intersubjectivity?

How would you account for the baby looking under the tray when she hears her mother's fingers tapping the base?

How could you use the concepts of primary and secondary intersubjectivity in your work with babies?

Infant language development

There is no language development without social interaction because language, gestures and sign language depend on sharing meaning with other people. Studies of abandoned infants show that children raised in institutions with minimal one-to-one contact with familiar adults suffer catastrophic language delay (Rutter et al., 2007). Generally the baby's ability to sound out the phonics p,b,g is apparent from two months old. They may be just accidental combinations of breath, lips and tongue but parents typically imitate and play with the sounds and echo them back to the baby – to the mutual delight of both! However, if they fail to get a response they may stop vocalising by six months babies can reproduce the full range all human sounds. Between six and nine months they begin to reduce this range of vocalisations to just those of their own mother tongue and register surprise when someone speaks in a foreign language (Gopnik et al., 1999).

Language learning follows a standard trajectory from babble to meaning making across all cultures as children play with the sounds and social gestures of their family and community. When they are in the company of children, adults often accompany their actions with a running commentary, emphasising key words as they speak (Wood, Bruner & Ross, 1976). This social interaction is vitally important in the early stages of learning language because it establishes the link between sound and meaning – for instance, the mmmm of babble is interpreted and repeated back to the child as mummy (or maman or mama or mammi) such that the sound gradually comes to represent or *symbolise* the person of mother in the mind of the child.

From the age of ten months, children become 'verbal' – they begin to refine babble into recognisable words and can often be heard practising the sounds of the day as they settle down to sleep. Children denied one-to-one social interaction during this early language-learning phase, such as the Romanian orphan children studied by Rutter (Rutter et al., 2007) are severely disadvantaged and may never catch up with their peers. Famous cases of 'feral' children brought up away from human contact, like Victor the Wild Boy of Aveyron (*c.* 1788–1828), suggest that after a certain age (Victor was 12) language, play and socialisation become impossible even with intensive teaching. Some argue that the initial rate of acquisition and the ultimate level of attainment depend in part on the age when learning begins (so-called *critical periods*). If these sensitive periods for learning language are missed, learning may be irregular and incomplete, suggesting that age-related loss in ability for language development probably reflects a progressive loss of neural plasticity in the brain because, as children grow older, their ability to develop language decreases dramatically as under-used neural pathways atrophy during the 'use it or lose it' phase of brain development (Long, 1990). Children with hearing and sight impairment, dyslexia and autistic spectrum disorders are particularly

Figure 6.2 Victor of Aveyron (c. 1788–1828). The story of this 'feral' boy who is believed to have lived alone in the wild for most of his life is truly fascinating!

Source: By Unknown - http://www.complex.com/ blogs/2009/05/28/politickin-with-john-brown-a-brief-history-of-feral-children/, Public Domain, https://commons. wikimedia.org/w/index.php?curid=8793091

vulnerable because they may not pick up on early pre-verbal communication such as pointing, or sharing eye contact, and without intervention they may suffer language delays and deficits in 'mind-mindedness' and reasoning about other people's mental states (Baron-Cohen, 1995; Shonkoff & Phillips, 2000).

First words

Most children utter their first words sometime between 10 and 15 months, beginning with naming words (nouns) – single words that may stand for a whole class of objects, such as calling every man 'daddy'. Soon this is followed by two-word utterances (daddy-car, mummy-shoe) and three-word utterances when they add action words (verbs) to the mix, such as 'mummy go office'.

For both adult and child at this stage, sharing meaning is more important than pronunciation. The adult provides encouragement and accepts early efforts enthusiastically (one friend accepted her baby son's pronunciation of 'Louisa' as 'weasel' and poor Louisa was known as Weasel for ever after). Later, the adult will 'correct' the articulation and pronunciation in a clear and simple form, by repeating the word and encouraging the child to copy, but for the most part the social act of making meaning and being understood is what counts, and the more the child is understood the more confident she will feel. There are several detailed accounts of the pattern of language development, most notably in Britain the Bristol Language Development Project conducted by Gordon Wells from 1974 to 1981.

Focus on Language development

One famous language development study was carried out by Roger Brown (1973), who exhaustively recorded the developing speech of three preschool children, dubbed Adam, Eve and Sarah. He described five stages of language development based on a child's mean length of utterance (MLU):

- 10–15 months – produces one-word utterances, naming objects (nouns).
- 15–30 months – produces two-word phrases (holophrases) that carry a wealth of meaning depending on context – for example, 'mummy car' may mean *mummy is leaving in the car, this is mummy's car* or *I want to go in the car with mummy.*
- 28–36 months – names actions (verbs). Adds morphological (word) markers – adding 's' to show more than one, or adding *ing* or *ed* to verb forms, or distinguishing the different forms *me, my* and *I.*
- 36–42 months – produces three-word utterances and asks questions: for example, '*Where daddy gone?*'
- 42–52 months onwards – produces complex sentences close to adult forms which relate one event to another: for example, 'Granny has a walking stick because her leg hurts'.

Why is it important for nurseries and preschools to provide a consistent carer or 'key person' for each child?

What kinds of play activities might help children practise their language skills at each stage?

Learning the grammar

From about 18 months of age, infants enter the 'word explosion phase', and over the next four years they will learn on average about nine new words each day so that by the age of six, they will have a vocabulary of around 14,000 words (Carey & Bartlett, 1978). Alongside the rapid growth in vocabulary, children are also discovering syntax (the grammatical patterns that govern language), and semantics (how meaning can change according to underlying rules). For example, a toddler understands that 'Mummy give …' has a different meaning from 'Give Mummy …', even though the words remain the same, because he has already internalised the pattern of syntax and intonation. Around age two, children will typically show an understanding of morphology (word structure) and, in English, will add 's' to denote plural nouns or 'ed' to denote tense. We can see them working hard on morphology when they make 'errors' – for example, when they generalise from what they already know to produce their own logical constructions: they have learned 'play-ed' and 'kick-ed', so it follows that 'catch-ed' and 'runn-ed' will follow the same pattern. Gradually, from about age four, children will recognise these 'exceptions that prove the rule' and will standardise words to match the dialect spoken around them. There is evidence from research with pre-lingually deaf children that grammar is harder for children to master the older they get (Cormier et al., 2012), which can bring long-term disadvantage.

Children have an inbuilt interest in the rhythms and patterns of language and delight in action rhymes, nursery rhymes, nonsense rhymes, songs and tongue twisters. Besides being a source of endless fun, playing with language improves their ability to distinguish between fine gradations of sounds (phonemes) needed later when they learn to read and inscribes grammatical constructions into their brains through repetition – for example, they hear three blind mice, not three blind mouses, and thus learn that there are irregular plurals in English.

Theories of language acquisition

Language is the defining characteristic that distinguishes humans from every other species on the planet. There have been numerous theories about *how* human children learn to reproduce language and whether other animal species can learn to communicate in a similar way. In the 1960s, in an effort to find out how children acquired language, various attempts were made to teach other primates to talk or sign – most famously the Gardner's work with a chimpanzee called Washoe (Gardner et al., 1989). The researchers suggested that chimps learned to communicate with humans through gesture, symbols and vocalisation at about the level of a two-to-three-year-old child. However, there is continuing controversy over whether this is 'real language use' or just a clever trick based on the chimps' learned responses to the researchers' repeated cues.

Behaviourist theories

In the 1950s the *behaviourist psychologist* B.F. Skinner argued that human children learn language through conditioned responses – when they accidentally produce an identifiable approximation of a word, positive reinforcement from adults essentially *conditions* or *trains* them to reproduce it again. This training process continues as they gradually learn grammar and intonation through imitation, receiving positive reinforcement from adults when they get it right.

Nativist theories

In the 1960s the *nativist* Noam Chomsky argued that behaviourist theories were too simple to account for the complexities of learning human language. Instead, he proposed that humans had an innate biological capability absent in all other species, which he called a *language acquisition device* (LAD) that primes us for understanding the basic structure of language – that is, the relationship between subject, object and verb (person, thing and action). Later, cognitive psychologist Steven Pinker pursued this idea in his book *The Language Instinct* (1994), where he argued that only humans have an innate facility for language; he refuted the evidence put forward that chimps can learn language and dismissed evidence from primate research as mere conditioning.

Constructivist theories

Piaget, the *constructivist psychologist* argued that language acquisition is an active intellectual process which begins when children first realise that a word stands as a *symbol* or *symbolic representation* of an object, person or action (Piaget and Inhelder, 1969). They then experiment with language, manipulating words and word order as they gradually piece together the way language works. Later, Tomasello (2003) pursued this constructivist line and showed that *preverbal thinking* is all about ordering, sequencing, classifying and recognising patterns; babies then apply this logic to verbal language, systematically picking out the words they hear stressed and emphasised during their parent/child interactions – IDS makes this process simpler. He argued that children construct language for themselves starting with the most obvious 'pivot' words (names of people and objects), before experimenting with 'noun combinations' like *daddy-car*, and then trying out 'verb islands' like *daddy go car*; in this way they learn the basic structural relationship between person/action/thing.

Social constructivist theories

Vygotsky took a *social constructivist* approach to language acquisition. He argued that language learning is a process of constructing *meanings* out of shared *social* activities; meanings are already shared before words appear and are communicated through relationships and emotions such that children understand the meaning of a raised voice or a soothing hand long before they understand speech. Later, Bruner (1983) showed how children and adults co-construct shared meanings through eye contact, body movement, gesture and vocalisations from moments after birth; these shared meanings become embodied in words – the mumbling lips at the breast become 'mumma', a *sound* infused with warmth and food and fondness. Gradually, through social exchange between the child and the family, these shared meanings are refined and categorised so that 'mumma' becomes a *word* representing a kinship relationship rather than a warm enveloping feeling.

None of these language acquisition theories is definitive; all of them are tied to the particular time and context of their authors. However, it is clear that initial language learning is an intense process requiring a close relationship between children and their significant carers. Once children reach a stage of 'talking about talking' (meta-language), they can acquire language purposefully and rapidly by asking for explanations about things that confuse them – specialised terminology, grammar, homophones, word derivations, definitions – so that they can incorporate into their own personal lexicon the words that are important to them.

Time to reflect

Sometimes people say they feel silly talking to a baby because babies can't understand. What do you think?

When parents say to a baby, 'wave bye-bye' or 'give granny a kiss', are they 'conditioning a response' as Skinner suggested or 'sharing a meaning' as Vygotsky believed?

Which do you think is more important for language learning among seven-year-olds – shared activities or word lists? Why?

Recall a play activity at home, in a nursery or at a school which prompted rich language learning. What do you think drove the learning?

Thought and language

Newspapers often carry stories about children coming to school or a nursery with 'poor language skills' which makes it difficult for them to take up the learning opportunities on offer. Some theorists have argued that language determines how we think and that different cultural linguistic groups understand the world in different ways. The implication is that language determines thinking; this idea transfers to theories about 'language deficit' and ultimately to theories that link limited language to limited thinking and poor school outcomes. How close is the link between language and thought? Do we think in 'words'? Can we grasp concepts like 'floating' and 'sinking' if we don't have the relevant vocabulary?

Focus on *Linguistic determinism*

Linguistic determinism (the idea that thinking is determined by the words available to the speaker) is most widely associated with the work of anthropologist Edward Sapir (1884–1939) and his student Benjamin Lee Whorf (1897–1941). They drew on studies of Native American languages – most famously they showed that having lots of words for different kinds of snow provided Native Americans with a sophisticated insight into the properties of snow that were invisible to English speakers. This led them to conclude that differences in language shape differences in thinking; by the 1950s the *Sapir–Whorf hypothesis* was widely accepted.

Basil Bernstein (1924–2000) investigated the Sapir–Whorf hypothesis through a study on class and language in London schools. He suggested that working-class families use a 'restricted code' of language (fewer words, shorter sentences, more instructions, fewer explanations) and middle-class families use an 'elaborated code' (more questioning, extended dialogue, detailed explanations, reasoned arguments). He argued that because formal schooling is based on 'elaborated codes' of the professional classes, the transition from family to formal education is easier for middle-class children and gives them an advantage over their working-class peers that persists throughout their schooling. He argued that 'elaborated codes' were better fitted for abstract thought and argument.

William Labov (born 1927), who studied black working-class children in New York, disagreed with Bernstein and argued that 'restricted code' was a pejorative term most often applied to dialect speakers of non-standard English; 'elaborated' code is the term used for 'standard' dialect of professionals. He showed that non-standard English is just as efficient at carrying complex abstract concepts as an 'elaborated code'. He believed that failure to make a successful transition from home to school was more likely to be the result of social prejudice associated with the use of non-standard English rather than any lack in the language itself.

More recently, Hart and Risley (1995) investigated language among preschoolers in the United Kingdom. They studied the number of words three-year-old children from different social classes heard *per hour* in a typical day at home. They found wide discrepancies – on average, children in welfare families heard 616 words per hour, children in families of manual labourers heard 1,251 words per hour and children in professional families heard 2,153 words per hour. Children in the welfare group had twice as many negative commands as those in the professional group; in addition, the MLU and structural complexity of the language used in the professional group was much greater than that in the welfare group. They concluded that the children from welfare families were linguistically disadvantaged and that this had implications for future learning.

Today many contemporary sociolinguists agree with the *weak* form of the Sapir–Whorf hypothesis, which says that language shapes thinking (see Gumperz & Levinson, 1996). However, Steven Pinker (1994) disagrees. He says that the idea that language is the *same as* thought is an absurdity. Instead, he believes that all humans think in a universal, electrochemical 'mentalese' and that words are only approximate 'translations' into a common language. He argues that most of the time we operate with the 'gist' of things rather than by slavishly decoding every word and phrase – therefore, we can be clear and logical thinkers whatever our sociolinguistic background.

Shonkoff and Phillips (2000) point to a wealth of recent evidence showing that young children who are *effective communicators* in the early years are better able to sustain play with other children, receive more attention from adults and are more likely to be successful at school. They argue that being an *effective* communicator at an early age has long-term implications for future confidence, self-esteem and learning.

Do you think having a wide vocabulary and sophisticated language (an 'elaborated code') makes someone a more effective communicator?

Can speakers of 'non-standard' dialects or 'restricted' codes think as effectively as speakers of 'standard' dialect?

Do you think children from professional families are likely to be more 'effective communicators' than children from welfare families?

How might your stance on these issues affect your professional judgement about children and families in your care?

There are powerful reasons for suggesting that health visitors, early education practitioners and social workers should keep a close eye on language in their developmental assessments of young children – but there are also powerful reasons for guarding against linguistic prejudice and class stereotyping. Family dialect may differ from the standard spoken and written forms, and children can feel sensitive and excluded if their language is perceived as 'non-standard', especially if others laugh or tease. Early childhood practitioners need to tread carefully and receive all children's spoken communications with the respect they deserve.

The interaction of play, language and social skills

The link between play, language and social skills has been a focus of many books on early childhood development (Isaacs, 1930; Piaget & Inhelder, 1969; Athey, 2003; Pellegrini, 2011; Broadhead & Burt, 2012). Piaget (1962) and Vygotsky (1978) recognised that play is the medium through which language and social development take place; in play children practise their skills and learn the behaviours of their culture (see also Chapter 10). Vygotsky showed that alongside an adult or among more skilful peers, play provides an ideal opportunity, to practise adult roles and behaviour, to develop self-control and above all to learn new concepts:

> In play, the child always behaves beyond his average age, above his daily behaviour; in play it is as though he were a head taller than himself. As in the focus of a magnifying glass, play contains all the developmental tendencies in condensed form and is itself a major source of development. ([1934] 1978: p. 102)

Bruner (1983) points out that the human infant spends much longer playing than the off-spring of other mammals and argues that as societies become more sophisticated children *need to play longer*. However, there is currently some concern that children get *less* time to play and socialise with peers than in the past, and there is evidence that free play opportunities in school and preschool programmes are in decline (Howes, 2011). Antony Pellegrini (2009) wonders whether a rise in incidences of attention deficit disorders, aggression and delinquency might be symptoms of societies that have forgotten how to play. He argues that play is an important site for fostering social bonding, adaptability and resilience because through their play children reward one another's prosocial behaviour and put limits on aggression.

Time to reflect

In your study group, discuss how you played as children.
How social was your play at ages four, six and eight?
Do the children you know play differently from the way you played?
Do you think unsupervised 'free' play is given a high enough priority in families, preschools and primary schools?

Play and social development

Language and socially appropriate behaviour become more critical as children gradually widen their social circle. Only children may find it more difficult to relate to their peers than children from large families because they spend more time in adult company and may find children of their own age alarming and unpredictable. Learning how to behave in acceptable ways, appropriate to circumstances, is a complex process of self-regulation – controlling emotions, choosing language carefully and responding to the needs of others – which requires huge effort for young children and proceeds in fits and starts with many slips along the way. Adults can model appropriate social behaviour by remaining calm and supportive and providing consistent care and affection. When boundaries are breached, a firm intervention from an adult can preserve harmony and prevent harm.

Table 6.1 Social development – relating to others

Babies	From around six months, babies enjoy the company of other babies and may sit together, smile and touch each other's faces. With adults they can play peek-a-boo, take turns and share games.
Toddlers	Toddlers laugh together and copy each other's actions.
	They begin to meet and greet; they learn to acknowledge giving with please and thank you (but only with prompting!).
2–3 years old	Children learn to join groups, first watching at a distance, then playing side by side, copying one another's actions. Adults can facilitate by introducing children to one another and offering help such as 'Here's a cup. You can pour water like the others too.'
	Instead of snatching, children begin to share, sporadically at first and gradually more reliably.
	Adults sustain harmony by providing a calm and orderly atmosphere and intervening in any aggressive or antisocial behaviour by providing alternatives and distractions to defuse the situation.
	Temper tantrums may take the form of wild flailing or holding their breath. This behaviour is alarming for other children, and adults should move them out of harm's way and wait quietly until the tantrum has passed before saying, 'Now that you are calmer, we can talk'.
	Children acknowledge private and public behaviour; they begin to understand that some behaviours like genital activity and toilet visits are private. Adults should be matter-of-fact and not shocked by young children's interest in their own and other people's bodies.
	Consistent routines with predictable boundaries keep children feeling safe and in control and makes socialising easier.
3–4 years old	At this age children are less likely to spit, bite, kick and hit when they feel angry. Socially mature children reliably show empathy and offer sympathy to a distressed playmate; these children are often popular, and other children will gravitate towards them. Socially immature children may be rejected; they can be helped to integrate by practising phrases like 'Can I have a go next?' or 'When you have finished, can I have a turn?'

Table 6.1 *(Continued)*

	Friendships develop as children recognise shared interests. Shared imaginary play and role play become more frequent as they learn to express their ideas aloud and to match their behaviour to other children's actions in order to sustain the make-believe.
	They can listen to a story in a group and recognise other children's needs by not interrupting or causing a commotion.
	Unexpected changes of plan, new situations or transitions to new settings or new friendship groups can still be upsetting and need sensitive management by adults.
	Signs of anger and frustration become rarer in social situations but may still be prevalent at home.
4–8 years old	Children increasingly rely on language to manage their social relations with adults and peers.
	They learn to be assertive without being aggressive or offensive; they can say 'Stop it!' firmly and without rancour. Children who are routinely mocked or physically chastised may in turn reproduce this negative behaviour with their peers and may find it difficult to be calmly assertive when they feel under threat.
	They show sensitivity to others and learn to hide their feelings when appropriate.
	They learn to ask for help without feeling inadequate and recognise that working as an apprentice in partnership with more skilful peers, or adults helps them to learn more quickly.
	They can be a follower or a leader as the social situation requires.
	They are proud of their achievements without being boastful; they tolerate other children's idiosyncrasies with good humour.
	They begin to manage envy and jealousy and no longer need the latest toy or fad to feel part of the group or to establish status.
	They gradually learn to manage changes of plan and disappointment with more equanimity.

Social play is essential for children's mental development because successful play with peers reflects back a positive self-image. In play with other children, they learn social rules of behaviour, different roles and new language. The kinds of play children engage in changes as the children become more socially mature: as babies and toddlers, they spend more time in solitary physical activity, exploring their environment and the things around them; as their language becomes more fluent and their social skills develop, they spend more time exploring the social worlds of friendship, shared interest and relationships. Once they can *decentre* and understand other people's needs, they can enter into social make-believe play, which requires them to listen carefully and to adapt their actions to fit in with playmates.

Play activities from birth to four

During the 'language explosion' from 18 months to four years, children simultaneously move from play with objects and people into a new kind of play – sometimes called *symbolic* or *imaginary* or *fantasy* play (see also Chapter 10). They begin to take on roles, being mother or father or pretending to be a superhero; they may turn an empty box into a rocket and set off into unknown universes; they may have an imaginary friend who has to be supplied with an extra cup and plate. As their language and social skills become more sophisticated, they engage more and more in pretend play with other children, taking on increasingly sophisticated roles; young children with good language and social skills can keep early cooperative play going for long periods (Bruner et al., 1976; Shonkoff & Phillips, 2000).

Mildred Parten (1932) famously studied free play among American preschool children, aged two to five. She identified six kinds of play linked to levels of social and linguistic engagement:

- *unoccupied play* – just watching and taking things in;
- *solitary play* – examining something closely or constructing something, or daydreaming with a favourite toy;
- *onlooker play* – watching and commenting from the sidelines, but not joining in directly;
- *parallel play* – playing alongside others, imitating their actions, but without interaction;
- *associative play* – engaging with others, perhaps commenting or giving a running commentary, but without coordinating the play;
- *cooperative play* – accepting particular roles in the game and coordinating with companions.

Parten saw these forms of play as 'developmental' or maturational, moving from simple to complex, with cooperative pretend play being the most advanced because it involves children *decentring* as they play – that is, matching up their own imaginary scenarios with those of their companions. In these games, children frequently move in and out of 'pretend' mode in order to regulate the behaviour and actions of their playmates; it requires endless negotiation to ensure that everyone is in the moment in the same imaginary space, operating with the same rules and conventions and not straying out of role. When the scenarios between the players become dislocated, disputes can arise or the game may be abandoned – skilled adults can intervene with helpful hints to prolong the play, perhaps offering props or a new direction. Although Parten thought cooperative play was the most developmentally advanced, more recent studies suggest that, depending on the familiarity of the social and linguistic context, cooperative play is evident in rudimentary form in children's social interactions from the beginning (Howes & Hamilton, 1992; Howes, 2011).

Play activities from four to eight

Vivian Gussin-Paley, an early childhood teacher and researcher in fantasy play and storytelling, documents the highs and lows of social play in her many books, most notably in *A Child's Work: The Importance of Fantasy Play, The Boy Who Would Be a Helicopter* and *Bad Guys Don't Have Birthdays: Fantasy Play at Four*. She shows that from four to eight years, children generally have the linguistic and social skills to behave in cooperative ways, taking into account other children's feelings: they know how to join in and when not to; they understand when to reveal their feelings and when not to (for example, in expressing polite pleasure when a present isn't quite what they wanted); they guard their tongues with their friends and don't make hurtful or disparaging comments; they show care for the feelings of others; they can be quietly assertive without being aggressive. Their social maturity now manifests itself in a strong desire to be accepted by the group and to modify their behaviour to fit in (often manifested in our consumer culture as having the latest toys or shoes). They can also take responsibility for younger or more vulnerable people and are more alert to potential danger.

From around age four, they are ready to play games with clear rules (chase, hopscotch, board games). They like to draw and to write and to read, to make models and to play computer games alone or in teams. As they get older, their social dramatic play becomes more complex, with elaborate rules and actions to support epic fantasies that can go on for days and weeks; these epic games are often very physical; they keep bodies fit and healthy and minds active and curious.

From around age six, children use play to develop friendships with like-minded people – having gangs, dens and secret societies like the characters in Enid Blyton's *Secret Seven* and *Famous Five* books, as well as making friendship bracelets and sharing and swapping collections of everything from figurines to computer games. Boys and girls often separate into single-sex play groups, learning from one another, sharing confidences and exploring their gender roles. At this age, children need to play in wide open spaces where they can exercise their limbs and perfect their motor coordination; they like to stretch themselves mentally and physically, staying just on the safe side of risk. They are often intensely competitive and desperate to win – in peer play, team games, individual sports, spelling tests, book reading marathons and making the most elaborate models or friendship bracelets. Some adults feel that competition creates winners and losers and should be discouraged, arguing that children should strive for only a personal best. However, children seem naturally to want to compete with one another at this age – to be tallest, oldest or best at skipping or catch, to climb the highest tree or kill the most enemies on their computer game. Everything is turned into a competition, and in the struggle for supremacy, they continually extend themselves, physically and mentally. Pellis and Pellis (2011), in their study of rough-and-tumble play, point out that although the competitiveness to win is intense, competitive play is a self-regulating system – the desire to win is balanced out with a desire to maintain cooperation (it rarely continues until one competitor is vanquished). The fun of this sort of play is in the rivalry itself and the desire to pit oneself against someone else, to reach beyond one's personal best and to aspire ever higher.

Case study: Epic fantasy play

In the playground a group of seven- and eight-year-old boys are pushing and shoving and squaring up to one another, roaring out threats and hollering loudly. One aims a high karate kick at his playmate. Suddenly, one shouts, 'Enemy!'

They all scatter, hiding behind other children or hunkering down among the dustbins. 'Over the top!' one yells, 'Get to the mound!'

Instantly they are rolling commando-style, then rising and running in a crouch towards the far side of the playing field. On the way, they swing themselves through the climbing frame, run across a slippery log, leap from tyre-island to tyre-island and pull themselves along the monkey bars. They race across the wet grass to a raised mound topped by a tree.

The first boy to reach it is the winner. He turns on his companions. He stretches out his arm, two fingers pointing, the other hand pulling a trigger at his elbow, 'Ackackackack!' The other boys dodge or fall to the ground in exaggerated death agonies. 'Gotcha! Gotcha! Die! Die!' One of the boys scrambles to his feet. 'Kerpow!' shouts the boy on the mound as he lobs an imaginary

▶

grenade; his victim dies a writhing, screaming death.

Suddenly the playground assistant appears. 'Boys! How many times have you been told? ... NO GUNS!'

Is the playground assistant right to discourage this kind of play? Why? Why not?

Discussion questions

Why do you think attack games and superhero play are so popular, particularly with boys? What functions might this kind of play serve? Should preschool settings and schools have policies that ban gun play?

Helping children to play

A small minority of children will need explicit instruction to help them integrate with their peers before they can play successfully – for instance, some children don't know how to join a group. They may barge in, they may be needy and clingy, or they may hang back, shy and diffident. Some children with social difficulties may exhibit tantrums, or anger; they may be demanding, or boastful and attention seeking. Others may feel they have to have the latest fashionable toy or item of clothing in order to be accepted. These children may be rejected by their peers and may need extra support from caring, non-judgemental adults who can facilitate their access into social groups. However, direct adult intervention may highlight the child's difficulties, and wherever possible it can be helpful to enlist the support of a popular child with accomplished social skills who can ease the child's passage towards acceptance.

In some harder cases, this may not be possible, and so adults will need to support the child in other ways. Some groups use *circle time*, where children take turns to say positive things about themselves and each other. Other approaches to integrating socially awkward children, like Creative Listening and Children's Hours pioneered by Rachel Pinney (1909–1995) or Nurture Groups introduced in the 1970s by Marjorie Boxall, were initially designed to help teachers to integrate children with special needs into mainstream schooling but have been taken up more widely. All these programmes emphasise the importance of *listening to children* and treating their concerns with respect (Lancaster, 2003). However, children hate being patronised and are very good at spotting well-meaning attempts at fostering inclusivity, so these programmes need to be used with care; otherwise, they may do more harm than good.

Broadhead and Burt (2012) describe how they created child-led play environments, places inside the classroom and outdoors that children could make into 'whatever you want it to be', where they could freely play together and explore shared interests and imaginary scenarios without adult interference. In these spaces, the authors suggest that children learn more about themselves and have the opportunity to find other children whose interests 'parallel and reflect their own' (p. 144), and through their reciprocal interactions and mutual trust they take their play to a higher level of complexity than they might have reached in adult-led play activities.

Socialisation, play, language and culture

The interweaving of socialisation, play and language prepares children to take forward the beliefs and values of their particular society (van Oers, 2010) because children integrate adult

Time to reflect

Design a play-based observation that will help you investigate how securely a child is integrated into their peer group. Focus on forms of play, language and social skills.

- *Aim*: What is the purpose of the study?
- *Objective*: What do you hope to uncover?
- *Ethics*: Whose permission do you need to carry out the observation?
- *Target group*: What age group will you choose?
- *Setting*: How will you observe?
- *Literature review*: How will you access relevant information on play and social integration?
- *Observational methods*: How will you collect and record your observations?
- *Findings*: How will you present and analyse your data?
- *Conclusions*: How will you relate your findings to previous studies?
- *Recommendations*: How will you use your literature review to recommend appropriate actions?
- *References*: How will you list the sources you have referred to in your study?

practices, values and norms they observe into their play. Barbara Rogoff et al. (2001) propose that play brings together the personal, interpersonal and community processes that prepare the child to live in a particular culture though a universal process of *apprenticeship*. First, children observe from the sidelines; then they practise their community language and roles in play; then they take their place alongside an adult or older child who guides them towards mastery until they can do the task for themselves. But different cultural expectations about children and their roles in relation to adults can lead to misunderstandings when different cultures come into contact. It can be disconcerting when a practitioner's cherished assumptions clash with strongly held beliefs drawn from a different culture.

Case study: A cultural misunderstanding

A Ugandan student commented disapprovingly on the 'disrespect' that English children show for their parents and teachers.

I suggested that what she called 'disrespect' was perceived by Western parents and teachers as healthy disagreement. I explained that in Britain, we often see challenge and disagreement as part of the process of growing up in a democratic society and that freedom of expression and respect for everyone's opinions, including children's, is part of our cultural story.

But my Ugandan student maintained that in her culture children are more polite. They are expected to conform to social rules of behaviour based on respect for adults. She said that learning to respect one's elders is part of learning to put others' needs first. In Uganda deference and submissiveness towards adults is deeply ingrained and highly val-

ued in children; the idea of holding a contrary opinion is almost inconceivable because everyone reveres age and experience, custom and tradition.

We then discussed how this cultural difference might have an impact in situations where children are asked to voice an opinion or where they are asked to report on abusive or neglectful behaviour by an adult.

Discussion questions

What do you make of these divergent views?

What effect might a Ugandan upbringing have on a child's behaviour in a Western setting?

Why is it important for professionals to understand the home cultural community of children in their care?

A. Bame Nsamenang (2004) points out that in sub-Saharan Africa, children's play is not policed by adults but is focused in mixed-age peer groups where children learn from one another, roaming freely, away from adult constraint. Far from a *Lord of the Flies* anarchy, he argues that this sociability with the wider group beyond the family and household encourages attitudes of social cohesion, interdependence and respect for adult norms; he contrasts this with the European and North American emphasis on family and individualism, where the elevation of the 'unique' child fosters competitiveness and weakens social ties. He suggests that the Western model of adult supervised play leads to family isolation and a fragmentation of community values, while the sub-Saharan African model is more likely to foster altruism and collective responsibility. He believes these values are under threat from the ubiquitous spread of Western early education and schooling programmes.

Sadly, outdoor, unstructured and unsupervised play in mixed-age peer groups is a luxury denied many children in Western societies – traffic, indoor computer games, adult anxieties about stranger danger and an education system that elevates formal academic skills above playing, socialising and creativity all conspire to restrict the time and space available for unfettered child play and child-led social learning.

For children and adults alike, play is important for mental and physical health; the social relationships fostered during play build self-confidence and well-being and feelings of being connected and supported in a wider community of sympathetic peers.

Summary

- Social interaction begins at birth and provides the foundation for play and language.
- Infant-directed speech (IDS), sometimes called parentese or motherese, is a universal adult style of talking to babies. Words and structures are simplified and delivered in a higher-pitched voice.
- The transition from primary to secondary intersubjectivity provides a platform for the development of mind-mindedness and meaning making.
- Language acquisition follows a universal pattern from single, naming words at around one year to complex adult forms by age four years.
- The interrelationship of thought and language is a hotly contested topic.
- Play offers opportunities for practising social interaction and for developing language.
- Social interaction, play and language provide the medium for the transmission of cultural values and beliefs.
- Free outdoor play in mixed-age peer groups, away from adult surveillance, is relatively rare for children growing up in the Western world.
- Play is important for the health and well-being of individual children and adults and for society at large.

Topics for further discussion

1 In settings you know, do you think child-directed play is given enough time and space in the curriculum for newborns to four-year-olds and for four- to eight-year-olds?

2 Bert van Oers believes play provides a site for children to explore the culture and values they observe in the adult world. Do you have any anecdotal evidence that supports this view?

3 What social skills might children learn through self-directed play that they could not learn through adult-directed play?

Assignments

1 Study the document 'What to expect, when? Guidance to your child's learning and development in the early years foundation stage' (4Children, 2015, https://www.actionfor children.org.uk/resources-and-publications/information-guides/what-to-expect-when-a-parents-guide/). What emphasis does it place on play? What guidance does it give for helping children's language development?

2 Make a video of someone talking to a pre-verbal baby. Can you identify any features of IDS in their interaction?

3 Find out about the language-learning patterns of hearing-impaired children. How can Makaton and Sign Language help their language, play and socialisation?

4 Access and read Laura E. Berk's classic article 'Vygotsky's Theory: the Importance of Make-Believe Play', in *Young Children*, November 1994: pp. 30–38. Summarise it for a presentation to colleagues.

Further reading

Classic texts on play, language and socialisation include Susan Isaacs' chapter 'Play and Growth', in *The Nursery Years: The Mind of the Child from Birth to Six Years* (1929); Vygotsky's *Play and its Role in the Mental Development of the Child* (1966); Mary Sheridan's two books *From Birth to Five Years: Children's Developmental Progress* (1973, updated in 2014, by Anjay Sharma and Helen Cockerill) and *Play in Early Childhood: from Birth to Six Years* (1997, 3rd edition 2011); and Janet Moyles' *The Excellence of Play* (1994, updated 2005).

Pelligrini, A. (ed.) (2011) *The Oxford Handbook of the Development of Play*. Oxford: Oxford University Press.

Developmental Psychology and Early Education (2012) by David Whitebread, covers the language debates in detail.

The Palgrave Handbook of Childhood Studies (ed. Qvortrup, Corsaro and Honig, 2011) has interesting chapters by William Corsaro on 'Peer Culture' and by Ann-Carita Evaldsson on 'Play and Games'.

Useful websites

Siren Films has produced DVDs about play, language and socialisation (www.sirenfilms.co.uk). National Children's Bureau 'Play England' supports and encourages play at www. playengland.org.uk.

References

Athey, C. (2007) *Extending Thought in Young Children*. London: Paul Chapman Publishing

Baron-Cohen, S. (1995) *Mindblindness: An Essay on Autism and Theory of Mind*. Cambridge, MA: MIT Press/Bradford Books

Berk, L.E. (1994) Vygotsky's Theory: the Importance of Make-Believe Play. *Young Children* November 1994: 30–38

Broadhead, P. and Burt, A. (2012) *Understanding Young Children's Learning Through Play: Building Playful Pedagogies*. London: Routledge

Brown, R. (1973) *A First Language: The Early Years*. Cambridge, MA: Harvard University Press

Bruner, J.S., Jolly, A. and Sylva, K. (1976) *Play – Its Role in Development and Evolution*. New York: Basic Books

Bruner, J. (1983) *Child's Talk: Learning to Use Language*. New York: W.W. Norton

Carey, S. (1978) 'The child as word learner', in J. Bresnan, G. Miller and M. Halle (eds) *Linguistic Theory and Psychological Reality* (pp. 264–293). Cambridge, MA: MIT Press

Cooper, R.P. and Aslin, R.N. (1990) Preference for Infant Directed Speech in the First Month after Birth. *Child Development* 61: 1584–1595

Cormier, K., Schembri, A., Vinson, D. and Orfamidou, E. (2012) First language Acquisition differs from Second Language acquisition in pre-lingually Deaf Signers; Evidence from Sensitivity to Grammaticality in British Sign Language *Cognition* 124(1): 50–65

DfE (2012) *The Statutory Framework for the Early Years Foundation Stage*. Crown copyright

Fogel, A. (1977) *Infancy: Infant, family and society*. St. Paul, MN: West Publishing in Gavin Bremner and Alan Fogel (eds) (2004) *Blackwell Handbook of Infant Development*. Oxford: Blackwell Publishing

Fogel, A. and DeKoeyer-Laros, I. (2007) The developmental transition to secondary intersubjectivity in the second half year: a microgenetic case study. *Journal of Developmental Processes* 2(2, Fall): 63–90

Gardner, R.A., Gardner, B.T. and Van Cantfort, T.E. (1989) *Teaching Sign Language to Chimpanzees*. Albany, NY: State University of New York Press

Gopnik, A., Meltzoff, A. and Kuhl, P. (1999) *How Babies Think*. London: Weidenfeld and Nicholson

Gumperz, J.J. and Levinson, S.C. (eds) (1996) *Rethinking Linguistic Relativity*. Cambridge: Cambridge University Press

Hart, B. and Risley, T. (1995) *Meaningful differences in the everyday experience of young American children*. Baltimore, MD: Paul H. Brookes Publishing (2004 printing)

Howes, C. (2011) 'Social Play of Children with Adults and Peers', in A.D. Pellegrini (ed.) *The Oxford Handbook of the Development of Play*. New York: Oxford University Press

Howes, C. and Hamilton, C.E. (1992) Children's Relationships with Caregivers: Mothers and Child Care Teachers. *Child Development* 63(4): 859–866

Isaacs, S. (1929) *The Nursery Years: The Mind of the Child from Birth to Six Years* (pp. 40–41). London: Routledge and Sons

Isaacs, S. (1930) *Intellectual Growth in Young Children*. London: Routledge

Labov, W. (1969) The logic of non-standard English. *Georgetown Monographs on Language and Linguistics* 22: 1–31. Reprinted in N. Keddie (ed.) (1973). *Tinker, Tailor … The myth of cultural deprivation* (pp. 21–66). Harmondsworth: Penguin

Lancaster, Y.P. (2003) *Promoting Listening to Young Children – The reader. Coram Family Listening to Young Children Project*. Maidenhead: Open University Press

Long, M. (1990) Maturational constraints on language development. *Studies in Second Language Acquisition* 12(3, September): 251–285

Mithen, S.J. (2005) *The Singing Neanderthals: the Origins of Music, Language, Mind and Body*. London: Weidenfeld & Nicolson

Nsamenang, A.B. (2004) *Cultures of Human Development and Education: Challenge to Growing up African*. New York: Nova Science Publications

Parten, M. (1932) Social participation among preschool children. *Journal of Abnormal and Social Psychology* 28(3): 136–147

Pellegrini, A.D. (2009) *The role of play in human development*. New York: Oxford University Press

Pelligrini, A.D. (ed.) (2011) *The Oxford Handbook of the Development of Play*. Oxford: Oxford University Press

Pellis, S.M. and Pellis, V.C. (2011) 'Rough-and-tumble play – training and using the social brain', in A.D. Pellegrini (ed.) *Oxford Handbook of the Development of Play* (pp. 245–259). Oxford: Oxford University

Piaget, T. (1962) *Play, Dreams and Imitation in Childhood*. London: Routledge and Kegan Paul

Piaget, J. and Inhelder, B. (1969) *The Psychology of the Child* (trans. Helen Weaver). New York: Basic Books

Pinker, S. (1994) *The Language Instinct; How the Mind Creates Language*. New York: Harper Perennial Modern Classics

Rogoff, B. (1990) *Apprenticeship in Thinking: Cognitive Development in Social Context*. New York: Oxford University Press

Rogoff, B., Goodman Turkanis, C. and Bartlett, L. (2001) *Learning Together: Children and Adults in a School Community*. New York: Oxford University Press

Rutter, M., Beckett, C., Castle, J., Colvert, E., Kreppner, J., Mehta, M., Stevens, S. and Sonuga Burke, E. (2007) Effects of profound early institutional deprivation: An overview of findings from a UK longitudinal study of Romanian adoptees. *European Journal of Developmental Psychology* 4(3): 332–350

Shonkoff, J.P. and Phillips, D. (2000) *From Neurons to Neighbourhoods: The Science of Early Development*. National Research Council, Committee on Integrating the Science of Early Childhood Development

Tomasello, M. (2003) *Constructing A Language. A Usage-Based Approach*. Cambridge, MA, and London: Harvard University Press

Trevarthen, C. and Hubley, P. (1978) 'Secondary intersubjectivity: Confidence, confiding and acts of meaning in the first year', in A. Lock (ed.) *Action, gesture and symbol: the emergence of language* (pp. 183–227). New York: Cambridge University Press

Trevarthen, C. (1993) 'The self born in intersubjectivity: an infant communicating', in U. Neisser (ed.) *The Perceived Self: Ecological and Interpersonal Sources of Self Knowledge* (pp. 121–173). New York: Cambridge University Press

van Oers, B. (2010) 'Children's enculturation through play', in L. Brookner and S. Edwards (eds) *Engaging Play*. Maidenhead: Open University Press

Vygotsky, L.S. ([1934] 1966) 'The role of play in the mental development of the child', in J.S. Bruner, A. Jolly and K. Sylva (eds) (1976) *Play – Its Role in Development and Evolution*. New York: Basic Books

Wells, G. (1986) *Bristol Language Development Study: the pre-school years (Language at Home and at School vol.2)*. Cambridge: Cambridge University Press

Wood, D.J., Bruner, J.S. and Ross, G. (1976) The role of tutoring in problem solving. *Journal of Child Psychology and Psychiatry* 17(2): 89–100

Emotional and moral development

Introduction

All children are unique, and their emotions, values and behaviours develop in different ways through a combination of individual temperament, family influences, and cultural expectations. At the core of emotional and moral development is the need for strong attachment ties, and many experts believe that secure emotional attachment is critical for mental health, emotional stability and maintaining satisfying social relationships. It is the constancy and consistency of first attachments which provide the foundations for developing a sense of self, for making wider relationships and for acquiring a moral framework. As children progress through infancy and childhood, they begin to take into account the effects of their words and behaviour on other people and to exercise conscious 'effortful' control over their emotions, tailoring their behaviour in prosocial ways to fit in with the shared moral values of the people around them.

This chapter looks at some of the ways children learn emotional control, prosocial behaviour and moral reasoning and considers the key role that EC professionals play in this development. For children in the age range from birth to eight, a secure attachment to the adults in their lives is crucial; parents provide the first attachment, but relationships with their key person in preschools and schools play an important part too. It is essential that the treatment children receive in their first forays into the wider social environment is warm, consistent and supportive if they are to make good friendships with their peers. Thoughtful, responsive and non-judgemental adults can provide the role models children need to become kind and helpful members of their communities who value and respect the needs of others.

Emotions

When we think about emotions, we usually think about words like affection, surprise, fear, anger, joy, sadness and so on – expressions of inner feelings that we all experience and that we communicate through words, body language, facial expressions and behaviour. But why are some children fearful, while others are full of derring-do? Are they born like that, or is their disposition a product of their upbringing?

Temperament and disposition

Mary Rothbart (2005) believes that babies are *differently reactive* and express innate temperament differences through different activity levels from the moment of birth. Some babies kick more, some are more attentive, some are more irritable or fearful, some are difficult to soothe and some are placid; she argues that these early reactive behaviours are *reinforced* by the responses of other people. She points out that extreme temperaments seem to be more stable – for example, an extremely passive baby may engage less and may be overlooked and ignored so that they retreat further into passivity as they grow older, while an extremely active child may seek and receive more social interaction and feedback (both negative and positive!) and may become even more active as nature and nurture reinforce one another. But others argue that for most young children temperament fluctuates with circumstance and that emotional behaviour is an *adaptive response* to context so that babies' temperaments develop in response to the care and nurture they receive (Bates & Wachs, 1994; Witherington et al., 2001; Crittenden, 2008).

Most early childhood professionals seem to operate with the belief that nothing is fixed, that obstacles can be overcome and that all children can flourish in responsive, supportive environments as long as their interventions match the children's needs. However, there are some basic social, physical and emotional requirements that need to be in place if children are to develop the emotional balance required to fulfil their potential as human beings. Psychologist Charles Maslow (1908–1970) showed that children can only become fully integrated, as people and as members of wider society, once all these needs have been met. Maslow (1943) produced a *hierarchy of needs*, showing how the physical basics of food, warmth and shelter have to be met in order for children to feel safe. Once they feel safe, they can then fulfil their emotional needs for love and kinship and

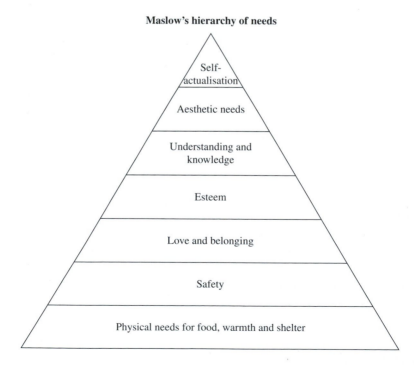

Maslow's hierarchy of needs

move on to satisfy their needs for esteem, knowledge and creative playfulness that culminate in 'self-actualisation', which is the development of a fully integrated self. When any of these needs remain unmet, the desire to fulfil them persists and interferes with the process of moving on.

When children come to school hungry, afraid or under-stimulated, they find it hard to 'fit in' with other people or to learn. It is a sad fact that children from the poorest families in the poorest neighbourhoods – even those who score highly in tests at 22 months – rapidly fall behind their peers; they suffer more physical and mental ill-health, more accidents and poorer educational outcomes (Griggs & Walker, 2008). Health visitors and early childhood specialists are the first point of contact for new parents and play an important role in helping them to understand the needs in Maslow's list. All parents and EC professionals need to be aware that physical and emotional security, love and kinship, play, talk and shared activities give children the foundations for a satisfying life and ultimately for 'self-actualisation'.

Emotional attachment

The importance of emotional attachment

Emotional attachment refers to the primary bond of trust and affection that develops between children and carers in infancy. Recent research from adoption studies around the world suggests that lack of close one-to-one interaction during the first two years may deprive children of the unique responses they need to develop this emotional attachment. For instance, if no one responds to a baby's cry, the baby eventually gives up crying; if no one responds to their babble, they stop babbling. It has been observed that children in overcrowded orphanages seem unnaturally still and passive and are generally developmentally delayed, especially in language (Rutter, 1998). The quality of attachment between child and carer is therefore of profound importance for every aspect of development.

Secure emotional attachment grows out of the responsiveness and playfulness between caregiver and baby, which is why before discharging new mothers from hospital, midwives check that this bonding process has begun by looking for eye contact, cuddling and talking. If bonding is problematic, perhaps after a difficult birth or when a child is born with some kind of impairment, families may need intensive professional support over an extended period to prevent rejection.

Figure 7.1 The Austrian zoologist, ethologist, and ornithologist Konrad Lorenz proved that attachment is a basic animal function. His experiments with greylag geese showed that the birds establish attachment bonds in the first twelve hours after hatching and that, in the absence of mother goose, they attach to the person who feeds them.

Source: By Eurobas - Own work, CC BY-SA 3.0, https://commons.wikimedia.org/w/index.php?curid=7311962

Theories of attachment

Various theories offer different explanations about the mechanisms that establish bonding, but all agree that the process is most intense during early infancy. *Freudian theories* suggest that babies are motivated to attach to the mother through feeding experiences and the gratification of libidinal drives. *Nativist theories* suggest that babies are naturally primed by evolution to attach to the person who feeds and protects them. Konrad Lorenz (1903–1989) studied attachment in animals and suggested that there is a window of opportunity, a 'critical period' very soon after birth, when the strongest attachment bonds are made.

Research in neuroscience suggests that human children establish the deepest attachment bonds during the first three years of life, when the right hemisphere of the brain (governing emotions) is most dominant. After this period, the possibilities for deep emotional attachment diminish as the left hemisphere (associated with language and logic) becomes more dominant. However, constructivist and social constructivist theories suggest that this position is too deterministic and that children can establish a variety of attachment bonds gradually over the first few years of life (and throughout their lives) as their social horizons expand and they learn to make distinctions between primary carers and 'strangers' (Rutter, 2002).

Bowlby's theory of attachment

John Bowlby (1907–1990) is sometimes called the father of attachment theory. His own life provides an illustration of how attachment can work. He was born at a time when middle-class mothers employed nannies and saw their children only for an hour a day. In his own case, his beloved nanny, his trusted attachment figure, left the family when he was four, and he later

Table 7.1 Bowlby's stages of attachment

0–6 weeks	The *recently birthed baby* attends to other people but shows no particular attachment.
6 weeks–2 months	The *babe in arms* shows indiscriminate social attachment by smiling, cooing and showing interest in everyone.
3–7 months	Sitting and reaching infants show attachment only to familiar people; they reserve smiles, coos and interest for people who appear frequently in their lives.
From 8–24 months	*Crawling, toddling infants* show intense attachment to the main caregiver; they try to maintain physical proximity at all times, they are wary of strangers; stranger anxiety peaks around 8–10 months. They use their caregiver as a secure base for forays into new territory and often cry when separated; separation anxiety peaks around 14–18 months.
From 24 months	*Talking infants* show some control over attachment feelings and don't cry inconsolably at separation. They begin to show 'multiple attachments', where they will accept consolation from trusted others. They have an 'internal working model' (IWM) of the absent parent and can maintain a sense of connection with a 'comfort blanket' that smells of home. They can be reassured and pacified with promises that 'mummy will be back' as long as they are confident in the bond of trust and affection with her. Securely attached children accept explanations for absences and gradually learn to manage their own reactions to separation.

(adapted from Bowlby (1969: p. 79))

recalled his feelings of abandonment, likening his loss to bereavement; he experienced further anxieties associated with separation when he was sent off to boarding school a few years later. These childhood experiences gave him a special insight when he began studying the emotional effects of separation on child evacuees during the Second World War, which led him to develop his theories of 'maternal deprivation' and 'attachment'. Over a long career, he came to believe that the reciprocal emotional attachment between mother and child was critical for mental health, emotional stability and maintaining satisfying social relationships in later life.

Theories of maternal deprivation and emotional attachment were ground-breaking at the time and had far-reaching consequences. For example, governments seized on the idea that mothers were the primary attachment figure to justify closing down state-supported nurseries for the children of poor families and to resist pressure for more childcare provision for working parents. More positively, hospitals changed their practices and encouraged parents to make more frequent visits to their sick children; social service personnel showed more reluctance to remove at-risk children into fostering and institutional care; and the wider population began to question the wisdom of adoption and emigration practices that saw 'deprived children' shipped off to countries like Canada and Australia for a 'better life'.

Although Bowlby's ideas about attachment and maternal deprivation were widely accepted, not everyone agreed. Feminist writers took issue with his emphasis on *mothers* as the key attachment figures, suspecting that it would provide a justification for keeping mothers out of the workforce. Men objected too; Rutter (1972) made the case for fathers to be recognised as emotional attachment figures too, and in his book *Maternal Deprivation Reassessed*, he provided evidence that babies form *multiple* attachments and that *both* parents (or even siblings and grandparents) could be primary attachment figures. Bowlby took these criticisms on board and accepted that any *consistent carer* could provide stable and secure early attachments. Of course, not all children can have consistent carers, and sometimes the attachment process is interrupted. However, evidence from adoption studies shows that children are resilient enough to grow attachment bonds with foster parents and adoptive families throughout childhood, although their chances are enhanced if they are placed in a family before the age of three (Werner & Smith, 1982; Rutter, 1998).

Parents and early childhood practitioners often express unease about very young children experiencing prolonged separation from their primary attachment figure, for example in day-care nurseries, fearing that it might be detrimental to emotional health and wellbeing. However, because emotional attachment is not exclusive to the mother–baby partnership, other people, including familiar 'key workers', can also provide secure attachment bonds that enable children to thrive (Dunn, 2002).

Mary Ainsworth and the Infant Strange Situation

Mary Ainsworth (1913–1999), a Canadian psychology graduate, began her career studying 'security theory' at the Institute of Child Study in Toronto, where she investigated emotional attachment between children and their parents, initially with the intention of discovering links between early attachment patterns and relationships in adulthood. When she married, she moved to London, where she joined John Bowlby at the Tavistock Clinic to study the effects of maternal deprivation on child development. There, she devised a famous experiment called the *Infant Strange Situation* to 'measure' the quality of attachment between infants and mothers.

Focus on *Attachment behaviour and the Infant Strange Situation*

Mary Ainsworth's study (1969) focused on *separation* and *reunion* patterns among 11–15-month-old children and their mothers. She set up an experiment under laboratory conditions to observe children's reactions to a 'strange situation'. First, she left the children to play with toys alongside their mothers. Then she introduced a stranger into the room. After a few minutes, the mother slipped away, leaving the child with the stranger. After a short while, the mother returned and was reunited with the child.

During the experiment, researchers recorded three key observations:

1. how children played before, during and after the mother's absence;
2. how they reacted to the stranger before, during and after the mother's absence;
3. how they reacted to separation and reunion with their mother.

Ainsworth observed three different patterns of attachment behaviour, which she labelled:

1. *Insecure-avoidant attachment* (Type A) – when the mother is present, the infant plays with the toys in a solitary fashion. He ignores both the stranger's arrival and his mother's departure. Play continues as before. The child accepts the stranger's attentions dispassionately; when his mother returns, he shows little interest.
2. *Secure attachment* (Type B) – when the mother is present, the infant explores and plays freely, showing her mother the new toys. She engages briefly with the stranger, using her mother as a secure base. When her mother leaves, she protests, abandons her play and spurns the stranger's attention but is soon comforted when her mother returns.
3. *Insecure-resistant* (Type C) – the infant doesn't settle or play; she shows anxiety before separation and becomes clingy and difficult. She is inconsolable when the mother leaves and shows resentment or helpless passivity during her absence, spurning the stranger's offer of comfort. When her mother returns, she resists all attempts at comfort and remains distressed.

Some years later, Ainsworth introduced a fourth category, of rather rare behaviour:

4. *Insecure-disorganised* (Type D) – the infant plays in an unfocused, desultory way, without showing any inclination to share the new toys with her mother. She mostly ignores both the parent and the stranger. During the mother's absence, the child seems surprised by the stranger's attempts to engage with her. When her mother returns, she seems confused and bewildered.

These observations led Ainsworth to theorise about separation and reunion situations:

- *Insecure-avoidant* children mask their distress and 'freeze' emotionally; they fear abandonment and avoid making a scene that might alienate others.
- *Securely attached* children feel free to express distress in the certain expectation that the parent will quickly return; they accept comfort with joy and relief.
- *Insecure-resistant* children vent their fear as anger; they resist or reject any attempts to comfort them.
- *Insecure-disorganised* children have no expectations that adults will behave in any predictably reliable or consistent ways towards them.

Some people argue that this theory ignores 'temperament' and cannot be taken as a proxy for emotional attachment. Do you think this is a valid criticism?

Some commentators point to cultural bias in the experiment. They suggest that Western infants brought up in nuclear families are more likely to register as *securely attached* on Ainsworth's scale than are children brought up in societies where childcare is more widely shared. Why might this be the case?

Very few children fall into the category *insecure-disorganised*. What factors might contribute to this rare form of infant *de*tachment behaviour?

Attachment and parenting

Patricia Crittenden, in her book *Raising Parents: Attachment, Parenting and Child Safety* (2008), argues that attachment patterns can be passed down through generations. Parents who experienced overly anxious or overly harsh parenting themselves may reproduce those behaviours and set up the cycle in their own children. She suggests that the patterns of attachment identified by Ainsworth represent children's *adaptive* behaviours towards the parenting they receive. She proposes that children who show anxious attachment patterns (Types A and C) are not 'poorly

---

Case study: Storybook Dads

Every year 20,000 children suffer traumatic emotional separation when a parent goes to prison. Half of all prisoners lose touch with their families; those who manage to maintain contact are six times less likely to reoffend.

In Dartmoor prison a visiting adult literacy teacher, Sharon Berry, introduced a scheme called *Storybook Dads* to help fathers keep in touch with their children through bedtime stories. Prisoners record themselves reading or telling a story onto DVD, sometimes with the help of puppets, sometimes using their computer skills to add sound effects, music and pictures. The scheme now operates in many other prisons.

'At first, I felt silly reading kids' books out loud', said Darren, 'it was even worse when I played it back. My voice was so boring!' But once he received positive reactions from his kids, he was keen to do the next one. 'It keeps me connected. They live too far away for visits, and their Mum can't afford the fares.'

Alice, aged five, listens to her dad every night before she goes to sleep. When he gets to the end of the story and says, 'Night, night, Alice, time for bed now, give Mum a kiss from me' she kisses his on-screen face and then kisses her mother. Whenever she feels sad because she is missing him, she puts on one of the DVDs. She sometimes plays them to her friends and they marvel that her dad is on the telly!

Discussion questions

How does this scheme support emotional attachment?
Can you think of other situations where this idea might be useful?
Can you think of any disadvantages associated with this scheme?

---

attached' but are actually expressing and responding to something they perceive as 'threatening' in their parent's behaviour towards them. She believes that children exhibiting Type D behaviours are at most risk of long-lasting emotional damage because their 'disorganised' responses may be indicative of deeply ingrained defence mechanisms towards emotionally inconsistent parenting, which may arise from periodic abuse, parental depression, neglect or institutionalisation.

She argues that early childhood specialists *should fix the environment before they fix the child*; crucially, they should help parents and carers to understand that calm, organised, affectionate and nurturing environments ensure the best chances for secure emotional attachment.

Secondary attachment – the role of the key worker

Richard Bowlby (2007), son of John, argues that children under the age of three who attend day care are particularly vulnerable to emotional stress; he points to research which identifies persistently raised levels of the stress hormone cortisol during periods of separation. Prolonged exposure to raised levels of cortisol in the bloodstream may damage the delicate structures of the brain and interfere with brain development; in addition, keeping children in a state of high anxiety may have long-term consequences for emotional health.

He suggests that prolonged stress may interfere with the attachment process and may result in a higher risk of emotional instability. He lists three risk factors for poor emotional health in children:

1 insecure attachment to the primary caregiver;
2 poorly handled separations;
3 lack of secondary attachment figures.

He suggests that when two or more of these factors are present, children may become withdrawn or aggressive and display behavioural problems and emotional instability that could persist into adulthood. However, *as long as the attachment to the primary carer is already secure*, children's emotional resilience can actually increase by having three or more secondary attachment figures. It seems that securely attached infants with good secondary attachments to other adults or siblings are more likely to be able to cope with the stress of temporary separation from their primary attachment figures. If we accept this position, we can see that EC professionals have an important role to play in ensuring that children who have difficulty separating from the parent and integrating with the group are given extra support by a consistent figure they can trust. It follows that providing a 'key person' or consistent secondary attachment figure that children and parents can get to know well is an important part of managing separations and transitions at nursery, preschool and school.

Time to reflect

In the United Kingdom, young children aged three and four are provided with free education and care for 15 hours each week. This provision is also offered to two-year-olds from disadvantaged or at-risk families.

What might be the advantages and disadvantages of day care for a two-year-old from a disadvantaged background?

If you were a working parent of a one-year-old at the end of your paid maternity period, would you prefer a nanny, a childminder or day-care nursery provision? Why?

Do you think there should be financial support beyond the statutory maternity period for parents or family members who want to look after their children at home? Why? Why not?

Emotional development

Parents generally report that their babies show primary emotions like interest, disgust and contentment from their earliest days. As they grow older and develop a sense of self, they begin to show secondary, self-conscious emotions like fear, surprise, joy, sadness and anger.

We should remember that both negative and positive emotions have a part to play in development. The table below (Table 7.2) sets out the general pattern for the appearance of various emotions.

Table 7.2 Emergence of emotions

Age	Expression of emotion
Primary emotions *0–18 months* 0–2 months	The newborn infant is at the mercy of his primitive instincts – these are sited in the interconnections between nervous system, limbic area and brain stem where early evolutionary patterns of flight, fight or freeze are located. As childhood progresses these early systems are connected to other brain regions (especially the neo-cortex) where thought and language bring them under conscious control (Thompson, 1998). Babies express feelings of hunger, sleepiness, cold, heat and contentment by crying or cooing. They show behaviours that indicate interest, distress, disgust, contentment. They turn their bodies away from unpleasantness and suck vigorously as they seek comfort; they wriggle and kick to show pleasure.
2–7 months	They show anger, sadness, joy, surprise and fear through voice, body and facial expression
7–12 months	They show delight in their discoveries and activities, but anger and sadness when frustrated. They move away from unpleasant situations and comfort themselves by sucking and chewing. The first signs of emotional regulation appear; children *co-regulate* their behaviour and take their emotional cue from others, exhibiting *social referencing* behaviour by checking to see how others react *before* reacting themselves.
Secondary or self-conscious *emotions 18–36 months*	Secondary or self-conscious emotions appear as the left hemisphere of the brain (language and logic) takes over from the right hemisphere (feelings). Once children are mobile, they will use their carer to help them to contain their emotions, returning to 'base' if something distresses them, or dragging their carer along while they investigate something new. They show *social referencing* behaviour by checking the emotional reactions of those around them *after* they have reacted themselves. At this stage, a *transition object* such as a 'comfort blanket', a dummy to suck on or a toy will provide reassurance and consolation (Winnicott, 1953). Gradually, from around 30 months, children use language to reassure themselves, giving a running commentary or talking to an *imaginary friend* although they may still seek comfort from a familiar transition object, particularly if separated from their carer (Vogler, Crivello & Woodhead, 2008).

Age	Expression of emotion
Around 12 months onwards	They show embarrassment, shame, guilt, envy and pride. This is the beginning of self-evaluation, arising from their perception of how their behaviour is valued by others (Witherington et al., 2001).
Around 18 months onwards	*Social referencing* now occurs *after* they have reacted as they seek confirmation of their own emotional responses. They learn to articulate feelings in words, and their carers adapt by offering more verbal reassurances, explanations and distractions. They begin to show some rudimentary awareness of the power of emotional display, intensifying their emotions to get their own way; suppressing them to hide their pain (Witherington et al., 2001).
3–4 years	As their social world expands children begin to exercise '*effortful control*' to fit into social situations – that is, they begin to consciously monitor and adapt their behaviour to match the demands of the context they find themselves in (Rothbart, 1989; Kochanska et al., 2001). By this age most children can regulate their emotions quite successfully; children with weak emotional control find it harder to maintain social relations; they may overwhelm their peers if they are too exuberant or distressed, or they may provoke negative reactions if they are too needy, or too withdrawn, or attention seeking. 'Effortful control' is encouraged by games like *Statues, What's the time Mr. Wolf?* and *Sleeping Lions.* Temperaments begin to stabilise, and behaviours become more predictable. They begin to manipulate their emotional responses: they tell fibs to cover up their misbehaviour; they shed crocodile tears; they disguise their true feelings to spare others or to mask disappointment. Most show empathy for others; children who are rated highly on emotional control and empathy at this age enjoy good relations with peers and adults.
4–5 years	Children begin to recognise that emotions may be influenced by factors such as tiredness, hunger, fear, anxiety, anticipation, pleasure and excitement. They begin to integrate the private and public selves as they learn to adapt to fit in (Rothbart et al., 2003).
5–8 years	By the time children reach school age, they can hide their own emotions and can understand the emotions of others around them. They reliably recognise other people's emotions from facial expressions and body movements; they begin to understand that emotion may stem from something that has happened in the past or elsewhere and that it is not necessarily rooted in the here and now. They are increasingly aware of acceptable and unacceptable displays of emotion in social situations (Eisenberg et al., 2010). They integrate facial expression, language and behaviour to express their feelings. They learn to manage 'mixed feelings' – for example, they can be happy at the prospect of a new baby, sad that their mother is away for the birth and anxious about impending change.

Emotional self-regulation – controlling feelings

Emotional development is not a smooth journey; even adults struggle with emotional self-regulation. 'Self-conscious emotions' like embarrassment, shame and guilt emerge in the second year and provide a basis for self-regulation as the child reflects on how their behaviour impacts on others.

Figure 7.2 By the time children reach school age, they can reliably recognise other people's emotions from facial expressions and body movements.

Source: Getty Images/iStockphoto Thinkstock Images/Alexey Avdeev

Children who can show empathy and altruism and who can self-regulate their emotions find it easier to fit into social situations and are likely to progress more quickly than children who are at the mercy of ungovernable passions (Eisenberg, 1986; Eisenberg et al., 2010). Self-regulation of emotions allows them to focus and attend to the task in hand and to be aware of the needs of people around them. Dunn and Herrara (1997) suggest that the more practice children have in discussing feelings, the more successful they are at negotiating and settling disputes with their peers. Early childhood practitioners can help the process by asking open-ended questions like 'How can we make you feel better?', 'Shall we take turns?' or 'How do you think Amy feels when she can't share?' These questions encourage children to reflect and to consider other people's feelings; adults who say 'Don't do that' or 'That's very unkind' only set up feelings of guilt or antagonism and are more likely to shame and humiliate than to offer a new way forward.

It is not just children who need to know how to rein in their passions; 'effortful control' (Rothbart et al., 2003) or conscious emotional self-regulation is important for adults too. Reactive behaviour is rarely productive when dealing with children or adults, whereas learning to bite one's tongue and to have a period of reflection to look at a situation from all sides is likely to have a better outcome for all concerned. People who are weak in 'effortful control' find it harder to maintain good social relations with peers and colleagues. Children with weak effortful control may be avoided or actively shunned when they react impulsively, speak out of turn or make inappropriate or negative comments. Before changing the child, practitioners should try changing the environment and their own attitudes because offering lots of opportunities to practise 'effortful control' might be enough to help children modify their behaviour.

Different cultures demand different forms of effortful control. For instance, Chinese parents may ignore certain competitive behaviours because they want to limit shame for the losers; American parents on the other hand may encourage competition because they prize individual achievement. Learning the cultural rules of social engagement provides the basis for developing an understanding of the moral framework of one's own society.

Time to reflect

What strategies can parents or professionals use to encourage young children to behave 'prosocially'?

How do adults model desirable social behaviour in their relations with children?

A child comes back from school and says with a sigh, 'They had another new rule at school today.' How should the parent react?

Supporting prosocial behaviour

In their study of children in care, Hodges and Tizard (1989) found that children with poor emotional self-regulation suffer from poor concentration, poor inhibitory control and a lack of empathy, all of which undermine social, cognitive and moral development and lead to antisocial behaviour. How can we help children to develop prosocial behaviour?

Numerous books offer help and advice on 'behaviour management' strategies; the advice generally falls into three broad categories:

- Ignore bad behaviour by withdrawing attention and affection to produce anxiety and reflection in the child.
- Assert power and set rigid boundaries to force good behaviour through punishment or reward.
- Initiate discussions that lead the child to consider the consequences of their behaviour and its effects on others.

Adults routinely use all of these methods depending on the situation, the age of the child or their own emotional state. Patterson (1982) found that parents who rely mainly on coercive strategies to control children's behaviours (those who say 'DON'T!' or who use physical punishment) seem to produce less empathetic children than parents who emphasise the social consequences of behaviour by saying things like 'Is that kind?', or 'How do you think it feels for the other person when you do that?'

Parke (1977) suggests that a mild reprimand and cognitive explanations about effects and outcomes produce the best results in promoting prosocial behaviour. The cognitive explanation gives the child the tools for moral reasoning and emotional regulation, while the mild punishment (such as withdrawal of privileges) provides a salutary reinforcement. Dunn suggests that discussing feelings, behaviour and consequences gives children the tools to manage their own behaviour and to understand the behaviour of others; she argues that children whose behaviour is ignored or punished are unlikely to develop an elaborated understanding of their own and other people's feelings and behaviour (Dunn et al., 1991; Dunn et al., 1995).

Crittenden (2008) suggests that many parents repeat the parenting patterns of their own childhoods without reflecting on whether it is fit for purpose. She suggests that managing behaviour should be a two-way process between the adult and child. Harsh words and a punitive regime may not work with a shy and sensitive child; on the other hand, explanations and appeals to conscience may not work with a fearless and impulsive child. She suggests we need to start with the carers – parents and professionals – when we talk about 'managing behaviour' and warns that, for the most part, coercive practices are counterproductive and lead to weak emotional self-regulation, poor behaviour and stunted moral growth for most children.

Bruno Bettelheim (1903–1990), a psychoanalyst from the Jungian tradition, showed in his book *The Uses of Enchantment* how fairy tales address children's fears and anxieties directly and how listening to them can help children to learn to control their feelings in the safety of an imaginary scenario. He pointed out that fairy tales embody children's deepest feelings – of fear and abandonment, love and hate, pride and jealousy – and address deep emotional conflicts that are universal in their reach. He suggests that fairy tales have an important part to play in providing children with comfort and hope by resolving terror through a happy ending (see also Chapter 10).

Time to reflect

Sometimes children ask to hear their favourite fairy tale over and over again. My own constant requests were for The Three Little Pigs, which held out the promise of triumphing over potential disaster through outwitting the enemy.
Which was your own favourite fairy story when you were a child? What need did it satisfy?
How can we account for the persistence and popularity of fairy tales in the Disney cartoons of today?
How do you think fairy tales might help children deal with deeply felt emotions?
How important do you think it is for children in the birth to eight age bracket to have fairy tales in their repertoire of stories?

Interventions

Non-judgemental partnerships between children, parents and professionals are likely to provide the best basis for interventions when children are in emotional difficulty. Early years programmes that are sensitive to the ecology of family, history and culture and where interventions are carefully tailored to individual circumstances may help parents to find new ways to manage children's behaviour. Formal interventions may range from home visits from health and social care workers, discussion groups organised through religious buildings, community centres and so on; classes put on by local authorities; and initiatives set up locally by day-care centres or nurseries. Most are designed to help parents feel confident in their parenting role: some educate parents about the stages of development that children pass through; others help to sensitise parents to the underlying significance of children's signals; others help parents prepare their children for preschool; others deal with emotional and behavioural management strategies; and others provide guidance on early literacy and numeracy so that parents can share their children's school experience. The key element in all intervention programmes is creating awareness – engaging in dialogue with children and adults, understanding the concept of emotional maturation, talking through problems, exploring possible solutions and above all providing safe, secure friendly environments where adults and children alike can express their fears and anxieties in the knowledge that they will receive a sympathetic hearing.

Understanding children's emotional development provides early childhood specialists and parents with the tools to help children along the path of self-control, which provides the foundation for prosocial behaviour and moral responsibility.

Moral development

As children develop, their physical and emotional relationship with the world changes, and they increasingly need to take account of the social rules that govern interactions with other people. Imagine what happens at the onset of crawling – children want to explore and assert their independence and mostly they are encouraged and praised. But sometimes they put themselves or others at risk, and then suddenly fear and anger is directed towards them. This prompts a fundamental readjustment in the emotional relationship as carers begin to behave as if their children are now consciously responsible for their own actions. Suddenly, and perhaps bewilderingly for the child, parents begin to ascribe intentionality and moral culpability to their behaviour and to label it good or bad, so children have to learn very quickly to distinguish between what is acceptable and unacceptable. Gradually they begin to understand that behaviour is governed by social rules of acceptability and that some behaviour yields moral disapproval.

What is moral development?

Once children are mobile, parents treat them as if they are acting with intention and have responsibility for 'moral' choices in their behaviour. They tell their children not to do things, because it is 'naughty' or 'unkind', and in doing so, they imply that the child has a choice about their behaviour. Morality is about choosing one course of action rather than another and making judgements that involve weighing one's own needs against the needs of others.

Moral development is about learning to treat others as you would like to be treated – with kindness, fairness and respect – and expecting to be treated well in return. In the past, 'bad' children were punished for their transgressions because bad behaviour was seen as a moral failing of the individual rather than as a sign of immaturity. Nowadays, we are less likely to think in terms of 'good' and 'bad' *children*, we are more likely to think in terms of good and bad *environments* which promote or hinder socially acceptable behaviours. We see morality and 'being good' as a gradual process of learning how to rein in emotion in prosocial ways for the benefit of both self and others in the community. Nancy Eisenberg (2000) argues that emotionality and emotion-related regulation underpin modern psychological studies of moral development and behaviour and that children who are treated with kindness, fairness and respect by adults are more likely to adopt this behaviour themselves.

As children learn to master their own emotions and to recognise emotions in other people, they begin to understand that their actions impinge on others and that moral concepts like fairness, kindness, truthfulness and altruism (benefiting others without benefiting oneself) are important. But how do they learn this moral code?

Time to reflect

In Europe eighteenth- and nineteenth-century writers produced moral tales for children based on the Ten Commandments of the Old Testament. These moral tales were designed to teach children how to be good by showing them the dire consequences of being bad.

Think about the stories children hear and see today.
Can you suggest any that carry a particular moral message for *children*?
Can you suggest any that carry a particular moral message for *adults* in relation to their treatment of children?
Think about *The Simpsons*. How do adults and children in the series deal with good and bad behaviour?

Theories of moral development

Theorists are divided as to whether moral, prosocial development is most influenced by cognitive maturity or by social experience. Piaget (1932/1965) identified a step-by-step cognitive maturation from selfish concern to social concern which characterised three distinct developmental stages of moral understanding in children:

- *pre-moral stage* (up to age five), when they egotistically follow their own inclinations and show little respect for other people's rules;
- *heteronomous morality* (around ages five to ten), when they believe rules are fixed and enforced by a higher authority like gods, police or parents; they fear punishment for themselves and are punitive and unforgiving in their turn when others break rules;
- *autonomous morality* (around ages ten to eleven) when they understand that rules and laws are made by common consent and can be legitimately challenged if they are not fit for purpose.

Kohlberg (1963, 1984) studied moral development in 10–16-year-old boys. He concluded that moral reasoning is not necessarily related to cognitive maturation but is a feature of an evolving understanding of wider societal issues related to children's opportunities to consider and reflect on complex social behaviours. As part of his study, he asked the boys to judge a moral dilemma told to them in story form. In the story, Heinz, too poor to buy a cancer drug for his suffering wife, stole the drug from the pharmacist. The boys were asked to say whether or not Heinz was right or wrong to steal in this instance. Kohlberg found that, far from reaching a point of moral 'maturity' linked to age or cognitive maturity, the group of boys exhibited all of Piaget's stages in their moral reasoning. Some boys argued that it is wrong to steal, whatever the circumstances; others believed that in this specific instance Heinz was justified in stealing to relieve the suffering of his wife; and yet others noted that 'stealing' is a social construction that can be interpreted differently according to custom or political persuasion – in this instance, the pricing of the drug could be construed as stealing from the poor.

Nancy Eisenberg also considers the social and emotional aspects of moral reasoning; she argues that emotional regulation and the development of *prosocial* behaviour provide the drivers for moral reasoning and are not necessarily linked directly to cognitive maturation but rather to the development of empathy for others. Even very young children will offer sympathy to a parent or sibling who is ill, showing that in specific circumstances they can put the needs of others before their own.

Table 7.3 Eisenberg's levels of prosocial moral reasoning

Level	Age	Behaviour and Response
Hedonistic	Infancy 0–2	Focus on own needs; offer help only if it benefits them (for instance, to get praise)
Needs oriented	Nursery 2–3	Recognise others' right to be helped but show no shame or guilt about refusing to help
Stereotyped/ approval based	Preschool 3–4	Hold stereotyped views of good and bad behaviour; concerned with behaving in ways that will be approved of by others
Empathy	Foundation stage+ 4–10	Show sympathy, make judgements on the basis of an emerging recognition of rights and obligations and the common good
Internalised values orientation	Post-primary/ adolescent 10+	Justify behaviour in terms of moral code, convictions, duties and individual responsibilities; realise that behaving against one's principles violates the self and damages self-respect

(adapted from Eisenberg, Lennon & Roth, 1983)

Case study: A moral dilemma

Three seven-year-old boys, Javid, Tom and Jake, were outraged when a classmate stole their friend's pen and hid it in his locker. They told the teacher, but she said she didn't want to listen to tale-telling. At break time, they hatched a plan. They would sneak into the classroom when the teacher was at lunch, retrieve the pen and return it to its rightful owner.

When the coast was clear, Javid and Tom entered the classroom while Jake stayed outside on the lookout for teachers. They were caught. The teacher was very angry that they had broken school rules and gone into the classroom without permission. She refused to listen to their justifications and made them stand at the front of the class as an example of bad behaviour.

Tom and Javid shamefacedly apologised and were allowed to go back to their seats. But Jake refused; he argued passionately that they had been righting a wrong – and besides he had not gone into the classroom but had stayed outside. He was told to remain standing at the front, facing his classmates, until he was ready to admit that he had done wrong. He stood there for an hour, red-faced and holding back tears. Suddenly, unable to bear the humiliation any longer, he fled.

When his mother came to collect him, he was nowhere to be found. After frantic searching, the police were called. Jake wasn't discovered until late in the evening, cold and distressed and lost. When the police brought him home, he ran to his bedroom and barricaded himself inside, distraught and refusing to be comforted. Over the next few days he expressed suicidal thoughts and refused to go to school.

The police liaison officer believed that the situation had been badly handled and advised the parents to acknowledge their son's good intentions and to provide him with support and distractions until he felt ready to face his classmates again. The head teacher disagreed and argued that the parents should present a united front with the school and join them in condemning his bad behaviour and avoid colluding in his defiance of authority.

Discussion questions

What moral dilemma were the boys trying to solve?

If you had been the teacher, how would you have handled the situation?

Can you make any observations about the boys' 'moral development' to explain why Jake, Tom and Javid reacted so differently to being called to account by their teacher?

Do you think the police liaison officer provided the right advice to the parents, or do you think the head teacher was right to insist that Jake had broken the rules and should face up to his crime?

Piaget focused on individual cognitive maturation as a key component in moral development and linked moral stages to chronological age. But Kohlberg argued that experience and dialogue can move children towards a more sophisticated form of moral reasoning regardless of age, while Eisenberg emphasised the ways that children's moral behaviour is linked to their *social* environments and *social* interactions with caring and responsive adults who model moral behaviour.

Changing views of emotional and moral development

The severe physical punishment meted out in eighteenth- and nineteenth-century Britain to control children's emotional and moral waywardness gave way in the twentieth century to a more empathetic stance towards children's emerging self-regulation and of the development of their moral understanding. A major change in child-rearing came with the development of psychoanalytic theories, when books like Susan Isaacs' *The Nursery Years* (1932) or Margaret Ribbles' *The Rights of Infants* (1943) encouraged parents to adopt a softer, more considerate approach in raising their children. Psychoanalysts advised parents to show affection, to value play and to show more indulgence towards children's individual foibles. In the second half of the twentieth century, work by Bowlby and others provided evidence that close contact between mothers and babies was essential for healthy emotional development in childhood; this emotional attachment was later extended to include close bonds with fathers and significant others. Healthy emotional development was seen as the basis of healthy moral or prosocial development, and the coercive practices of earlier generations were called into question. Relationships between parents and children gradually became less authoritarian and more cooperative and informal. Today child–adult structures are less hierarchical, and this has led to changes in family life and in school life – for example, Elias (1998) argues in *The Civilising of Parents* that the focus on children as persons with rights rather than as possessions of parents has led to a belief that physical punishment of children should no longer be tolerated.

These changes mean that adults are expected to show self-restraint in their dealings with children: as a consequence, children are expected to show more self-restraint themselves, regulating their emotions and moral actions in accordance with the needs of others and of their own individual conscience. Today, advice to parents and EC professionals has changed from 'command and control' to a rather more a humane and friendly approach – although detractors may apply the term 'permissive'. When children can be comfortable in the presence of adults, when they can expect to be treated if not equally then at least with respect and kind concern, it seems likely that they will learn to value and model self-control and consideration in their own dealings with others.

Summary

- A secure attachment to a trusted and consistent carer provides the best foundation for emotional and moral development – this carer is usually a parent, but children can form multiple attachments with anyone who loves and understands them.
- Parents and children co-regulate one another's emotions and behaviours from the outset.
- Babies and infants have little control over their expressions of emotion.
- Once children are mobile, parents treat them as if they are acting with intention and have responsibility for 'moral' choices in their behaviour.
- 'Self-conscious emotions' like embarrassment, shame and guilt emerge in the second year and provide a basis for self-regulation as the child reflects on how their behaviour impacts on others.
- In the preschool years, games linked to emotional control can help children self-regulate their behaviour.
- Fairy tales can help children explore their darkest fears in the safety of a narrative with a happy ending.
- Theorists are divided as to whether moral, prosocial development is most influenced by cognitive maturity or by social experience.
- Children who show empathy and altruism and who can self-regulate their emotions find it easier to fit into social situations and are likely to progress more quickly than are children who are at the mercy of ungovernable passions.
- Explanation and discussion are better than coercion in fostering moral or prosocial behaviour.
- Sensitive, non-judgemental interventions by professionals working alongside parents and young children can provide information and education to promote emotional and moral development.
- Attitudes towards children's emotional and moral development depend on the prevailing ideology of time and culture. Authoritarian and coercive strategies have been replaced by a belief in fostering autonomous self-regulation.

Topics for further discussion

1 Children often use comfort objects to help them manage emotions. What advice would you offer to a parent who is worried that her three-year-old still insists on using a pacifier?

2 Managing separations from parents and transitions into new environments are peak times of stress for children. Children who have been encouraged to be independent (feeding, dressing, making choices, talking about feelings, understanding the rules of prosocial behaviour) are at an advantage when faced with new situations. Devise a checklist of activities and competencies to guide parents in preparing their children for a childminder setting, a nursery or a school.

3 Can superhero play be a useful vehicle for emotional and moral development? What lessons might be learnt?

Assignments

1 Find the Children's Society's *Good Childhood Inquiry* at www.childrenssociety.org.uk. The inquiry is ongoing (you might even want to contribute to their online conversation). What threads are currently trending?
2 Professor Judy Dunn writes about social, emotional and moral development. Find out more about her and present her ideas to colleagues.
3 'Behaviour management' is a concern for many parents and early childhood specialists. Is 'behaviour management' a term you feel comfortable with? Collect behaviour policies and advice leaflets from local centres. What are the common underlying principles? What are the current core messages for parents?

Further reading

From Neurons to Neighbourhoods (2000) edited by Jack Shonkoff and Deborah Phillips
The Blackwell Handbook of Infant Development (2001) edited by Gavin Bremner and Alan Fogel.
The Handbook of Moral Development (2006) edited by Melanie Killen and Judith Smetana

Useful websites and resources

The Secret Life of Children series, Channel 4, covers all aspects of development including emotional and moral development.
Siren Films DVD on Attachment (**www.sirenfilms.co.uk**).
For one mother's view of the adoption challenge, go to *Attachment and resilience – the power of one*: Dr Erica Liu Wollin at TEDX Hong Kong 2013 **https://www.youtube.com/watch?v=C-ZIUtJr8nE**

References

Ainsworth, M.D.S. and Wittig, B.A. (1969) 'Attachment and exploratory behaviour of one-year-olds in a strange situation', in B.M. Foss (ed.), *Determinants of Behaviour IV* (pp. 111–136). London: Methuen
Bates, J.E. and Wachs, T.D. (1994) *Temperament: Individual differences at the interface of biology and behavior*. Washington, DC: American Psychological Association
Crittenden, P. (2008) *Raising Parents: Attachment, Parenting and Child Safety*. Cullompton: Willan Publishing
Bowlby, J. (1969) *Attachment and Loss: Vol. 1 Attachment*. London: Hogarth Press
Bowlby, R. (2007) Babies and toddlers in non-parental daycare can avoid stress and anxiety if they develop a lasting secondary attachment bond with one carer who is consistently

accessible to them. *Journal of Attachment and Human Development* 9(4). Special Issue: The Life and Work of John Bowlby: a tribute to his centenary.

Dunn, J. (2002) 'Emotional development in early childhood: A social relationship perspective', in R. Davidson, H.H. Goldsmith and K. Scherer (eds) *The Handbook of Affective Science* (pp. 332–346). Oxford: Oxford University Press

Dunn, J., Brown, J.R. and Beardsall, I. (1991) Family talk about feeling states and children's later understanding of others' emotions. *Developmental Psychology* 27: 448–455

Dunn, J., Brown, J.R. and Maguire, M. (1995) The development of children's moral sensibility: Individual differences and emotion understanding. *Developmental Psychology* 31: 649–659

Dunn, J. and Herrara, C. (1997) Conflict resolution with friends, siblings, and mothers: A developmental perspective. *Aggressive Behaviour* 23: 343–357

Eisenberg, N. (1986) *Altruistic emotion, cognition, and behavior*. Hillsdale, NJ: Erlbaum

Eisenberg, N. (2000) Emotion, Regulation and Moral Development *Annual Review of Psychology 2000,* 51: 665–697

Eisenberg, N., Lennon, R. and Roth, K. (1983). Prosocial development: A longitudinal study. *Developmental Psychology* 19: 846–855

Eisenberg, N., Valiente, C. and Egglum, N.D. (2010) Self-regulation and school readiness. *Early Education and Development* 21: 681–698

Elias, N. (1998) 'The Civilising of Parents', in J. Goudsblom and S. Mennell (eds) *The Norbert Elias Reader* (pp. 189–211). Oxford: Blackwell

Griggs, J. and Walker, R. (2008) *The costs of child poverty for individuals and society: a literature review.*

Hodges, J. and Tizard, B. (1989) Social and family relationships of ex- institutional adolescents. *Journal of Child Psychology and Psychiatry* 30: 77–97

Isaacs, S. (1932) *The Nursery Years* (2nd edn) London: Routledge and Kegan Paul

Killen, M. and Smetana, J.G. (2006) *Handbook of Moral Development*. Mahwah, NJ: Lawrence Erlbaum Associates

Kohlberg, L. (1963) The development of children's orientations toward a moral order: I. Sequence in the development of moral thought. *Vita Humana* 6: 11–33

Kohlberg, L. (1984) *Essays on moral development: Vol.2 The psychology of moral development*. San Francisco, CA: Harper and Rowe

Kochanska, G., Coy, K.C. and Murray, K.T. (2001) The development of self-regulation in the first four years of life. *Child Development* 72: 1091–1111

Maslow, A.H. (1943) A theory of human motivation. *Psychological Review* 50: 370–396

Parke, R.D. (1977) 'Some effects of punishment on children's behaviour – revisited', in E.M. Hetherington and R.D. Parke (eds) *Contemporary readings in child psychology*. New York: McGraw Hill

Parke, R.D. and O'Neil, R. (1997) 'The influence of significant others on learning about relationships', in S. Duck (ed.) *The Handbook of Personal Relationships* (2nd edn). New York: Wiley

Patterson, G.R. (1982) *Coercive family processes*. Eugene, OR: Castilia Press

Piaget, J. (1932/1965) *The moral judgment of the child*. London: Free Press

Ribble, M. (1943) *The Rights of Infants*. New York: Columbia University Press

Rothbart, M.K. (2005) Early Temperament and Psychosocial Development. Published online 12 July 2005 at www.child-encyclopedia.com/temperament/according-experts/early-temperament-and-psychosocial-development. Accessed 10 October 2012

Rothbart, M.K., Ellis, L.K., Rueda, M.R. and Posner, M.I. (2003) Developing mechanisms of temperamental effortful control. *Journal of Personality* 71(6): 1113–1143

Rutter, M. (1972) *Maternal Deprivation Revisited* (2nd end). New York: Penguin Books

Rutter, M. (2002) Nature, nurture, and development: From evangelism through science toward policy and practice. *Child Development* 73(1): 1–21

Rutter, M. and the English and Romanian Adoptees (ERA) Study Team (1998) Developmental catch-up, and deficit, following adoption after severe global early privation. *Journal of Child Psychology and Psychiatry* 39(4): 465–476

Shweder, R.A., Mahapatra, M. and Miller, J.G. (1990) 'Culture and moral development', in J. W. Stigler, R.A. Shweder and G. Herdt (eds) *Cultural psychology: Essays on comparative human development* (pp. 130–204). Cambridge: Cambridge University Press

Thompson, R.A. (1998) 'Early sociopersonality development', in W. Damon (series ed.) and N. Eisenberg (vol. ed.) *Handbook of child psychology: Vol 3: Social, emotional, and personality development* (pp. 77–97). New York: Wiley

Vogler, P., Crivello, G. and Woodhead, M. (2008) *Early Childhood Transition Research: A Review of Concepts, Theory and Practice*. Bernard van Leer Foundation http://oro.open.ac.uk/16989/1/. Accessed 30 December 2016

Werner, E. and Smith, R. (1982) *Vulnerable but Invincible: a study of resilient children*. New York: McGraw Hill

Winnicott, D. (1953) Transitional objects and transitional phenomena. *International Journal of Psychoanalysis* 34: 89–97

Witherington, D.C., Campos J.J. and Hertenstein M.J. (2001) 'Emotional Development' in G. Bremner and A. Fogel (eds) *Blackwell Handbook of Infant Development*. Oxford: Blackwell

IN THE BEST INTERESTS OF THE CHILD: SHAPING CHILDREN'S LIVES

Children and families in context

Introduction

Part 2 showed how the individual child develops. In Part 3 we will look at the way in which sociology has changed the focus from individual development to the study of children as part of a social order of family, neighbourhood and culture. Sociology shows us that children do not develop in a vacuum but are subject to influences from a wide variety of social contexts and social constructs. The chapter discusses the changing nature and plurality of modern family forms and introduces some key sociological themes. It ends by considering some of the interventions designed for disadvantaged families with young children.

A sociological understanding

Sociology is the systematic study of human societies; societies can be studied along several dimensions from the *macro*-level of political and economic organisation to the *micro*-level of individual family structure. It looks for explanations of human behaviour in *social structures* (families, neighbourhoods, culture) and in the social influences that shape values and aspirations. It asks questions about how things like wealth, gender, class, culture, status and power impact on people's lives.

Ask yourself these questions:

- Are you young?
- Are you white?
- Are you female?
- Are you from a professional family?
- Do you have a part-time job?

Many of you will have answered yes to all these questions – you are probably at university and are likely to come from a family that places a high value on education. If you answered no, you may be older, perhaps combining study with parenting. Or if you are male, from an ethnic minority or from a working-class family, you may have had to struggle to convince yourself and your family that getting a degree in Early Childhood Studies is an aspiration worthy of considerable financial investment. Your social background will have informed your ideas and opinions, but it will not have *determined* them.

Within each social category of class, gender or culture, every child is in some sense a self-determining entity able to make choices, to have *agency*, but social background may limit or expand the options open to them. Sociologists look at the way in which people are able to make choices, to what extent they accept or resist the social structures that bind them and to what extent they can alter the direction of their lives. Structure and agency are twin pillars of modern sociological studies.

Developing a sociological imagination

C. Wright Mills (1959) coined the term *sociological imagination* to describe the ability to develop a vivid awareness of the links between what people experience and the kind of society they live in. A sociological understanding can be liberating because it encourages what Paulo Freire (1970) called *problematisation* (critical questioning) and *conscientisation* (raising consciousness about previously unquestioned assumptions), which enable people to stand in the shoes of others to see the world as they see it. A sociological understanding provides the tools for analysing how individuals and society operate – for example, to understand how limited opportunities for children lead to limited educational outcomes; how poverty, poor play spaces and lack of amenities can contribute to poor mental and physical health; or how a chaotic home life makes it more difficult to make friends.

Sociology also alerts people to different cultural practices, values and beliefs so that they can show greater cultural sensitivity towards people of diverse backgrounds. And perhaps most importantly, sociology brings self-enlightenment, so that groups and individuals feel empowered to try to act on the circumstances of their own lives and the lives of those they represent (Giddens, 2006).

In the past 20 years, a particular strand of sociology, the sociology of childhood, has encouraged a 'critical stance' towards children and childhood by providing an analysis of the historical, social and contemporary discourses that adults have constructed around them. Recent studies into the sociology of childhood have shown how children have traditionally been rendered invisible and voiceless by adults who assume that they are too immature to have anything valuable to contribute (Mayall, 2002; James & Prout, 2004; Corsaro, 2004; Kehily, 2008; Moran-Ellis, 2010; Qvortrup et al., 2011). In contemporary Western societies, it is now generally accepted that children, even very young children, can make informed choices and should be consulted about decisions that affect them.

Socialisation

Socialisation (see also Chapter 6) is the process through which children gradually learn the values, beliefs and social behaviours of their society, initially from the family and then through peers, the media and wider society – psychologists like Bandura, Piaget and Kohlberg and sociologists like Mead and Merton wrote extensively on the ways in which socialisation is transmitted down the generations. More recently, sociologists of childhood such as Kehily (2008), Hengst (2011), Alanen (2011), Mayall (2011) and Clark and Kehily (2013) have examined the effect of rapidly changing social and political cultures on parenting, child-rearing and socialisation.

Through play and games, children develop both a sense of self and an understanding of the social roles of other people. Young children practice social behaviours through *role play*; they copy their parents or siblings, pretending to make picnics for their stuffed toys or to be engine drivers with toy trains, and as they do so, they practice appropriate language and social roles. As they get older and find themselves in social contexts outside the home, they learn to take other people into consideration: they learn to keep quiet during story reading or to share and take turns. Once they begin to play more complex games, like board games or team games, they learn that there are specific rules of conduct that control their own roles and the roles of other people involved in the game. For example, a child playing striker in a football match learns that chasing the ball all over the pitch is less helpful than lurking around the goal area of the opposing team waiting for teammates to bring the ball forward. As they learn to modify their own behaviour in relation to others, they simultaneously learn to take other people's behaviour into account.

A new generation

Although children pick up the ways of their families and the wider behaviour of their neighbourhoods and communities, they also position themselves as a *generational group* separate from the adult world (Honig, 2011). Each new generation is *socially located* in a particular historical time frame (Mannheim, 1952, in Mayall, 2002), which produces its own new culture: for example, girls and boys born into a post-feminist world will act out male and female roles differently from children in their grandparents' generation. Children pick up all sorts of cues from the society they find themselves in and incorporate them into their generation's version of society.

Social contexts

Families

Children learn their social behaviour in many different contexts – family, peers, religious institution, school, health centre, supermarket, street and each context makes different social demands. But the basic unit of enculturation and socialisation is the family.

Modern families come in all shapes and sizes. Until the mid twentieth century, most children in Western countries were born within monogamous marriages with a bread-winning father and a mother whose chief responsibility was the care of children. In the post-war period (from 1945 onwards) social, legal and economic changes led to a gradual change in family roles as a larger proportion of women took up paid work; in addition, divorce made single-parent families more common (Jensen, 2011). Although the two-parent family, supported by a local extended family (where grandparents, uncles, aunts and cousins live nearby) is still the norm for most children, poverty, ill health, migration, war, famine, disease or global catastrophe leave many children in the world without strong family networks and reliant on their own resources or the charity of strangers (OECD, 2009).

Many alternative family forms exist in Britain today – children may be raised in families with cohabiting parents, step-parents, LBGT parents, adoptive parents or a single parent. Families are smaller, parents are likely to be older and both parents are more likely to work. Although most children in Britain live with two biological parents, a substantial number are cared for by a single parent or live in step-families generally consisting of a natural mother and a step-father (ONS, 2015). Sometimes families are blended from two or more families, and children grow up with half- or step-brothers and sisters. Families are more geographically dispersed than they were in the past because changing employment patterns or migration force them to move away from the place parents were born. This variety, sometimes referred to as *pluralisation* of family forms is a feature of postmodern Western communities and confounds the stereotype of a nuclear family consisting of 'Mum, Dad and the kids' living out their lives within a long and stable marriage. The changing profile of families leads to changing patterns of socialisation for children. Anthony Giddens (2006) summarises the global changes in families as follows:

- Clans and other kin groups are declining in influence.
- There is a general trend towards the free selection of a spouse and arranged marriages are in decline.
- There is a wider acceptance that women have rights in marriage and in the family.
- There is more sexual freedom for men and women in previously restrictive societies.
- There is a general trend towards extending human rights to children.
- Same-sex partners are gradually gaining acceptance in more societies.

Time to reflect

What changes have you observed in family structures in your own cultural community from your grandparents' generation through to your own?
What factors have driven the changes in your family structure?
What factors driving contemporary social changes are likely to affect the present generation of children in your locality?

Green (2009) points to evidence showing that on many measures (school outcomes, physical health, emotional well-being and involvement in crime) children prosper best in stable two-parent families because these generally provide the most secure *economic* framework, the most stable *emotional* framework and the most stable *social* framework. Although any variety of supportive family can supply children's needs satisfactorily, it is possible to list *clusters of negative factors* like low income, substance abuse, single-parent status, family mental ill health, impoverished neighbourhoods and poor living conditions which, when taken together, reduce the quality of children's lives. A single one of these factors may not have a significant impact, but an

Figure 8.1 Families come in many forms - not just the nuclear family of 'Mum, Dad and the kids'.
Source: Photodisc/Getty Images

accumulation of factors is likely to reduce life chances in the long term. Family poverty combined with neighbourhood poverty seems to be a particularly poisonous combination (Shonkoff & Phillips, 2000). However, we should remember that as long as children are provided with the basic needs of shelter, food, warmth and secure relationships, most will thrive.

Parenting

There are multiple and competing styles of parenting ranging from very strict to laissez faire. Culture and family tradition, the size of the family, the mix of sons and daughters, cultural expectations about male and female roles will all affect the ways that parents choose to bring up and socialise their children.

Beyond the home, children may encounter parenting styles that conflict with their home experience – children who are used to being consulted and expressing their views may find it difficult to accept adult directives, while children who expect firm guidance may find it difficult

---

Focus on *Parenting*

Diana Baumrind (1971) produced a *taxonomy of parenting styles* after studying the parents of preschool children in London. She noted that parents offered four dimensions of *control, nurture, communication* and *expectations* in their parenting and combined them in a variety of ways to produce four distinct parenting styles – *authoritarian, permissive, authoritative* and *rejecting/neglectful*:

- *Authoritarian* parents command and control their children. They expect unquestioning obedience and use punishment and threats to enforce good behaviour. Authoritarian parents rarely consult their children and are sparing with praise and affection.
- *Permissive* parents exercise minimal control over their children and see themselves as advisers and consultants. They are generally loving and affectionate. They may be inconsistent about discipline and may hand over responsibility for behaviour to the children themselves. Other people may regard them as over-indulgent and neglectful because they fail to set boundaries.
- *Authoritative* parents set firm boundaries and encourage discussion about the limits they enforce. They are generally warm and affectionate and have high expectations about what their children should achieve as they mature. They tend to reason with their children using age-appropriate language and show high levels of empathy, involvement and sensitivity.
- *Rejecting-neglectful* parents provide only minimal levels of supervision and engagement. They provide physical care but little emotional support. They ignore their children for the most part and fail to provide regular routines and clear guidelines. They expect their children to absorb social rules and rarely explain the principles underlying decisions.

How far do you accept Baumrind's *taxonomy of parenting*?

Do you think these categories would apply in every culture?

Do parents vary their parenting styles with different children in their family?

Why might parents opt for permissive or authoritarian styles?

Do you think parenting styles are subject to sociohistorical fashions?

How might different parenting styles shape the socialisation of children?

---

to behave in self-directed ways or may feel anxious about stating preferences. Responding to these different expectations among children can present particular challenges for professionals working in families with diverse backgrounds and cultures.

Secondary socialisation

Secondary socialisation refers to the factors outside the home that help shape a child's relations with the wider social context. Some of these will be direct agencies of socialisation, like schools and religious institutions; others will be indirect, like the media or government policies.

Urie Bronfenbrenner (1917–2005), a key figure in the sociology of childhood, showed how individual children are *socially located* at the centre of an *ecological system* (Bronfenbrenner,

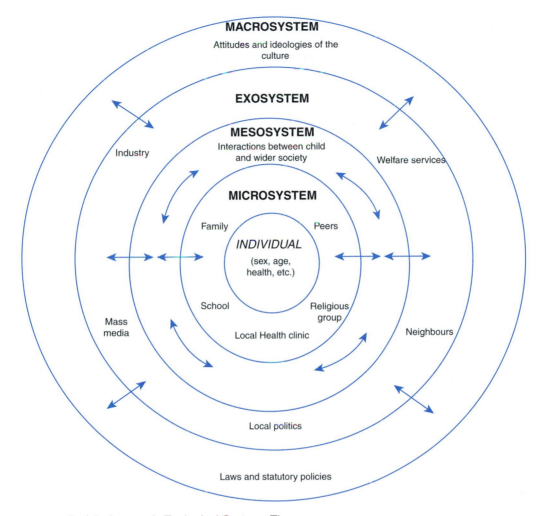

Figure 8.2 Bronfenbrenner's Ecological Systems Theory
Source: Based on Bronfenbrenner, 1979

1979) which is unique to them. Just as a plant or animal occupies a particular ecological niche of soil and climate that can promote or stunt development, so too children occupy a particular ecological niche in society that will help or hinder their progress.

Bronfenbrenner's *ecological systems theory* shows the factors feeding into the social context for each child. Children are initially influenced by the *micro-system* of direct personal contacts in the family, school and community in which they grow up. They are also affected by the *meso-system*, which determines the variety and quality of opportunities available to them through the childcare, schooling and amenities in their immediate neighbourhood. These facilities depend in large part on the *exo-system* of government policies, public opinion and media which deliver messages about how society values children and families. All this is contained in a *macro-system* of culture that shapes the dominant ideological beliefs of the time.

Case study: From rags to riches – a true story

Michaela DePrince was born in 1995 in war-torn Sierra Leone. Aged three, she lost both parents and was sent to an orphanage. She was badly mistreated by staff, who thought she was the 'devil's child' because she suffered a skin pigmentation condition called *vitiligo*. Her most treasured possession was a picture of a ballet dancer in a pink tutu torn from a magazine. At the orphanage she became deeply attached to another little girl, and at age four, they were both adopted into an American family. The family consisted of seven other adoptees and two birth children. Her adoptive parents took her to ballet classes: 'Dancing helped me share my emotions and connect to my family, it helped me to feel like I was special and not the "devil's child"'.

At one of her classes, she overheard someone say, 'We don't put a lot of effort into the Black girls, because they end up getting fat'. She was aware that there were very few Black ballerinas in her classes and struggled with the fact that she was Black in a predominantly White community. She later learned of two famous contemporary Black dancers, Misty Copeland and Lauren Anderson, who achieved starring roles in ballet productions in the United States, and she took inspiration from them.

As a young dancer, she moved to Europe and is now a professional ballerina with the Dutch National Ballet.

She has written a memoir, *Hope in a Ballet Shoe* (2015). Faber and Faber want to use the proceeds to set up a dance school for children in Sierra Leone. She goes into schools to talk to children about her life in dance because, as she says, 'there are practically no Black people in ballet, so I need to speak out'. She likes being a role model: 'When I see that I've inspired young people to dance, especially young Black dancers, that's amazing for me.'

(Based on an interview by Corinne Jones, *The Observer*, 8 February 2015)

Using Bronfenbrenner's ecological systems theory and your sociological imagination, explore the shaping social factors in Michaela DePrince's life.

Discussion questions

Why do you think 'rags to riches' fairy tales are so satisfying, particularly for children?
Can you recall an inspirational story or fairy tale that sustained you in childhood?

Cultural reproduction

Educational settings socialise children directly and indirectly in a variety of ways, sending out messages about relative status and value. Most obviously, children are segregated into age cohorts in a social hierarchy with adults at the top and the youngest at the bottom, so they quickly learn where they belong in society's 'pecking order'. Child minders and practitioners in schools and nurseries are the arbiters of 'good' and 'bad' behaviour and pass on values about what is socially acceptable – for example, well-behaved children are picked as 'helpers' and given special responsibilities; badly behaved children have to sit on the naughty step; poor readers are put in a group with other poor readers; and sporty children are picked for the school team. Children get a constant drip-feed of judgements and underlying messages about what society values and, indirectly, of their own worth. Robert K. Merton (1910–2003), an American sociologist, called these messages *self-fulfilling prophecies* and warned that they can have lifetime consequences for children's self-belief and aspirations.

Many sociologists have shown a particular interest in the way schools socialise children. For instance, Ivan Illich (1973) argued that schools value only a narrow spectrum of curricular knowledge and often unconsciously exclude children whose traditional forms of knowledge are different.

A famous ethnographic study called *Learning to Labour: How Working Class Kids get Working Class Jobs* showed how schools reproduce low educational aspirations in working-class children (Willis, 1977). In Basil Bernstein's significant book *Class, Codes and Control* (1971), he described the language of the uneducated as a 'restricted code' which put speakers at a disadvantage in the classroom where the 'elaborated code' of the educated classes prevails. Similarly, William Labov showed in his book *The Study of Non-standard English* (1969) how schools reject the language and culture of Black children, leaving them feeling marginalised and worthless (see also Chapter 6).

It seems that schools and other institutions may help perpetuate social and economic inequalities through a system of *cultural reproduction*. Bourdieu (1986, 1990) pointed out that children from working-class backgrounds and minority groups have a much wider gulf to bridge between home and school than do children from more privileged homes whose cultural backgrounds are more in tune with the expectations of schools and professionals. He argued that social value depends on the different kinds of *capital* people bring with them. He called these different kinds of *capital* – *social capital* (community networks), *symbolic capital* (status and value), *economic capital* (income), *cultural capital* (libraries, schools, arts and music) and *human capital* (knowledge, skills and competence). He argued that *human capital* begins to grow where *cultural, symbolic, economic* and *social capital* intersect; it follows that children (and societies) with limited forms of *capital* at their disposal start much lower down the ladder and, without intervention, may be destined to remain impoverished and powerless.

Bourdieu's analysis provides one explanation for the wide gap between educational outcomes for children from different backgrounds – it is not talent but opportunity that is lacking. The belief that *cultural* capital builds *human* capital and pays dividends for both individuals and society is used to justify an expansion of investment in education, particularly *early childhood education* (OECD, 1998; UNICEF, 2003).

Time to reflect

At age 22 months, four children score the same on a developmental test:

- a street child in Kampala
- a child of migrant Vietnamese parents in Australia
- a child born to a wealthy aristocratic family in New York
- a child with cerebral palsy born to a family in middle-England

How might Bourdieu's five forms of *capital* intersect in each case?
How are the children's life chances affected by their store of *capital*?
How can we maximise each child's potential for 'self-actualisation'?

Peer groups

The tendency for children to coalesce into peer groups is a feature of many children's stories – think of *Little Women*, *The Famous Five*, *Lord of the Flies*, *Harry Potter*, and *His Dark Materials* – and to make their separateness distinct, adults are usually conveniently absent. Peer groups have a powerful socialising influence on children. All parents know that sinking feeling when their child gets in with the 'wrong crowd'. In contemporary Western societies, many children spend more and more time in day care and in after school clubs, interacting with children of their own age and spending less time with family. This marks a departure from earlier generations when children spent their free time with family and friends, learning beliefs and values in a more intergenerational way.

William Corsaro (2004) puts peer groups at the centre of his analysis of the sociology of childhood: he shows how groups of children throughout history have collectively constructed new versions of society out of the shared cultural cues around them. A contemporary example might be sharing the culture of Disney animations – each peer group will have its own generational tropes of, perhaps, *Mickey Mouse*, *Bambi* or *Frozen*. Alongside, fans will have imbibed different social understandings peddled by the films – children brought up on *Cinderella* or *Beauty and the Beast* will have a different view of women's roles than children brought up on *Frozen*. In an article called *My Mother and Father Are African, But I'm Norwegian*, Corsaro (2013) shows how this process of peer group socialisation leads children in ethnically mixed peer groups to create their generation's unique understanding of national identity in multicultural Europe. In this way, children are at the forefront of social change and may hold very different views from their parents; adults may think they are shaping the next generation, but children are doing it for themselves.

Media

The media is another powerful tool of socialisation. Children around the world receive information about the lives other people lead through the media of advertising, films and television programmes, the Internet, comics, newspapers and books. They are faced with multiple and contradictory representations of roles and values that may conflict with what they are learning at home and in the community. They are bombarded with consumer information that makes it seem that everyone else has the latest product; young children are particularly vulnerable to product placement, and the phrase 'pester power' has entered the language to reflect this.

Nsamenung (2004) argues that the dominating influence of Western media is spreading a message of individualism around the world which undermines cooperative community values in more traditional societies; he believes that individualism places a great burden on children to believe that they stand or fall by their own efforts and obscures the limiting factors of their social background. While individualism offers more people more opportunities to shape their lives than was the case when gender, social class, ethnicity and religious affiliation largely determined the direction of someone's life, it also brings feelings of risk and anxiety (Beck, 1992).

David Buckingham (2000) points out that the present generation of children are the first *natives* of the Internet age, and they have unprecedented power to think independently without the restrictions placed on them by adults in the physical world. In addition, their *native* status reverses the roles between adult and child so that they find themselves teaching their parents and grandparents. The virtual world that they explore so easily provides both opportunities and risks; there is considerable adult anxiety around children's access to online sites, fears

about cyber-bullying and 'grooming', moral panics about the damaging and corrupting possibilities of video-nasties and ideological angst about 'brainwashing'. Technological changes
come so fast that adults are in danger of being left behind while their children forge ahead in a
brave new world of virtual realities.

Time to reflect

It is not uncommon to see families sitting together playing companionably, but independently, on some form of lap-top device or mobile phone.

What effect might 'online' childhoods have on the present generation of children under
eight?
Should adults restrict the amount of time children spend online?
Cyber-bullying is a problem for many children. How can we help children to develop resilience in the face of a cyber-bully? Should society insist that Internet providers protect children online?

Social constructs

Although groups of children may be subject to similar social influences, their gender, ethnicity,
health, wealth and age will provide them with distinct perspectives that affect their personal
social constructs. Social constructs are the way we understand reality and our place in it – as well
as the way society constructs *us* as members of the social fabric (Berger & Luckman, 1966).

As early as 1837, the English sociologist Harriet Martineau (1802–1876) alerted her readers
to the idea that women, children and non-white people construct, and are constructed by,
society in very different ways from white, male adults. In the 1970s, this theme was taken up by
feminists, civil rights activists and champions of minority interest groups who began to examine
the mechanisms that constructed particular social groups as 'other' – notably, women, Black
people, the disabled and latterly *children*.

Gender

Gender is a modern concept, developed by feminists to analyse the ways in which women and
girls are *culturally* and *socially* defined in contrast to men and boys as 'other'. Gender shapes
beliefs and attitudes in overt and covert ways. For instance, before children learn to identify
themselves as a boy or girl, they receive a host of gendered cues – they are handled differently,
spoken to differently, given different toys and admired for different attributes. Everything
around them is gendered – men and women dress differently, speak differently and often perform different roles. One study observed the different reactions to a six-month-old baby presented alternatively as Beth or Adam. When the baby was Adam, he was offered trains; when
she was Beth, she was offered dolls; the adults commented on Adam's lusty cry and described
Beth as sweet; they smiled more at Beth than at Adam (Will et al., 1976).

It is not until children are four or five that they can reliably understand that gender is linked to anatomy – it is not uncommon to hear preschool girls say they want to be boys when they grow up and vice versa. However, they have already received countless messages about themselves as gendered individuals and even by the age of two, they can demonstrate a cultural understanding of gender; they can say whether they are a boy or a girl and can point to social differences in roles and interests and expectations. For instance, even when both their parents work, they will say that mummy is *at home* and daddy is *at work* because this is the general social message they have received about gender roles.

Time to reflect

Sajid and Sidra are eight-year-old twins who both attend a London primary school. They share a house with their parents, grandmother and two uncles. Their mother has very little English and almost no formal education. Their father runs a small company selling car parts. His English is heavily accented, and he prefers to do business with people from his own community.

Sajid prays four times a day and reads his Koran at the mosque every day after school. On weekends he learns his Koran for three hours until he knows his set text off by heart; he recites it to his mother, and if there are any errors, he must repeat the learning until he is word perfect. His parents encourage him to be disciplined about his schoolwork because they want him to get a good job, to be a good father and to be respected in the community. He values the limited free time he gets to play football with his friends in the park.

Sidra also goes to the mosque each day after school and reads her Koran to learn how to be a good Muslim. On weekends she does not have to learn the Koran like her brother but instead spends her time helping her mother with cleaning, cooking and other household chores. She enjoys the responsibility and is looking forward to being a wife and mother herself. She sometimes goes to a friend's house but is not allowed to play unsupervised in the park. She has asked her father if she can be a dentist when she grows up because she admires the Muslim woman who examines her teeth at the local dental practice. Her father has given his blessing for the plan, but her grandmother and uncles have misgivings.

How do *generation* and *gender* intersect in the lives of Sajid and Sidra?
Why do you think Sidra's grandmother and uncles are worried about her having a career?
Should early childhood specialists try to *persuade* parents that boys and girls should have equal opportunities?

Girls and boys may be *relatively* different, but they are *absolutely* equal. We should celebrate their differences and value each for the unique qualities they bring as individuals – deriding pink fairies and banning guns and superhero play may send the right adult messages but will do little to build the confidence of children who *choose* and enjoy this sort of play.

Ethnicity

We all belong to an ethnic group, and we are all ethnocentric in the sense that we all have a cultural construct that may make us feel awkward when we encounter other people's cultural beliefs and practices – but armed with a *sociological imagination*, we can at least try to understand and empathise with other people's cultural perspectives.

The terms 'ethnicity' and 'race' are often used as if they are interchangeable, but they are not. 'Race' has echoes from historical pseudoscientific beliefs that people differed significantly at a biological level; perceptions of 'racial' difference are often associated with stereotyping, racism, prejudice and discrimination. Ethnicity, on the other hand, denotes a group organised around a particular culture, history, family kinship, language and/or style of dress. People *learn* their ethnicity through socialisation; it is not a consequence of their biology (Banton, 1987; Baldock, 2010). Sociologists and anthropologists point out that custom, history and family account for ethnic differences; modern geneticists support this view by pointing out that there are greater biological variations *within* ethnic groups than there are between them.

However, we have to recognise that social experiences and social attitudes are all affected by perceptions of body shape, skin colour, dress code and religious observances (Brown, 1998). Everyone has the right to be treated with equal respect and an obligation to offer equal respect to others. Adults working with children have a duty of care and protection to ensure that no child is undervalued or subject to discrimination on the grounds of 'difference', and any breaches should be dealt with firmly to provide a model of fairness for children to follow.

Migration has brought an increasing ethnic diversity to the towns and cities of most Western countries. In Britain we have people from Commonwealth countries, from Europe, from Asia, from Africa, people of every skin colour, ethnic culture and religious persuasion. Official profiling forms designed to monitor equal opportunities or for census purposes now ask people to 'self-identify' under headings of White; Mixed/Multiple Ethnic; Asian/Asian British; Black/African/Caribbean/Black British; Other (including Arab). It is hard to see how useful these bureaucratic categories are since they seem to mix skin colour, continent, nationality and parentage in a rather arbitrary fashion.

Impairment and disability

Impairment and disability affect the way people construct, and are constructed by, society. Medical, behavioural, developmental and learning impairments may present barriers to social participation – for instance, in many countries 'disabled' children are far less likely to go to school or to participate in the social life of their wider communities than 'abled' children.

In the past, a medical model of individual disability held that a 'disabled' person required medical care and support to help them adapt in an 'able-bodied' world. The medical model has been superseded by a social model which says that although we cannot ignore the physical or mental impairment itself, 'disability' is exacerbated by unjust exclusion from the able-bodied world and requires environmental and social adjustments to enable everyone to participate equally. Rather than focusing on disability, the emphasis should be on people's capabilities and on providing the right conditions for them to participate (Nussbaum, 2003; Nutbrown & Clough, 2013). This shift in understanding puts the onus on organisations to remove the barriers that prevent full participation by providing things like ramps, dropped kerb edges, adapted washrooms, hearing loops and large print books, or specialist staff with the expertise to support children with impairments to make life more equitable.

In Britain, children with impairments are welcome in all settings and are less likely to attend special segregated units than in the past. Part 6 of the Equality Act 2010 gives all children a right to equal opportunities in schools and specifically outlaws discrimination on the grounds of disability. Children with learning difficulties may have a statement of educational needs (SEN) or an education, health and care plan (EHC) for those with more complex needs. Schools and nurseries provide a named SENCO (special education needs coordinator) to help practitioners and parents to provide for the particular needs of children who find it difficult to access the opportunities on offer.

Practitioners should remember that these children will have a unique perspective into their own condition and the difficulties facing them. They will have much more expertise than any practitioner could possibly have, and it is imperative that, first and foremost, they should be consulted and asked about their concerns and needs before any plans are made or any decisions taken on their behalf.

Poverty

Poverty presents a special barrier to children's 'self-actualisation'; the social constructs around poverty are almost entirely negative, and children from poor homes are, and feel, stigmatised.

The World Bank (2008) estimates that around the world 1.5 billion, nearly a fifth of the global population, lives in *absolute* poverty, existing at a subsistence level without healthcare, welfare support or education. In the economically developed world, where populations are more affluent, the proportion of children living in *relative* poverty is rising as the income gap between rich and poor grows wider. Britain has some of the worst poverty figures in Western Europe, with high numbers of children living in low income households, either on welfare or with employed parents earning less than a living wage (Aldridge et al., 2011). Poverty puts health, welfare and educational achievement at risk: children growing up in poverty are more likely to die before they are five; they are more likely to suffer obesity and accidents and poor health; and they have poorer educational outcomes.

The National Children's Bureau (2010) found that the gap in potential between children from low- and middle-income families is already evident among babies of 22 months, and the gap widens as they get older. Poverty is more likely to afflict single-parent families struggling to keep themselves afloat on a single income, and the mechanisms of *cultural reproduction* suggest that disadvantage is passed on to the next generation (Bourdieu, 1986; Marmot, 2010). Children who suffer multiple negative effects – such as disability or being in care, or whose parents are in prison – are more likely to have poor educational outcomes in childhood and poor social and economic outcomes in adulthood.

Social class

'Social class' is a way of stratifying society; it is a term used by sociologists to describe inequalities between different groups (Giddens, 2006). A social class shares common characteristics of wealth and status – the *upper class* (around 3 per cent of the population) typically owns most of the wealth and power. The *middle class* makes up the largest group and consists broadly of white collar professionals who have higher levels of education; the *working class* is a smaller group and consists of blue collar or manual workers; the '*underclass*' is a minority group of people living under severe deprivation on the margins of society. In some societies a *caste system* fixes an individual's status at birth, but in class-based societies there is the potential for social mobility so that people with particular talents can achieve a different class position from the one they were born into – this is the basis of *meritocracy*, sometimes called the *American Dream*. However, social mobility in class-based societies is mostly of a rather limited range, and children tend to follow the patterns of wealth and occupation, attitudes and values of their parents (Giddens, 2006).

Sylva et al. (2014) found in their study Effective Pre-school, Primary and Secondary Education (EPPSE) that the 'home learning environment' is the most significant factor for children's learning because parents who read, talk and play with their children offer the best foundation for development. Parents in all social classes can and do provide this kind of home learning environment. The EPPSE research also shows that access to good-quality preschooling from age two can be a critical factor correlating with later outcomes for children; researchers found that the greatest gains went to the most disadvantaged classes, but middle-class children benefited significantly too.

Time to reflect

You are chairing a discussion about free nursery places. The first speaker says, 'If you want to send your kids to nursery, you should pay. Why should the tax-payer pick up the tab?' The second speaker says, 'I think one of you should stay at home when your children are small, not pack them off for somebody else to look after.' The third speaker says, 'If I didn't get free places for mine, I couldn't afford to send them. And I'd have to give up my part-time job. It's not much, but it makes all the difference.'

How would you respond to these remarks?
Who should bear the cost of early childcare – parents, the state or a mixture of both?
What sociological evidence could you provide to make a case for universal childcare for all preschool children?

Discourses around children and childhood

In the past, social analyses largely ignored children's roles in the social order and left them *voiceless* and *disempowered* (Mayall, 2002). In the 1980s and 1990s, sociologists turned their attention towards the *sociology of childhood* (Qvortrup, 1985; Prout & James, 1990; Jenks, 1996). They analysed the discourses of childhood, forensically examining the *constructs* adults use when they talk about children. They showed how children were defined by words like *immature, inexperienced* and *incomplete*, words that implied that children's status and value in society lay primarily in their potential to become useful adults. This led to the suggestion that we should redefine children in a way that recognised their human rights, thinking about them as human *beings* rather than human *becomings*. Jens Qvortrup (1985) pointed out that children are, in reality, full-time workers in education. He argued that schoolwork is an important economic investment for society, which relies on children to be committed and productive learners from a very young age. Without their contribution, society would collapse. This paved the way for a new sociology of childhood that proposed that children have a different, but equally valid, world view that adults should take into account when dealing with children's issues (Prout & James, 1990; Lee, 2001).

Focus on *Children's voice and participation*

In contemporary sociology, children's *voice* and *participation* are key concepts for early childhood professionals.

Make a collection of policy documents from your field of interest which focus on children's *voice* and *participation*. Try to find out from practitioners how they listen to children and promote participation.

How are the opinions of children canvassed?
Can you find any examples where children have been empowered to have their ideas recognised and acted on?
In your experience, do adults really listen to children, or do they just pay lip service to the idea of *children's voice* and *participation*?

Discourse analysis – a sociological tool

Discourses are the shared stories we tell ourselves about reality: sociologists use *discourse analysis* to uncover the implicit *cultural constructs* or assumptions underlying our ways of seeing the world. By *deconstructing discourses* like historical writings, political speeches, policy documents, mission statements, newspaper reports, film, television and even daily conversations, we can uncover the dominant discourses shaping our attitudes, values, beliefs and misconceptions (MacLure, 2003). For example, discourse analysis helped to expose the ways in which children were silenced and disempowered by powerful adults in child abuse cases when survivors testified that they could not get their voices heard because the dominant discourse of the time led police and professionals to believe adults before children and led to their accusations being ignored or dismissed as fantasy.

Discourses of disgust

Discourse analysis is a useful tool for debunking the myths that grow up around certain groups – groups who are often excluded from mainstream society and spoken of in terms of disgust. Any neutral word can be turned into an expression of disgust if the dominant social discourse encourages it: words like immigrant, feminist and kids can all be used as terms of abuse. The disgust is expressed through stereotypes that work by diminishing power and status (MacLure, 2003). Dominant discourses use words like *benefit scroungers* or *feral* to dismiss families and children from disadvantaged groups. This sort of language can quickly lead to

- marginalisation
- mockery and cruel humour
- dismissive and demeaning treatment
- physical, sexual, emotional and financial abuse
- restrictions in opportunities for decision making and 'agency'.

Any of these can inflict serious long-term emotional harm on the victims. Practitioners have a duty to challenge labelling and stereotyping in the workplace in order to protect children and their families from abuse. They can counter some of the negative effects felt by socially excluded groups by making sure that all children and families get a chance to participate on equal terms by

- listening to and respecting everyone's opinions
- ensuring that everyone has opportunities for making their own choices
- respecting the choices they make
- encouraging integration
- normalising equal opportunities so that no one is left out
- challenging negative stereotyping.

Time to reflect

Nothing classifies somebody more than the way he or she classifies.
(Pierre Bourdieu, 1990: p. 132)

What do you think Bourdieu meant?
Consider the word 'chav'.
How have you heard it used?
What can we say about the attitude of a speaker who uses the word?
How could you address issues of labelling and stereotyping in the workplace? What practical steps might you take?

For further analysis of the term 'chav', read

- 'Chav Mum, Chav Scum' by Imogen Tyler (2008) in *Feminist Media Studies* 8(1): 17–34;

- *Chavs: the Demonisation of the Working Class* by Owen Jones (2011).

An ecological view of families and children in context

This chapter tried to show how individuals are shaped by social contexts and social constructs. The question remains how we can best support children to fulfil their potential in society today.

The idea that young children represent the *human capital* of a community is widely accepted, and since the 1990s, policies in education, healthcare and social care around the world have been increasingly focused on families and young children 'in need'. It seems that long-term gains for individual children and for society as a whole can be made through the targeted provision of high-quality programmes for families (Shonkoff & Phillips, 2000; Penn et al., 2006).

However, some commentators (Peirson, 2010; Campbell-Barr, 2012) suggest that it might be better to focus on whole communities rather than on individual children and families. They argue that we need to reframe the way we talk about 'disadvantage'; instead of focusing on individual 'victims', we need to look at disadvantage as a community problem and to find ways to make communities stronger and more resilient. They argue for an ecological approach where social policies are targeted at whole neighbourhoods. The benefit of this approach is that it treats deprivation as a social and political problem rather than as a failing of particular families and individuals. Including marginalised families alongside more stable and affluent families brings 'at-risk' groups into the mainstream without stigmatising them with targeted provision.

In 2012, the OECD report *Starting Strong III: A Quality Toolbox for Early Childhood Education and Care* looked at variations in approach to meeting the needs of 'dysfunctional' social groups. They concluded that childcare should be a concern of *all* government agencies from highways to health. They argued that policymakers should shift their focus away from individual children and families towards *community*, directing resources towards providing rich social and cultural environments for all children.

In Europe the most successful models for society-wide support systems are found in Scandinavia (Moss & Petrie, 2002; Repo, 2004; OECD, 2006). Significantly, taxation is very high in Scandinavia, and state investment in social infrastructure is strongly supported by the electorate. In many other Western countries, the electorate votes for lower taxation and a smaller state budget in the belief that private initiatives offer better value for money than state initiatives.

This is where the insights of sociology rub up against the practicalities of politics as we decide how best to organise society in the best interests of children and families. Although early years practitioners cannot directly influence the way societies are configured or the economic and political decisions that shape the kinds of childhoods children enjoy, they do have an important part to play in supporting discussions with children, parents and colleagues that lead to practical measures for ensuring that all the children and families in their care experience a sense that they are valued and included in their immediate community.

Summary

- Sociology is the systematic study of human societies.
- Developing a sociological imagination enables practitioners to better understand themselves and others.
- Children learn about identity and social roles through observation and role play.
- The basic unit in society is the family.

- There has been a pluralisation of family forms over the past half-century due to changing attitudes towards divorce, single parenting, remarriage and same-sex marriage.
- Primary socialisation takes place in the family.
- Different parenting patterns promote different kinds of socialisation.
- Secondary socialisation takes place beyond the home, through peer groups, neighbourhoods, schools, media and the arts.
- Bronfenbrenner's ecological systems theory shows how each individual exists at the centre of a network of social structures that influence potential development.
- Bourdieu identified five forms of social capital which intersect to shape an individual's life chances – *cultural capital* is the fertiliser that grows *human capital*.
- Early years provision has been identified as a significant site for cultivating *human capital* through education, care and family support.
- Social perspectives differ according to age, class, ethnicity, gender, ability and wealth.
- Children's perspectives have traditionally been ignored, but a new sociology of childhood has emerged to explore what it means to give children a voice.
- Discourse analysis is a useful tool for uncovering the hidden assumptions that underpin dominant social attitudes towards children and families.
- The discourse of 'disadvantage' is focused on individual families who are deemed to be 'failing', but sociological research suggests that 'disadvantage' is a structural phenomenon, not an individual one.
- An ecological approach to 'disadvantage' would seek to break cycles of deprivation in neighbourhoods by offering good housing, good schools, a wider social mix, good transport links and good services to strengthen communities for the benefit of *all* young children and their families.
- Practitioners have a part to play by acknowledging and understanding the social structures within which we all live and by providing inclusive settings where everyone feels valued.

Topics for further discussion

1 Think about school and preschool provision for children in your local area. Can you identify any stratification among settings?

2 Share newspaper reports and government policy documents reporting on the future of early childhood education and care. Is the emphasis on ecological provision for whole communities or on targeting individual children and families?

3 In your groups, share newspaper articles that deal with families and young children on the margins of society. Summarise the article in a few words. Do the voices of the marginalised come through? What are the underlying assumptions made in the article? Are there alternative *discourses* that could have been brought into play?

4 In your groups, brainstorm about a current TV soap opera. How many different kinds of family are portrayed? What social stratification is apparent? What parenting styles are portrayed? How accurately does the programme reflect society today? Can you uncover what

the programme makers think of each family? Is there a 'discourse of disgust' they want to share with viewers?

Assignments

1   Find out about CAFCASS (Children and Family Court Advisory and Support Service). How does CAFCASS give children a voice? How far do you think children should contribute to discussions about custody arrangements?
2   Read 'Combining Work and Family in Two Welfare State Contexts: a Discourse Analytical Perspective' by Katja Repo in December 2004, in *Social Policy & Administration*, 38(6): 622–639. Why does the author use *discourse analysis* to compare the different ways parents experience the welfare state in two different countries? How does it help us to understand the social structures of family care in England and Finland?
3   Read the 'Field Report' (*The Foundation Years: preventing poor children becoming poor adults. The Report of the Independent Review on Poverty and Life Chances*) by Frank Field (2010). How does the report propose to improve life chances for the next generation of disadvantaged children?
4   Read *The Grapes of Wrath* (1939) by John Steinbeck, which explores the effects of the Great Depression on a 'decent, hard-working' family.
5   Read *Shame* (2007) by Jasvinder Sanghera, which provides an insider view of caste culture and the consequences of rejecting family values in a traditional society.

Further reading

Corsaro, W. (2004) *The Sociology of Childhood*, Thousand Oaks, CA: Pine Forge Press (new edition 2014)

Mayall, B. (2002) *Towards a Sociology of Childhood: thinking from children's lives*, Buckingham: Open University Press

DfE/DH (Department for Education/ Department of Health) (2011) *Supporting Families in the Foundation Years*. www.education.gov.uk. Accessed 9 November 2012.

DH (Department of Health) (2012) *Report of the children and young people's health outcomes forum*. https://www.gov.uk/government/uploads/system/uploads/attachment_data/file/216852/CYP-report.pdf. Accessed 30 December 2016.

Useful websites

Policy Studies Institute: www.psi.org.uk
Joseph Rowntree Foundation: www.jrf.org.uk
The Poverty Site: www.poverty.org.uk

References

Alanen, L. (2011) 'Generational Order', in J. Qvortrup, W.A. Corsaro and M.-S. Honig (eds) *The Palgrave Handbook of Childhood Studies* (pp. 159–174). Basingstoke: Palgrave Macmillan

Aldridge, H., Parekh, A., MacInnes, T. and Kenway, P. (2011) *Monitoring poverty and social exclusion*. York: Joseph Rowntree Foundation.http://www.npi.org.uk/publications/income-and-poverty/monitoring-poverty-and-social-exclusion-2011/. Accessed 28 December 2016

Baldock, P. (2010) *Understanding Cultural Diversity in the Early Years*. London: Sage

Banton, M. (1987) *Racial Theories*. Cambridge: Cambridge University Press

Baumrind, D. (1971) Current patterns of Parental Authority. *Developmental Psychology* 4(1, Pt 2, January): 1–103

Beck, U. (1992) *Risk Society: Towards a New Modernity*. London: Sage Publications

Berger, P. L. and Luckmann, T. (1966) *The Social Construction of Reality: A Treatise in the Sociology of Knowledge*. Garden City, NY: Anchor Books

Bernstein, B. (1971) *Class, Code and Control: Volume 1 – Theoretical Studies Towards A Sociology Of Language*. London: Routledge and Kegan Paul

Bourdieu, P. (1986) 'The Forms of Capital', in J. Richardson (ed.) *Handbook of Theory and Research for the Sociology of Education* (pp. 241–258). New York: Greenwood

Bourdieu, P. (1990) *In Other Words: Essays Towards a Reflexive Sociology*. Cambridge: Polity Press

Bronfenbrenner, U. (1974) Developmental research, public policy, and the ecology of childhood. *Child Development* 45(1): 1–5

Bronfenbrenner, U. (1979) *The Ecology of Human Development: Experiments by Nature and Design*. Cambridge, MA: Harvard University Press

Brown, B. (1998) *Unlearning Discrimination in the Early Years*. Stoke on Trent: Trentham

Buckingham, D. (2000) *After the Death of Childhood: Growing Up in the Age of Electronic Media*. Cambridge: Polity

Campbell-Barr, V. (2012) Early years education and the value for money folklore. *European Early Childhood Research Journal* 20(3): 423–437. http://dx.doi.org/10.1080/1350293X.2012.704764

Clark, A. and Kehily, M.J. (2013) 'Home and Family', in Alison Clark (ed.) *Childhoods in Context* (2nd edn) (pp. 53–108). Bristol: Policy Press

Corsaro, W. (2004) *The Sociology of Childhood*. Thousand Oaks, CA: Pine Forge Press

Corsaro, W. with Johannesen, B. O. and Appoh, L. (2013) 'My Mother and Father Are African, But I'm Norwegian': Immigrant Children's Participation in Civic Society in Norway. *Sociological Studies of Children and Youth*, Vol. 16. Bingley, UK: Emerald Group Publishing

Freire, P. (1970) *Pedagogy of the Oppressed*. Reprinted 2006. New York: Continuum

Giddens, A. (2006) *Sociology* (5th edn). Cambridge: Polity Press

Green, D.G. (2009) *Individualists who cooperate: Education and welfare reform befitting a free people*. London: Civitas: Institute for the Study of Civil Society. www.civitas.org.uk. Accessed 9 November 2012

Griggs, J. and Walker, R. (2008) The costs of child poverty for individuals and society: A literature review. October 2008. http//:www.jrf.org.uk/sites/default/files/jrf/migrated/files2301-child-poverty-costs.pdf. Accessed 16 November 2016

Hengst, H. (2011) 'Collective Identities' in J. Qvortrup, W.A. Corsaro and M.-S. Honig (eds) *The Palgrave Handbook of Childhood Studies* (pp. 202–214). Basingstoke: Palgrave Macmillan

Honig, M.-S. (2011) 'How is the Child Constituted in Childhood Studies', in J. Qvortrup, W.A. Corsaro and M.-S. Honig (eds) *The Palgrave Handbook of Childhood Studies* (pp. 62–77)). Basingstoke: Palgrave Macmillan

Illich, I. (1971) *Deschooling Society*. New York: Harper & Row

James, A. and Prout, A. (eds) (2004) *Constructing and Reconstructing Childhood* (2nd edn). London: Routledge/Falmer

Jenks, C. (1996) *Childhood*. Abingdon: Routledge

Jensen, A-M. (2011) 'Pluralization of family forms', in J. Qvortrup, W.A. Corsaro and M.-S. Honig (eds) *The Palgrave Handbook of Childhood Studies* (pp. 140–155). Basingstoke: Palgrave Macmillan

Jones, O. (2011) *Chavs: The Demonization of the Working Class*. London: Verso

Kehily, M.J. (ed.) (2008) *An Introduction to Childhood Studies* (2nd edn). Maidenhead: Open University Press/McGraw-Hill

Kehily, M.J. (2011) Childhood in crisis? Tracing the contours of 'crisis' and its impact upon contemporary parenting practices. *Media, Culture and Society* 2(32): 171–185

Labov, W. (1972) *Language in the Inner City: Studies in the Black English Vernacular* Philadelphia, PA: University of Pennsylvania Press

Lee, N. (2001) *Childhood and society: growing up in an age of uncertainty*. Buckingham: Open University Press

MacLure, M. (2003) *Discourse in Educational and Social Research*. Buckingham: Open University Press

Marmot, M. (2010) *Fair Society, Healthy Lives: Strategic Review of Health Inequalities in England post 2010, The Marmot Review*. www.instituteofhealthequity.org. Accessed 22 October 2012

Martineau, H. (1837) *Society in America*. Reissued 2009, Cambridge: Cambridge University Press

Maslow, A.H. (1943) A theory of human motivation. *Psychological Review* 50: 370–396

Mayall, B. (2002) *Towards a Sociology of Childhood: thinking from children's lives*. Buckingham: Open University Press

Mayall, B. (2011) 'Generational Relations at Family Level', in J. Qvortrup, W.A. Corsaro and M.-S. Honig (eds) *The Palgrave Handbook of Childhood Studies* (pp. 175–187). Basingstoke: Palgrave Macmillan

Merton, R.K. (1949) *Social theory and social structure*. New York: Free Press

Moran-Ellis, J. (2010) Reflections on the Sociology of Childhood in the UK. *Current Sociology* 58(2): 186–205

Moss, P. and Petrie, P. (2002) *From Children's services to Children's Spaces*. London: Routledge/Falmer

National Children's Bureau (2010) *Principles for engaging with families.* London: NCB. http://www.socialserviceworkforce.org/system/files/resource/files/engaging_with_families_0.pdf. Accessed 30 December 2016.

Nsamenung, A.B. (2004) *Cultures of Human Development and Education: Challenge to Growing up African.* New York: Nova Science Publishers

Nussbaum, M. (2003) Capabilities as fundamental entitlements: SEN and social justice. *Feminist Economics* 9(2–3): 33–59

Nutbrown, C. and Clough, P. (2013) *Inclusion in the Early Years.* London: Sage

OECD (1998) *Human capital investment: An international comparison.* Organisation of Economic Co-operation and Development, Paris: Centre for Educational Research and Innovation

OECD (2006) *Starting Strong II: Early Childhood Education and Care.* www.oecd.org/edu/school/startingstrongiiearlychildhoodeducationandcare.htm. Accessed 28 December 2016

OECD (2009) *Doing better for children* www.oecd.org/els/family/doingbetterforchildren.htm. Accessed 18 February 2015

OECD (2012) *Starting Strong III: A Quality Toolbox for Early Education and Care.* http://www.oecd.org/edu/school/startingstrongiii-aqualitytoolboxforearlychildhoodeducationand-care.htm. Accessed 30 December 2016

ONS (Office for National Statistics) (2015) Statistics Bulletin. *Families and Households*, 2014. www.ons.gov.uk/peoplepopulationandcommunity/birthsdeathsandmarriages/families/bulletins/familiesandhouseholds/2015-01-28. Accessed 11 November 2016

Peirson, L. (2010) 'Community Psychology', in Geoffrey Nelson and Isaac Prilleltensky (eds) *In Pursuit of Liberation and Well-being.* Basingstoke: Palgrave Macmillan

Penn, H., Burton, V., Lloyd, E., Potter, S., Sayeed, Z. and Mugford, M. (2006) 'What is known about the long-term economic impact of centre-based early childhood interventions? Technical report', in *Research Evidence in Education Library.* London: EPPI-Centre, Social Science Research Unit, Institute of Education, University of London

Prout, A. and James, A. (1990) 'A new paradigm for the sociology of childhood? Provenance, promise and problems', in A. James and A. Prout (eds) *Constructing and Reconstructing Childhood: Contemporary Issues in the Sociological Study of Childhood.* London: Falmer

Qvortrup, J. (1985) 'Placing children in the division of labour', in P. Close and R. Collins (eds) *Family and Economy in Modern Society* (pp. 129–145). London: Macmillan

Qvortrup, J., Corsaro, W.A. and Honig, M.-S. (2011) 'Why Social Studies of Childhood? An Introduction to the Handbook', in J. Qvortrup, W.A. Corsaro and M.-S. Honig (eds) *The Palgrave Handbook of Childhood Studies* (pp. 1–18). Basingstoke: Palgrave Macmillan

Repo, K. (2004) Combining Work and Family in Two Welfare State Contexts: A Discourse Analytical Perspective. *Social Policy and Administration* 38(6, December): 622–639

Shonkoff, J.P. and Phillips, D.A. (2000) *From Neurons to Neighbourhood: The Science of Early Childhood Development.* Washington, DC: National Academy Press

Sylva, K., Melhuish, E., Sammons, P., Siraj I. and Taggart, B. (2014) *Educational and Developmental Outcomes at Age 16* for The Effective Pre-school, Primary and Secondary Education Project (EPPSE 3–16+), DfE RR 354. https://www.gov.uk/government/

uploads/system/uploads/attachment_data/file/351496/RR354__Students__educational_and_developmental_outcomes_at_age_16.pdf. Accessed 28 December 2016

Tyler, I. (2008) Chav Mum, Chav Scum. *Feminist Media Studies* 8(1): 17–34

UNICEF (2003) *A seven-fold return on investment: the best start in life for every child.* www.unicef.org/earlychildhood/files/CARD_early_childhoodENG.pdf. Accessed 28 December 2016

UNICEF (2005) *Child Poverty in Rich Countries 2005, Report Card No. 6.* Florence: Innocenti Research Centre

Will, J., Self, P. and Datan, N. (1976) Maternal behaviour and perceived sex of infant. *American Journal of Orthopsychiatry* 46(1): 135–139

Willis, P. (1977) *Learning to Labour: How Working Class Kids get Working Class Jobs.* Farnborough: Saxon House

World Bank (2008) Poverty data: A supplement to World Development Indicators 2008. http://siteresources.worldbank.org/DATASTATISTICS/Resources/WDI08supplement1216.pdf. Accessed 28 December 2016

Wright Mills, C. (1959) *The Sociological Imagination.* Reprinted 2000, Oxford: Oxford University Press

Representations of childhood

Introduction

Our understanding of children and childhoods is complex and often contradictory. But it is important for us as early childhood specialists to try to get to grips with the hidden and sometimes unconscious ideas that lie behind the metaphors and concepts that we use to talk about children. We might think of childhood as a time of carefree pleasures and innocence, or we may be more concerned that it is a time of preparation for adulthood in the future. Whatever our beliefs, they will shape the way we see children and how we relate to them. Understanding something of the history of adults' representations of children provides us with a perspective on our own contemporary versions of childhood.

The history of childhood has often been characterised by what we would now regard as cruel and inhuman treatment but which at the time was considered to be in the best interests of children. In different times and places, adults' beliefs about bringing up children have been couched in terms of growth and nature, taming and moulding, training and inspiring, and preparation for future citizenship. All these beliefs coexist, but sometimes one view prevails, sometimes another. These beliefs underlie the way adults treat children and what provision they make for them.

Perhaps the most salient feature of contemporary childhoods, particularly in the West, is the expansion of children's rights and the inclusion of children's voices in decisions that directly affect the quality of their lives.

Memories of childhood

Sometimes adults present a romantic view of what it means to be a child. They look back at their own childhoods nostalgically, remembering long warm summers of innocence and carefree pleasure as we can see from this verse from the poet A.E. Housman (*A Shropshire Lad*, 1923):

That is the land of lost content,
I see it shining plain,
The happy highways where I went
And cannot come again.

Our own memories may be influenced by notions of idealised childhoods drawn from films, books, or photos in the family album, and when unhappy memories surface we may be left feeling conflicted and cheated. But memory is an unreliable witness, and Hilary Mantel thinks we should guard against an overly simplistic account of our memories of childhood. She reminds us that

> When you were a child you had to create yourself from whatever was at hand. You had to construct yourself and make yourself into a person, fitting somehow into the niche that in your family has always been left vacant... Much of what happened to you, in your early life, was constructed inside your head. You were the passive observer, you were the done-to, you were the not-explained-to; you had to listen at doors for information, or sometimes it was what you overheard; but just as often disinformation, or half a tale, and much of the time you probably put the wrong construction on what you picked up. How then can you create a narrative of your own life? (*Giving up the Ghost: A Memoir*, 2003: p. 223)

For some adults, childhood is remembered as a halcyon time of sunny days and unfettered play; for others it is remembered as a time of frustration, fear and anxiety recalled in 'misery memoirs' like *Angela's Ashes* or *A Child Called It* or in earlier novels like *Jane Eyre* or *David Copperfield*. Claerwen James, a portrait artist who spends long hours observing the children she paints, said,

> I am a long way away from my childhood now, but a lot of children are not that happy, and I didn't like being a child much either. It is an uncomfortable state, not knowing who you are yet, and not being able to articulate things or have any power. (*Observer*, 10 February 2013: p. 11)

We should remember that children don't describe themselves as inhabitants of a mythical land of Green Ginger called childhood; they see themselves as *people* with the same needs and emotions and desires as everyone else.

Defining childhood

We make a distinction between childhood and adulthood without really stopping to question what the differences are or indeed if there are any differences at all. When does childhood begin and end? We can all agree that babies and infants are biologically immature and dependent and spend their time in play like other young mammals, but when do adults stop referring to them as 'children'? Is it when they reach puberty or earlier or later? Is it when they make a contribution to the family chores? Or is it only when they become economically independent? Do parents *ever* see their own children as adults? We could argue that childhood is a rather fluid category. In the past, white males have referred to women and non-white people as 'childlike' and used the concept of childishness to exclude whole groups from the rights and privileges that they themselves enjoyed. In our own society, childhood is often thought of as a space between infancy and puberty, when adults hold most of the power – and our laws and regulations are shaped to recognise the space as 'not-adult' with all that entails in terms of legal rights and obligations. But as we shall see, the space is ill-defined and culturally flexible.

Long and short childhoods

Childhood is defined by the UNCRC (1989) as between birth and age 18, which is the standard length of schooling and financial dependency in the West. But around the world there are reports and pictures of 'child' labourers, 'child' brides and 'child' soldiers living out 'adult' roles, and it is clear that in many societies the distinction between childhood and adulthood is less clear-cut than the UNCRC definition would suggest.

Figure 9.1 Kenneth Thomas Gubb aged 3, *c*.1927
Source: Author's own.

Viviana Zelizer (1985) argues that in the West, as families have grown smaller and education has grown longer, the *short childhoods* of the past have been replaced by the *long childhoods* of the present, making children 'economically worthless but emotionally priceless' (p. 3). Hendrick (2011) argues that as societies become more sophisticated, a longer period of training is required to prepare them for adult roles and the 'schooled child' comes into existence, opening up a space for 'childhood' between infancy and the end of formal education. But in many societies around the world (and sometimes in our own – for example, where 'children' care for disabled parents) 'short childhoods' remain the norm because many children make domestic and economic contributions to help support their families from a very early age.

Time to reflect

The division between adulthood and childhood is a slippery concept, as we can see from the following statements:

> The UNCRC defines childhood as the period between birth and age 18.
> Children's wards in English hospitals include infants and young people up to 16.
> The English justice system treats children as adults from the age of ten.
> In many countries, children work full-time alongside adults from age five, making a contribution to the family economy.

Under Islamic Sharia law, children can be married once they reach puberty.

Discuss these different concepts of childhood.
Do your parents still see you as 'children'?
Is there a particular age at which children should be party to decisions made on their behalf by adults?
What criteria would you use to define the beginning and end of childhood?

In my own family album is this picture (Fig. 9.1), taken in 1927, of my father at age three wearing the gown that marked him as an infant. Soon after the picture was taken, he was 'breeched' and swapped the dress for trousers. Along with the trousers came his first responsibilities on the family farm – sorting potatoes, gathering eggs and running errands. Toys, books and school took second place to 'jobs' – especially during planting and harvest. As he got older, he earned his keep and helped to provide for the wider family. His was a 'short' childhood marked by obedience to adults and few choices; adulthood began officially at 13 when he left school and took up full-time work on the farm.

The invention of childhood

Phillipe Ariés (1914–1984), an art historian, famously suggested in his book *Centuries of Childhood* (1962) that in medieval Europe, 'the idea of childhood did not exist .... [A]s soon as the child could live without the constant solicitude of his mother, his nanny or his cradle rocker, he belonged to adult society' (1962: p. 125). He argued that childhood is an 'invented' or artificial adult construct and that rather than being a watertight category, the boundary between childhood and adulthood shifts according to societal needs of time and place. He suggested that the medieval mind made little distinction between adults and children, noting that until the 1600s 'children' were portrayed in paintings as *miniature adults*, with adult faces and adult clothes.

Ariés examined documents, court records and paintings to construct his theory that childhood is an 'invention' and argued that because medieval adults and children shared a communal public space where nothing was hidden from view (including bawdy behaviour, bodily functions and sexual acts) there was no division between adults and children – they shared the same stories, the same spaces, the same culture, the same games, the same lack of shame about their bodies and sexuality. He pointed out that it was only after the 1600s that European children began to appear in paintings as a separate category occupying a space between infancy and full maturity. He suggested that in Europe the distinction between adults and children began when upper-class families built private spaces for themselves in their homes and when their

Figure 9.2 *Madonna and Child*, by Berlinghiero Berlinghieri of Lucca, 1230, in which we can see the depiction of the child as a 'miniature adult'.

Source: By Berlinghiero Berlinghieri - Metropolitan NY, Public Domain, https://commons.wikimedia.org/w/index.php?curid=6618282.

Focus on *Neither dolls nor miniature adults*

Read this passage from A.S. Byatt's *The Children's Book* (p. 29), which describes middle-class family life circa 1900.

> Children in these families, at the end of the nineteenth century, were different from children before or after. They were neither dolls nor miniature adults. They were not hidden away in nurseries, but present at family meals, where their developing characters were taken seriously and rationally discussed, over supper or during long country walks. And yet, at the same time, the children in this world had their own separate, largely independent lives, as children. They roamed the woods and fields, built hiding places and climbed trees, hunted, fished, rode ponies and bicycles, with no other company than that of other children. And there were many other children. There were large families, in which relations shifted subtly as new people were born – or indeed, died – and in which a child also had a group identity, as 'one of the older ones' or 'one of the youngest ones'. The younger ones were often enslaved or ignored by the older ones, and were perennially indignant. The older ones resented being told to take the younger ones along. (p. 29)

In this extract, A.S. Byatt says that middle-class Edwardian children were 'neither dolls nor miniature adults'. What do you think she means by this?

She talks about *'children in these families'* and *'other'* children. Who are the *other* children she is talking about? Do you think these *other* children shared a similar 'separate and independent' childhood?

How do childhoods in the UK today compare with the Edwardian childhoods described by A.S. Byatt?

---

children began to be schooled in a separate place away from their families. He concluded that only when 'Family and school together removed the child from adult society' (p. 397) could they be placed in a separate category called 'childhood'.

The Disappearance of Childhood?

Neil Postman, in his book *The Disappearance of Childhood* (1982), suggests that we are returning to a time, similar to the medieval world described by Aries, when the distinction between adulthood and childhood is once more blurred. He argues that adults and children once again share the same public space: They share the same programmes on television, and they are exposed to the same knowledge of news, violence and sex. The childhood of popular imagination, a time of protected innocence, no longer exists. He argues that what we imagine 'childhood' to be is a mirage, heavily influenced by sentimental Victorian notions of childhood innocence where children are kept in a 'walled garden' separating them from 'adult knowledge' (p. 141), particularly sexual knowledge. Postman wrote his book before the dawn of the Internet and focused on the way television brings images of sex and violence into children's lives to show that the sentimental notion of childhood as a time of doll-like innocence has all but disappeared. We might argue that the Internet has now taken the place of television to raise anxieties in the minds of parents and opinion makers about the corruption of an idealised understanding of what it means to be a child.

While not everyone agrees with Ariés or Postman, both highlight the possibility that childhood is an artificial concept imposed by adults to demarcate boundaries about what is appropriate and inappropriate for the young, particularly the access to sexual knowledge. In our modern, industrialised Western societies, the 'long childhoods' of the twenty-first century may last well into the teens and twenties, with parents still feeling responsible for, and making choices for, their adult 'children'.

Nightmare childhoods

Lloyd de Mause, a psycho-historian wrote that

> The history of childhood is a nightmare from which we have only recently begun to awaken. The further back in history one goes, the lower the level of childcare, and the more likely children are to be killed, abandoned, beaten, terrorised and sexually abused. (de Mause, 1974: p. 1, in Heywood, 2001: p. 41)

Similarly, in Steven Pinker's book *The Better Angels of Our Nature: a History of Violence and Humanity* (2012), he identifies a trend in human history for a decrease in violence (including violence towards children) over time – he argues that since the earliest historical records there has been a decline in aggression towards ethnic minorities, women, homosexuals, animals and children. He suggests that the global spread of literacy, trade, international law and increasing cosmopolitanism helps us to empathise with 'other' groups and to dismiss toxic ideologies by deploying reason – in this way we are more likely to negotiate our way forward rather than use violence to compel others to agree. As far as children are concerned, this means that there is a tendency towards including them in discussion rather than issuing orders backed up by threats of physical punishment.

Linda Pollock (Pollock, 1983, in Heywood, 2001) takes a less optimistic view and argues that 'nightmare' childhoods are ever-present and that any society in any age is capable of brutality towards children. She suggests that there is a duality in our thinking about children which, at the extremes, means adults still see children as 'good' or 'bad', either as 'little angels' or as 'little devils '. This duality makes it difficult to see children as people in their own right, people who, like adults, are a complex mixture of conflicting desires and contradictory behaviours.

In the best interests of the child

Fogel (2001) argues that in every generation, adults balance what *they feel* for their children, against what they think is *good for them* so that, depending on the prevailing social circumstances, the treatment of children and expectations about childhood change. He points out that the history of childhood is littered with examples of what we might now consider cruel and inhuman treatment towards children, often carried out by well-meaning adults 'in the best interests of the child' – smacking children to help them learn right from wrong, caning them in schools for misdemeanours to reinforce the message that certain behaviours are unacceptable, removing them from feckless families 'for their own good'. All of these instances are predicated on the idea that 'adults know better' and children belong to a separate category of 'not-knowing', the inference drawn from this separation of adult from child is that children need to be controlled and regulated without consultation.

Focus on *The Stolen Children*

In 2009 Prime Minister of Australia Kevin Rudd apologised to what were called the *Stolen Children* and *Forgotten Australians* for past treatment at the hands of the state.

The *Stolen Children* and *Forgotten Australians* comprised an estimated 500,000 children put into institutional care over the twentieth century. Many were migrant children from impoverished British families and orphanages. They were sent alone to make a new start in the colonies in the belief that they would have a better chance of a good life. They were cared for by religious orders and charitable organisations in large institutional children's homes, and many were told that their parents had died. Some were adopted into kind and caring families, but others experienced physical, emotional and sexual abuse. The trauma they experienced remained with them and blighted their adult lives. In some cases, survivors' partners and children felt the impact of the child abuse as the survivors meted out the treatment they had received themselves, passing it on to the next generations.

What can we learn about adults' understanding of the 'best interests of the child' from this example?
How can we understand the parents who send unaccompanied children to enjoy a 'better life' in the West?

Children in their own right

Contemporary debates about Western childhoods focus on the changes in the way adults and children relate to one another during the process of maturation between infancy and adolescence. Allison James (2011, in Qvortrup 2011) suggests that since the 1970s, there has been a profound theoretical shift in childhood studies which entails seeing children as 'social actors' – not just recipients of adult guidance but as people in their own right who behave as active agents in relationships and decisions. This idea of children having 'agency' implies that they can make changes in the way the generations interact and can alter the hierarchical relationship between adults and children (Mayall, 2002). Children's rights and needs are at the centre of the debate, and parents and teachers, health professionals and social workers find themselves having to redefine their notions of childhood – it is no longer acceptable to treat children as objects or possessions or to expect their unquestioning obedience. Instead, adults now have a duty enshrined in policy documents and in international law to listen, explain, discuss and negotiate *with children* before making decisions that affect them. This represents a revolutionary change in the relationship between adults and children and a corresponding redefinition of what childhood means (James et al., 1998).

Historical shifts in adults' concepts of childhood

Having some historical perspective on the changing ways adults have seen childhood provides some context for examining the way we see childhood today. In Cunningham's book *The Invention of Childhood*, he traces the history of childhood through the ages and explores the way adults' concepts of childhood are in continual flux. Although these 'schools of thought' about the prevailing relations between children and adults are presented under separate historical headings, it is important to remember that at any one time there are always multiple opinions in existence about the role of adults in children's lives. In our own time the boundaries are being policed in debates about 'tiger mothers' and 'helicopter parents' or about the 'play versus work' balance in early education or about the parent–child balance in decisions about custody arrangements. In the brief history of childhood that follows, we should bear in mind that at one and the same time, people played multiple variations on the theme of how best to treat their children.

Ancient Greeks and Romans

In ancient Greek and Roman times, childhood was seen largely as a preparation for adulthood. Two traditions of child-rearing were significant for the ancient Greeks: the Spartan tradition emphasised valour and was designed to produce patriotic warriors, and the Athenian tradition emphasised learning and thinking skills and democratic citizenship. The Spartans believed that harsh treatment of children would strengthen mind and body and instil discipline, while the Athenians, like Socrates and Plato, believed that encouraging children to reason would foster self-discipline and develop a healthy mind in a healthy body. The Romans were inclined towards the Spartan approach and infanticide was lawful during the early Roman Empire under the law of *patria potestas*, or 'power of the father' (Fogel, 2001), where each newborn child was presented to the father, who decided whether they lived or died – any sickly or unwanted babies were left on the Roman hillsides to perish. Later Romans, like Cicero and Quintilian (35–100 CE), adopted the kinder, Athenian approach favouring encouragement and reasoning and rejecting the use of corporal punishment for children.

The European middle ages

As Christianity spread throughout Europe, it brought a different set of adult representations of childhood. St. Augustine (354–430 CE) who preached the Christian doctrine of love and tolerance also preached the doctrine of *original sin*, which holds that children are born tainted with evil from Adam and Eve's first disobedience in the Garden of Eden (Heywood, 2001). The act of sexual congress and the subsequent passage of the child through the vagina of the mother passed this evil to the child and required absolution from the church. Hence, babies were baptised soon after birth to ensure their place in Heaven; otherwise, unbaptised babies would spend eternity in *limbo*. For the next thousand years, Christian parents and teachers believed they should tame the wild bodies and bawdy behaviour of young children to ensure that they would spend their afterlife in Heaven: – children were punished 'for their own good' to save them from the alternative afterlife of hellfire and damnation. The eternal soul rather than the physical child was the focus of adult attention, and childhood was the time for instilling a healthy fear of an all-seeing God and to ensure a moral and virtuous adulthood and a heavenly reward after death.

The Renaissance (c. 1300–1600)

In the Renaissance (the 'rebirth' of classical civilisation in Europe), educators and philosophers rediscovered the ideas of the ancient Greeks and Romans. Writers, scientists and philosophers of the time questioned religious beliefs and explored humanist perspectives that shifted the focus away from God and eternity towards the individual in the here and now (Fogel, 2001). The humanist perspective led philosophers like Erasmus to publish 'books of manners', describing how children should be treated, how they should behave and how they should be educated. For the sons of the relatively wealthy, like William Shakespeare, childhood now became a distinct phase synonymous with 'schooling', a period between mewling infant and sighing lover:

> All the world's a stage …
> … And one man in his time plays many parts,
> His acts being seven ages. At first, the infant,
> Mewling and puking in the nurse's arms.
> Then the whining schoolboy, with his satchel
> And shining morning face, creeping like snail
> Unwillingly to school. And then the lover,
> Sighing like furnace, with a woeful ballad
> Made to his mistress' eyebrow...
> (*As You Like It*, Act 2, scene 7, William Shakespeare)

As religious faith and superstition encountered the power of science and the scientific method, struggles between Enlightenment thinkers and religious thinkers produced two profoundly different views of children. Fundamentalist Christians, who believed children were born evil and should be raised in fear of Hell and damnation and should be helped along the paths of righteousness with liberal doses of physical punishment, were challenged by Enlightenment thinkers (like the rationalist John Locke), who believed on the contrary that children were born innocent, blank slates for life to inscribe. Enlightenment figures argued that kindness and reason, rather than fear and punishment, were better ways to guide the young.

The child of Nature (c. 1750–1830)

Jean Jacques Rousseau took issue both with the Christian doctrine of *original sin* and with John Locke's emphasis on *rationalism*. He dismissed both the idea that children should be brought up in fear of damnation and the idea that children should be led through reason because he thought that both approaches would interfere with the *natural* development of their faculties (Heywood, 2001). He saw children as *creatures of nature*, born innocent rather than sinful, imaginative rather than rational. In his treatise *Emile*, he described children as 'noble savages'. He believed that nothing should be done to mould them; instead, they should spend their childhood in a *state of nature*, doing what comes *naturally* – running, jumping and shouting to their heart's content. Rousseau believed that children were creatures of *instinct* and *sensation* and that with Nature as their teacher, they would grow strong and healthy in the open air, learning as they played.

Rousseau spawned a revolutionary movement called Romanticism, which spread across Europe and the United States and which still affects our representations of what it means to be a child today. Romanticism was an aesthetic and philosophical movement, a reaction against both the Enlightenment obsession with reason and the Christian obsession with moral training. The Romantics wanted individual freedom, equality and dignity for all – men, women, slaves and *children*. Romantic writers took up Rousseau's ideas about the essential goodness of children's *natures* and about *natural* childhoods lived in *Nature's* outdoor classroom. Here we have Coleridge promising his newborn son a life of Nature and freedom:

> *But thou, my babe! shalt wander like the breeze*
> *By lakes and sandy shores, beneath the crags*
> *Of ancient mountain, and beneath the clouds*
> ('Frost at Midnight', Coleridge)

The Romantics believed that childhood is the wellspring for everything that follows in adulthood, or as Wordsworth wrote, 'the child is father of the man'. Romantics mourned the loss of childhood and envied children the imagination that connected them directly to both Nature and the divine, a sensation that was hard to recapture in adulthood. Wordsworth expressed it thus:

> *There was a time when meadow, grove and stream,*
> *The earth, and every common sight*
> *To me did seem*
> *Apparelled in celestial light,*
> *The glory and the freshness of a dream.*
> *It is not now.*
> ('Ode: Intimations of Immortality from Recollections of Early Childhood', Wordsworth)

However, others scoffed at the Romantic representations of idyllic childhood and pointed out the darker elements of most childhoods of the eighteenth and nineteenth centuries. For instance, William Blake contrasted the Romantic celebration of unconfined and uncorrupted childhood with the bleak reality of most children's lives in his *Songs of Innocence and Experience*:

> When my mother died I was very young.
> And my father sold me while yet my tongue,
> Could scarcely cry 'weep 'weep 'weep 'weep.
> So your chimneys I sweep, & in soot I sleep.
> ('The Chimney Sweeper', William Blake)

In a similar vein, Elizabeth Barrett Browning pointed out that life for the children of the factories, mines and streets was entirely unnatural:

'For oh', say the children, 'we are weary,
And we cannot run or leap -
If we cared for any meadows, it were merely
To drop down in them and sleep ...'
('The Cry of Children', Elizabeth Barrett Browning)

For all their flaws, the Romantics pricked the consciences of many adults, changing the way their generation saw the childhoods of the poor and setting in train the great reform movements around child labour and education of the nineteenth century.

The child of the evangelists (c. 1750–1830)

As Wordsworth's Romantic vision of the child as 'A naked Savage, in the thundershower' (*Prelude*) gained a hold in the popular imagination, a particularly vehement version of Christian fundamentalism called evangelism emerged in opposition. In 1779 Hannah Moore, a leading evangelist and educator, wrote:

[It is] a fundamental error to consider children as innocent beings, whose little weaknesses may perhaps want some correction, rather than as beings who bring into the world a corrupt nature and evil disposition, which it should be the great end of education to rectify.
(in Benziman, 2012: p. 55)

Mrs Sherwood, another evangelist and a popular author of moral tales, wrote a story in which children were taken, for their 'improvement', to contemplate the rotting corpse of a criminal swinging on a gibbet (*History of the Fairchild Family*, 1818). If that wasn't enough to convince them that 'the Wages of Sin is Death', her prayer against pride and envy should have done the trick:

Oh Lord God, Almighty Father! hear the prayer of a poor wicked, proud child! I know that my heart is full of sin, and that my body is corrupt and filthy, and that I must soon die and go down into the dust: and yet I am so foolish and so wicked as to wish to be great in this world. I wish to have a fine house to live in, and a great many servants to wait on me, and to be of great consequence, and to be made a great deal of: and yet I know, that, if I had what I deserved, I should now at this moment be in hell fire ... make me lowly and humble in heart, content and thankful for what I have.
(Mrs. Sherwood, in Hunt, 2001: p. 23)

Childhood, according to the evangelists, was no time to spare the rod, and their fierce moral tales were widely bought and read (especially in Sunday Schools and Christian institutions set up for the children of the poor, who were deemed to be in more need of moral guidance!). Indeed Christian magazines like the *Boys Own Paper* and the *Girls Own Paper* survived until 1965 (Hunt, 2001), carrying their salutary messages of sin and punishment.

The child of Victorian England (1837–1901)

The Victorian period was a time of great cruelty, neglect and exploitation, as we can see in the work of Gustave Doré's illustrations in *London* (1872) – but it was also a time of unprecedented sympathy for the 'child as victim', as well as a time for adults to sanctify the notion of childhood . In many paintings and books of the early Victorian period, concern for children was often expressed in mawkishly sentimental terms: children are cloyingly sweet, helpless, impossibly good and saintly; they are *dolls* rather than *miniature adults.*

Children and their concerns provided the content for many Victorian novels: Dickens wrote about the cruelty and abuse meted out to poor children in books like *Oliver Twist* and *Nicholas Nickleby*; Charles Kingsley wrote about the great divide between rich and poor children in *The Water Babies*; and Charlotte Brontë exposed the plight of orphans in *Jane Eyre*. The historian G.M. Trevelyan wrote that 'Enlarged sympathy with children was one of the chief contributions made by the Victorian English to real civilisation' (1944, in Wullschlager, 1995: p. 13).

The early Victorians tended to see poverty as a moral failing and divided the poor into the 'deserving' poor of hard-working God-fearing families who had fallen on hard times through no fault of their own and the 'undeserving' poor of the godless, feral and feckless who were too lazy or immoral to look after their own families. But towards the end of the nineteenth century, this distinction began to fade as social research showed that poverty was in fact a structural failing built into the social and economic fabric of society. Victorian social activists like Joseph Rowntree, Charles Booth and Henry Mayhew carried out surveys on the conditions of the poor in the factories and slums of the major cities in England and were shocked by the pitiful plight of the children they met. Their publications contributed to parliamentary campaigns against child labour enacted in the *Factory Acts*, which marked the first steps towards making 'childhood' a protected space and a universal right (Hendrick, 1997).

Figure 9.3 *Bubbles*, by Sir John Everett Millais. During the Victorian period, childhood was often depicted in a sentimental way.

Source: By John Everett Millais - Public Domain, https://commons.wikimedia.org/w/index.php?curid=5139164.

Case study: Henry Mayhew and the little watercress girl

Henry Mayhew (1812–1887) interviewed workers in the streets of London in Victorian times. One of his interviewees was a girl of eight, selling bunches of watercress to help support her family. Here is an extract from 'The Little Watercress Girl':

> The little watercress girl who gave me the following statement, although only eight years of age, had entirely lost all child-ish ways, and was, indeed, in thoughts and manner, a woman. There was something cruelly pathetic in hearing this infant, so young that her features had scarcely formed themselves, talking of the bitterest struggles of life, with the calm earnestness of one who had endured them all. I did not know how to talk with her. At first I treated her as a child, speaking on childish subjects: so that I might, by being familiar with her, remove all shyness, and get her to narrate her life freely. I asked her about her toys and her games with her companions; but the look of amazement that answered me soon put an end to

any attempt at fun on my part. I then talked to her about the parks, and whether she ever went to them. 'The parks!' she replied in wonder, 'where are they?' I explained to her, telling her that they were large open places with green grass and tall trees, where beautiful carriages drove about, and people walked for pleasure, and children played. Her eyes brightened up a little as I spoke; and she asked half-doubtingly, 'Would they let such as me go there-just to look?' all her knowledge seemed to begin and end with watercresses, and what they fetched.

From Henry Mayhew's *London Labour and the London Poor*, 1861–1862, p. 47)

Discussion questions

Why is Mayhew taken aback by his encounter with the little watercress seller?
Why does he find it difficult to talk to her?
How does the watercress girl challenge his understanding of childhood?

The movement for universal education gathered pace, and in 1870 Forster's Education Act gave every child the right to elementary education up to the age of 12. Many parents and employers resisted, and many children remained in work. But by 1880 elementary education was made compulsory, and a *childhood for all* became both a social principle (that everyone was entitled to a childhood) and a social fact (that childhood was a time exclusively set aside for schooling). Towards the end of the century, the ill-treatment and neglect of children became a punishable crime under the *Prevention of Cruelty to, and Protection of, Children Act 1889*, and the state began to take some responsibility for children, gradually eroding fathers' rights to own their children as exclusive property to do with as they wished (Hendrick, 1997).

Children's literature and the cult of childhood

Gradually, 'childhood' came to be seen as a protected time free from work and adult concerns and as a right for every child. Children came to be seen in the popular imagination as innocents occupying a prelapsarian idyll, an earthly version of the Garden of Eden called childhood. Hunt argues that this led to a change in the way literature for children was written, as writers searched 'for a tone appropriate to a changing relationship between adults and children' to replace the commanding tones of the moralists of earlier generations (Hunt, 2001: p. 240). *Alice in Wonderland* (1865) marks the beginning of literature for and about children which is sympathetic to their concerns as children. Children are no longer preached at with dreadful warnings, nor sentimentalised as 'poor little victims'; instead, writers tried to give them an authentic voice. In America, *What Katy Did* (1872), *Little Women* (1868–1869) and *Tom Sawyer* (1876) all presented children's points of view. In Britain, R.L. Stevenson's *Child's Garden of Verses* (1885) and Andrew Lang's *Fairy Books* (1889–1910) were hugely popular. The Edwardian authors, Edward Lear, J.M. Barrie, Kenneth Graham and A.A. Milne (all men, incidentally) idealised and idolised childhood; they set their tales in a fantasy preindustrial landscape where it was always summer and children played endlessly in the fresh country air. Childhood was idolised as a state of purity, a pre-sexual life of moral simplicity, a land of and lost content, yearned for but denied to adults (Wullschlager, 2001). This *cult of childhood* made a Wonderland and Neverland of children's lives that still runs deep in our thinking today – we associate childhood with Narnia and The Secret Garden, with the Yellow Brick Road and the Land of Green Ginger, where children are protected by their innocence from the horrors of adulthood. Like Peter Pan, we want childhood to last forever and for children *always to have fun*!

Time to reflect

It is great fun to trace the history of adults' representations of childhood through the representations of children's lives in stories and pictures from different periods. Children's books offer some surprising insights into the way adults think about children and childhood.

Consider a favourite book from your childhood. Can you remember why you liked it as a child?
How do you feel about it now?
How do the text and pictures represent childhood?
Could this book have been written or illustrated in any other era?
What books would you like all children to know?

Twentieth-century concepts of childhood

Smart et al. (2001) suggest that for most of the twentieth century, our view of childhood was dominated by an *embryonic model* which inclined us to see children as immature and unformed *potential* persons who have to be guided and shaped by adults for *future* citizenship. This approach can be seen in the child study movement, where children's growth and maturation patterns were studied in minute detail. Cyril Burt (1883–1971), a leading British psychologist, summed up the approach:

> superintending the growth of human beings is as scientific a business as cultivating plants or training racehorses. (in Cunningham, 2006: pp. 198–199)

Notions of 'training' children were taken up enthusiastically. For example, health workers advised parents to potty-train newborns by applying a cold potty rim to the baby's bottom and promised that there would be 'no soiled napkins after the first week or so, and very few wet ones' (Cunningham, 2006: p. 199). In New Zealand, Dr Truby King (1858–1938) set up the Mothercraft Training Society to teach mothers to train their children to feed and sleep by the clock: he advised parents to ignore any night-time interruptions and to impose regular feeding habits as a foundation for instilling future obedience (Cunningham, 2006). In America, John Watson (1878–1958), a behavioural psychologist, gave the following advice to parents:

> There is a sensible way of treating children. Treat them as though they were young adults. … Never hug and kiss them, never let them sit on your lap. If you must, kiss them once on the forehead when they say goodnight. Shake hands with them in the morning. (in Cunningham, 2006: p. 198)

Children, like puppies, had to be trained into good habits, manners and obedience through firm and rigid routines applied by dispassionate and authoritarian adults.

But others disagreed. Psychoanalytic theories highlighted the important role of emotion in children's lives, and in response, child-rearing advice gradually became more relaxed. Margaret Ribble, in her book *The Rights of Infants* (1943), stressed the importance of warmth and affection between mothers and children for the development of emotional and social stability. Dr Benjamin Spock, who wrote *Baby and Child Care* in 1946, advised mothers to feed babies on demand, to enjoy their children and to think about the world from the child's point of view. Similarly, psychoanalyst Donald Winnicott wrote *The Ordinary Devoted Mother* (1949), in which he coined the term 'good enough parenting' to reassure parents that they could rely on love and instinct to raise their children. Work on infant attachment by John Bowlby and Mary Ainsworth (see Chapter 7) showed that positive bonding between mothers and children laid the foundations for successful learning and was a powerful predictor of mental health and stability. And 40 years later, the focus on the mother–child bond shifted when Rutter (1981) pointed out that fathers had an equally important role to play in raising well-adjusted children. The second half of the century saw a kinder attitude towards children and a growing sensitivity to their psychological needs.

Contemporary debates about childhood

The history of childhood has been one of increasing visibility and improving conditions overall as children's concerns became more clearly recognised in the adult consciousness. A major driver in redefining contemporary concepts of childhood was the United Nations Convention on the Rights of the Child (UNCRC, 1989). Children's rights are now enshrined in policy documents and in international law, and parents, teachers, health professionals, social workers and police officers find themselves having to revisit their own representations of childhood. They are now expected to listen, explain, discuss and negotiate *with children* before making decisions about their futures. In the United Kingdom, the Children Acts (1989 and 2004), along with the *Every Child Matters* initiatives, have shifted the power balance between adults and children so that now the interests of the child are *paramount*, even in the face of opposition from their parents.

Not everyone is comfortable with the children's rights agenda. The idea that children have rights is faintly alarming to many adults because it implies that children can legitimately challenge the traditional hierarchical relationship between the generations (Mayall, 2002). Some people (particularly from countries where community *inter*dependence comes before individual independence) believe that too much emphasis is placed on individual children's rights and too little emphasis is put on conformity to the traditional norms and practices of the collective group (Nsamenang, 2004). Some argue that current representations of childhood make too much of the *unique* child's *rights* and make too little of children's obligations to family, neighbourhood and society (Gabriel in Parker-Rees et al., 2010).

In a recent article, one Taiwanese teacher expressed her doubts about this prevailing twenty-first-century view of childhood individualism:

> When I first started teaching, a good child was a child who would simply obey and follow the rules. ... Now being a good child is not about following the rules. Parents and most young teachers believe that rigid rules will kill children's creativity and sense of independence. Now a good child is all about being creative and becoming independent. (Ah-Hui, quoted in Lee & Tseng, 2008: p. 190)

Since the 1970s, a new sociology of childhood has argued that children are *social actors* with agency and power to define themselves and to influence the adults around them; they may have less power than adults in many spheres, but they are actively engaged in building their own relationships and identities separately from adults. As they do so, they form their own distinct generation and their own versions of society, which will be different from that of their parents (James, 2011), and thus children have an important part to play in the evolution of societies.

Future childhoods

Romantic ideas continue to influence our beliefs about children and childhood, and contemporary early education and child-rearing practices emphasise the importance of warm adult–child relationships, creativity, imagination and a close communion with the natural world to support children's holistic development (Halpin, 2006, 2008). However, in our work with children, we are bound to meet other adults from cultures with widely differing perspectives, and we need to be aware that our own beliefs grow out of our own particular set of circumstances. These different perspectives determine how people relate to children and how they define childhood (Kehily, 2008).

Clearly, a major development in the way adults relate to children in the twenty-first century is the emphasis on listening to children and addressing their concerns seriously. But of course, not everyone will agree that this is a positive development, and as a practitioner you will find yourself treading a fine line as you try to balance your own passionately held beliefs with the demands placed upon you by adults who hold equally passionate but different beliefs about what childhood means.

Let's leave the last words to children themselves. An international survey asked children around the world what constituted a good childhood. Here is what they said:

- Strong, safe, loving relationships
- Equal treatment, dignity and respect
- Good schools and good teachers

- Food and decent living conditions in decent neighbourhoods
- Freedom from child labour, mistreatment and exploitation.
  (United Nations Development Group, 2013)

Summary

- Memories about childhood may be unreliable; adults often look back to a golden age of childhood.
- Childhood may be short or long; children in emerging economies generally have shorter childhoods than children in developed economies.
- Childhood is an 'invented' construct that marks children off from adults; the boundary between childhood and adulthood shifts according to social conventions of time and place, and the boundaries are policed by adults who make decisions about what can be expected of children of different ages.
- The universal availability of electronic images to adults and children alike have led to the disappearance of childhood innocence.
- Nightmare childhoods were common in the past and still exist where powerful adults exploit children.
- The mistreatment of children has often been justified on the grounds that it is in their best interests.
- It is no longer acceptable for parents to treat children as possessions; the law now recognises children's rights to participate in decisions which affect them.
- The history of childhood shows that at any one time several conflicting versions of childhood exist.
- Adults who believed in 'original sin' took a punitive and moralistic stance towards children; Enlightenment thinkers encouraged adults to reason with children; Romantic thinkers emphasised childhood as a time for creativity and imagination as each child developed their own unique *nature* as they learned *naturally* from *Nature*.
- Nineteenth-century reformers and writers campaigned for the right of every child, rich or poor, to enjoy a childhood free from work and exploitation.
- A cult of childhood emerged where children were imagined as occupants of a fantasy world of eternal summer; any transgression against children was seen as a corruption of childhood and punishable by law.
- Some child experts thought of children as a homogenous group who could be successfully trained into desirable behaviour; others believed, on the contrary, that each child had different emotional needs and that adults should tailor their approaches to the individual.
- The history of childhood has been a battleground between those who believe adults should be in a position of power over children and those who believe children are entitled to a voice. Children's rights are enshrined in the UNCRC (1989), but some commentators think these rights are applicable only to children in economically advanced nations; others think that the emphasis on individual rights weakens community ties and undermines adults.

- A sociology of childhood shows how children construct themselves separately from the adults around them to form their own new generation with their peers.
- Contemporary early childhood practices are heavily influenced by Romanticism, but other points of view are widespread too. Working with children demands that practitioners should be critically aware of their own and other people's representations of childhood.

Topics for further discussion

1 What significant factors inform your own beliefs about childhood?
2 Choose a headline story about children that is currently in the news. What does it reveal about the writer's internal representation of what childhood means?
3 Do you think children's views are given as much weight as those of adults? Can you think of any examples where children have significantly challenged adult attitudes?

Assignments

1 Review a parenting book or a television parenting programme. Explain what appear to be the author's understanding of the desirable power balance between children and adults.
2 Make an online collection of paintings, sculptures, photographs and advertisements to show how children have been portrayed over the centuries. What conclusions can you draw?
3 Find Lewis Carroll's photographs of Alice Liddell and compare them to Mary Cassat's picture, '*Girl in a blue armchair*'. How do they strike you from a twenty-first-century perspective?

Further reading

The Invention of Childhood by H. Cunningham (2006). London: BBC Books
A History of Childhood by Colin Heywood (2001). Cambridge: Polity Press
An Introduction to Childhood Studies (2nd edn) by Mary Jane Kehily (2008). Buckingham: Open University Press
Hendrick (2011) 'The Evolution of Childhood in Western Europe c. 1400–c. 1750' in J. Qvortrup, W.A. Corsaro and M.-S. Honig (eds) *The Palgrave Handbook of Childhood Studies* (pp. 99–113). Basingstoke: Palgrave Macmillan

Useful websites

The Family and Parenting Institute is an independent charity which monitors current issues about childhood and families. It produces an annual Family Report Card for the UK – **www. familyandparenting.org/**

Look at the online journal *Global Studies of Childhood*, Volume 1, no. 4, 2011, Special Issue: Childhood in Literature, Media and Popular Culture at http://gsc.sagepub.com/

References

Ariès, P. (1962) *Centuries of Childhood*, Pimlico edition (1996). London: Random House

Benziman, G. (2012) *Narratives of Child Neglect in Romantic and Victorian Culture*. Basingstoke: Palgrave Macmillan

Buckingham, D. (2009) 'Children and Television', in J. Qvortrup, W.A. Corsaro and M.-S. Honig (eds) *Palgrave Handbook of Childhood Studies* (pp. 347–359). Basingstoke: Palgrave Macmillan

Byatt, A.S. (2009) *The Children's Book*. Vintage Edition (2010). London: Random House

Cunningham, H. (2006) *The Invention of Childhood*. London: BBC Books

de Mause, L. (1974) 'The evolution of childhood' in Heywood, C. (ed.), *The History of Childhood* (p. 41). New York: Psychohistory Press.

Fogel, A. (2001) 'The History (and Future) of Infancy', in G. Bremner and A. Fogel (eds) *Blackwell Handbook of Infant Development* (pp. 726–757). Oxford: Blackwell Publishing

Gabriel, N. (2010) 'Adults' concepts of childhood', in R. Parker-Rees, C. Leeson, J. Willan and J. Savage (eds) *Early Childhood Studies* (3rd edn) (pp. 137–151). Exeter: Learning Matters

Halpin, D. (2006) Why a *Romantic* conception of education matters. *Oxford Review of Education* 32(3, July): 325–345

Halpin, D. (2008) Pedagogy and the Romantic Imagination. *British Journal of Educational Studies* 56(1, March): 59–75

Hendrick, H. (1997) *Children, Childhood and English Society, 1880–1990*. Cambridge: Cambridge University Press

Hendrick, H. (2011) 'The Evolution of Childhood in Western Europe c. 1400–c. 1750', in J. Qvortrup, W.A. Corsaro and M.-S. Honig (eds) *The Palgrave Handbook of Childhood Studies* (pp. 99–113). Basingstoke: Palgrave Macmillan

Heywood, C. (2001) *A History of Childhood*. Cambridge: Polity Press

Hunt, P. (ed.) (2001) *Children's Literature: An Anthology 1801–1902*. Oxford: Blackwell Publishing

James, A. (2011) 'Agency', in J. Qvortrup, W.A. Corsaro and M.-S. Honig (eds) *The Palgrave Handbook of Childhood Studies* (pp. 34–45). Basingstoke: Palgrave Macmillan

James, A., Jenks, C. and Prout, A. (1998) *Theorising Childhood*. Cambridge: Polity

James, C. (2013) Interview. *The Observer*, 10 February 2013, p. 11

Kehily, M.J. (2008) *An Introduction to Childhood Studies* (2nd edn). Buckingham: Open University Press

Lee, I.-F. and Tseng, C.-L. (2008) Cultural conflicts of the child-centred approach to early education in Taiwan. *Early Years* 28(2, July): 183–186

Mantel, H. (2010) *Giving up the Ghost: A memoir*. London: Fourth Estate Harper Collins

Mayall, B. (2002) *Towards a Sociology of Childhood*. Buckingham: Open University Press

Mayhew, H. (1861–1862) 'The Watercress Girl', in R. Douglas-Fairhurst (ed.) *London Labour and the London Poor: A selected Edition* (p. 47–50). Oxford: Oxford University Press

Nsamenang, A.B. (2004) *Cultures of Human Development and Education: Challenge to Growing up African*. New York: Nova Science Publishers

Pinker S. (2012) *The Better Angels of Our Nature: a History of Violence and Humanity*. London: Penguin Books

Pollock, L. (1983) 'Forgotten Children: Parent-Child Relations from 1500 to 1900', in C. Heywood (ed.) *A History of Childhood*. Cambridge: Polity Press

Postman, N. (1982, republished 1994) *The Disappearance of Childhood*. New York: Vintage/Random House Press

Ribble, M. (1943) *The Rights of Infants*. New York: Columbia University Press

Rousseau, J.-J. (1991) *Emile or On Education* (trans. Allan Bloom). Harmondsworth: Penguin

Rutter, M. (1981) *Maternal Deprivation Revisited* (2nd edn). New York: Penguin Books

Sherwood, M.M. (1818) 'History of the Fairchild Family or, the Child's Manual: Being a Collection of Stories to Show the Importance and Effects of a Religious Education', in Peter Hunt (ed.) *Children's Literature: An Anthology 1801–1902* (pp. 17–23). Oxford: Blackwell Publishing

Smart, C., Neale, B. and Wade, A. (2001) *The Changing Experiences of Childhood – Families and Divorce*. Cambridge: Polity

Trevelyan, G.M. (1944) 'English Social History', in Jackie Wullschläger (ed.) *Inventing Wonderland* (p. 13). London: Methuen

Spock, B. (1946) 'The Common Sense Book of Baby and Child Care' in H. Cunningham (ed.) *The Invention of Childhood* (p. 202). London: BBC Books

United Nations Development Group (2013) *A Million Voices: The World We Want*. www.worldwewant2015.org. Accessed 6 March 2015

Winnicott, D. (1949) *The Ordinary Devoted Mother and her Baby*. Nine Broadcast Talks. Republished in *The Child and the Family and the Outside World*. London: Tavistock Publications, 1957. New York: Basic Books

Wullschläger, J. (2001) *Inventing Wonderland: the Lives of Lewis Carroll, Edward Lear, J.M. Barrie, Kenneth Grahame and A.A. Milne*. London: Methuen

Zelizer, V. (1985) *Pricing the Priceless Child: The Changing Social Value of Children*. New York: Basic Books

Early education

Introduction

In most countries around the world, early education (and care) for newborns to eight-year-olds has become a focus of attention for governments and policymakers. This chapter provides an overview of the emergence of early education in its various forms and discusses some of the principles underlying important debates about the role of parenting, play and teaching that contribute to the contemporary picture. This chapter will give you some sense of the tremendous struggle that has taken place over more than a century to make quality education for young children a high priority.

Historically, early education has drawn on an eclectic mix of ideas and good practice from all over the world (see Chapter 3). Contemporary research and practice follows this tradition, and nowadays the Internet offers instant access to a host of ideas from specialists in the field who maintain a lively global debate sharing insights about new developments in the field. You can find from UNESCO (United Nations Educational, Scientific and Cultural Organisation), OECD (Organisation for Economic Co-operation and Development), UNICEF (United Nations Children's Fund), ILO (International Labour Organisation), WHO (World Health Organisation) and World Bank websites comparative data about what is on offer in different countries.

In England, early education and care is governed by the requirements of the Early Years Foundation Stage (birth to age five) and the National Curriculum KS1 (five to seven). Similar documents, but with different emphases, cover Scotland, Wales and Northern Ireland. However, the area is in constant flux, and it is important to consult the relevant websites to keep abreast of the latest developments.

The emergence of early childhood care and education in the United Kingdom

For over a hundred years, there have been campaigns for the state provision of nursery education and care, particularly for the children of the poor. For example, the 1870 *Elementary Education Act (Forster Act)* made provision for all children aged five to 11 to attend school. When attendance was made compulsory in 1880, very young children who were previously minded by older siblings at home now accompanied them to school – to the consternation of many teachers! In 1905 the *Report of the Consultative Committee on Infant and Nursery Schools* addressed this problem and advised that children under five should not attend infant schools, because doing so prevented them from having fresh air, exercise, movement and sleep – in addition, it was felt that the rigid style of rote learning dulled their intellectual curiosity.

In 1908 the *Acland Report: School Attendance of Children below the Age of Five* stated that the proper place of children under five was at home with their mothers – although the report suggested that children from 'unsatisfactory' homes would benefit from nursery school. The report advised that nurseries should permit free movement, inside and outside play and sleep, but that there should be no formal reading, writing or arithmetic.

In 1933, the Hadow Report on *Infant and Nursery Schools* set out the case for a national programme of nursery schooling for children under five (particularly in deprived areas) based on play, socialising and learning to be independent. Psychologists Cyril Burt and Susan Isaacs made important contributions to the report, emphasising the particular emotional needs of children under seven.

In 1967 the *Plowden Report: Children and their Primary Schools*, although not specifically aimed at the nursery years, laid out the founding principles of active, play-based, experiential learning for young children which still influence educational programmes today.

Until the late twentieth century, UK provision for children under five was a patchy mixture of privately and publicly funded arrangements of nannies and private nursery schools, grandparents and ad hoc family arrangements, childminder services, voluntary playgroups and, for the most disadvantaged families, 'social services welfare groups'. Early education has now moved to centre stage. Gradually over the past 30 years, the state has taken over more of the responsibility for funding 'universal' provision. In England, all three- and four-year-olds (and disadvantaged two-year-olds) are now entitled to 15 hours of free education and care per week (with plans to increase this to 30 hours). The mixture of private and voluntary provision which exists in most local authorities has been supplemented in the most deprived areas of the country by Children's Centres and Sure Start Centres, which provide health, welfare and educational support for vulnerable parents and their children.

In 1988 the *Education Reform Act* introduced a National Curriculum and standard attainment tests for seven-year-olds. Faced with these tests, schools exerted downward pressure on voluntary preschools, playgroups and nurseries to turn away from *play* and to include more formal literacy and numeracy learning. In 1990, the *Rumbold Report: Starting with Quality* advised the government to set up a national framework for early education to ensure quality across all local authorities, and in 1996 the *Desirable Outcomes for Children's Learning on Entering Compulsory Education* provided the first formal guidance for what could be expected from children in the foundation stage of ages three to five. This was followed in 2000 by *Curriculum Guidance for the Foundation Stage*, which set out early learning goals and advised on the stepping stones required to achieve them. In 2003, the non-statutory guidance *Birth to Three Matters* emphasised that babies and infants are *active* learners from the outset and that nurseries should supply a full range of play activities and language development opportunities, delivered primarily through a key person who would build a strong emotional connection with each child.

Following alarm about child safety, the document *Every Child Matters* was published in 2003. This charged local authorities with putting in place a multidisciplinary framework in health, social care and education to bring practitioners together to safeguard children. Success would be measured on 'five goals' for children – being healthy; being safe: enjoying and achieving; making a positive contribution; and having economic well-being. Early years practitioners were expected to play a full part in monitoring and assessing children at risk of neglect and abuse and liaising with other child support agencies.

In 2006 the *Rose Report* into language and literacy learning was published. This emphasised the need for a rich language environment for the foundation stage based on speaking and listening skills to increase children's language skills in readiness for reading. For children entering reception and in KS1, it recommended a formal 'synthetic phonics' approach to reading based on sound discrimination and 'blending' to enable children to decode (read) or encode (write) words. The report led practitioners to include more and more activities designed to improve school readiness by introducing young children to formal reading, writing and numbers.

In 2007 the Department for Education published the first EYFS framework, *The Statutory Framework for Early Years Foundation Stage: Setting the Standard for learning, development and care for children from birth to five*, which combined the previous *Curriculum Guidance for the Foundation Stage* and *Birth to Three Matters* into one document. The EYFS covers learning and development and early learning goals; it details assessment requirements for monitoring progress, and it sets out safeguarding and welfare responsibilities, including the assignment of a key person for every child.

There is a good deal of evidence that children receiving high-quality early education and care experience improved social and cognitive outcomes (Sylva et al., 2010; Vandell et al., 2010; Melhuish, 2011). Early intervention in high-quality, long-term provision brings advantages, particularly for children at risk of low educational achievement. Improved educational outcomes seem to be associated with the quality of adult–child relationships and the opportunities available for *shared sustained thinking* (Siraj-Blatchford et al., 2002). Evidence from the Effective Provision of Pre-School Education (EPPE) Project (Sylva et al., 2004) suggests that preschool can play an important part in combating social exclusion by offering disadvantaged children, in particular, a better start to primary school.

But the evidence needs to be treated with caution (NESS, 2008, 2010, 2012). Efforts to measure the success of these schemes and to decide what constitutes best practice is difficult because of the wide variety of factors that need to be taken into account: culture, family background, individual differences, as well as the beliefs and practices of practitioners (Penn, 2011; Lewis, 2011). In 2011 the *Tickell Report* reviewed the evidence for effectiveness of early years provision and concluded that the early years curriculum was best delivered through planned, purposeful play with a balance of adult-initiated and child-initiated activities where children are supported to progress at their own pace. The review advised that the assessment procedure should be simplified and that the transition from the play-based foundation stage curriculum to the more formal Key Stage 1 should be managed carefully.

As more money has been allocated to early years care and education, so too have more efforts been made to control and prescribe what is provided and to measure what outcomes have been achieved. Assessments of children's progress and inspections of early education provision by Ofsted are part of this drive to make providers and schools accountable for the considerable sums of money being invested. It is clear that in the United Kingdom, early years education is now firmly established as an important part of children's learning journey. It has also become an important part of the social fabric: it frees parents to work, and it is the site for the delivery of health, education and social services. Some argue that it is provided less for children than for parents because the wider involvement of women in the workforce has driven the agenda for childcare and education rather than children's own needs; others have argued that provision for children under five is part of a strategy to get poorer women off benefits and into work. However, we can see that over the past century there has been a genuine altruistic desire to improve the health, welfare and education of the nation as a whole and that part of the strategy for achieving this has been more and more investment in the education and care of the youngest children and their families – particularly those who are vulnerable and at risk of falling by the wayside. This focus on investment in early years is repeated around the world by governments that recognise the importance of supporting mothers and young children as part of their strategies to produce strong and adaptable people in a rapidly changing global environment.

Early education programmes across the world

Early years care and education in the United Kingdom draws on a rich exchange of ideas from across the world. Thanks to the Internet, cross-cultural links are available to everyone, and it is relatively easy to keep up with the latest developments in every continent – but be aware that prescribed and centralised early education programmes are particularly characteristic of wealthier countries and that in poorer countries different community and neighbourhood schemes are being developed (Leadbeater, 2010).

In the United Kingdom, investment in early years care and education in the 1990s was heavily influenced by findings from the Head Start programme in the United States (see Schweinhart et al., 1993 and 2005). This programme began in 1965 and was originally a summer holiday catch-up programme for disadvantaged children to prepare them for infant school. It later grew into a full-time early years programme designed to provide support for disadvantaged children. It aimed to enhance children's ability to make the most of their educational opportunities by addressing their wider social needs. It offered highly qualified staff, low child/adult ratios, a richly resourced environment and a support programme for parents. The programme was very expensive to run, but longitudinal data suggests that it was successful and that for every dollar spent in the early years (UNICEF, 2003), seven dollars could be saved in social support expenditure during school and teenage years. Sure Start programmes and Children's Centres were set up in disadvantaged areas of the United Kingdom as a direct response to findings from Head Start (although funding has been gradually withdrawn over the last decade of austerity).

Also from the United States, an approach called Developmentally Appropriate Practice (see Copple & Bredekamp, 2009) became influential in the 1980s and 1990s. At its heart is the process of matching milestones in child development with effective teaching strategies; starting with close observation, adults tailor their interventions to the individual, assessing each child's level of understanding and supplying materials and activities to take the child to the next level. The programme, widely used in the United States, was revamped in 2009 but is criticised for relying too heavily on adult-led activities.

Two other influential programmes, *Te whariki* and Reggio Emilia have fed into the EYFS curriculum. *Te whariki*, developed by Margaret Carr, Helen May and Tamati and Tilly Reedy was introduced in New Zealand in 1996. *Te whariki* means 'woven mat' and refers to the many strands of experience that children bring with them into the nursery. It is an early childhood education curriculum which values what families and communities have already contributed to their children from birth. It puts particular emphasis on children's learning dispositions rather than on what they 'know'. Margaret Carr developed *Learning Stories* (2001) to document children's dispositions in five key areas – interest, involvement, persistence, expression and responsibility. These areas, rather than knowledge, skills and competencies, form the basis for assessment. The underlying philosophy has similarities with Reggio Emilia, which puts community, expression and creativity at the heart of early education and celebrates the many ways children express themselves through dance, art, play and music, which Loris Malaguzzi, the founder of the programme, calls the *hundred languages of children*. Malaguzzi recorded children's development through photographs, artwork and written records of conversations rather than keeping 'scores' to show how children progress. This portfolio approach for assessing progress has been widely adopted in nurseries and schools in the United Kingdom in tandem with more formal assessments based on competencies in specified areas of learning and behaviour.

More recently, early education has adopted aspects of the Forest School movement originating in Scandinavia. Forest Schools connect children with nature and use outdoor activities to foster social skills and self-confidence. They may be especially relevant for children who lack opportunities for outdoor play or who present challenging behaviour. The programmes encourage team building and cooperation, risk management, project planning and outdoor play. The Forest School idea, with its belief in connecting children with nature and the importance of *bio-therapy* for physical and mental well-being has been extended to encompass animal therapy programmes (Friesen, 2010). Animals are non-judgemental, and building relationships with them helps children to develop empathy and to read body language. Animal therapy is particularly promoted for children with social and behavioural delays such as attention deficit hyperactivity disorder. The programmes aim to build trust and confidence, first with animals and then with people, through the development of *non-verbal* social skills like caring and responsibility.

Case study: Outdoor play and the Forest School movement

At Forest School a student was asked to play alongside a young girl (aged four) who refused to speak at nursery. They painted trees with water, crawled through undergrowth like rabbits, and watched mini-beasts in the leaf litter. One day, they made insects out of sticks. The girl indicated to the student that she had forgotten to put antennae on her insect; the student added two sticks, and the girl smiled. The following week, the girl was engrossed in watching a trail of ants

▶

crawling up a tree trunk. 'Where are they going?' she suddenly asked. The student said, 'Perhaps they are sipping the sap', and she scraped off some resin to show her. The child turned it over in her hands, 'It's sticky!' Later, she addressed the student again. Over the next few weeks, she talked a little more each time she went to Forest School. And then one day, to everyone's delight, she found her voice at nursery.

How do you account for the child breaking her silence at Forest School?

Children have fewer opportunities for outside play nowadays. Many preschool children are over-weight and have low levels of physical activity (RCPCH, 2013). It seems that we have a genera-tional dislocation from nature; parents worry about traffic and stranger danger; children walk less; play is often confined and sedentary; and many homes lack gardens or access to outdoor space. Forest Schools aim to give children the chance to spend time among woodland trees.

Historically, the movement draws inspiration from those who believed that nature has an important part to play in child development – from Rous-seau and the romantics in the eighteenth century to Leslie Paul and the Woodcraft Folk in the twen-tieth. Without space and opportunity to run and jump and climb, motor skills and coordination may be impaired, and children may never learn the pleasures and pains of physical play in the open air. Forest Schools offer physical challenges and the chance to learn about the relationship between humans and the natural world.

Share your experiences of Forest School visits with colleagues.

Discussion questions

Do you think children get an authentic experi-ence of nature, natural play and discovery in the Forest School settings you have visited?

How far does our society recognise children's need for nature and outdoor play in their plan-ning decisions for schools and neighbourhoods?

Figure 10.1 Children have fewer opportunities for outside play nowadays. Without space and opportunity to run and jump and climb, children may never learn the pleasures and pains of physical play in the open air.

Source: Image Source/HEIDE BENSER CM

Charles Leadbeater (2010) sees a growing trend towards the imposition of centralised, national curricular models of education which, he argues, hark back to a nineteenth-century view of education based on teaching facts to a largely passive and ignorant audience. He argues, in an inspirational TED (technology, entertainment and design) talk, that the West has much to learn about education from programmes in the slums of South America, India and Africa, where the challenges facing millions of children have prompted new innovations in learning. He singles out the Pratham model in India, devised by Madhur Chavan, which serves 21 million children and the Harlem Children's Zone led by Geoffrey Canada – both offer different, innovative education programmes to the children and families and communities they serve by encouraging peer-to-peer learning around strategically placed computers and Internet access. Leadbeater suggests that our own system, controlled from the centre and hidebound by prescriptive 'national curricula', is desperately old-fashioned and stifles imagination and creativity. He also points out that our Western systems entrench social stratification and inequality by valuing only a narrow range of skills and competencies, and in doing so we waste many of our most talented youngsters from the outset.

Focus on *A new way of doing early education*

Find Charles Leadbeater's 2010 talk *Educational Innovation in the Slums* at https://www.ted.com/talks/charles_leadbeater_on_education.

Watch the talk with your group.
Does it change your 'vantage point'?
What can we learn from the way early education is organised in other places?
What have you learned from Leadbeater's analysis?

The Statutory Framework for the Early Years Foundation Stage (2014)

The Early Years Foundation Stage (EYFS) covers the years from birth to five, that is, from birth to the end of the reception year. Three *prime areas* of learning are communication and language; physical development; and personal, social and emotional development. These are first assessed at the two-year progress check. Four *specific areas* of learning are listed under the headings of literacy; mathematics; understanding the world; and expressive arts and design, and these are assessed through play-based teacher observations at the end of the year when a child turns five. Assessment is ongoing and diagnostic, so that practitioners can adapt their approach for those children who need extra support or more challenge and forms the basis of the *Early Years Foundation Stage Profile*, which is handed over at the end of the reception year to Year 1 teachers to help them produce individual learning plans for children in the transition to the more formal requirements of the KS1 curriculum designed for six- to eight-year olds.

In 2011 the *Tickell Review* made a case for a slimmed down version of the 2007 EYFS. As a result, children are now assessed against 17 early learning goals (previously 69) at three levels of proficiency – namely, *emerging*, *expected* or *exceeding*; these goals are set at a level that most children achieve. The 2014 EYFS document was been welcomed for its clarity and the simplicity of its assessment procedures. The supporting document, the non-statutory *Development Matters in the Early Years Foundation Stage* (British Association for Early Childhood Education, 2012), provides excellent guidance to support practitioners and incorporates the most up-to-date research on effective teaching strategies matched to child development. Play underpins the philosophy of the EYFS, and the document makes clear that *playing and exploring* come first in any new learning but that teaching is part of learning too. Supportive adults, who challenge and extend children's thinking and who help them to develop the skills of self-control and cooperation with others, have a key role to play in developing confident learners with good learning dispositions of curiosity, perseverance and focus.

> **Focus on** *Early Years Foundation Stage (from birth to age five)*
>
> Access the latest version of the EYFS. Read through the document and provide a summary of the main themes.
>
> What are the underlying principles?
> Do you think the document is child centred?
> Do you approve of its general approach? Or do you have reservations? Give reasons.
> Look at the Foundation Stage Profile to be completed by teachers at the end of reception year. How far do the assessments support the general principles of the document?
> What does the Foundation Stage Profile offer to children, parents, teachers, inspection teams and government policy planners?

The EYFS (2014) emphasises partnership between parents and practitioners and gives educators leeway over the way they balance play and teaching with child-led and adult-led activities. It is individualist in its philosophy, but at the same time, it recognises that children need to learn to behave cooperatively and considerately before they are ready to work in the more formal atmosphere of the KS1 classroom. The overarching theme is that practitioners should ensure children have child-centred and play-based education but that adults have a role in facilitating a mixture of child-led and adult-led activities which contribute to a rich learning environment. The EYFS states that

- every child is a **unique child** who is constantly learning and can be resilient, capable, confident and self-assured;
- children learn to be strong and independent through **positive relationships**;
- children learn and develop well in enabling environments, in which their experiences respond to their individual needs and there is a strong partnership between practitioners and parents/carers;

■ **children develop and learn in different ways and at different rates**, and the framework covers the education and care of all children in early years provision, including children with special educational needs and disabilities.

The premise of the document is that in a positive atmosphere with clear rules of conduct and structured challenging activities, any child can develop confidence, self-esteem, perseverance and curiosity – the basic requirements of a healthy learning disposition. The latest version, (EYFS, 2014) puts more emphasis on the role of teaching in the learning process and promotes 'teaching and learning to ensure children's "school readiness"' (p. 5). This focus on the role of the teacher is reflected in a demand for higher entrance requirements for students wanting to become Early Years Educators (at a minimum they need to hold a C grade at GCSE level in maths and English). The role of the parent in the child's learning continues to be a focus and settings are expected to forge strong practitioner–parent partnerships. The Common Inspection Framework was introduced in 2015 to ensure that all settings adhered to the same high standards of teaching, learning and behaviour expectations so that all children entering school are ready to learn and cooperate with their peers.

The key person

At the heart of the learning experience in early education outside the home is the key person who takes the place of the parent. When children first arrive in an early childhood setting, they may be fearful, suspicious, doubtful, sensitive, anxious and perhaps lonely. Their greatest need is to feel close to the people around them. It is important for them to be able to identify someone who is optimistic, kind and understanding. Kindness is the essential ingredient – when children are frightened or lonely, there is nothing more devastating for them than to feel that the people around them are cold, indifferent or preoccupied.

The key person gets to know the child well and builds good partnerships with parents, teachers and other staff on their behalf – this is particularly important during the birth-to-three phase, when children are learning language and social skills. The key person understands their child's personality, their idiosyncratic language patterns, their desires and their fears and builds a strong bond to help in the unfamiliar social situations and emotional upsets that are a normal part of the nursery day. This one-to-one intense relationship creates trust and promotes learning by drawing the key worker and child together so that they can talk, play and learn in a friendly and relaxed way. The need for a key person does not disappear as children get older; in KS1 they still require the support of an understanding person – a classroom helper, a teacher or a friend – to help them through the school day. The key person sees the child in his or her whole social context and is best placed to foster positive relationships and to provide an enabling environment that will allow them to develop and learn in different ways and at different rates, in a way that is unique to them.

Dahlberg et al. (2007) suggest that providing good-quality care and education depends on adults' seeing children as human beings, listening to them and allowing them to discover things for themselves, not imposing adult explanations before they have had time to explore their own. They cite the Reggio Emilia approach as a good example of quality care and education where relationships, language and self-expression are given a higher priority than curricular content and knowledge. They argue that children need socially supportive spaces to best develop a sense of confidence and power in their own abilities (Dahlberg & Moss, 2005).

Time to reflect

If you were choosing a preschool or school for your child, what factors would be most important to you?
Would the same factors be important to your child?
How would you judge whether or not the setting provided an *enabling environment*?
How would you assess the *quality of relationships* in the setting?
Would you apply different criteria to choosing a preschool and choosing a school? In what ways might they be the same? In what ways might they be different?

Parent partnerships

The relationship between key person, child and parent is germane to the effective delivery of both EYFS and KS1 programmes. Parents are their children's 'first educators' (Alexander, 2008), and personal, social and emotional *relationships* lie at the heart of the learning process. The opening paragraph of the *Statutory Framework for the Early Years Foundation Stage* (EYFS, 2014) states that 'Good parenting and high quality learning together provide the foundation children need to make the most of their abilities and talents as they grow up' (para. 1, p. 2).

And in Dame Clare Tickell's review (2011), she writes, 'The contribution of parents and carers to their child's early development cannot be overstated. Strong bonds between parents and their children, forged from the outset, are critical for the development of wellbeing' (ch. 3, para. 4, p. 20).

Early years practitioners need to respect parents' insights and to work closely in partnership with them because a strong reciprocal relationship provides a starting point for making the right decisions for individual children.

Good parenting and high-quality learning

What is 'good' parenting, and how does it contribute to high-quality learning?

Bruner (1996) suggests that children and parents are *naturally tuned to each other*: children are primed to ask for help, and parents are primed to respond at an appropriate level. He explains that parents and children instinctively collaborate and adopt four basic modes of teaching/learning:

1 *Apprenticeship* – children work alongside a parent to learn something like paring vegetables or how to operate a computer, asking questions as they go.
2 *Abstract thought and experiment* – children discuss things like how to spend their birthday money or try things out like testing whether things float or sink in the bath.

3 *Accessing prior knowledge and building on it* – children may wonder why some balloons sink to the ground and others soar away, and parents explain that some gases are lighter than air. They may then apply this knowledge when they see smoke rising from a bonfire and open up further discussion about the density of hot and cold gases.

4 *Instruction or transmission of information* – children receive explicit fact-based information or instructions delivered by a more knowledgeable person.

Bruner points out that *parents* use all four of these modes without ever giving it too much thought, but *teachers* rely mainly on one: the instruction and transmission mode.

When practitioners see themselves as 'teachers', they can easily slip into transmission mode, instructing children and providing facts and explanations rather than offering them opportunities to make their own contributions and to come to their own conclusions. Teacherly instruction has its place, but used too frequently, it may limit children's opportunities for discovery and impair their confidence by making them think there is only one correct way of thinking about things – the teacher's way. Of course some things do require 'teaching', but in the foundation stage, when children are learning how to learn, it forms only a small part of the whole learning experience. The danger for practitioners is that in 'transmission mode' they fail to take account of children's own understanding and focus instead on the curricular 'learning goals' rather than on the child.

Figure 10.2 *Apprenticeship*, one of Bruner's four basic modes of teaching/learning, involves children working alongside a parent to learn something like how to operate a computer, asking questions as they go.

Source: PhotoDisc/Getty Images

Parenting interventions

The Early Years Foundation Stage (2014) emphasises the importance of practitioners' working in partnership with parents, and to this end a booklet titled *What to expect, when?* (4Children, 2015) provides guidance for parents on children's learning and development in the early years. The booklet covers the prime areas of learning (personal, social and emotional development; physical development; communication and language) and the specific areas of learning (literacy; mathematics; understanding the world; expressive arts and design). It guides parents on ways to enhance the values of play and exploration, active learning, creativity and critical thinking and helps them to understand how those working in early years – whether in a nursery, at a preschool, as a childminder or in a reception class – are supporting their children to achieve 'school readiness'.

The focus on parent partnership raises the question of what constitutes 'good' parenting. A study of parenting interventions within the Sure Start system in Wales (Hutchings, 2007) found that being taught 'parenting skills' had great benefits in reducing problem behaviour in young children. Parents learned to

- increase positive child behaviour through praise and incentives;
- improve parent–child interaction through relationship building;
- set clear expectations and limit threats and sanctions for noncompliance;
- apply consistent gentle consequences for problem behaviour.

In Graham Allen's report (Allen Report, 2011), *Early Intervention: The Next Steps*, the member of parliament makes the case for government money to be spent on improving *parenting skills*, particularly among those caring for children under three. He argues that intervention at this stage will forestall persistent social problems passed from generation to generation because good parenting practices benefit children in the here and now and provide them with a role model when they become parents themselves:

> What parents do is more important than who they are. Especially in a child's earliest years, the right kind of parenting is a bigger influence on their future than wealth, class, education or any other common social factor. (Allen Report, 2011: p. xiv)

Findings from the National Evaluation of Sure Start (NESS, 2012) in the United Kingdom suggest that parenting classes can be successful – on the whole, parents who took part in parenting programmes tended to be less harsh in disciplining their children than before and tended to provide more stimulating environments at home. There was evidence too that there was a reduction in the prevalence of chaotic home environments, which led to improved life satisfaction for both parents and children.

However, not everyone is convinced that this emphasis on 'training' parents is a good idea (see Focus on/Parenting below).

The importance of play in the early years

There has been support for the principles underlying the EYFS since its arrival in 2007 –the emphasis on a balance of play-based experiences has met practitioners' approval even though some

Focus on *Parenting*

Frank Furedi, a UK Professor of Sociology, is critical of twenty-first-century early years political discourse around parenting. He detects a belief in *'parental determinism'* – the idea that every parental action in the early years has an indelible effect on children and determines everything from job prospects to happiness in adulthood. Out of this comes a belief in *'parenting deficit'*, which leads to intervention.

He argues that politicians, healthcare workers, social workers, educators and child experts have colonised childhood with all sorts of conflicting advice about what constitutes good parenting, and in doing so, they have undermined parents. These experts do not merely provide guidance – they are consulted by officials, and their views may be enshrined in legislation and policies affecting health, care, education and the welfare of children in families. He questions the 'scientific knowledge' surrounding childcare, arguing that it makes parents feel incompetent and gives 'experts' too much power.

He points out that the core assumption behind initiatives like parenting classes is that child-rearing consists of a set of practices that can be learned and skills that can be taught by professionals. He argues that, on the contrary, child-rearing is essentially about building relationships; that relationships evolve and change over time; and that by focusing on 'experts' and 'professional' training, we undermine parents and make them less confident about relying on intuition and experience.

He concludes that *'deficit parenting'* has become an all-purpose explanation for social ills and allows governments to dodge the truth that social problems arise from social structures and cultural attitudes, not from the way individuals parent.

(From Furedi, F. (2012) *Parental Determinism: a most harmful prejudice.* http//www. frank-furedi.com/index.php/site/article/553. Accessed 31 January 2013)

What is *parental determinism*?

Is the concept of *deficit parenting* one that you would subscribe to?

Do you think parenting can be taught? If so, what would you include in a parenting course?

If parenting can't be taught, how would you help parents who experience difficulties around their child?

Ivan Illich (1977) famously argued in *Disabling Professions* that professionals *disable* laypeople by undermining their confidence in their own abilities. Do you think this might be a danger in promoting formal parenting classes?

feel that in practice, the insistence on *targets* and *outcomes* militate somewhat against the child-centred spirit of the document (Brooker *et al*, 2010). However, the emphasis on 'school readiness' and 'teaching' in the latest 2014 version has made some practitioners suspect that the play-based learning may be under threat. There is a popular consensus among many early education specialists that the principles of a play-based curriculum could be usefully adapted and extended for children up to eight years old but the demands of the National Curriculum has made this difficult to achieve.

When Susan Isaacs wrote 'Play is indeed the child's work, and the means whereby he grows and develops. Active play can be looked upon as a sign of mental health; and its absence, either of some inborn defect, or of mental illness'(1929,p 10), she was reacting against the adult-directed, sedentary, rote- learning that characterised much of the education of her time.

Play-as-work is still a much discussed topic in early education (Moyles, 1994; Brown 2003; Wood, 2010; Brooker, 2010; Burghart, 2010; Pellegrini, 2011; Broadhead & Burt, 2012; Bateson & Martin, 2013). Piaget identified three phases of play which matched his *constructivist* theories of children developing cognitive abilities – *practice play* (from birth to age two), where children repeat physical actions over and over again; *symbolic play* (ages two to seven), where they imagine and pretend; and *rule-bound play* (seven onwards), where games are controlled by strict boundaries (Piaget, 1962). Vygotsky (1968, 1978), on the other hand, took a *social constructivist* approach and observed that children are not bound by Piagetian 'stages' but can move beyond their developmental age when they are supported in their play by dialogue with a peer or adult. This idea that learning can be speeded up through the *dialogue* of play/work lies behind the notion of 'sustained shared thinking' (Siraj-Blatchford et al., 2002).

The literature is full of references to different categories of play, although deciding what constitutes play and what constitutes work is more difficult (Hughes, 2012). Play can be solitary, parallel or cooperative (Parten, 1932); it may be symbolic (using a banana as a gun), epistemic (taking something apart to see how it works) or ludic (acting out a fantasy role) (Hutt et al., 1988); it may be child-initiated free play or adult-initiated structured play. The important thing to remember is that the most satisfying play is all-absorbing.

There is strong evidence for delivering early education through play, not least because play starts naturally at the level of the child's own development (Tickell Review, 2011). When adults (or peers) build from this starting point, by modelling, demonstrating or asking appropriate questions, they help children to learn to *do something they couldn't have done or thought of by themselves*. There are debates to be had about the exact mix of adult-initiated and child-initiated play appropriate for different ages, but it is generally agreed that play, both indoor and outdoor, is an important element in all learning – even for adults.

The 'free play' which characterised many playgroup and preschool approaches in the 1970s and 1980s has gradually fallen out of favour. Time for unstructured free play remains part of the preschool day, but structured play and adult-directed activities are now generally considered to be an appropriate and essential part of a child-centred curriculum for the twenty-first century. Kathy Sylva, in *Childwatching at Playgroup and Nursery School*, questions the educational value and learning potential of 'free play', which too often descends into the mere repetition of previous play episodes. Drawing on Vygotsky and Bruner (see Chapter 3), she argued that the potential for learning through play was enhanced only when children engaged in thoughtful dialogue with more knowledgeable adults or peers. Her research shows the positive impact that early education can have, not only on children's knowledge, but on their problem solving, social skills and disposition to learn when they find themselves in the care of well-qualified and reflective practitioners who understand the value of supported and directed play. Her ideas have fed into the work of the EPPE project and have had a major influence on the Statutory Framework for Early Years Foundation Stage.

The questions remains, how far should children be left to learn through playful experiment and discovery, and how far should adults direct play towards learning the skills covered in the curriculum? Every practitioner has to weigh up the different approaches to find their own way of balancing work and play for the individual children in their care.

Role play and story play

Vivian Gussin Paley, an influential American early education specialist (see Chapter 6) puts stories and make-believe at the centre of early learning: 'Story playing and storytelling has become the curriculum of any classroom in which I am the teacher' (Paley, 1990: p. 4). She believes that pretend play is 'story in action', while storytelling is 'play in narrative form' and both are crucial for building a sense of self: 'In play, the child says, "I can *do* this well; I can *be* this effectively; I can *understand* what is happening to me and to the other children. In story telling a child says, "This is how I interpret and translate right now something that is on my mind"' (Paley, 1990: p. 10). She points out that being able to sequence a narrative is essential for logical thought and that through role play and storytelling, children are practising their powers of reason to work out the order of events, the salient details and the possible outcomes and consequences.

One particular kind of story, the fairy tale, has a special place in the early years. Psychoanalyst Bruno Bettelheim argued that fairy tales have evolved to address primitive and universal fears and longings and to offer resolutions which help children develop hope, optimism and emotional resilience (Bettelheim, 1976). There is a wealth of literature to suggest that fairy tales perform an important protective function in helping children to maintain a healthy mental

Figure 10.3 Fairy stories such as Sleeping Beauty have fallen out of favour somewhat; however, there is a wealth of literature to suggest that they perform an important protective function in helping children to maintain a healthy mental balance.

Source: Henry Meynell Rheam [Public domain], via Wikimedia Commons

balance – writers like Marina Warner and Jack Zipes have written extensively on their psychological and cultural significance. All early education practitioners rely heavily on story books and picture books for a variety of purposes – to entertain and amuse, to open up discussion or to explain – but the fairy tale has fallen out of favour somewhat perhaps because fears about stereotyping gender roles have given them a bad name. However, the simple structure of fairy tales, beginning 'once upon a time' and ending 'they all lived happily ever after', gives children the basic logic for ordering a sequence of events into a narrative framework – with the added bonus that everything always turns out right in the end.

Rhymes and rhythms for literacy learning

Playing with language and finding rhymes and connections between words seems to be a natural, universal feature that all children seem to delight in. In Wood's chapter 'The literate mind' (1998), he cites research that shows children who lack phonological awareness will find learning to read and write more difficult. Recognising rhyming words and alliterations like 'Peter Piper picked a peck of pickled peppers' and being able to discriminate the tiny sound differences between jog/dog or pin/pan or the word endings like felled/felt or heard/hurt provide the building blocks for our phonetic writing and reading system. Wood points to research that shows that 'children with poor phonological awareness are likely to become backward readers' (1998, p. 215). Playing with words, making nonsense words, repeating new words over and over just for the pleasure of hearing them is an important part of learning language. Nursery rhymes and songs help children articulate the sounds of language and to recognise rhythms and then to fine-tune their discrimination of sounds and words so that when they begin the process of learning to read, they can more easily detect the differences associated with each letter of the alphabet. In addition, reciting rhymes and singing songs in unison with other children bestows a sense of belonging and, above all, is great fun.

> ### *Time to reflect*
>
> Children love rhymes, poems and action songs. The more they know, the easier it will be for them to learn to read because getting the words right involves an acute ear for the fine phonic distinctions they will need when they start to read.
>
> With colleagues, compile an online resource folder of favourite rhymes, poems and action songs. Divide them into groups suitable for babies, toddlers, three- to four-year-olds, five- to six-year-olds and seven- to eight-year-olds.
>
> Discuss how they might contribute to literacy learning.

Transition from foundation stage to Key Stage 1

In many countries, the foundation stage lasts until children are six or seven when they are judged to be sufficiently emotionally stable, socially competent and physically and personally capable of listening attentively, working alongside others and showing good self-control.

Finnish children, for example, who have the highest educational outcomes in Europe, begin formal academic schooling at age seven (*Starting Strong III*, OECD, 2012). In England the transition to Key Stage 1 takes place at age five at the end of the reception year when children move towards more formal learning with a focus on literacy and numeracy skills.

Key Stage 1 is the label given to the two years of schooling in England, Wales and Northern Ireland that cover ages five to seven (Year 1 and Year 2), and all children follow the National Curriculum laid down under the *Education Act (2002)*. At present, this consists of the statutory study of the English language, maths, science, information and communication technology, design technology, history, geography art and design, music, physical education and religious education (parents can withdraw their children from RE if they wish). At the end of Year 1, teachers assess children's progress towards literacy with phonics screening, followed at the end of Year 2 by SATs (standard assessment tasks) in reading, writing, speaking and listening, maths and science. The results are used diagnostically by teachers to gauge whether children need extra support and by head teachers and Ofsted (Office for Standards in Education, Children's Services and Skills)inspectors to track learning and teaching standards. Results for all schools are tabulated into league tables to help parents make an informed choice about schools and to help inspection teams monitor school performance nationwide.

In a study by Brooker et al. (2010), practitioners expressed anxiety about the perceived difficulties of making the transition from a play-based curriculum to the more formalised learning environment of National Curriculum KS1. Teachers felt pressure to get results in phonics screening in Year 1 and in SATs in literacy, mathematics and science at the end of Year 2. KS1 teachers were less likely to be trained in play-based learning and were fearful about abandoning the formal approaches that have worked for them in the past. Tickell recommended that the National Curriculum Review should address this issue to *reinforce the connections* between the foundation stage and KS1 so that the transition can be managed more smoothly. This may herald an opportunity for foundation stage practitioners to exert an upward pressure on their KS1 colleagues so that some of the best and most-appropriated play-based approaches can be extended to five- to seven-year-olds (Orlandi, 2012) – but in reality it seems to have exerted a downward pressure on the foundation stage to introduce more formal tasks in the service of 'school readiness'.

Recent visits to Year 1 and Year 2 classrooms remind me that the passive listening and learning that takes place during 'transmission of information' times can be a trial for many children, particularly boys. The EYFS document foregrounds play, active discussion, hands-on experience and the sharing of emerging understanding rather than just the 'delivery' of information. At KS1, although *play* is still important, it is most often teacher directed, and the demands of the curriculum and the requirement to reach goals squeezes out time for free play and role play that fills so much of the day in nursery and preschool. In addition, the design of school classrooms and the number of children in each class means that free movement is severely restricted, and teacher pupil ratios mostly prevent children from accessing the outdoors during lesson time. In KS1 classrooms playing takes the form of playing on computers, engaging in table-top activities which present educational concepts in playful ways or playing with concepts in group and class discussions – exploring ideas, sharing understanding and debating conflicting evidence. The teacher's role is to provide structure and resources, to answer questions and to provide opportunities for 'sustained, shared thinking', which includes time for 'playful' shared activities with classmates.

Focus on *Key Stage 1 National Curriculum (Year 1 and Year 2)*

Access the most recent version of the National Curriculum for KS1. Look at the areas of learning (section 6).

Plan a series of playful activities suitable for seven-year-olds around the theme of nuts and seeds or wool (or any other topic that appeals to you).

How will you ensure that every area of the curriculum is covered?
How will you ensure that there is a balance between teacher-led and child-led activities?
How might you bring everything together at the end of the project so that everyone shares their learning?

Make a spider diagram showing how each activity connects with each area of the curriculum and which learning goals they address.

It is always exciting to be involved in early childhood education. On a personal level, nothing is more satisfying than seeing a child's delight when he or she masters something new. But it is easy to lose sight of the unique child among the myriad demands to cover the 'learning areas' and to achieve targets. Insights from play-based early learning show us how understanding grows out of creative opportunities to explore and to share ideas with other people in an atmosphere of reciprocal respect and warmth. This approach has implications for learning at every level because adults, as much as children, need to play creatively with new concepts as they struggle for understanding. Even Google and Apple have discovered the advantages of encouraging their workforces to learn through play.

Summary

- *Any child* who enjoys positive relationships in a stimulating, enabling environment will learn and develop.
- The contribution of parents and carers to their child's early development cannot be overstated.
- In a child's earliest years, parenting is a bigger influence on their future than wealth, class, education or any other common social factor.
- The role of the key person in early childhood settings is crucial because every child needs a sensitive, responsive adult who knows them well enough to effectively support their learning and extend their understanding.
- Children who benefit from high-quality nursery education – especially those from disadvantaged backgrounds – are more likely to succeed in primary school.

- Over the past century, early childhood education has assumed more and more importance and has attracted the attention of policymakers and legislators; globally, it is now given very high priority.

- Early years care and education in the United Kingdom has been influenced by ideas and practices from around the world. However, Western practices do not have a monopoly on quality or relevance.

- In England, early education and care is governed by the requirements of the *Statutory Framework for Early Years Foundation Stage* (for newborns to five-year-olds), and the *National Curriculum in England: Key Stages 1 and 2 Framework* (for ages five to seven and seven to 11).

- Play underpins the EYFS. Playing and exploring come first. But the role of teaching in learning has been given more emphasis in the 2014 EYFS curriculum document.

- Stories and make-believe help children to explore themes and to develop logical, sequential thinking.

- Rhythm, rhyme and playing with language are important in developing aural discrimination in preparation for learning to read and write.

- The *Statutory Framework for the Early Years Foundation Stage* focuses on the learning areas of personal, social and emotional development; communication and language; and physical development. Children are assessed at the two-year progress check and again at age five through the Foundation Stage Profile.

- The National Curriculum (KS1) covers the two years of schooling from age five to age seven. Assessment occurs through teacher-administered phonics screening in Year 1 and standardised testing in English language, maths and science in Year 2. Assessments are both individually diagnostic and useful for monitoring whole school progress.

- Research into play offers useful pointers for engaging all learners – children, students and workplace employees – and puts the emphasis on active learning and creative interactions rather than on listening and instruction.

Topics for further discussion

1 Recall your play as a child (where, when, how, what). What did you learn as you played? As an adult, how do you define the difference between work and play? Do you have a good balance between work and play in your life? How does 'play' help you to learn as an adult?

2 Draw up a plan of indoor and outdoor space for your ideal Key Stage 1 (KS1) classroom. What would you include? How much free access would you permit (to the outdoors, to the painting equipment, to the home/cooking corner, to the library, to the toilets and so on)? How would you achieve a balance between child-led and adult-led activities? How does your plan and approach reflect your philosophy of early childhood education?

3 Think about parent–practitioner partnerships. How would you ensure that you involved both fathers and mothers (fathers sometimes feel excluded in early education settings)? How can you make sure that the parent–professional relationship is a genuine partnership? What

difficulties might arise between 'professional' and 'parent'? What strategies might you use to create a level playing field between you?

Assignments

1   Access the OECD (2012) *Quality Matters in Early Childhood Education and Care: United Kingdom* at www.oecd.org/education/school/50165861.pdf. How does the United Kingdom compare with other countries in the OECD? What do we need to do better? What progress has been made since 2012?

2   Try to remember how you learned to read. Write a brief account. Now familiarise yourself with the literacy sections in the current EYFS and the National Curriculum KS1 documents. Are there differences in emphases? Find out about 'learning to read' and the debates around *real books* and *phonics* (the *Rose Report* is a good place to start). Summarise the arguments, and share your findings with your group. Share your knowledge of the reading methods used in local settings and schools. Are there differences in approach?

3   Observe children playing in the sand pit. What are they doing? What are they saying?
Are they wrestling with mathematical concepts of size and volume and speed of flow, or are they pretending to be bulldozer drivers? How could you engage in *shared, sustained thinking* with them? How would you do it? What might be your purpose?
Record what happens when you come alongside and enter into their play. Do any learning opportunities arise? What can you learn from your encounter? Remember, even negative data have a story to tell!

Further reading

Development Matters in the Early Years Foundation Stage (EYFS) (2012) Early Education, The British Association for Early Childhood Education. https://www.early-education.org.uk/development-matters-early-years-foundation-stage-eyfs-download. Accessed 28 December 2016

Contesting Early Childhood, a series edited by Peter Moss and Gunilla Dahlberg

Wood, D. (1998) *How Children Think and Learn* (2nd edn.) Oxford: Blackwell Publishing

Giardello, P. (2013) *Pioneers in Early Childhood Education: the roots and legacies of Rachel and Margaret McMillan, Maria Montessori and Susan Isaacs*. Abingdon: Routledge

Nutbrown, C., Clough, P. and Selbie, P. (2008) *Early Childhood Education: history, philosophy and experience*. London: Sage.

Useful websites

National Evaluation of Sure Start at www.ness.bbk.ac.uk/
Department for Education (DfE) at www.education.gov.uk/
The British Association for Early Childhood Education at www.early-education.org.uk

References

4Children (2015) *What to expect, when? Guidance to your child's learning and development in the early years foundation stage.* http://www.foundationyears.org.uk/files/2015/03/4Children_ParentsGuide_2015_WEB.pdf. Accessed 30 December 2016

Alexander, R. (2008) 'Pedagogy, Curriculum and Culture', in K. Hall, P. Murphy and J. Soler (eds) *Pedagogy and Practice: Culture and Identities* (pp. 3–28). London: Open University/Sage

Allen, G. (2011) *Early intervention: the next steps.* www.gov.uk/government/uploads/system/uploads/attachment_data/file/284086/early-intervention-next-steps2.pdf. Accessed 10 March 2015

Bateson, P. and Martin, P. (2013) *Play, Playfulness, Creativity and Innovation.* Cambridge: Cambridge University Press

Bettelheim, B. (1976) *The Uses of Enchantment: The Meaning and Importance of Fairy Tales.* New York: Knopf

British Association for Early Childhood Education (2012) *Development Matters in the Early Years Foundation Stage.* www.foundationyears.org.uk/files/2012/03/Development-Matters-FINAL-PRINT-AMENDED.pdf. Accessed 28 December 2016

Broadhead, P. and Burt, A. (2012) *Understanding Young Children's Learning Through Play: Building Playful Pedagogies.* London: Routledge

Brooker, L. (2010) 'Learning to play or playing to learn: children's participation in the cultures of home and settings', in L. Brooker and S. Edwards (eds) *Engaging Play.* Maidenhead: Open University Press

Brooker, L., Rogers, S., Ellis, D., Hallet, E. and Robert-Holmes, G. (2010) *Research Report DFE-RR029: Practitioners' experiences of the EYFS.* London: DfE

Brown, F. (2003) *Playwork: Theory and Practice.* Buckingham: Open University Press

Bruner, J. (1996) 'Folk Pedagogy', in *The Culture of Education* (pp. 44–65). Cambridge: Harvard University Press

Burghardt, G.M. (2011) 'Defining and recognising play', in A.D. Pellegrini (ed.) *The Oxford Handbook of the Development of Play.* Oxford: Oxford University Press

Carr, M. (2001) *Learning Stories.* London: Sage

Copple, C. and Bredekamp, S. (2009) *Basics of Developmentally Appropriate Practice in Early Childhood Programs Serving Children from Birth through Age 8.* Washington, DC: National Association for the Education of Young Children (NAEYC)

Dahlberg, G. (2011) 'Policies in Early Education and Care: Potentialities for Agency, Play and Learning', in J. Qvortrup, W.A. Corsaro and M.-S. Honig (eds) *The Palgrave Handbook of Early Childhood Studies.* Basingstoke: Palgrave Macmillan

Dahlberg, G., Moss, P. and Pence, A. (2007) *Beyond Quality in Early Childhood Education and Care: Languages of Evaluation* (2nd edn). Abingdon: Routledge

Development Matters in the Early Years Foundation Stage (EYFS) (2012) Early Education, The British Association for Early Childhood Education. www.early-education.org.uk. Accessed 10 March 2015

DfE, Department for Education (2014) *Statutory Framework for the Early Years Foundation Stage* (EYFS). https://www.gov.uk/government/uploads/system/uploads/attachment_

data/file/335504/EYFS_framework_from_1_September_2014__with_clarification_note.pdf. Accessed 30 December 2016

Friesen, L. (2010) Exploring Animal assisted Programs with children in School and Therapeutic Contexts. *Early Childhood Education Journal* 37(4): 261–287

Furedi F. (2012) Parental Determinism: a most harmful prejudice. www.frankfuredi.com/index.php/site/article/553. Accessed 31 January 2013

Hughes, B. (2012) *Evolutionary Playwork and Reflective Analytic Practice* (2nd edn). London: Routledge

Hutchings, J. (2007) Parenting interventions in Sure Start services for children at risk of developing conduct disorders: pragmatic randomised control trial. *British Medical Journal* 334: 678. www.bmj.com

Hutt, J.F., Tyler, S., Hutt, C. and Christopherson, H. (1988) *Play, Exploration and Learning: A Natural History of the Pre-School.* London: Routledge

Isaacs, S. (1929) *The Nursery Years: Birth to Six Years.* London: Routledge

Leadbeater, C. (2010) *Educational Innovation in the Slums.* www.ted.com/talks/charles_leadbeater_on_education?language=en. Accessed 18 July 2016

Lewis, J. (2011) From Sure Start to children's centres: an analysis of policy change in English early years programmes. *Journal of Social Policy* 40(1): 71–88

Melhuish E.C. (2011) Preschool matters. *Science* 333: 299–300

Moyles, J. (1994) *The Excellence of Play.* Buckingham: Open University Press

NESS (National Evaluation of Sure Start) (2008) *The Impact of Sure Start Local Programmes on Three-year-olds and Their Families*

NESS (National Evaluation of Sure Start) (2010) *The impact of Sure Start Local Programmes on five-year-olds and their families.* November 2010 DFE-RB067

NESS (National Evaluation of Sure Start) (2012) *The Impact of Sure Start Local Programmes on Seven-year olds and their Families* Institute for the Study of Children, Families and Social Issues, Birkbeck, University of London

Nutbrown, C. (2012) *Foundations for Quality: the independent review of early education and childcare qualifications* (Nutbrown Review). https://www.gov.uk/government/publications/nutbrown-review-foundations-for-quality. Accessed 7 March 2013

OECD (2012) *Starting Strong III: A Quality Toolbox for Early Childhood Education and Care.* www.oecd.org/edu/school/startingstrongiii-aqualitytoolboxforearlychildhoodeducation-andcare.htm. Accessed 8 March 2013

Orlandi, K. (2012) *Onwards and Upwards: Supporting the transition to Key Stage One.* Abingdon: Routledge

Paley, V.G. (1990) *The Boy Who Would Be a Helicopter.* Cambridge, MA: Harvard University Press

Parten, M. (1932–1933) Social participation amongst pre-school children. *Journal of Abnormal and Social Psychology* 27: 243–269

Penn, H. (2011) *Quality in Early Childhood Services: An International Perspective.* Maidenhead: McGraw Hill International

Pellegrini, A. (ed.) (2011) *The Oxford Handbook of the Development of Play*. Oxford: Oxford University Press

Schweinhart, L.J., Barnes, H.V., Weikart, D., *Significant Benefits: the High-Scope Perry Preschool Study Through Age 27*. Ypsilanti, MI: High/Scope Press

Schweihart, L.J., Monti, J., Xiang, Z., Barnett, W.S., Belfield, C.R., Nores, M. *Lifetime Effects: the High/Scope Perry Preschool Study Through Age 40*. Ypsilanti, MI: High/Scope Press, 2005

Siraj-Blatchford, I., Sylva, K., Muttock, S., Gilden, R. and Bell, D. (2002) *Researching Effective Pedagogy in the Early Years*. Nottingham: DfES. dera.ioc.ac.uk/4650/1/RR356.pdf

Sylva, K., Melhuish, E., Sammons, P., Siraj-Blatchford, I. and Taggart, B. (eds) (2010) *Early Childhood Matters: Evidence from the Effective Pre-school and Primary Education Project*. London: Routledge

Sylva, K., Melhuish, E.C., Sammons, P., Siraj-Blatchford, I. and Taggart, B. (2004) The Effective Provision of Pre-School Education (EPPE) Project: *Technical Paper 12 – The Final Report: Effective Pre-School Education*. London: DfES/Institute of Education, University of London

Sylva, K., Roy, C. and Painter, M. (1980) *Childwatching at Playgroup and Nursery School*, Vol. 2. Oxford Pre-school Research Project. High/Scope PR

Tickell, C. (2011) *The Early Years: foundations for life, health and learning* (Tickell review). www.educationengland.org.uk/documents/pdfs/2011-tickell-report-eyfs.pdf. Accessed 30 December 2016

UNICEF (2003). A Seven Fold Return on Investment: the Best Start to Life for Every Child. www.unicef.org/early childhood/files/CARD_early-childhoodENG.pdf

Vandell, D.L., Belsky, J., Burchinal, M., Steinberg, L., Vandergrift, N. and NICHD Early Child Care Research Network (2010). Do the Effects of Early Child Care Extend to Age 15 Years? Results from the NICHD Study of Early Child Care and Youth Development. *Child Development* 81: 737–756

Vygotsky, L. (1968) *Thought and Language* (trans. E. Hanfmann and G. Vakor). Cambridge, MA: MIT Press

Vygotsky, L. (1978) 'The Role of Play in Development', in *Mind in Society* (trans. M. Cole) (pp. 92–104). Cambridge, MA: Harvard University Press

Wood, D. (1998) *How Children Think and Learn* (2nd edn). Oxford: Blackwell Publishing

Wood, E. (2010) 'Developing integrated pedagogical approaches to play and learning', in P. Broadhead, J. Howard and E. Wood (eds) *Play and Learning in the Early Years*. London: Sage

CHILDREN IN SOCIETY: EVERY CHILD MATTERS

IV

Early childhood social policy

Introduction

To study social policy is to study the ways in which governments seek to alter conditions for individuals in the interests of society as a whole. At their most benign, social policies provide solutions to the social problems which hinder the full participation of adults and children in the society in which they live. Children's lives are to a great extent influenced by social policy because they and their families are principal recipients of welfare services in education, care, health, justice and housing. Their experiences in these areas will have a major impact on their present and future well-being.

Social policies are always in flux – they are adapted and changed to meet new expectations as society changes, as governments change and as the economic climate changes. Policymakers draw on research evidence to guide their proposals, but they are also influenced by the politics and economics of the day. In democracies, successful and sustainable social policy builds on customs, habits and traditions which resonate with the values of the people, culture and times and are enshrined in law. As nations face increasing globalisation, international law and the principles underpinning it – equality, fairness and human dignity – play an increasingly important role in the formation and implementation of policy.

Beliefs about children's needs and rights have changed radically since the nineteenth century, as have the structure of families and the organisation of society. The purpose of this chapter is to consider how changing social policies shape the lives of young children and families.

In the United Kingdom, powers over health and social services, education, training, housing and local government are devolved to assemblies in Scotland, Wales and Northern Ireland; decisions about taxation and social security are made by the UK government. As you read this chapter, it is worth remembering that local variations exist in the regions and that these may have a significant effect on the way children and families experience welfare reforms in your area.

Defining social policy

Social policies deal with welfare issues in society – education, health, social care, housing, environment and income – and define what the government thinks is the best way of building a just and stable society. It is concerned with the ways in which governments distribute resources (taxes) to keep the economy thriving at the same time as maintaining social control and providing for the most vulnerable (Hill & Irving, 2009). The basic unit of social policy for children is the family, and every government tries to strike a balance between family responsibilities and state obligations when it decides how best to allocate state funds.

Time to reflect

'We should think hard about how far we are willing to see the state interfere in the way we raise our children, otherwise we may find that it starts to meddle where it should not. Most people want to live decent lives. They want to have children who do not get into trouble, who are upright citizens and who will have jobs when they leave education. The state's task is to help people do what they want to do, not mould people into a particular pattern' (Kennedy, 2005: p. 239).

How far do you agree or disagree with the general principle of Helena Kennedy's position here?
How far should parents have rights over their own children?
How far should governments be responsible for children?

Policy literacy

Early childhood practitioners need a certain level of 'policy literacy' in order to deconstruct the issues and principles behind changes in policy and to understand how these might impact on children's lives. Hill and Irving (2009) suggest that when addressing social policy changes, we need to consider some major philosophical themes:

- *morality and social justice* – the extent to which those in power distinguish between 'deserving' and 'undeserving' cases when they make decisions about providing support for those who have fallen on hard times;
- *family obligation* – how far policy enshrines a notion that families are responsible for their own support and welfare and how far the state is responsible;
- *settlement* – how far society has an obligation to citizens through place of birth and family ties;
- *stigma and social control* – how policy is designed to promote harmony or to prevent disharmony and how far individual decisions about lifestyle are 'vilified' as unacceptable in order to maintain the social fabric;
- *work and welfare* – the basic questions about the relationship between work, making a contribution to society and level of wages and taxation, in return for state support in times of hardship;
- *administration and bureaucracy* – decisions about central control and local control in implementing the policies agreed by governments.

When faced with a change in social policy, we need to ask some key questions:

- Who designed the policy changes?
- Whose interests are being served?

■ Who are the intended targets?

■ What is the purpose and intended outcome?

■ What effects might this policy change have on different sectors of society?

■ How might particular groups in society be affected in the long term?

■ What alternatives are available?

■ How might the policy be challenged?

■ How do other countries address the same issues?

In order to assess the likely impact of policy changes on children and services, we need to understand the relationship between the individuals who are the 'subject' of social policy, the institutions set up to implement them and the wider historical, economic and cultural structures in which they exist. Policies may seem fair to one group and unfair to another, or they may fit with a general spirit of the times but be opposed by special-interest groups. For example, the introduction of the free National Health Service was welcomed by those who could not afford healthcare but was opposed by a majority of doctors who feared a loss of autonomy and income; more recently, many people opposed the Adoption Act (which allowed same-sex couples to adopt) because of anxieties about children being 'morally corrupted' by growing up in the households of homosexual parents. In the United Kingdom, free healthcare is now defended by most people, including the medical profession, and same-sex adoptions are accepted. But in many countries there is still opposition to these policies.

How social policy is made in the United Kingdom

The drive for new social policies comes from political pressure, public opinion, lobby groups, media reports, practitioners' opinions, research evidence and academic reviews of practice at home and abroad. Political parties identify the social changes they want to make and outline their intended policy solutions in their manifestos (although they may later abandon them for economic or political reasons).

Once in office, the government draws up a timetable of policy changes. They ask experts for reviews and reports (known as Green Papers) addressing the relevant social policy issues. Civil servants and consultants then draft a document called a White Paper, indicating the government's firmer intentions. Ministers then have to persuade their colleagues that their new proposals are fair, sound and workable. Once accepted by a majority of MPs, lawyers draw up a bill, which then appears in the Queen's Speech at the beginning of a new parliamentary year. The bill is debated and amended, with due regard to EU and international law, in both houses of Parliament (the Commons and the House of Lords) through a series of readings. Once both Houses are satisfied, the bill receives Royal Assent and becomes law through an Act of Parliament.

In the United Kingdom, Parliament and equivalent bodies in Wales, Scotland and Northern Ireland determine the final shape of the Act while the executive branch (ministers and their departments) ensure that Parliament's intentions are conveyed to local authorities. The local authorities then provide information, guidelines, training and advice to practitioners. Regulatory bodies like OFSTED (Office for Standards in Education) or the CQC (Care Quality Commission) check that the government's intentions are being correctly implemented.

Practitioners and researchers implement the guidelines and show that they are following the policies by providing a paper trail of evidence – for example, records of staff training, records of client or pupil outcomes, records of consultation with service users, audits of resources and case studies of good practice. This information then feeds back into the debate and may lead to further reforms. Campbell-Barr (2010) calls this ongoing process the 'research, policy and practice triangle'. She cites as an example, the response of practitioners and researchers in challenging plans to increase the ratio of children per adult in settings outlined in the policy document *More great childcare*. The outcry from the sector forced the government into a U-turn, and ratios remained as before.

It is increasingly common for children to be part of this triangle and to be canvassed for their opinions, either in the early consultation phase or when assessing the impact of policy changes. This is in recognition of their right under the UNCRC article 12 to be consulted on decisions that directly affect them. For example, 3000 children and young people were asked for their views during the consultation phase of *Every Child Matters*, and several young respondents made the point that because the consultation was in writing, many younger children were excluded from the process from the outset. As a result, 62 country-wide focus groups were set up with children aged four to 18 so that they could have their say. Their key message to policymakers was that children should be involved in all decisions that impact on their lives. The focus groups revealed that the consultation document had overlooked several areas that proved to be a major worry for children – their safety on their way to and from school, the lack of security in parks and playgrounds on weekends and the lack of consultation before information was passed on about them to other staff, their parents and other authorities. Some of the respondents suggested that being consulted was not the same as being heard.

Historical shifts in UK social policy

If we are to make sense of what is happening to young children and families today, we need to be aware of the historical origins and development of social policy. In the past, governments generally confined themselves to spending the taxes they collected on matters of defence and trade; the idea that the state should intervene in family matters has always been viewed with suspicion. This tension between public and private responsibility for children can be traced back to the earliest Elizabethan Poor Law (1601) and is ever present in decisions about how far the state should intervene in the way families choose to live (Baldock, 2011).

For example, there was resistance from parents and from employers to the nineteenth-century Factory Acts, which sought to limit the working hours of child labourers. Similarly, there was opposition to the Education Acts, which made universal education for five- to 11-year-olds compulsory because older children were often required to look after younger ones while parents worked or were required as seasonal labourers in rural areas. Various Children Acts from the earliest *Prevention of Cruelty to, and Better Protection of, Children Act* (1899) have met with criticism because many parents felt that they represented an unwarranted intrusion into family life and the right for parents to discipline their own children in the way they thought fit.

The Children Act of 1948, which placed a duty on local authorities to care for orphans and for children at risk of harm at the hands of their parents, was carefully worded so as not to give the impression that the policy interfered with or undermined the sacrosanct power of parents over their own children. Most recently, there have been debates about the Children Act (1989), which made children's needs *paramount* in cases where abuse is suspected and extended local authority powers to remove children from families even in the face of opposition from their parents. The Act allowed for children to be consulted themselves and to have a say in any decisions made about their futures. The Act was updated in the wake of the death of Victoria Climbié, the inquiry which followed (Laming Report: DoH, 2003) and the subsequent publication of the policy document *Every Child Matters*. This led to the Children Act (2004), which extended safeguarding obligations to education, health and social care practitioners by requiring them to share information about children they believed to be at risk of family ill-treatment. Again, there were objections about how far the authorities should be allowed to go in interfering with families and particular concerns were voiced about the confidentiality issues around sharing information between services.

Case study: Rights and responsibilities in family and state

Figure 11.1 Parents in the UK are urged, but not compelled, to vaccinate their children.
Source: BANANASTOCK

In France and the United States, children can attend school only on production of a valid vaccination certificate, but in the United Kingdom, this is not the case. The primary aim of vaccination is to protect the individual from disease. The secondary aim is to provide 'herd immunity' – the more people who are vaccinated, the fewer sites of new infection and the less likelihood of an epidemic.

Parents in the United Kingdom are urged, but not compelled, to vaccinate their children. Health professionals base their advice to vaccinate on large population studies that show the benefits of herd immunity. But parents base their refusal to take up the vaccination on their perception of individual risk; they worry about an adverse reaction in their own child. Since 1998, UK parents have exercised their individual right to refuse vaccination for their children in the light of (now discredited) research by Andrew Wakefield that the triple MMR vaccine (measles, mumps, rubella) was linked to autism.

Measles is dangerous for children; rubella is dangerous for pregnant women; mumps can cause sterility in men. Recent outbreaks of all three diseases have caused alarm among health officials because the rate of vaccination in the United Kingdom has fallen below the level necessary for herd immunity. Health workers have renewed their efforts to persuade parents to get their children vaccinated in order to avoid an epidemic of what can be a life-threatening disease for children, a health hazard for unborn babies and a painful and life-changing condition for men.

Various factors persuade parents to distrust the 'paternalistic' approach of health officials and the government – the fact that medical practitioners are paid extra for meeting targets for high levels of vaccination, a general mistrust of 'science' and 'experts' in the wake of various medical scandals involving children and a generalised unease about living in a 'risk society' where hazards seem to proliferate.

Discussion questions

How confident are you in the case made for MMR vaccination?
Should MMR vaccination be made a compulsory condition of attending preschool and school?

There is always a debate about how far government should take responsibility for the welfare of citizens and how far citizens should be held responsible for their own welfare. In high tax countries, like the Nordic countries of Europe, state support for families tends to be higher than in lower tax countries like the United Kingdom and the United States. Where income tax is high, governments argue that social welfare is a societal obligation and that the state has a responsibility to provide universal support for all families. Where income tax is kept low, governments argue that when people keep more of their income, they can make their own choices about how to spend on their own welfare and that any government spending should be targeted only at vulnerable families in extremis.

This polarity between *targeted* support for the most vulnerable and *universal* support for all families sets up a tension in the delivery of welfare. In the contemporary United Kingdom, all families receive some universal support such as child benefit payments, free maternity and birth services, 15 hours of free early years education and care for preschool children, free schooling for children aged five to 18, and free health, dental and welfare services. But any further funding is progressively targeted towards families with special needs, so that by the time children reach school, only vulnerable families will be receiving extra direct funding to cover things like free 'wrap-around' childcare (i.e. before and after school care), free school meals, tax credits, housing benefits or extra payments for children with special needs.

Social policy before the welfare state

Before the nineteenth century, social welfare was traditionally left to church and charity and was not regarded as a responsibility of the state. But throughout the nineteenth century, reformers agitated for better working conditions, better housing, better health and better education, and successive governments passed reforming legislation to improve conditions for families. In particular, they addressed the needs of children: for example, Factory Acts (from 1802–1901) gradually improved health and safety for child labourers and reduced the number of hours they could work. Similarly, Education Acts (1870–1891) legislated for free elementary (primary) education for all children between the ages of five and 11. In addition, there were concerns about the treatment and exploitation of children by parents and others such that in 1899 the government introduced a law to protect children through *The Prevention of Cruelty to, and Better Protection of, Children Act*. Some adults at the time regarded these reforms as an unwelcome intrusion into family life and complained that parents' rights over their children were being eroded and that the restrictions on child labour were driving poor families deeper into poverty (Baldock, 2011).

Health and education were twin concerns for the United Kingdom in an age of Empire. For much of the nineteenth century, *public health* was the focus of government attention, and government investment in sanitation and clean water supplies had a major impact on the nation's health overall. For individuals suffering acute illness, only Poor Law infirmaries and workhouses were available, and most people regarded a stay in those as a fate worse than death. Family health issues were brought to a head when recruitment drives for men to fight in the Anglo-Boer Wars (1899–1902) in South Africa revealed shocking levels of poor health among British volunteers when it was discovered that as many as one in three was stunted, under-nourished or ill (Hill & Irving, 2009). This, together with fears about the quality of British 'breeding stock', provided the impetus for governments to urgently examine the state of children's health across the nation. In 1904 a report from the Interdepartmental Committee on Physical Deterioration urged the government to establish a school medical service and to provide school meals for the poorest children; a few years later, amid accusations of meddling in the private lives of families, the government passed the Children Act (1908), which made the parental neglect of children's health punishable by law. But medicine, doctors and hospitals cost money, and although from 1911 employed men were covered under a National Health Insurance scheme for sickness and medical treatment, there was no such provision for women and children.

After the First World War (1914–18) the health of families declined alarmingly as widows were left to bring up children without the support of a breadwinner and infant mortality, malnutrition, anaemia and rickets among children increased. Mortality rates among the poorest families were much higher than those of wealthier families (Cunningham, 2006). Part of the problem was poor housing – during the Industrial Revolution, many people moved from the countryside into cities, and during the nineteenth century, private landlords built huge numbers of dwellings for rent. These were mostly poorly constructed, unsanitary and overcrowded with many families able to afford to rent only a single room (Alcock, 2014). Initiatives like the Garden City movement inspired the 1909 Housing and Town Planning Act to provide better quality housing and more pleasant environments; and later, during the First World War, the pressures of working class rent strikes led government to introduce rent controls to curb the greed of landlords. After the war, there was a worsening housing crisis, and a new Housing and Town Planning Act (1919) ushered in an era of publicly owned housing to provide 'homes fit for heroes' returning from the trenches. Besides building millions of homes, there was a concerted effort to clear the worst of the slums and replace them with terraces and tenements where families could live in dignity. By 1939 the state had accepted responsibility for housing and many people were living in local authority housing or in subsidised, privately built, owner-occupied homes.

Child poverty in low-paid or unemployed families remained stubbornly resistant to change over the nineteenth century and the early twentieth century. Novels by Dickens, Mrs Gaskell and Kingsley lodged images of starving children roaming the streets, prey to corruption and crime, into the minds of readers. Gradually the cold charity of the old Poor Laws with their stigma of idle fecklessness were replaced by insurance-based protection for the unemployed, sick and elderly. But it was limited to the working poor, and assistance for the destitute still came via Poor Law channels re-named Public Assistance. By the 1930s there was some relief available, but it was seen as undignified and undesirable to be dependent on it.

Although many children received some sort of schooling during the nineteenth century, elementary education was made compulsory in a series of Education Acts from 1870 onwards for children aged between five and eleven. Reading, writing, arithmetic and religious instruction were provided so as to ensure a steady stream of literate, numerate and morally upright workers to service the Empire. However, nothing was provided for younger children, and those with working parents were cared for in a variety of ways – by older siblings or relatives, in elementary schools alongside their siblings or by more or less suitable paid minders. There were various scandals associated with unsafe and unsanitary 'baby farms', where large numbers of children were supervised and where they were at risk of injury and disease. The plight of poor infants and toddlers who needed care while parents worked led to a growing agitation for better nursery care. Pioneers like the McMillan sisters (Rachel and Margaret) exposed the poor physical and mental development of mothers and infants in inner cities and set up exemplary outdoor camps and nurseries to provide good-quality food, washing facilities, play spaces and a little learning to give them a better start in life. In 1933 Susan Isaacs wrote a report (*Report of the Consultative Committee on Infant and Nursery Schools*) for the Haddow Committee on the importance of nursery education for the physical, social, intellectual and emotional development of children (Parker-Rees & Willan, 2006). In it she described the provision made for young children in other countries where nursery education was more advanced, and she advised that children under age five in the United Kingdom needed similar care and education (ideally free for them and funded by the state) to make the most of their lives. In 1937 she wrote the pamphlet *The Educational Value of the Nursery School*, which was to have a significant impact on nursery provision in the future.

The welfare state

The poor state of the nation's children once again became starkly apparent to the authorities when large numbers were evacuated from the city slums to the countryside to escape the bombs during the Second World War (1939–45). In 1942 social reformer William Beveridge produced a 'Report on Social Insurance and Allied Services', commonly known as the Beveridge Report. This hugely influential report, together with his report 'Full Employment in a Free Society' (1944), laid the foundations for the welfare state in the post-war United Kingdom. It outlined ways in which the government could tackle the five 'giant evils': want, disease, ignorance, squalor and idleness. Reforms were introduced in the post-war period to combat these 'giant evils':

- The National Health Service (NHS) to fight disease
- full employment to combat idleness
- state education up to age 15 to combat ignorance
- public housing to eliminate squalor
- social benefits payments (National Insurance and Assistance, Family Allowance) to combat want.

The idea that the state should be ultimately responsible for its citizens and should control economic factors to ensure their welfare was a radical left position advocated by Fabians like Beatrice and Sidney Webb (who set up the London School of Economics and later its Department of Social Science and Administration) and liberal economists like Maynard Keynes; this position was vigorously disputed by those on the right who believed in individual responsibility, free markets and the ideas of the capitalist economist Adam Smith (who wrote *An Enquiry into the Nature and Causes of the Wealth of Nations* in 1776). The election of a post-war Labour government in 1945 – under Prime Minister Clement Atlee, close associate of the socialist Fabians, Keynes and the Webbs – marked a watershed in the development of British social policy. Atlee committed the new government to implementing Beveridge's vision and funding welfare support out of general taxation, an unprecedented decision, which still reverberates in the way governments allocate tax revenues today (Alcock, 2014).

Support for mothers and children underpinned Beveridge's vision (sometimes called the Keynes/Beveridge Welfare State) for a more generous post-war society – a society in which individual hard work, thrift and full employment would be supported by a compassionate state in times of hardship. Beveridge argued that a *universal* welfare system, paid for through social taxation, was the best way to ensure the health and wealth of the nation. His reports paved the way for Atlee's post-war Labour government to introduce free maternity care, a free National Health system, free secondary education for all children aged up to 15, a council house building programme for affordable homes, sickness and unemployment benefits, comprehensive social services for families in difficulty and means-tested social security benefits for families in financial need.

Beveridge's underlying conviction that every person in the land should be employed, decently housed, well educated and cared for in sickness and in health made the post-war United Kingdom a more equal and fairer society than ever before. The influence of the voluntary sector (church and charity) diminished, and the state took over their functions to provide a comprehensive welfare system for all. However, private medicine, private maternity care, private education and favourable subsidies for home owners meant that wealthier citizens could opt out of the system and buy more privileged services for themselves. Despite the welfare state, many children in the 1950s and 1960s still lived in poor accommodations, in insalubrious neighbourhoods where schools were poor and health services overburdened, and although provision for babies and school age children improved dramatically, there was still little attention paid to the needs of the majority of preschool children.

Market forces: social policy 1979–97

In 1979, Margaret Thatcher led a Conservative government into office. Free market ideas were in the ascendancy. The welfare state was expensive and required high levels of taxation to pay for it; critics argued that high taxes reduced the money available for business investment and made the United Kingdom poorer by squeezing the jobs market and putting more people on unemployment benefits. They also argued that free welfare services only encouraged the feckless to become dependent on the state and to take no responsibility for their own protection or financial security and that a state monopoly on the provision of services led to increasing expense for governments because there was no competition to keep costs down. In the late 1970s, there were fears that these views would lead to a dismantling of the welfare system, but in fact the broad consensus across all political parties that welfare services were a mark of a humane society held and throughout the Conservative years under Margaret Thatcher comprehensive public support for health, education, social security and social services remained intact (Alcock, 2014).

Housing and education were the twin prongs of Conservative reforms. In an effort to encourage people to take responsibility for themselves, the Conservative government abolished rent controls to encourage more house building and introduced a plan to allow those who could afford it to buy their rented council properties at favourable discounts; unfortunately, as economic circumstances changed, many people found themselves with mortgage arrears during the 1990s; repossessions reached over 75,000 per year; and many families found themselves homeless and hopelessly in debt (Alcock, 2014). Alongside the sale of council houses, housing associations were given grants to provide homes for the poorest, and gradually they took over the supply of most social housing. In the poorest areas, council houses remained in Local Authority control, but without investment, they soon became run-down, and many of the poorest children lived on 'sink estates' where unemployment and social problems made life difficult.

From 1979 to 1997, the number of children living in poverty in the United Kingdom tripled, and it was estimated that one child in three was affected, the highest proportion in any European country (Bradbury & Jantti, 1999). Social assistance payments rose inexorably – from 4 million claimants in the 1970s to 8 million in the 1980s and 10 million in the 1990s, with many families receiving means-tested income support, family credit and housing benefits, either because they were on low income or because they had particular needs such as disability. As state support grew, some critics argued that it encouraged people to make fraudulent claims, and others argued that state support contributed to a poverty trap and provided a perverse incentive to remain unemployed or on low wages because extra earnings brought a reduction in benefits (Alcock, 2014). Between 1979 and 1990, the continuing changes in family life (more women in the workforce, rising divorce rates, the proliferation of reconstituted families, increasing numbers of single-parent families, increasing numbers of workless households) led to increasing expenditure on welfare support and a rise in the numbers of children being cared for in Local Authority homes and foster families.

Education was also in need of reform as old industries like mining and manufacturing declined and technological innovations grew. The government was determined to improve education for the majority so that a highly skilled workforce would be in place to take advantage of the growing demands in new industries. In 1988 the government introduced a National Curriculum and then Standard Attainment Tests to measure the quality of teaching and the progress of primary school pupils. This was overseen by an inspection service (OFSTED) tasked with measuring and improving standards in schools (see Chapter 10). However, less attention was given to preschool children – they continued to be cared for in an ad hoc fashion by childminders and by private, public and voluntary organisations under the general surveillance of Social Service departments. But the clamour for preschool care was growing. In the post-war expansion of universities, women had taken up higher education and professional careers, but once they became mothers, they were often forced to swap careers for childcare. The voluntary system of childcare mushroomed (it was accompanied by a cacophony of disapproving voices (Friedan, 1982) on both sides of the Atlantic, protesting that 'feminists' were abandoning their children in pursuit of careers and money.

Healthcare and social workers became concerned that large numbers of children were being cared for in dangerous, insanitary premises under the care of unqualified people. In addition, various scandals where parental neglect and abuse led to the deaths of children (notably Maria Colwell in 1973 and Jasmine Beckford in 1984) prompted the development of a new Children Act (1989) to strengthen the authorities' powers to intervene in families where children were at risk of harm or neglect (Piper, 2008). The Act removed parents' 'rights over' their children and instead charged parents with 'responsibility to' them and made the child's needs 'paramount' over and above the parents' wishes in cases where the child was at risk of harm. Although social workers were encouraged to do everything possible to keep children in their families, the Act bestowed new powers to intervene in families so that children could be removed for their own safety if necessary. This marked a major shift in the intervention of the state into family life.

Academics and politicians, keen to raise educational standards and the physical and mental health of the next generation, called for quality (and standardisation) in early years provision. Teachers implementing the National Curriculum reported poor 'readiness' among children starting school, and there was growing pressure for childcare and education for preschoolers; schools set up their own preschools, and there was downward pressure on other preschool settings to better prepare children for formal education. In 1990 the Rumbold Report *Starting with Quality* outlined ways of improving care and education for three- to five-year-olds. Six years later, in 1996, the *Desirable Outcomes for Children's Learning on Entering Compulsory Education* outlined the Early Learning Goals (ELG) that children should reach before entering school. This marked a changing emphasis from care to education for children aged three to five. There was a brief attempt at increasing the supply of nursery education when parents were offered childcare vouchers to stimulate growth in the sector, but a growing economic crisis and rising male unemployment pushed the issue out of sight, and reforms stalled (Baldock, 2011).

The Third Way: social policy 1997–2010

In 1997 a 'New Labour' government came into power with Tony Blair as prime minister and Gordon Brown as chancellor of the exchequer. They promised to eliminate child poverty by 2020 and committed to finding a different way of providing welfare – somewhere between the right-wing pro-market approach and the left-wing state monopoly approach. They called their reforms the Third Way. They recognised that there was not a one-size-fits-all solution to welfare and that there was room to strengthen voluntary, private and state provision to meet the needs of different families. Reforms in health, education and social care were based on 'what works' rather than a particular economic ideology. The *National Childcare Strategy* (DfEE, 1998) outlined a plan for integrating children's services by encouraging settings to 'combine nursery education, family support, employment advice, childcare and health services on one site' (DfEE, 1998: p. 7). In addition, the intention was to introduce nursery grants, to reform regulation of providers and to improve the quality and diversity of the workforce (Baldock, 2011).

Figure 11.2 The 1997 'New Labour' government, led by Tony Blair, promised to eliminate child poverty by 2020 and committed to reforming the provision of welfare.
Source: Müller/MSC

The following were New Labour's key themes for welfare reform:

- a shift away from state provision to more personal responsibility;
- a focus on mixed public, private and voluntary-sector provision;
- a system of audits and inspections to ensure that basic standards were being met;
- an emphasis on choice so that service users could choose services according to need;
- a commitment to 'joined-up services' to reduce inefficiencies.

Early years care and education

New Labour put good-quality childcare and education for preschool children at the heart of their reforms. They abolished the voucher scheme and funded an expansion of 'educare' (education and care) for all four-year-olds and later extended this to three-year-olds. They produced a *National Childcare Strategy* (DfEE, 1998), which emphasised the need for multi-professional cooperation through Neighbourhood Nurseries, Early Excellence Centres and Sure Start Children's Centres where children and parents could get education, healthcare and social support. Providing more childcare had two aims – it would give parents the freedom to take up paid work to get their families out of poverty and it would give preschool children a head start in educational and social skills. This drive for an integrated approach to childcare was given a further impetus in the Child Care Act 2006, which encouraged authorities to listen to local parents' voices and to provide suitable one-stop facilities where parents could access the childcare services they needed.

The government transferred responsibility for early years from social service departments (who were mostly concerned with health and safeguarding issues) to the Department of Education, thereby emphasising 'education' over 'care'. Drawing on the Rumbold Report, they introduced the *Curriculum Guidance for the Foundation Stage* (QCA/DfEE, 2000) which became the *Early Years Foundation Stage* (DfES, 2007, updated 2012, 2014). Funding was provided for 15 hours of free educational care for all three- to five-year-olds. Extra funding was linked to a 'welfare to work' strategy aimed at persuading parents (particularly single mothers on benefits or in low-income households) to take up employment.

In disadvantaged areas, generously funded local Sure Start centres were set up to provide high-quality health, education and social care for young children, together with advice for their parents about child development, housing, social support benefits and employment opportunities. An *Extended Schools Initiative* (DfES, 2002) proposed the expansion of before- and after-school care on school premises to offer more childcare for working parents. The intention was to reduce child poverty by supporting parents with funding targeted at those 'marginal' families most in need of support (Eisenstadt, 2012).

Focus on *The benefits of nursery education and care*

An independent study from Lancaster University followed 15,500 children from the millennium cohort (children born in 1990) and compared test and exam results of children who did and did not attend nursery. The study showed that children from poorer homes who attended nursery benefited significantly, achieving better results in their National Curriculum tests at age 11 and in their GCSEs at age 16 than those of similar children who did not attend nursery. The report suggests that nursery education makes little difference for 'middle-class children' but is significantly beneficial for 'poorer children'.

(*The Impact of Pre-school on Adolescents' Outcomes: Evidence from a Recent English Cohort* by Patricia Apps, Silvia Mendolia, Ian Walker (October 2012) Discussion Paper No. 6971, October 2012 at http:// www.iza.org)

Another study from the National Institute of Child and Human Development in the United States followed 1200 children. They found that children who spent *long hours* in good-quality day care did indeed show improved cognitive/linguistic abilities, but they also found that long hours in day care were detrimental to socio-emotional behaviour and that many children showed high levels of stress and aggression. They concluded that *limited time* in day care had positive gains for children but that extended hours of day care could be damaging. They argued that government social policy should aim to expand rights to parental leave and support parents of young children through the tax system to spend more time at home.

(Belsky, J. (2006) Early child care and early child development: Major findings of the NICHD Study of Early Child Care. *European Journal of Developmental Psychology* 3: 95–110)

What questions do these conflicting pieces of research pose for makers of social policy?

Do you think 'wrap-around care' is a good solution for the children of working parents, or would it be better for parents to receive funding to support part-time work so that they can spend more time with their children?

Should funds be targeted at providing more free early childhood care and education for 'disadvantaged' children, or should all children have a right to free full-time preschool care?

Although safeguarding had been an important part of early years remit under the guidance of Social Services, the death of Victoria Climbié in 2000 focused minds on the neglect and abuse of children in their own homes. Lord Laming's report (2003) showed that although police, teachers and social workers had visited her, a lack of communication between them had contributed to her death. The Laming report set in motion New Labour's *Every Child Matters* (ECM) agenda (DfES, 2003), which set out the ways in which joined-up children's services could cooperate and share information about 'at-risk' children. The ECM document fed into the Children Act (2004), which put a duty on all professionals in education, social services, justice and health to share information about children. Some parents and professionals opposed the document, fearing that it would compromise a family's right to confidentiality. Sadly, the death of 17-month-old Peter Connelly in 2007 showed that it was more difficult to share information across agencies than had been envisaged; as a result, the Common Assessment Framework (CAF) was drawn up to provide a common language and a standardised form for multi-agency professionals across social care, health and education to identify vulnerable children and to make it easier to act more quickly. The National Society for the Prevention of Cruelty to Children (NSPCC) reports that around 70 children still die each year at the hands of those who care for them. Since 2007, efforts to prevent a repeat of Baby Peter's death have resulted in a yearly increase in the number of children placed on child safeguarding registers (DfE, 2015).

Joined-up services

In 2004 the government published *Choice for parents: the best start for children – a ten year childcare strategy* (HM Treasury, 2004), which encouraged providers to set up more nurseries. In 2007, they published *Every Parent Matters* (DfES, 2007) to bring together education, health and social services childcare training, childcare information for parents, support systems for teenage parents and counselling services for parents in abusive relationships. Trained Parent Support Advisers were established in schools, and Family Nurse Partnerships provided one-to-one support for parents experiencing difficulties (Crowley, 2012). A further document, the *Healthy Child Programme: pregnancy and the first five years of life* (DoH, 2009) emphasised a renewed focus on mothers' and children's health in the first years.

In 2010 compelling evidence from the EPPE studies showed that high-quality staff and intensive educational provision could improve educational outcomes for disadvantaged children (Sylva et al., 2010), and this led to calls for better training for the workforce and special leadership qualifications for managers in preschool settings (Nutbrown, 2012).

The verdict on New Labour's early childhood policies

An OECD (2011) report, *Doing Better for Families*, confirmed that child poverty in the United Kingdom, under New Labour, had fallen faster than in any other OECD country. In addition, the quality and quantity of early childhood provision had improved immeasurably. But some critics believed that the government had been too interventionist – they argued that the reforms had put us in danger of *micro-managing* childhood because the insistence on measurements, targets and outcomes put undue emphasis on developmental norms with the result that children felt under pressure to perform and felt like failures when their performance was called into question (Moss, 2009).

In 2008, global financial difficulties forced a recession, and as the economy shrank in the United Kingdom, it became clear that with rising unemployment, a growing elderly population and smaller tax revenues, public expenditure on social welfare would need rethinking. This was bound to affect early childhood provision.

The Big Society: social policy 2010–2015

In 2010 a coalition government between Conservative and Liberal Democrats, led by David Cameron, took office. There was an early emphasis on the idea of the Big Society, where charities, voluntary organisations and private providers were encouraged to take over some of the services previously administered by the state. The underpinning belief was that these organisations were more nimble than government in responding to specific local needs. However, the new government promised to keep the Labour pledge to eliminate child poverty by 2020. It also followed up on the *Nutbrown Review* (2012) by publishing *More great childcare: Raising quality and giving parents more choice* (DfE, 2013), which outlined steps to increase childcare for women who want to work and to improve the quality of the early years workforce.

The case for targeting health, social care and education funding on early years as a way of improving outcomes for the most disadvantaged was made in five key independent reviews (Field, 2010; Marmot, 2010; Tickell, 2011; Allen, 2011; Munro, 2011), which were welcomed by the government. The reports pressed the government to concentrate their efforts on providing extra support for the youngest and most disadvantaged children and families, who are most vulnerable to the long-term effects of deprivation (Hevey & Miller, 2012). Unfortunately, continuing economic difficulties forced the coalition government to admit that the child poverty target would be missed for the foreseeable future.

They set out their own plans to address child poverty in the *Child Poverty Strategy for 2014–2017*. Their welfare reforms were all designed to cut state expenditure. They identified the root causes of child poverty as unemployment, low earnings and educational failure and argued that the best way to combat all three was to discourage a 'dependency' culture by reducing state support and returning welfare responsibility to individual families. However, critics argue that lack of employment, under-employment and particularly young adult unemployment are serious *endemic* problems that disproportionately affect young families in both the short-term and the long term (Parekh et al., 2010). Others point out that the government had adopted a simple rhetoric of dividing people into 'shirkers and workers', which was unfair and disparaging because many people receiving benefits, such as child tax credits and income support, are actually working multiple jobs on minimum wages, trying their best to provide for their families. In fact, it is families with children (who necessarily rely most on the state) who have suffered the greatest reduction in household income as a result of welfare changes (Hirsch, 2013). Welfare cuts hit vulnerable families hardest – the BMA reports that more young children die in the United Kingdom than in any other European country, and record numbers are taken into care (BMA, 2013); in addition, the cuts to housing benefit forced large numbers of children into temporary accommodations, where they suffered very high levels of stress and deprivation (Housing Statistical Release, 2014: www.gov.uk).

Case study: Welfare reforms and individual consequences

Titina Nzolameso, a divorced, single mother of five children aged between two and ten years lived in council property in Westminster, London. In 2013 the government introduced a £500 weekly benefits cap to encourage claimants back into work. This meant that the rent on the family flat became unaffordable. She was offered a relocation to Milton Keynes, 50 miles away. She refused on the grounds that her children were settled in their London schools and that she relied heavily on her network of friends for support. Westminster Council decreed that by refusing, she had made herself intentionally homeless. She appealed but was overruled. Her children were taken into care, and she was housed in a hostel for the homeless. In 2015 the Supreme Court quashed the local authority decision, arguing that it had not properly discharged its duty to secure accommodation for its tenant. The council argued that in order to accommodate the family, they would have to ignore more deserving families on the waiting list who had a more pressing need to stay in the area because of employment (*The Independent*, 20 March 2015).

Why was the change in benefits policy introduced?

What was the intended outcome? What are the unintended consequences?

What is the dilemma for the council?

What long-term effects can you envisage for the children?

Do you think it is reasonable for councils to move families out when they have no employment ties to the area? What else could have been done?

Critics argue that the government's cap on benefits means in effect that council authorities are being forced into *social cleansing* by moving the poorest out of high-rent areas. Is this a fair criticism? How do other countries deal with issues like these?

Some of the coalition government's social policy reform proposals – such as the establishment of privately run 'free schools', changes to childcare ratios, allocating SEN budgets to families rather than to schools, the closure of Children's Centres, the possibility of funding grandparents to provide childcare, private agencies for childminder 'chains', an increased interest in 'apprenticeship' models of work-based training for EYFS teachers and practitioners, proposals to limit funding to only the most 'difficult' families – suggested that the focus on the welfare of preschoolers was wavering (Baldock, 2011).

Time to reflect

The *Children and Families Act* (2014) sets out new arrangements for adoption, children in care, children with special educational needs, parental leave, ante-natal care and flexible hours for working parents.

The Act removes the explicit requirement for social workers and adoption agencies to consider a child's ethnic and religious background when placing them for adoption. Are there risks associated with this?

The Act allows for a 'personal budget' for parents of children with special needs. How might this work in practice? What are the funding implications for schools and settings?

The Act makes provision for employers to offer more flexible working conditions for parents with childcare responsibilities. Think about a workplace you know. How might a request for flexible working be construed?

Do you think the Act is child centred or parent centred?

Welfare under the Conservative government 2015

In 2015 the Conservatives formed the governing party in the United Kingdom. They made a commitment in their manifesto to increase the number of hours of free childcare and education from 15 to 30 hours per week, but these have not yet materialised, and we are told not to expect them until 2017. The main thrust of their policies so far seems to be to roll back state interventions, to reduce public expenditure and to offer carrots and sticks to encourage individuals to take care of their own welfare (regardless of their circumstances). To this end, the government has raised the minimum wage, offered incentives for home-ownership, raised the personal tax allowance and planned a Universal Credit to allow people receiving benefits to make their own budget decisions. Cost-cutting measures designed to take pressure off public finances were a key priority, however, and various measures like cutting benefits, limiting child tax credits to the first two children, and introducing a bedroom tax/spare-room subsidy have been put in place. A report *Losing in the long run* (Action for Children, 2016) suggests that since 2010, central government funding of early support services for families has been cut dramatically. The authors believe that the cuts have contributed to a rising number of children being taken into care or pushed into poverty and that this will, in the long run, cost more for the state and the individual in terms of school exclusion, child protection, mental health and crime.

A work in progress

Social policy is of course always a work in progress. The central questions remain the same, but economic crises, both global and domestic, can upset the best laid plans of any government. The following are some of the questions that social policy has to address for every generation:

- How can we best deliver support for children and families in the face of competing claims for funds?
- How can we best balance the obligations of state and family?
- How can we weigh up long-term benefits against short-term costs?
- How far should we improve conditions for all families, and how far should we focus our efforts on the poorest?

Although children's lives, especially poor children's lives, have improved immeasurably since the nineteenth century, we are still a long way from being a child-centred society. In the United Kingdom, the most disadvantaged children still suffer in comparison to their more fortunate peers on every measure from infant mortality to school performance and job prospects. One problem may be that poor and socially excluded children remain invisible to most of our policymakers. Alcock (2014) points out that in the United Kingdom, the people who make the policies (the politicians and their civil servants) come from a narrow spectrum of society; they tend to be socially unrepresentative in terms of gender, ethnicity, disability, schooling and income. Their collective lack of knowledge about the challenges faced by ordinary families necessarily colours their judgement when they make decisions on behalf of the majority of children.

As Helena Kennedy (2005) points out, people do not behave better, or look after their children better, if they are made poorer. Or, as Nelson Mandela said, 'We must move children to the centre of the world's agenda. We must re-write strategies to reduce poverty so that investments in children are given priority' (2002).

Summary

- Social policy is concerned with the ways in which governments distribute resources (taxes) in response to a perceived need; it is, ideally, concerned with improving human welfare.
- Beliefs about children's needs and rights have changed radically since the nineteenth century alongside changes in the structure of families and the organisation of society; social policies reflect those changes.
- Since Victorian times, there has been a gradual improvement in health, education and welfare provision for children. In the first half of the twentieth century, there was some nursery provision for deprived children.
- The welfare state was set up after the Second World War to fight the five 'giant evils'. It was particularly concerned with supporting mothers, infants and children. It made provision for children's departments, a national health service, secondary education and a social insurance system for those in sickness and unemployment.
- Pressure for early education and care came from working women and feminists. In the 1960s and 1970s, childcare was provided by private or voluntary organisations and regulated by Social Service departments.
- During the Thatcher years, concerns about 'school readiness' drove an agenda for nursery provision and an increasing interest in early preschool education. Under New Labour, early education and care was transferred from Social Services to the Department of Education.

- New Labour made eradicating child poverty by 2020 a central target. They concentrated efforts on early education and care. They set up Sure Start centres in disadvantaged areas to provide multidisciplinary support for parenting, child health, education, housing, employment, social services and income issues.
- Local Sure Start centres were replaced by a national system of Children's Centres in deprived areas to provide more standardised support for disadvantaged children. Evidence shows that early childhood support is particularly beneficial for children in disadvantaged households.
- The coalition government sought to dismantle a centralised 'one-size-fits-all' service for children. Policymakers focused on rebalancing the partnership between families and the state to make individuals responsible for their own life choices.
- The Conservative government has focused on reducing the welfare budget and increasing employment to try to break the cycle of 'dependency on the state'.
- When social welfare expenditure is reduced, those in the most disadvantaged households, whether in work or out of work, get poorer. This has long-term effects on health, welfare and educational outcomes for children.
- The future for family welfare support is uncertain, and there are fears that child poverty is growing as the welfare state is reformed.

Topics for further discussion

1 Discuss the competing cases for universal versus targeted early provision for young children and their parents in the United Kingdom. What are the social implications for targeting one group of children for special investment? Who decides which groups fulfil the criteria of disadvantage?
2 The Victorians categorised the poor as 'deserving' or 'undeserving'. How does current political rhetoric categorise the poor? How might children be affected by these categories? Do you think our society is becoming more, or less, supportive of families who fall on hard times?
3 Parenting involves responsibilities and life-long commitment. Inadequate parenting has long-term adverse effects on children and society. How can we identify struggling parents? Should we intervene? What prevents us from intervening?

Assignments

1 In the United Kingdom, preschool care comes in all sorts of varieties. Look up the information held on local provision by your nearest Children's Centre. Do you think the variety of childcare on offer is a strength or weakness? How much does cost influence parents' choice of provision? How is provision in your area reflective of social diversity and integration?
2 Find out about CAFCASS (Children and Family Court Advisory and Support Service), which deals with the adoption, care and custody of children. Whose needs are given priority – child, parent or society?
3 Consider a topical family welfare issue. Find out which current social policies address the issue. What solutions are proposed in the policies? What do you think the outcomes will be for families?

Further reading

Piper, C. (2008) *Investing in Children: Policy, law and practice in context*. Cullompton: Willan Publishing

Miller, L. and Hevey, D. (eds) (2012) *Policy Issues in the Early Years*. London: Sage

Baldock, P. (2011) *Developing Early Childhood Services: Past, Present and Future*. Maidenhead: Open University Press/McGraw Hill

Social Policy and Society is an important journal for discussing the tensions and contradictions which lie beneath policy changes.

Useful websites

www.oecd.org provides a wealth of information on early childhood provision around the world through its *Starting Strong* reports.

www.gov.uk brings together all social policy information in one place and lets you navigate easily to your area of interest.

https://www.jrf.org.uk/reports on poverty and well-being.

References

Action for Children, National Children's Bureau and The Children's Society (2016) *Losing in the long run: trends in early intervention funding*. London: Action for Children, National Children's Bureau and The Children's Society

Alcock, C., Daley, G. and Griggs, E. (2008) *Introducing Social Policy* (2nd edn). Harlow: Pearson Longman

Alcock, P. with May, M. (2014) *Social Policy in Britain* (4th edn). London: Palgrave Macmillan

Allen, G. (2011) *Early Intervention: the Next Steps*. www.dwp.gov.uk/docs/early-intervention-next-steps.pdf. Accessed 30 December 2016

Apps, P., Mendolia, S. and Walker, I. (2012, October) *The Impact of Pre-school on Adolescents' Outcomes: Evidence from a Recent English Cohort*. Discussion Paper No. 6971 October 2012. http://www.iza.org. Accessed 10 June 2013

Baldock, P. (2011) *Developing Early Childhood Services: Past, Present and Future*. Maidenhead: Open University Press/McGraw Hill

Belsky, J. (2006) Early child care and early child development: Major findings of the NICHD Study of Early Child Care. *European Journal of Developmental Psychology* 3: 95–110

Beveridge, W. (1942) Report on Social Insurance and Allied Services. http://www.sochealth.co.uk/national-health-service/public-health-and-wellbeing/beveridge-report/. Accessed 28 December 2016

Beveridge, W. (1944) Report on Full Employment in a Free Society. https://books.google.co.uk/books?id=CjicBQAAQBAJ&pg=PT56&source=gbs_toc_r&cad=4#v=onepage&q&f=false. Accessed 28 December 2016

Bradbury, B. and Jantti, M. (1999) *Child Poverty across industrialised nations*. Innocenti Occasional Papers. Florence: UNICEF

British Medical Association (BMA) (2013) *Growing up in the UK: ensuring a healthy future for our children*. https://www.bma.org.uk/collective-voice/policy-and-research/public-and-population-health/child-health/growing-up-in-the-uk. Accessed 28 December 2016

Campbell-Barr, V. (2010) 'The research, policy and practice triangle in early childhood education and care', in R. Parker-Rees, C. Leeson, J. Willan, J. Savage (eds) (3rd edn) *Early Childhood Matters*. Exeter: Learning Matters

Children Act 2004 www.legislation.gov.uk/ukpga/2004. Accessed 4 July 2013

Childcare Act 2006 www.legislation.gov.uk/ukpga/2006. Accessed 4 July 2013

Child Poverty Strategy for 2014–2017. https://www.gov.uk/government/publications/child-poverty-strategy-2014-to-2017

Crowley, M. (2012) 'Parenting policy and skills strategies', in L. Miller and D. Hevey (eds) *Policy Issues in the Early Years* (pp. 77–90). London: Sage

Cunningham, H. (2006) *The Invention of Childhood*. London: BBC Books

DfE (2013) *More Great Childcare: Raising quality and giving parents more choice*. https://www.gov.uk/government/publications/more-great-childcare-raising-quality-and-giving-parents-more-choice

DfE (2015) *Characteristics of children in need, 2014–15*. SFR 41/ 2015. https://www.gov.uk/government/statistics/characteristics-of-children-in-need-2014-to-2015

DfEE (1998) *The National Childcare Strategy*. http://webarchive.nationalarchives.gov.uk/20100407010852/http:/www.dcsf.gov.uk/everychildmatters/publications/green-papers/1998greenpaper/

DfES (2002) *Extended Schools Initiative*. https://www.gov.uk/government/uploads/system/uploads/attachment_data/file/350462/Extended_schools.pdf

DfES (2003) *Every Child Matters*. London: DfES

DfES (2007) *Every Parent Matters*. Nottingham: DfES

DfES (2007) *Statutory Framework for the Early Years Foundation Stage*. London: DfES (updated 2014)

DoH (2009) *Healthy Child Programme: Pregnancy and the first five years of life*. https://www.gov.uk/government/publications/healthy-child-programme-pregnancy-and-the-first-5-years-of-life

Eisenstadt, N. (2012) 'Poverty, social disadvantage and young children', in L. Miller and D. Hevey (eds) *Policy Issues in the Early Years* (pp. 13–27). London: Sage

Field, F. (2010) *The Foundation Years: Preventing Poor Children Becoming Poor Adults*. http://webarchive.nationalarchives.gov.uk/20110120090128/http:/povertyreview.independent.gov.uk/media/20254/poverty-report.pdf. Accessed 4 July 2013

Friedan, B. (1982) *The Second Stage*. Cambridge, MA: Harvard University Edition (1998)

HM Treasury (2004) *Choice for Parents: the Best Start for Children – A Ten Year Childcare Strategy*

Hevey, D. and Miller, L. (2012) 'Reconceptualising policy making in the early years', in L. Miller and D. Hevey (eds) *Policy Issues in the Early Years* (pp. 169–179). London: Sage

Hill, M. and Irving, Z. (2009) *Understanding Social Policy* (8th edn). Chichester: Wiley Blackwell

Hirsch, D. (2013) *A Minimum Income Standard for the UK in 2013*: Joseph Rowntree Foundation (JRF). https://www.jrf.org.uk/report/minimum-income-standard-uk-2013? Accessed 30 December 2016

Housing Statistical Release (2014) https://www.gov.uk/government/statistics/local-authority-housing-statistics-year-ending-march-2014

Isaacs, S. (1937) *The Educational Value of the Nursery School.* London: The Nursery School Association of Great Britain, first edition 1937, second 1938. (Reprinted in Isaacs, S. (1948) *Childhood and After* (pp. 47–63). London: Routledge and Kegan Paul

Kennedy, H. (2005) *Just Law: The Changing Face of Justice – and Why it Matters to Us All.* London: Vintage Books

Laming, Lord (2003) *The Victoria Climbié Inquiry Report*, Cm. 5730, The Stationery Office

Macmillan, R. (2013) *Making Sense of the Big Society: perspectives from the third sector.* Working Paper 90. Birmingham: Third Sector Research Centre. http://www.birmingham.ac.uk/generic/tsrc/documents/tsrc/working-papers/working-paper. Accessed 30 December 2016

Mandela, N. (2002) *The State of the World's Children.* UNICEF. http://www.inicef.org/sowc02 summary/index3.html

Marmot, M. (2010) *Fair Society, Healthy Lives.* http://webarchive.nationalarchives.gov.uk/20130107105354/http:/www.dh.gov.uk/prod_consum_dh/groups/dh_digitalassets/documents/digitalasset/dh_128840.pdf. Accessed 4 July 2013

Miller, L. and Hevey, D. (eds) (2012) *Policy Issues in the Early Years.* London: Sage

Moss, P. (2009) *There are alternatives! Markets and Democratic Experimentalism in Early Education and Care.* The Hague: Bernard van Leer Foundation. www. bernardvanleer.org/. Accessed 3 March 2013

Munro, E. (2011) The Munro Review of Child Protection: Final report. https://www.gov.uk/government/uploads/system/uploads/attachment_data/file/175391/Munro-Review.pdf. Accessed 30 December 2016

Nutbrown, C. (2012) *Foundations for Quality: The Independent Review of Early Education and Childcare Qualifications. Final Report.* London: DfE

Organisation for Economic Cooperation and Development (OECD) (2011) *Doing Better for Families.* Paris: OECD

Parekh, A., MacInnes. T. and Kenway, P. (2010) *Monitoring poverty and social exclusion.* Joseph Rowntree Foundation (JRF). https://www.jrf.org.uk/report/monitoring-poverty-and-social-exclusion-2010. Accessed 30 December 2016

Parker-Rees, R. and Willan, J. (eds) (2006) *Early Years Education: Major Themes in Education, Vol. 1* (pp. 134–156). Abingdon: Routledge

Piper, C. (2008) *Investing in Children: Policy, law and practice in context.* Cullompton: Willan Publishing

QCA/DfEE (2000) *Investing in the Future: Curriculum Guidance for the Foundation Stage.* QCA Publications

Sage, D. (2012) A challenge to liberalism? The communitarianism of the Big Society and Blue Labour. *Critical Social Policy* 32(3): 365–382

Sylva, K., Melhuish, E., Sammons, P., Siraj- Blatchford, I. and Taggart, B. (2010) *Early Childhood Matters: Evidence from the Effective Provision of Pre-school and Primary Education Project.* London: Routledge

Tickell, C. (2011) *The Early Years Foundations for Life, Health and Learning.* https://www.gov.uk/government/publications/the-early-years-foundations-for-life-health-and-learning-an-independent-report-on-the-early-years-foundation-stage-to-her-majestys-government. Accessed 30 December 2016

Diversity and inclusion 12

Introduction

We are *all* different, but we all deserve to be treated with equal respect, and we are all entitled under the law to take our part in an inclusive society. Early years professionals are expected to promote inclusive and anti-discriminatory practice for the children and families in their care and, just as importantly, for colleagues in their workplace. In practice, this means removing the barriers that lead to exclusion so that everyone has an equal opportunity to take part.

UNICEF (2010: 1) states that the true measure of a nation's standing is how well it attends to *all* its children by protecting them during their vital, vulnerable years of growth and ensuring their health and safety; material security; education and socialisation; and sense of being loved, valued *and included*. Children who face prejudice through personal, structural or institutional discrimination on the grounds of ethnicity, gender, ability or family circumstances may suffer physical or mental harm. Legislation goes some way towards addressing inequalities by setting out the parameters designed to help everyone participate in society irrespective of birth or background. However, legislation is not enough on its own and professionals need to understand how discrimination operates in practice.

This chapter sets out to explore how inclusion can be promoted in early years provision.

Equality and inclusion

In our society, it is tempting to take equality for granted, because the idea that human rights are 'common sense' and that equality legislation is an expression of 'natural justice' is mostly accepted. But a brief look at history suggests that, in the past, *in*equality was more likely to be understood as natural justice and common sense. At various times it was believed that men held dominion over women, that white people could dominate black, that heterosexuals could criminalise homosexuals, that able people could make decisions about the disabled and that parents had jurisdiction over children. These 'common-sense' principles kept everyone in their place and prevented them from questioning their status or entertaining ideas above their station. Equality for diverse groups has been hard won over centuries and continues to be fought for as new groups come forward to claim discrimination against their human rights. Children are one of the most recent, among a long list, to have won the right to be listened to and consulted (Clark, 2008; Williams, 2009).

There are different ways of justifying equality of opportunity and equality of treatment (Freeman, 1997, 2007). We might justify it on *moral* grounds, arguing that treating people unequally is plain *wrong* and that everyone should be treated equally, regardless of circumstance because this *feels right*. Or we could justify it on *utilitarian* grounds, arguing that treating people equally provides 'the greatest good for the greatest number'. Or we could take a *rights* approach by saying that each and every child has a right to be treated equally, irrespective of moral or utilitarian arguments, because the law says so. Most of us operate with a mixture of all three justifications in the belief that a more equal and inclusive society is a fairer society where the needs and rights of individuals are recognised and respected. Offering equal opportunities to all children and working towards an inclusive society provides the best chance of producing healthy, educated and well-balanced citizens in the future, citizens upon whom our own prosperity will one day depend.

All around the world, children live in deeply *un*equal societies where cultural prejudices about poverty, gender, ethnicity and physical or mental ability can affect how they are included or excluded from the mainstream. Inclusion is not the same as integration or assimilation. Integration and assimilation are based on the premise that diverse groups should fit in and *adapt* to the culture of the majority as far as possible. Inclusion, on the other hand, involves accepting people's differences and *removing the barriers* that prevent them from taking part in mainstream culture; the onus lies with authorities and institutions to ensure that their services are accessible to all. In practice, inclusion depends on the way society *enables* people to engage in their community; it is expressed in the day-to-day adaptations and compromises made to ensure that everyone – poor and rich, adult and child, black and white, disabled and abled, boys and girls, regardless of belief or background, is enabled to participate (Siraj-Blatchford, 2014).

Being excluded can happen for a variety of reasons. It may be for *interpersonal* reasons; for instance, a child who is shy or awkward in company may be excluded because they find it difficult to engage with other people. It may be for *structural* reasons; for instance, a child with limited mobility may find it harder to access the space and activities on offer unless the facilities have been adapted for their needs. It may be for *institutional* reasons; for instance, in the past disabled children were regularly turned away from schools on the grounds that they would require too much attention from teachers to the detriment of other children's education.

The task of early childhood specialists is to remove barriers and to provide an environment where everyone, as far as possible, can enjoy a satisfying childhood in the present and a fulfilling adulthood in the future (DfES, 2004a).

Children's legal right to equality

Under the United Nations Convention on the Rights of the Child (1989), all children are entitled to equal opportunities and protection from unfair discrimination. The Convention is based on four binding principles of adult obligations towards children:

- *prevention* – of harm, ill-health, abduction and discrimination;
- *participation* – in society and decisions about their own welfare;
- *protection* – from abuse, conflict and exploitation;
- *provision* – of basic needs, education and security.

These four principles (the four Ps) form the basis of children's rights to life and dignity, to identity, to autonomy from parents, to their own views, to civil rights, to care, to mental and physical protection, to social welfare and to protection from exploitation. The Convention is clear that rights begin in the cradle and that all babies and young children have a right to life and deserve to enjoy a childhood free from neglect, exclusion, exploitation and abuse. Although the Convention recognises that the family is the primary space for nurture, it also states that where families fail in their duty of care, it is the responsibility of communities and governments to support children and, in extreme cases, to provide direct care by removing children from abusive families in order to give them the best chance of leading a satisfying life.

As discussed in Chapter 11, in the United Kingdom, children's rights have evolved out of the earliest Prevention of Cruelty to Children Act of 1889. Currently, equal opportunities and protection from unfair discrimination are covered by the Children Act (1989), the Human Rights Act (1998), the Children Act (2004) and various Welfare and Education Acts (Powell & Uppal, 2012). The Children Act (1989) included for the first time the notion that children's needs should be 'paramount' and that their welfare should take precedence, even over the wishes of their parents. When family customs and beliefs come into conflict with children's rights, the law presumes in favour of the child. The Children Act (2004) draws on the agenda of *Every Child Matters* (DfES, 2004b) and establishes the requirement that all professionals (from health, social care, welfare, education and the criminal justice system) should work together and share information to meet the needs of children at special risk of being excluded – children in care, children with mental and physical disabilities and children at risk of maltreatment or neglect. The Equality Act (2010) makes it illegal to discriminate on the grounds of 'protected characteristics' like age, disability, race, religion and gender. All these contribute to a strong legal framework to protect children, especially vulnerable children.

Time to reflect Children's rights?

In the United Kingdom, it is legal for parents to administer 'reasonable chastisement' in the form of a light smack. Unreasonable punishment is classed as a smack that leaves a mark or involves the use of an implement like a belt or cane. A parent can also give another person (such as a grandparent or babysitter) consent to use 'reasonable chastisement' on their child.

It is illegal for a teacher to smack a child, although a proposed change in the law may make it possible for them to use 'reasonable force' to restrain a child who is being disruptive, committing a crime, causing damage or harming someone.

Critics argue that the present law of 'reasonable chastisement' violates the child's rights by denying them the legal opportunity to bring a charge of common assault against the perpetrator (as an adult victim of common assault could do).

The NSPCC and other children's charities have campaigned for a total ban on physical punishment, citing evidence that it causes psychological harm and perpetuates a cycle of abuse down the generations.

In light of the four Ps of the UNCRC (1989), do you think the United Kingdom violates the principles of the Convention by permitting the use of 'reasonable force' and 'reasonable chastisement'?

The NSPCC has campaigned against corporal punishment for many decades. Why do you think the state is so reluctant to introduce legislation?

If you saw an adult smacking a child in a supermarket, how would you react?

Diversity

Working with other people's children obliges us to be critically aware of our own deep-rooted attitudes and beliefs. We will certainly come across parents, colleagues and children who are different from us in terms of gender, abilities, income or social and cultural background. It is important to acknowledge these differences. After all, we are not all the same, because we all experience the world differently, but none of us should be discriminated against because of our differences (Lindon, 2012). Clearly we have a duty to make any sort of intolerance or harassment totally unacceptable whether this comes from the majority group towards minorities or from minorities towards other groups.

Young children often think in simple stereotypes (Brown, 1998), such as women have long hair and wear dresses and men have short hair and wear trousers. One of the tasks for supporting diversity is to challenge this unsophisticated thinking from the outset:

- gender – boys can dress up in skirts; girls can be superheroes;
- religion – there is no 'right religion' for everyone;
- race/ethnicity/culture – everyone can be what they want to be, such as Asian boys can be basketball players, an Afro-Caribbean girl can be prime minister, white working-class girls can be doctors, and Chinese children can be actors;
- income/poverty – many famous people have overcome disadvantage to become successful and fulfilled;
- language – it is normal for many children to speak more than one language, and that multilingualism is an asset not a deficit.

Although everyone feels comfortable around people who are like themselves, we must guard against the natural tendency to avoid what is unfamiliar. One way to get children to enjoy difference is to encourage them to be curious about new and diverse experiences by giving them opportunities to discover and explore uncertainties.

Figure 12.1 Adopting gender stereotypes.
Source: blue jean images/Lane Oatey/Blue Jean Images

Cultural diversity

We are, of course, all ethnic; we all have an ethnicity based on unifying features such as a culture, religion and language which affects the way we are included in society. In the United Kingdom, Section 9 of the Equality Act (2010) is entitled 'Race', and the accompanying note explains that 'race' includes colour, nationality and ethnic or national origins (Explanatory Notes for Section 47: legislation.gov.uk). However, the word 'race' is problematic when used about different groups of people, because there is no scientific evidence for categorising people into different races. But sometimes we want to distinguish between people on the basis of ethnic identity for the purposes of uncovering inequalities between groups and in order to root out discriminatory practices. Siraj-Blatchford (2014) suggests that some early years professionals are unwittingly contributing to disadvantage for some children because they fail to recognise the ethnic diversities of the children in front of them and fall back on treating them 'all the same' – which is not the same as treating them equally. For example, there is no provision in the EYFS assessments for bilingual children to demonstrate their skills in their first language and, by assessing them in the 'same way' as everyone else, there is a danger that EAL children (children for whom English is an additional language) will be seen as less able than their English-speaking peers.

In order for children to develop a sense of belonging and value, they must see themselves and their families represented in their settings through books, artwork, family sets, dolls, cooking equipment, print from their own written languages, workbook illustrations and so on. These images should be available throughout the setting – including in parent handbooks, annual reports and training materials so that all families feel recognised, represented and included. Discrimination is often unconscious, because of a lack of acknowledgement that we live in multi-ethnic societies; Siraj-Blatchford reminds us that *all* children and families attending early years settings should be encouraged to be proud of, and to value and celebrate, their ethnic heritages.

Time to reflect

Why is treating children *all the same* not equivalent to treating them equally?
Is special treatment discriminatory?
Is there a case to be argued for positive discrimination towards potentially excluded groups?
How can professionals address children's unwitting prejudices?

In the Equality and Human Rights Commission report *How Fair is Britain?*, the authors suggest that nearly 10 per cent of British children are growing up in a mixed-race household and that as society has grown more diverse, Britons have become more tolerant of difference and more welcoming of diversity (Equality and Human Rights Commission, Triennial Review, 2010). However, media reports of 'hate' crimes suggest that prejudice towards ethnic minorities is still a factor in national life – it seems to be a universal truth that wherever there is a significant ethnic minority anywhere in the world, there are issues of exclusion and discrimination when sections of the indigenous population feel their way of life is somehow under threat. Understandably, many parents from ethnic minority groups feel anxious about how their children will be treated outside the family.

In the United Kingdom, every organisation is expected to provide equality and diversity policies and a checklist of criteria against which to measure compliance. But sometimes these policies and checklists become routine, a matter of ticking boxes rather than providing a starting point for serious professional reflection and judgement. Unless professionals really *feel* and *understand* the rights of diverse groups to be equally included, it is unlikely that equality policies will translate into any life-changing or significant actions for those individuals who are most at risk of exclusion (Baldock, 2010).

Case study: Addressing cultural diversity

A parent asks you to hand out birthday party invitations at break time. The children are all very excited and rush to put their invitations in their home bags. Cara remains at the table, forlorn, her lower lip trembling. There is no invitation for her. She is the only child in the class to be excluded. She is a child from the Traveller Community and has had some difficulties settling into the school. She is quiet and watchful most of the time, but she occasionally has an angry outburst, and her behaviour can seem erratic. She puzzles the other children, and they often leave her to play alone, not sure whether she wants to join in or not. Some of the children are overtly hostile, and she is subject to name calling. Teachers are quick to condemn any name calling they hear. Parents are wary of the Traveller Community, and you have noticed that they seem slightly uncomfortable around Cara's mother, who stands apart when she collects Cara from school. When you raise the issue with colleagues, they say that Travellers keep to themselves and don't want to integrate with the wider community.

Discussion questions

Should you have a quiet word with the parent of the birthday child and try to get Cara included? How could you and your colleagues address the exclusion in the long term so that the Cara is able to be more successfully included?

Are there any steps you might take with Cara's family to encourage more involvement in the school community?

Where could you get advice to address the particular issues around inclusion and Traveller families?

In many situations, dialogue provides the key to inclusion. Professionals can go some way to overcoming ignorance about other ethnic groups by listening to parents and children; asking questions in a positive, interested way; or asking about dietary customs and religious observances. Simple things can promote inclusivity and contribute to the education of staff and children alike – for example, offering a selection of books from different parts of the world or providing toys that include characters with different skin tones; celebrating religious festivals from different faiths; or inviting parents from different ethnic groups to share food and cooking skills. Open dialogue is itself a way of showing inclusiveness and can have the effect of building confidence in both professionals and families by modelling and demonstrating inclusion in action, thus underlining the principle that everyone's opinion is valued (Clark et al., 2005).

Income diversity

Children born into families whose income is insufficient for basic needs have an unequal start in life and reduced expectations in terms of health, development and well-being (Marmot, 2010). The language used to refer to poor people by MPs and journalists sometimes suggests we have not moved very far from the Victorian concepts of deserving and undeserving poor (see Chapter 11). It is easy to find examples of attitudes that imply that poverty is a lifestyle choice and that poor people are legitimate targets for casual vilification; laughing at poor people is a staple of British humour as we can see from the endless 'chav' jokes on the Internet. Poor people and their children can easily lose hope under the constant barrage of derogatory remarks. Children are only too aware, even at an early age, of the disparaging terms applied to them and their families – with devastating consequences for their sense of inclusion and their self esteem.

Poverty is difficult to define. *Absolute poverty* is a term used to describe the precarious situation of families who suffer hunger and lack shelter. *Relative poverty* refers to those families who lack the resources and material comforts typical for their community. Few children in Britain live in absolute poverty, but large numbers live in relative poverty (ONS, 2015). Children in poverty are more likely to live in one-parent families, often in overcrowded accommodation where adults are stressed and anxious and where there is little spare energy or money to enjoy life to the full. In spite of difficulties, we should remember that parents from every income group love their children and want the best for them and that children themselves are enormously resilient and manage to make the best of things in unpromising situations.

Poorer neighbourhoods are often blighted by high crime levels; they often have fewer amenities like parks and playgrounds and sports centres, and fewer facilities like libraries, medical centres, playgroups and nurseries; they often lack infrastructure like bus routes and supermarkets. As a way of addressing this kind of social disadvantage, the *Every Child Matters* strategy encouraged local authorities to establish children's centres in deprived communities and extended school opening times for before- and after-school clubs (so-called wrap-around care) to help working parents manage their childcare responsibilities. Children's centres offer health services, education and social spaces for parents and children and provide a hub for information and expertise to help them access services for their children and training and employment information for themselves. There is evidence that these centres have a positive effect on outcomes for poor children, but there is also evidence that families who would benefit most are less likely to use them. However, these centres are currently under threat from funding cuts, and there seems to be little political will to retain them (4Children, 2014); politicians on the right often argue that voluntary local initiatives are more successful than wholesale state initiatives.

Professionals working with poor families may be inclined to elevate the significance of expensive, centrally managed initiatives put in place by governments and backed by academic studies so that they overlook the homespun 'bottom up' activities that grow out of community effort. But community schemes can be very successful at involving hard-to-reach families who may think the mainstream official provision is not for them. These community schemes often begin with the families in the flats or streets in a particular neighbourhood; they may be based around churches, mosques, temples and synagogues, community halls and sports venues. They provide local support in familiar surroundings where families can come together naturally; they enable communities to grow networks where they can exchange information and skills in an informal way. Sometimes these less structured organisations nurture a sense of pride and ownership in the locality and a commitment to the children and families living there. Once embedded, they become the focus for lifelong support systems because people feel a sense of ownership which they may not feel in the client/professional relationship of more formal organisations (Tunstall, 2009).

Professionals cannot solve the problems of poverty on their own, but they can use their empathy and imagination to alleviate some of its burdens. Simple steps like providing boots and coats in a range of sizes for outdoor play, offering clothes and uniform swaps, supplying toy libraries and second-hand equipment exchanges or providing access to online free-cycle sites make a huge difference to families living on limited incomes. Schools and nurseries can help by protecting poor families from extra costs. It is not difficult to arrange ways to subsidise trips and outings or to provide low-cost activities like neighbourhood walks or visiting speakers as part of the curriculum. It is easy to provide opportunities for parents to demonstrate their cooking skills, to talk about their work or country of origin or to explain festivals and customs. When children see their parents and other members of their community valued and respected, they feel valued and respected themselves.

Ability/disability

Children with mental and physical impairments were largely neglected under the Education Act of 1870; they were generally regarded as uneducable and often referred to as 'defective'. Work by pioneers like Maria Montessori showed that with the right support and encourage-ment, children with impairments could progress and learn (Pound, 2011).

In the first half of the twentieth century, local authorities set up special segregated schools and nurseries for impaired children; these schools provided medical expertise and therapies to help children cope with their conditions in practical ways, but there was little in the way of education. It wasn't until the second half of the century that responsibility for these children was transferred from health departments to education. Impaired children were no longer seen solely as medical cases; instead, they were recognised as having special needs requiring specialist educational support (Wall, 2011). Special schools with specialist staff were set up for those for those suffering deafness or blindness or those with cerebral palsy or with educational and behavioural disorders (EBD). Attitudes gradually began to change; for example, children with autistic spectrum disorders who were once classified as *imbeciles* or *defectives* began to be seen differently as their condition became the subject of study.

Focus on Autism: the emergence of a concept

Autism is a lifelong developmental disability that affects how people communicate with, and relate to, others. It affects the way people understand the world around them. People with autism often experience over- or under-sensitivity to sound, touch, taste, smell, light and colour. These differences can cause them considerable disorientation and anxiety. Autism is a spectrum condition such that the condition can be expressed in a range of ways: some people with autism will lead relatively normal lives; others will always need support. Chil-dren with autism often have difficulties with social communication, social interaction and social imagination, which lead others to label them as being unresponsive or lacking in empathy, and the children themselves often feel misunderstood and unfairly judged.

In the past, children we now recognise as having autistic spectrum disorders were often labelled uneducable and excluded from society in asylums or special units. Gradually, over the past century, the nature of their disorder has become clearer, and they are now sup-ported and offered assistance to develop and progress in mainstream community settings. The population at large now understands the condition more sympathetically as a result of books and films which have brought it to general attention.

- In 1911 Swiss psychologist Eugen Bleuler introduced the term autism to describe severely withdrawn individuals lacking in social skills.
- In 1943 Austrian psychiatrist Leo Kanner established autism as a childhood disorder and hypothesised that it is caused by cold and unresponsive parenting, by *'refrigerator mothers' and undemonstrative fathers*.
- In 1944 Austrian paediatrician Hans Asperger published important work on high-achieving people with autism, giving his name to Asperger's syndrome.
- In 1950 Austrian-born psychologist Bruno Bettelheim published work in the United States suggesting that parental rejection and lack of love causes autism.
- In 1962 in the United Kingdom, Dr Lorna Wing, a psychologist and mother of a daughter with autism, set up the National Autistic Society to study the condition and to support parents and children's understanding. Together with her collaborator, Judy Gould, she became the pre-eminent expert in the fields of autism and Asperger's syndrome.
- In 1979 a study by Lorna Wing and Judy Gould suggested that autism is a spectrum disorder involving a triad of impairments in social interaction, communication and imagination, which has little to do with parenting styles.
- In 1988 the film *Rain Man*, starring Dustin Hoffman, brought autism to a wider audience.
- In 1998 surgeon Andrew Wakefield produced a report linking autism to the MMR triple vaccine. Many parents withdrew their children from the vaccination programme, prompting an epidemic of measles. The research was later discredited.
- In 2003 Mark Haddon's *The Curious Incident of the Dog in the Night-Time*, narrated by a boy with Asperger's syndrome, gave millions of readers an insight into living life with an autistic spectrum disorder.
- In 2007 scientists found a genetic link for autism. One in 100 in the United Kingdom and the United States is thought to be affected – earlier estimates had put the figure at five in 10,000.
- In 2009 the *Autism Act* became the first disability-specific law in England that conferred a duty on local authorities and the National Health Service to recognise and continue to support people with autism beyond the school-leaving age of 18.

Some children with autism will have challenging behaviour; this may be controlled with prescription drugs or by behaviour management techniques. All children on the spectrum need extra help with communication and social skills. Early years practitioners have a special role in encouraging these children to be as independent as possible and to help them to overcome the maladaptive behaviours that lead to their social isolation.

What can the practitioner do? Practitioners may need to give special support to individuals to help with

- anger management
- changes in routine
- dealing with uncertainty.

They may also give instruction and training to help children to

- recognise non-verbal cues like smiling and frowning;
- understand common behaviour patterns like sharing or queuing or offering help;
- practise social skills like encouraging them to role play common social interactions like meeting and greeting, sharing, turn-taking and conversation or walking away from conflict.

Every child is unique; the child with autism needs a uniquely tailored programme of interventions worked out in consultation with their families and relevant paediatric services.

Special Educational Needs and Disabilities (SEND)

A breakthrough for the education of mentally and physically impaired children was marked by the publication of the Warnock Report (1978). Radically, the Warnock committee consulted children and parents rather than relying solely on expert opinion. Overwhelmingly, parents and children expressed a wish to be included in mainstream education. The Warnock Report recommended that wherever possible, all children, as far as their disability allowed, should be *integrated* in mainstream schools with their peers and helped to *adapt* to school life. The report suggested that support should begin in the home at the earliest opportunity to give each child the best chance of school readiness. Warnock abandoned the deficit terms *handicapped, maladjusted* and *educationally subnormal* and used the term special educational needs (SENs) to reinforce the idea that all children could benefit from education as long as they were properly prepared and supported.

The 1981 Education Act continued to talk about *integrating* children. The Act set out three conditions for children with special needs to be offered places in schools and nurseries – if that was what *their parents wanted*; if *schools had the necessary resources*; and if the presence of SEN children would *not impair the learning* of other children. Some schools were reluctant and continued to turn away children with disabilities, or segregated them into remedial units during lesson time, arguing that teachers were not trained to take up the challenge of including these children in 'normal' classrooms.

Focus on *Portage*

The National Portage Association was set up in 1983 in the wake of the *Warnock Report*. Portage is an outreach service for preschool children with additional support needs. Portage home visitors are employed by local authorities and charities to support children and families within their local community.

Portage is characterised by

- regular home visiting;
- supporting the development of play, communication, relationships, and learning within the family;
- supporting the child and family's participation and inclusion in the community;
- working with parents within the family and responding flexibly to their needs;
- helping parents to identify what is important and planning goals for learning and participation;
- keeping a shared record of the child's progress and any issues about their care.

Portage support is offered on a long-term basis to children suffering severe disabilities which prevent them from attending a regular school. Portage home visitors access wider professional support through regular team meetings and offer links to other organisations.

(National Portage Association at www.portage.org.uk)

In 1988 the terminology in National Curriculum documents changed from *integration* to *inclusion*; and practitioners, settings and schools were expected to *adapt to, and provide for*, the SENs of individual children to promote inclusion by *removing barriers* to participation. Schools could no longer refuse admission on the grounds of poor facilities or lack of specialist expertise as they had done under the 1981 Education Act. The Special Needs Code of Practice (DfEE, 1994) recommended that schools identify children with special needs and provide a written Individual Education Plan (IEP) showing how schools would adapt lessons, teaching styles, resources and buildings to cater for particular SEN pupils. Schools and settings were required to have a person designated as Special Educational Needs Co-ordinator (SENCO) who could oversee provision and be a first point of contact for children, parents and practitioners. For the first time, parents were given the opportunity to be fully consulted. In the Revised Special Needs Code of Practice (DfES, 2001), this right to consultation was extended to children themselves so that they could contribute to their IEPs and comment on their progress reviews. Statements of special educational needs are currently under review and may be replaced with Education, Health and Care (EHC) plans, which will allow parents and children to manage their own budgets to buy in services from local authorities for support. The intention is to reduce the numbers of children registered as having special educational needs on the grounds that every child is 'special' in some way and requires an independent learning plan (some critics, including Warnock, believed that some schools had cynically exaggerated the numbers of SEN pupils in their schools in order to attract extra funding). The plan is to restrict registration to the most severely impaired children so that resources can be targeted at those in greatest need – this has led to increasing tensions (and legal challenges) between parents and local authorities over the eligibility of their children for extra funding.

Case study: Lucas: Paralympics torch bearer

Lucas was chosen to be a torch bearer in the Paralympics. He suffers from frontal nasal cranio-facial dysplasia, a deformity of the head and face, a mid-line deformation that occurred as he was developing in the womb. His parents, extended family and their friends prepared him for a normal life by helping him to talk clearly, to manage solid food (difficult with his condition) and to socialise with his peers. But when he joined his village primary school, he was bullied, excluded and mocked, even by children he already knew from preschool.

The under-the-radar punching, spitting, name calling and teasing got him down so much that he was unable to function. Teachers seemed unable to intervene, and no action was taken against his tormentors. Towards the end of his primary school life, he walked out of his classroom and refused to return. He believed that teachers, parents and children found his difference just too difficult to manage.

Lucas was a very bright boy but he was falling behind his classmates because of the oppressive school environment. Lucas was referred to the organisation Changing Faces, who arranged to go into his school to run workshops for staff and pupils in an effort to make them understand how Lucas felt and to find a way past the discrimination he had suffered.

Later, when Lucas transferred to secondary school, he asked if someone from Changing Faces could address the whole school at the first assembly of the term to explain his disfigurement and to help teachers and pupils respond appropriately. This approach paved the way for an inclusive and supportive experience where Lucas was treated in the same way as everyone else and suffered no further discrimination.

Discussion questions

Understanding his disfigurement helped teachers and children to accept him.
Read Lucas's story and hear him speak at www.changingfaces.org.uk.
Why do children sometimes discriminate against children they perceive as different?
What steps can practitioners take to help children accept and include a child they have previously shunned?

Listening to parents and children is an important part of matching children to the right provision for their particular needs (Savage & Brodie, 2015). Practitioners cannot be experts in every condition, but by taking the lead from parents and other professionals involved in the child's care, the majority of special needs children can be accommodated successfully in main-stream settings. However, not all children and parents want to be included in the mainstream; sometimes they feel their needs would be better met in specialist schools where their condition is understood well, where there are others facing the same difficulties and where there is access to specialist help. Some years after writing her report, Warnock (2005) retracted some of her recommendations and said that specialist schools had an important role to play and that parents and children should be entitled to make their own judgement of which school system would best suit their needs.

Gender

It is common to see children playing in same-sex groups or gravitating towards same-sex adults. Children as young as two already identify themselves as boy or girl (Skelton & Hall, 2001), although gender identity may remain a fluid category for some. Some scientists argue that boys and girls are *biologically* primed to behave in gendered ways, while some social scientists argue that children *learn* their gender roles through social interaction and observation. Rutter (2006) argues that nature and nurture are so intricately entangled that any attempt to argue either of these positions is unhelpful; some characteristics *are* genetically heritable, but those characteristics are subject to 'gene environment interplay' such that individuals are a product of both biology and socialisation.

For practitioners, stereotypical views about gender roles and gendered social behaviour are unhelpful. Children actively construct their own gender identities – sometimes choosing to follow *same-sex* patterns of behaviour, sometimes deliberately choosing to identify with *opposite-sex* role models and sometimes just going their own way – rejecting some attributes, accepting others and sometimes actively seeking out behaviours that reinforce their sense of difference from the accepted stereotype. They *choose* to identify with particular groups, reflecting on the pluses and minuses of belonging to one group rather than another, weighing up the pressures exerted by adults, the media and peers and coming to their own conclusions about how things work for them.

Recently, there has been an increasingly loud debate over the 'feminisation' of early child-hood provision; some commentators argue that boys spend too much of their early childhood in female company (girls do too…). Roberts-Holmes (2009) considers the absence of men from early years to be a particular difficulty facing boys; he suggests that more should be done to make the profession attractive to men. His underlying assumption is that women have differ-ent social styles and behaviours and that the lack of male role models has a detrimental effect on boys and gives girls an advantage. He argues that the 'domestication' and 'feminisation' of pri-mary schools and nurseries means that boys suffer a form of hidden discrimination. There is evidence of discriminatory practice – boys are reprimanded more than girls, boys are more likely to be labelled hyper-active, the school curriculum favours cooperative (female) rather than competitive (male) activities and, *on average*, boys have poorer educational outcomes than girls (Holland, 2003). Other commentators argue that just because there are more women in early years care and education, it does not follow that boys are disadvantaged. Skelton (2002) points out that boys/girls, men/women and mothers/fathers are not homogenous groups. They are diversified through class, ethnicity, sexuality, and beliefs about masculinity/femininity. She provides evidence to show that poor educational outcomes are most noticeable among working-class white boys, and she argues that family background factors such as different forms of masculinity and class-based educational expectations are more likely to be responsible than the preponderance of female professionals in schools and nurseries.

Men and women share many common attributes, and we should beware of accepting glib stereotypes about the feminisation and domestication of care and education among female workforces. Perhaps we do need more men in the workforce – not because of rather culturally laden arguments about feminising and domesticating but because both boys *and girls* could benefit from being taught and cared for by both genders.

Creating an inclusive culture

Equality legislation and policies do not necessarily translate into consistent and universal inclusion practices. It is not simply a matter of 'delivering' equality but of recognising the often unthinking discrimination that takes place on a daily basis and constantly reviewing and reflecting on what it is to be truly anti-discriminatory and inclusive; adults and children have to *embody* these principles in their behaviour, actions and conversation.

The overall message to children should be *to expect respect from everyone and to treat everyone with respect.* This message should be clearly modelled in the behaviour of staff and reinforced with simple guidelines. All children can be encouraged to understand that *everyone is different and being different is normal* (Nutbrown & Clough, 2009) and that to discriminate on the grounds of difference is a form of bullying. Simple steps can help children understand their role in combating discriminatory behaviour, and a code of conduct for young children might include the following directives:

- If something is upsetting you, talk about it to an adult you trust.
- If you feel like being nasty to someone, find something else to do.
- If you have bullied someone, apologise.

Children who feel insulted or excluded may develop low self-esteem and display poor behaviour which may be difficult to handle. When an incident occurs, Siraj-Blatchford and Clarke (2000) suggest the following course of immediate action:

- Do not ignore sexist, racist or derogatory comments. Take the abusive child aside and explain why the remark was hurtful.
- Provide comfort and support to the abused child.
- Explain in clear and appropriate terms why the behaviour was unacceptable and ask the abused child how they feel so that both children can reflect actively on the incident.

Figure 12.2 Children who feel insulted or excluded may develop low self-esteem and display poor behaviour.

Source: Stockbyte Royalty Free Photos

■ Follow up by working alongside both children at some point during the day. Let them both know that they are valued.

■ Involve parents when a child has shown unwelcome prejudice. Explain the incident and emphasise your equality policy. Point out that discriminatory behaviour invites sanctions and is harmful to their child.

In the long term, professionals should develop strategies that reinforce a general ethos of inclusiveness so that children and parents understand that discriminatory behaviour is unacceptable.

■ Discuss equality policies with new parents and children at the outset.

■ Read stories and organise activities that deal with similarities and differences. Encourage children to discuss the issues raised.

■ Show an interest in different dress codes, different religious celebrations, different family rituals and different foods.

■ Create an ethos where everyone is valued for their contribution, regardless of difference.

■ Involve children and parents in the development of equality decisions.

■ For each new activity, make a note of how to include any children who are at risk of being left behind – for example, children with motor or mental difficulties or EAL children.

An equal opportunities policy

An equal opportunities policy can help ensure that the equality rights enshrined in law are actively promoted. An equal opportunities policy should include the following:

- details about meeting the individual needs of all children (including how those children who have a disability or have special educational needs will be included, valued and supported and how reasonable adjustments will be made for them);
- the name of the SENCO (if appropriate);
- details of inclusive practices designed to promote and value diversity and difference;
- arrangements for reviewing, monitoring and evaluating the effectiveness of inclusive practice;
- arrangements for dealing with inappropriate attitudes and practices (including those of staff, parents or children);
- how the provision encourages children to value and respect others;
- how the provider incorporates British values under the Prevent duty (DfE, 2015) which requires all schools and childcare providers to prevent extremism or 'the vocal or active opposition to fundamental British values including democracy, the rule of law, individual liberty and mutual respect and tolerance of different faiths and beliefs'.

It is important that the policy is shared with all new parents and staff at the outset and that its principles be communicated to children through day-to-day interactions. Poverty, gender, ethnicity, religious practices and special educational needs all present sites for unconscious and unintended discrimination, and professionals need to monitor their provision to make sure that no one is excluded or discriminated against. *Partnership* between parents and professionals is a key area for addressing questions of cultural and social inequality because it is only through genuine dialogue with parents that professionals can really understand the needs of individual children in a culturally diverse community (Dahlberg & Moss, 2005; Siraj- Blatchford et al., 2007).

Time to reflect *Removing barriers to provide enabling environments*

Scenario

You are responsible for Eloise, aged four, who is wheelchair bound because of cerebral palsy. She suffers deafness, which is partly alleviated by her hearing aids. She is bright and interested and has some limited control over her hand movements. Her speech is indistinct, but she has learnt to sign proficiently and communicates well with her family. Her older brother is in another class and will interpret if necessary. A classroom assistant is equipped with a microphone that allows Eloise to hear her in the hubbub of the classroom. Neither you nor your assistant is familiar with British Sign Language or Makaton (a speech-based system of signs and symbols to aid communication), but by speaking slowly and facing Eloise directly, you both manage to communicate successfully with her. Eloise is making good progress in literacy and numeracy and has good IT skills.

How would you develop your communication skills with Eloise?

How would you encourage other children to work and play with her?

What practical things could you do to ensure that her environment is enabling?

You have agreed a learning plan with Eloise and her parents. What kind of things would you look out for, listen for and note to show the progress she makes and the difficulties she encounters? How might you enable her to contribute to her assessment profile?

Children excluding children – you can't say you can't play

Children can be very quick to point out difference. Their own need to 'belong' to a particular group and to establish their own identity seems to drive them to exclude 'others' who do not share their own characteristics. This can lead to victimisation and bullying of children who are 'different' for some reason and it can be very hard to counteract bullying once it has begun. Prevention is better than cure and professionals should concentrate on providing an inclusive atmosphere where they themselves model non-judgemental and non-discriminatory behaviour though a generous, warm acceptance of all the staff, children and parents who form their community (DCSF, 2008; DfE, 2014). Simple procedures like showing respect, expressing interest, listening attentively to *every* child and adult can go a long way towards providing a democratic ethos where children are less likely to bully or to be the victims of bullying.

> ### *Time to reflect* You Can't Say you Can't Play
>
> Vivian Gussin Paley, in her book *You Can't Say You Can't Play*, writes,
>
> > Turning sixty, I am more aware of the voices of exclusion in the classroom. 'You can't play' suddenly seems too overbearing and harsh, resounding like a slap from wall to wall. How casually one child determines the fate of another.
> >
> > 'Are you my friend?' the little ones ask in nursery, not knowing. The responses are also questions. If yes, then what? And if I push you away, how does that feel?
> >
> > By kindergarten, however, a structure begins to be revealed and will soon be carved in stone. Certain children will have the right to limit the social experiences of their classmates. Henceforth a ruling class will notify others of their acceptability, and the outsiders learn to anticipate the sting of rejection. Long after hitting and name calling have been outlawed by the teachers, a more damaging phenomenon is allowed to take root, spreading like a weed from grade to grade.
> >
> > Must it be so? This year I am compelled to find out. Posting a sign that reads YOU CAN'T SAY YOU CAN'T PLAY, I announce the new social order, and from the start, it is greeted with disbelief.
> >
> > Only four out of twenty-five in my kindergarten class find the idea appealing, and they are the children most often rejected. The loudest in opposition are those who do most rejecting. But everyone looks doubtful in the face of this unaccountable innovation.
> >
> > —Vivian Gussin Paley (1992) *You can't say you can't play.* Cambridge, MA, and London: Harvard University Press p. 3–4

Discuss the passage above with your group.

Do you think Vivian Gussin Paley is right to decree that in her classroom 'you can't say you can't play'?

What difficulties can you envisage?

Do you think saying 'you can't say you can't play' would encourage children to be more inclusive?

A workplace audit

In 2015 the UK government charged all childcare and educational settings, including childminders, with the duty of promoting British values as part of the Prevent duty strategy aimed at identifying families and children at risk of radicalisation (DfE, 2015). This presents practitioners with a difficult balancing act between valuing children's home cultures and championing liberal democratic values such as children's rights, gay rights and gender equality.

One practical way of opening up discussions about diversity and inclusiveness among families and practitioners about inclusiveness and diversity is to examine the current situation in your own workplace by asking yourselves the following questions::

Policy

- Are equality policies in place and up to date?
- Are all staff, parents and children aware of the policies?
- Is there a children's version of the policy? Is it on display?

Workforce

- Does the team reflect the cultural diversity of the catchment area?
- Do we have both men and women on the team?
- Do we make it possible for disabled people to participate in our workforce?

Resources

- Do we supply a diverse range of dolls, puppets and 'small-world people'?
- Are there clothes from all cultures in our dressing up box?
- Is the home corner equipped in a way that reflects the diversity of children's homes and cultures?
- Do the puzzles show different ethnic groups?
- Do the musical instruments come from a broad range of cultures?
- Do the books show racial/ethnic diversity?
- Can the paint colours be used to represent all the skin tones in the group?

Practice

- Has everyone received equality awareness training in the past year?
- How easy is it for staff, parents and children to voice their concerns about unfair practices?
- What steps are in place to address discriminatory behaviour?

■ How do you deal with discriminatory language?

■ How do you record examples of discrimination when they occur?

■ What sanctions are in place for staff, parents or children who contravene equality guidelines?

Even when everything is in place, we should remember that it is the respect shown between individual adults and children that cements real equality in early childhood settings. Children take their cue from the adult behaviours they see around them, and it is important that professionals model inclusive and non-discriminatory behaviour.

Helping children to grow up without prejudice

We live in an unfair society where shape, colour, accent, dress and a host of other differences can unleash all sorts of unthinking prejudice, exclusion and discrimination. We are all prejudiced in some sense because none of us can escape the assumptions of our own narrow individual viewpoint. Sometimes the media and politicians deliberately stoke anxieties about difference, and it can be difficult to remember that people are individuals, not caricatures of some groupspeak. It is not easy to challenge our own or other people's assumptions; it requires reflection, intellectual effort, sensitivity and insight. We can move on only if we address the prejudice in ourselves, in our workplace and in our relations with others.

Ignorance and fear are at the root of prejudice. Children who grow up celebrating diversity, rather than fearing difference, are more likely to show respect to others and to value each individual for all their remarkable variety.

Summary

■ Diversity is a fact of life, and all children and adults are unique.

■ Everyone is equal under the law.

■ Equality is justified by moral, utilitarian and human rights arguments.

■ Assimilation and integration imply a requirement that everyone should adapt to mainstream culture; inclusion means recognising difference and removing the barriers that prevent people from fully engaging in society.

■ Children's rights to equal treatment are covered under the four tenets of the UNCRC: *prevention* of discrimination; *participation* rights; *protection* from harm; *provision* for needs.

■ Gender, ethnicity, income inequality and disability are common sites for potential discrimination.

■ Equality in the United Kingdom is governed by the Equality Act (2010), and discrimination towards those with 'protected characteristics' is outlawed.

■ Inclusivity in early childhood settings extends to providing books, toys and activities that represent the whole gamut of human experience, including disability, gender and ethnicity.

■ Creating an inclusive culture depends on zero tolerance of discrimination among staff, children and parents.

■ Monitoring equality and inclusivity is part of day-to-day quality control.

- Adults need to reflect on their own cultural prejudices and to familiarise themselves with the different cultural viewpoints of parents and the children in their care.
- Children often take their cue from the adult behaviours they see around them, and so it is important that professionals model inclusive and non-discriminatory behaviour.
- Implementation of the requirements of Prevent duty and British values presents practitioners with a delicate balancing act between respecting children's home culture and promoting those Western values enshrined in law.

Topics for further discussion

1 Share your knowledge of books, toys and activities directly concerned with issues of gender, disability or ethnicity. What would you recommend to colleagues?
2 How can we deal with children who feel victimised by other children? How can we manage their tormentors? Share experiences of good practice.
3 Look at the DfE (2015) Prevent duty document. How does it fit in with your ideas about equality and inclusion?

Assignments

1 Collect some equality policies. They might be from health, social services or education (including your college/university). What do they have in common? How well do they promote a culture of equal opportunities? Do they cover inclusion at the personal, structural and institutional levels? Are there steps in place to monitor inclusivity in practice?
2 Think about gender and the early childhood workforce. What positive steps could encourage more men to take up employment in health, social care and education workforces for young children? Can you identify any barriers that might make it more difficult for men to engage in early childhood settings? Do you think the lack of men in the sector for newborns to eight-year-olds disadvantages boys?
3 Discuss the idea of 'you can't say you can't play' with children. What views do they come up with? Do they think it is fair? How would you summarise their responses?

Further reading

Holland, P. (2003) *We Don't Play with Guns Here: War, Weapon and Superhero Play in the Early Years*. Milton Keynes: Open University Press

Gussin Paley, V. (1992) *You can't say you can't play*. Cambridge, MA, and London: Harvard University Press

Pugh, G. and Duffy, B. (eds) (2010) *Contemporary Issues in the Early Years* (5th edn). London: Sage

Warnock, M. and Norwich, B. (2010) Chs. 1–3: 'Special Educational Needs: A New Look'; 'A Response to "Special Educational Needs: A New Look"'; 'Response to Brahm Norwich' in L. Terzi (ed.) *Special Educational Needs: A New Look*. London: Continuum

Useful websites

www.equalityhumanrights.com/en provides advice and updates on equality regulations. It has a YouTube link where you can find training videos as well as interviews with people like Alison Lapper or Gok Wan talking about their experiences of discrimination.

www.gov.uk provides links to equality policies in health, education and social care for England, Scotland, Wales and Northern Ireland.

References

4children (2014) *Sure Start Children's Census 2014.* http://cdn.basw.co.uk/upload/basw_21518-10.pdf. Accessed 30 December 2016

Baldock, P. (2010) *Understanding Cultural Diversity in the Early Years.* London: Sage

Brown, B. (1998) *Unlearning Discrimination in the Early Years.* Stoke on Trent: Trentham

Clark, A. (2008) *Why and how we listen to young children.* Listening as a way of life leaflet series. London: National Children's Bureau

Clark, A., Kjorholt, A.T. and Moss, P. (eds) (2005) *Beyond Listening: Children's Perspectives on Early Childhood Services.* Bristol: Policy Press

Dahlberg, G. and Moss, P. (2005) *Ethics and Politics in Early Childhood Education.* London: Routledge Falmer

DCSF (Department for Children, Schools and Families) (2008) *Bullying Involving Children with Special Educational Needs and Disabilities. Safe to Learn: Embedding Anti-bullying Work in Schools.* London: DCSF Publications

DfE (Department for Education) (2014) *Statutory Framework for the Early Years Foundation Stage* (EYFS) www.gov.uk/government/uploads/system/uploads/attachment_data/file/335504/EYFS_framework_from_1_September_2014__with_clarification_note.pdf. Accessed 30 December 2016

DfE (2015) *The Prevent duty: Departmental advice for schools and childcare providers.* https://www.gov.uk/government/uploads/system/uploads/attachment_data/file/439598/prevent-duty-departmental-advice-v6.pdf. Accessed 30 December 2016

DfEE (1994) *Special Needs Code of Practice.* London: DfEE

DfES (Department for Education and Schools) (2001) *Revised Special Needs Code of Practice.* London DfES

DfES (2004a) *Removing Barriers to Achievement: the Government's Strategy for SEN.* Nottingham: DfES Publications

DfES (2004b) *Every Child Matters: Change for Children.* London: DfES

Equality Act (2010) *Explanatory Notes for Section 47.* www.legislation.gov.uk/ukpga/2010/15/notes/contents. Accessed 19 July 2013

Equality and Human Rights Commission (EHRC) (2010) *How Fair is Britain? Equality and Human Rights Commission Triennial Review 2010.* www.equalityhumanrights.com/en/publication-download/how-fair-britain-report. Accessed 19 July 2013

Freeman, M. (1997) *The Moral Status of Children: Essays on the rights of the Child.* The Hague: Martinus Nijhoff Publishers

Freeman, M. (2007) *The Best Interests of the Child*. The Hague: Martinus Nijhoff Publishers

Gussin Paley, V. (1992) *You can't say you can't play*. Cambridge, MA, and London: Harvard University Press

Holland, P. (2003) *We Don't Play with Guns Here: War, Weapons and Superhero Play in the Early Years*. Milton Keynes: Open University Press

Lindon, J. (2012) *Equality in Early Childhood: Linking Theory and Practice* (2nd edn). London: Hodder Education

Marmot, M. (2010) *Fair Society, Healthy Lives*. http://webarchive.nationalarchives.gov.uk/20130107105354/http:/www.dh.gov.uk/prod_consum_dh/groups/dh_digitalassets/documents/digitalasset/dh_128840.pdf. Accessed 4 July 2013

Nutbrown, C. and Clough, P. (2009) Citizenship and Inclusion in the Early Years: Understanding and Responding to Children's Perspectives of 'Belonging'. *International Journal of Early Years Education* 17(3): 191–206

ONS (2015) *Persistent poverty in the UK and EU, 2008–2013*. http://webarchive.nationalarchives.gov.uk/20160105160709/http://www.ons.gov.uk/ons/rel/household-income/persistent-poverty-in-the-uk-and-eu/2008–2013/persistent-poverty-in-the-uk-and-eu—2008–2013.html. Accessed 30 December 2016

Powell, J. and Uppal, E. (2012) *Safeguarding Babies and Young Children: A Guide for early Years Professionals*. Maidenhead: Open University Press/McGraw Hill Education

Roberts-Holmes, G. (2009) 'People are suspicious of us': a critical examination of father primary carers and English early childhood services. *Early Years: Journal of International Research and Development* 29(3): 281–291

Rutter, M. (2006) *Genes and Behaviour: nature-nurture interplay explained*. Oxford: Blackwell

Savage, K. and Brodie, K. (2015) 'Some practical steps towards a more inclusive practice', in K. Brodie and K. Savage (eds) *Inclusion and Early Years Practice* (pp. 190–195). Abingdon: Routledge

Siraj-Blatchford, I. (2014) 'Diversity, Inclusion and Learning in the Early Years', in G. Pugh and B. Duffy (eds) *Contemporary Issues in the Early Years* (6th edn) (pp. 151–164). London: Sage

Siraj-Blatchford, I., Clarke, K. and Needham, M. (2007) *The Team around the Child: Multi-agency Working in the Early Years*. Stoke on Trent: Trentham

Skelton, C. (2002) The 'feminisation of schooling' or 're-masculinising' primary education? *International Studies in Sociology of Education* 12(1): 77–96. Abingdon: Routledge

Skelton, C. and Hall, E. (2001) *The Development of Gender Roles in Young Children: A review of Policy and Literature*. Manchester: Research and Resources Unit, Equal Opportunities Commission

Tunstall, B. (2009) *Communities in recession: the impact on deprived neighbourhoods*. Joseph Rowntree Foundation. www.jrf.org.uk/sites/default/files/jrf/migrated/files/communities-recession-impact-neighbourhoods.pdf. Accessed 29 June 2016

UNESCO (1950) *The Race Question* hhttp://unesdoc.unesco.org/images/0012/001282/128291eo.pdf. Accessed 19 July 2013

UNICEF (2010) *The Children Left Behind: A League Table of Inequality in the World's Richest countries*, Innocenti Report Card 9. Florence: UNICEF Innocenti Research Centre

UNCRC (United Nations Convention on the Rights of the Child) (1989). http//www.unesco.org/education/pdf. Accessed 17 November 2016

Wall, K. (2011) *Special Needs and Early Years: A Practioner's Guide* (3rd edn). London: Sage

Warnock, M. (Chair) (1978) *Special Educational Needs* (The Warnock Report). Report of the Committee of Enquiry into the Education of Handicapped Children and Young People. London: Her Majesty's Stationery Office

Warnock, M. (2005) *Special Educational Needs: a new look*. London: Philosophy of Education Society of Great Britain

Williams, L. (2009) *Developing a listening culture*. Listening as a way of life leaflet series. London: National Children's Bureau

Health and well-being 13

Introduction

International research suggests that early childhood is a crucial time for establishing health and well-being if children are to enjoy a fulfilling childhood and a satisfying adulthood. Health and well-being begins in the womb, where the mother's good physical and mental health offers the best conditions for a good start to her child's life. Children's experiences in the first eight years of life influence their ability to make the most of their opportunities and have an effect on future generations when children grow up to become parents themselves. Individual health and well-being does not exist in isolation; it is bound holistically to structures of self, family, community and the state. This chapter explores some of the factors that affect health and well-being and indicates some ways in which practitioners can help to provide healthy, positive environments where young children can flourish.

The state of the world's children

Only 15 per cent of the world's 1.5 billion children live in rich countries. Around the globe, child mortality is highest where children live in 'absolute' poverty, without access to regular food, clean water, sanitation and healthcare. In 2015, nearly 4.5 million children under the age of five died, three quarters of them from preventable causes such as pneumonia, diarrhoea, neonatal sepsis, pre-term delivery, malaria and birth-related asphyxia (WHO, 2015). The risk of a child dying in the first year of life was highest in the WHO African Region (55 per 1000 live births), but globally the infant mortality rate has been declining from an estimated rate of 63 per 1000 live births in 1990 to 32 per 1000 in 2015. This represents remarkable progress but masks the fact that even in rich countries a *social gradient of health inequalities* exists, which means that those children in lower socioeconomic groups are at higher risk of mortality or ill-health than children in higher income groups.

In the past, population health was measured in statistical terms – infant mortality rates, deaths from childhood diseases, poverty indices, income and GDP. But these 'hard facts' missed other, 'softer' cultural indicators that are just as important for health and well-being. In 2007, UNICEF began to measure health and well-being across six *quality of life* dimensions – these included material well-being; health and safety; educational well-being; family and peer relationships; behaviours and risks; and subjective well-being. For the first time, the survey canvassed the views of young people themselves about their 'subjective sense of their own well-being' – a measure that put children in the United Kingdom at the bottom of the 21 countries surveyed.

The latest Human Development Report (UN 2013), uses a multidimensional poverty index (MPI) to explore global dimensions of disadvantage, health and well-being, and it concludes that the number of children living in absolute poverty around the world is declining thanks to a *combination of medical and social interventions* – interventions such as the development of schools, health clinics, better housing and infrastructure, improved access to water and improvements in the distribution of international trade. The report indicates that children's health and well-being is best promoted where a proactive state encourages social programmes in health and education alongside democratic participation rights for all citizens, better conditions for women and better access to trade and technological innovation. However, although the report is optimistic about the apparent improvement in *average* global well-being, it points out that at local levels, within rich and poor societies alike, the gap between the richest and poorest is actually widening, and without considerable state support, the health and well-being of the very poorest children born into *any* society in the twenty-first century will likely be compromised.

The national picture

Although children and young people growing up in England today are healthier than they have ever been before, the most disadvantaged are still at risk of a poor start in life, and improvements are slower than in other EU countries. Four recent reports (Field, 2010; Marmot, 2010; Allen, 2011; Tickell, 2011) put good ante-natal care and early childhood support at the centre of their recommendations for improving the health and life chances of the next generation of children. The *Report of the Children's and Young People's Health Outcomes Forum* (Lewis & Lenehan, 2012) showed that too many children in the United Kingdom have poorer health outcomes than children from comparable countries – with higher mortality rates, higher obesity rates and poorer rates of daily physical activity. Poorer health varies with social factors such as the socioeconomic status of the family, and the poorest health outcomes occur among children in care: nearly half have a mental health disorder, and two-thirds have at least one physical health complaint. Variations in quality of health for children from different backgrounds is unacceptable in a rich country like the United Kingdom, and the clear evidence that pregnancy and the earliest years are critical to their future health and well-being suggests that we should provide more early interventions for those most in need.

A social gradient of health inequalities

Poor health and well-being are linked closely to poverty – poverty of income, opportunity, housing and all the social ills that can arise from these. Poverty is not a personal problem; poverty is a phenomenon of social organisation, economic structure and government policy

(JRF, 2012). But it is a difficult phenomenon to control, and governments sometimes find it easier to construe it as a failing of individuals. Under the barrage of negative rhetoric, it is easy for any one of us to slip into a moral mindset that construes poverty as deserved, a result of laziness and fecklessness, and that likewise wealth and success are also deserved, the just rewards of hard work and diligence. But if we look closely at the facts, we can see that in the United Kingdom, poverty is heavily concentrated in particular regions of the country (where jobs are scarce or out of reach) and in particular families (where impoverished environments offer little stimulation for adults and limited experiences for children). These structural inequalities are reproduced over and over and contribute to a *social gradient* of inequalities, including inequalities in health and well-being. Put simply, children further down the social and economic scale have poorer life chances and health outcomes than children higher on the scale. Poorer children are demonstrably more at risk of mortality and morbidity in both developed and developing countries (whether from the 'new' factors like sudden infant death, accidents and behaviour problems or the 'old' factors like infection and malnutrition) than their more fortunate peers.

Marmot (2010) shares the view that health inequalities arise from a complex interaction of factors, including physical and mental health, housing, income, education, social inclusion and individual resilience. He argues for interventions and action at a community level, believing that holistic, universal programmes will bring better health to more children than a system geared towards interventions with 'at risk' families. Holistic community initiatives might include transport to alleviate isolation for families who can access services only on foot; local sustainable food production and outlets; zero carbon homes that are warm and cheap to heat; or libraries, parks and centres for recreation with safe routes for children. The review suggests that these wider public health initiatives from governments and local authorities will contribute most significantly to the health and well-being of the nation's children.

Time to reflect

Can you think of any local initiatives in your area that contribute to improved health and well-being for children and families?
Are the initiatives generated by local people, local agencies or a combination of both?
Do you agree with Marmot that broad community initiatives are more likely to foster good health than authority-led targeted interventions with 'at-risk' families?

The effects of extreme neglect

Research from the field of epigenetics (how environmental factors affect development at a cellular level) shows how extreme neglect (such as an absence of sensory, emotional or cognitive stimulation) alters the physical and chemical structure of DNA responsible for switching genes on and off and can have long-term effects on brain development. Extreme neglect results in smaller brains and abnormal development of the cortex and is particularly critical from conception to age eight.

Focus on *Severe neglect and brain development*

Nowadays, neurologists use CT scans to examine brain development. A CT scan is a computerised tomography scan. It is a special type of X-ray using a scanner and computer equipment to take pictures of the brain. It differs from a standard X-ray in that it produces pictures of cross-sections of the brain. The CT images below show the devastating effects of neglect on the developing brain.

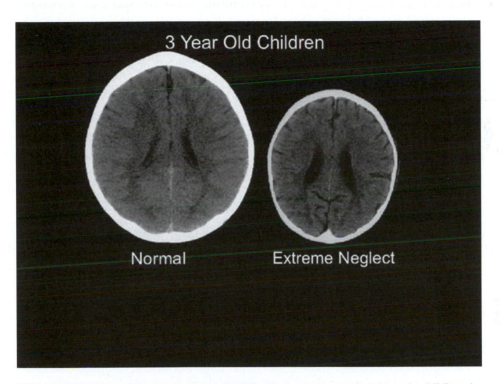

Figure 13.1 Abnormal brain development following sensory neglect in early childhood.
Source: Perry, B.D., (2002) Childhood experience and the expression of genetic potential: what childhood neglect tells us about nature and nurture. *Brain and Mind* 3: 79–100

These images illustrate the negative impact of neglect on the developing brain. In the CT scan on the left is an image from a healthy three year old with an average head size (50th percentile). The image on the right is from a three-year-old child suffering severe sensory-deprivation neglect. This child's brain is significantly smaller than average (3rd percentile) and has enlarged ventricles and cortical atrophy. (Perry, B.D. (2002) Childhood experience and the expression of genetic potential: what childhood neglect tells us about nature and nurture. *Brain and Mind* 3: 79–100)

Neurologist Bruce Perry (2002) distinguishes between the effects of global neglect (very rare) and of chaotic neglect (more common) on brain development. Children who suffer *global neglect* are most likely to have been in institutions since birth; they have generally had little exposure to touch, language or social interaction. Children who suffer *chaotic neglect* are more likely to be subject to inconsistent patterns of social, emotional, physical and cognitive support in neglectful families. Globally neglected children have a much smaller frontal-occipital circumference (FOC) or head size, a proxy measure for brain size; chaotically neglected children show no difference in FOC when compared to the norm.

Perry found that when children suffering global neglect were placed in supportive environments, they recovered some ground. However, their likelihood of recovery was inversely proportional to their age – that is, the earlier in life they were removed from the neglectful situation, the more robust their recovery. They had the best chance of recovery if they were fostered or adopted into family environments before age two.

This CT image is frequently reproduced (see The Allen Report; 2011), without further explanation, to show the effects of neglect on infants. Why might this be misleading?

A number of recent adoption studies (the *Canadian–Romanian Adoption Study:* Morison, Ames and Chisholm, 1995; the *English and Romanian Adoptees* (ERA) study: Rutter et al., 1998; *Children Adopted from the Former USSR:* McGuinness et al., 2000) found that early neglect had lifelong consequences. However, all the studies found that if neglected children were adopted into supportive families *before age two*, the worst effects of early deprivation could be overcome.

Focus on English and Romanian Adoptees (ERA) study: Rutter et al., 1995 and continuing

The ERA study followed the lives of 165 Romanian orphanage children under the age of three-and-a-half who had been adopted into UK families. Its aim was to examine the extent to which children could recover when extreme deprivation in early life was followed by a middle childhood within a safe family environment. The progress of these adoptees from Romanian orphanages was compared to a control group of 52 UK adoptees of the same age who had not been in any type of institution.

Most of the Romanian adoptees showed motor, personal-social and language delays at the time of adoption but showed significant developmental catch-up after adoption. The control group did not show the same pattern of delays. Children who were older than six months when they were adopted from institutions experienced autistic-type problems: they had difficulty in forming appropriate attachments and social relationships; they suffered inattention, over-activity and poor mental functioning; and one third of them needed educational, psychological or psychiatric interventions.

The results showed that children adopted before the age of six months in both groups made good progress and 'caught up' with peers by age four. However, the Romanian children who *were older than six months* when they were adopted showed significant developmental delays at age four and beyond. Follow-up studies continued from 2003 to 2009, and the results gave reason for optimism about the human ability to overcome early disadvantage throughout childhood and adolescence. However, a significant number of older adoptees continue to show impairments. The team concluded that *early* adoption could help children overcome the privations they had suffered during their first year; later adoptees suffered more delays but still benefitted. (See Rutter et al., 1998, 2012)

Currently, in the United Kingdom, high numbers of vulnerable children are being removed from families by social service departments However, the number of children available for adoption has fallen. This apparent anomaly has resulted from a court ruling that local authorities should consider whether a child's interests could be better served by being raised safely and permanently within their wider extended family rather than being offered for adoption to an *un*related family. The need to explore the possibility of placing a child with blood family has slowed the adoption process for vulnerable children, resulting in their spending longer in institutional care.

Time to reflect

What risks and benefits are associated with placing vulnerable children within their extended family, where they are cared for by grandparents, aunts and uncles or adult siblings?

Health and well-being: bio-medical and ecological perspectives

What do we mean by health and well-being? How do we decide whether a child is healthy and enjoying a good quality of life? What factors contribute to a good-quality childhood environment? How can we provide the best conditions for children? Do children and adults share the same beliefs about what factors support health and well-being?

Medical historian Henry E. Sigerist (1941) famously suggested that 'health is not simply the absence of disease: it is something positive, a joyful attitude toward life, and a cheerful acceptance of the responsibilities that life puts upon the individual'. His words are echoed in the World Health Organization's definition that health and well-being make up 'a state of complete physical, mental and social well-being and not merely the absence of disease or infirmity' (1948). These definitions suggest that health and well-being need to be regarded holistically and should include questions about a person's spiritual, emotional and social relationship with self and community.

Time to reflect

What would you want to include in a definition of 'good health'?

It is tempting to think of health and well-being in bio-medical terms, assuming that health is an *individual* phenomena inscribed in the body, treatable with medicine, surgery or psychiatric support. However, some commentators (Brancaccio, 2000; Furedi, 2004) suggest that such a narrow bio-medical view of health in the West may be contributing to the rise in diagnoses of modern 'diseases' such as attention deficit hyperactivity disorder, which, they suggest, is rare or non-existent in non-Western countries. They point to figures showing that a significant subset of children are medicated to control symptoms of 'aberrant' behaviour and argue that the explanation for this behaviour might lie in cultural factors such as parenting styles, schooling practices, changes in cultural expectations about modern childhood and the way children are perceived by adults, rather than in individual pathologies.

Focus on *Attention deficit hyperactivity disorder (ADHD)*

ADHD is a group of behavioural symptoms that include inattentiveness, hyperactivity and impulsiveness. It is believed to be linked to chemical malfunctions in the brain, particularly in those areas of the prefrontal cortex, which is responsible for reasoning, self-control, organising, planning and problem solving. For the past 50 years, the psycho-stimulant methylphenidate (commonly known by the trade name Ritalin) has been given to children to reduce ADHD symptoms. It has a good safety record and high efficacy in the treatment of ADHD and is approved for use in the United States and the United Kingdom. ADHD became increasingly recognised and diagnosed by health professionals from the 1990s onwards. Since then, the use of Ritalin-type prescriptions has risen markedly – between 2007 and 2012 prescriptions in Britain rose by 50 per cent. Several legal actions have been initiated against its widespread use on various grounds – such as the inadequate availability of information on side effects, failure to get informed consent, misdiagnosis and coercive pressure from schools to put children forward as ADHD sufferers.

The increasing use of drugs like Ritalin to control children's behaviour is a cause for concern among many professionals working with young children. Frank Furedi (2004) argues that the rise in diagnoses of ADHD is part of a medicalisation of childhood, brought about by a lack of clarity about roles and relationships between adults and children. He argues that health professionals and schools have redefined the normal problems of childhood (such as poor self-discipline, wayward behaviour, inattentiveness) as medical conditions requiring pharmacological intervention. He argues that ADHD is not a sign of bio-medical ill-health but a natural reaction in children to the mixed messages they receive from the adults around them who struggle with conflicted feelings about when, or if, they should exercise their authority. (Furedi, F. (2004) *Therapy Culture: Cultivating Vulnerability in an Uncertain Age*)

How comfortable are you with Furedi's analysis?

What support would you offer a parent who expressed fears that their child might have ADHD?

How would you support a child who was diagnosed with ADHD?

Find out more about ADHD. Do you think it is a bio-medical condition or a symptom of adult *dis*-ease with modern childhood?

Weisner (2002) reminds us that a narrowly bio-medical view of health ignores all the ecological, social and cultural factors that contribute to 'wholeness'. He points out that physiological aspects of health and well-being account for only some of the differences between being able (or unable) to enjoy a fulfilling childhood. He suggests that children's healthy physical, emotional, intellectual and social development depends on a host of factors, such as the demographic profile of the community, adult work patterns, children's labour practices, childcare arrangements, schooling programmes, play spaces and opportunities, attitudes towards women and girls, cultural beliefs about children and childhood and varying practices around rearing child.

From disease prevention to health promotion

Of course, health and well-being do in part depend on physiology, and *disease prevention* is an important part of achieving good health and well-being. More children now survive thanks to public health initiatives such as sanitation, clean water, birth hygiene, immunisation programmes and the provision of medicines. Disease prevention continues to have notable successes resulting in more children surviving into healthy adulthood – the near eradication of smallpox and a massive reduction in malaria, typhus and cholera. An understanding of germ theory, together with simple practices like hand washing, food hygiene and toilet cleanliness prevent many other kinds of illness that in previous generations might have resulted in deaths among children. As disease has become better controlled, attention has shifted towards community *health promotion* by educating people through hygiene and health programmes delivered by schools and health centres. It is generally recognised that the greatest gains in health and welfare for a population are made when well-informed individuals, families and communities take responsibility for their own social, mental and physical well-being.

Focus on *Health promotion*

Health promotion is the process of enabling people to increase control over, and to improve, their health. To reach a state of complete physical, mental and social well-being, an individual or group must be able to identify and to realize aspirations, to satisfy needs, and to change or cope with the environment. Health is, therefore, seen as a resource for everyday life, not the objective of living. Health is a positive concept emphasizing social and personal resources, as well as physical capacities. Therefore, health promotion is not just the responsibility of the health sector, but goes beyond healthy life-styles to well-being. (WHO (1986) *Ottawa Charter for Health Promotion*. http://www.who.int/healthpromotion/conferences/previous/ottawa/en/)

The UNCRC urges member states to reduce infant mortality and to prevent ill-health by

- providing pre- and post-natal maternity care;
- providing primary healthcare;
- protecting children from environmental pollution;
- providing clean water and safe food;
- providing information and education on healthcare such as breast feeding, hygiene, sanitation, child health and nutrition, causes of risk and accident;
- providing preventative healthcare (family planning and immunisation programmes);
- making efforts to persuade adults to abandon unhealthy traditional practices (such as female genital mutilation);
- supporting populations in developing countries through international aid, education and equitable trading agreements.

(Article 24 of UNCRC (1989) www.crin.org/docs/resources/treaties/uncrc (accessed 26 March 2013)

Can you think of any local initiatives in your area that successfully promote community health?

How far do you think community health is linked to economic priorities?

Investing in child health – through health promotion, family intervention, disease prevention, immunisation, health screening, improved living conditions, parental intervention programmes, increasing democratisation – is seen as the best way to invest in health, well-being and welfare for individuals and for whole communities. The international programme Child to Child (CtC) argues that health promotion is best effected through education programmes focused on *children* because they are well placed to transfer their knowledge about hygiene, sanitation, vaccination, nutrition, play and exercise to the whole community and will put it into practice when they become parents themselves.

At the heart of this approach is a shift away from medical services towards social services, with health being seen as a community effort encompassing safeguarding, housing, play space, early years care, health services and general education. Public health programmes are increasingly being taken out of the hands of the medical profession and made the responsibility of local authorities. In the United Kingdom, health education in the community is based on a 'life course perspective' (DfES, 2003; DOH, 1997, 2004; DoH, 2009; NICE, 2012) in the belief that tackling disadvantage before birth and during the early years alleviates immediate health inequalities and goes some way to breaking the cycle of deprivation by improving the health and well-being of all children as they grow towards adulthood and begin to have families of their own.

Promoting health and well-being in early childhood

In 2009 Layard and Dunn published *A Good Childhood*, which presented opinions from children aged 5–17 about what they thought was most important for health and well-being. Love came out on top, making human relationships the single most important factor in children's own assessment of health and well-being. They believed that feeling valued and secure, enjoying good quality family relationships and feeling included and respected were key components for a healthy life.

Resilience

A recent study (Sabates & Dex, 2012) followed children at ages three and five from the Millennium Cohort Study, who were exposed to more than two risk factors – risk factors such as parental depression, parental disability, smoking during pregnancy, alcohol, domestic violence, financial stress, unemployment, teenage parenthood, poor parental basic skills and overcrowding. Where more than two risk factors occurred, children's cognitive and behavioural development was compromised. A combination of low income and several other risks was particularly implicated in negative effects on child development.

However, resilience can help children to flourish despite the presence of risk factors. Resilience is a recognised psychological term used to describe the capacity of an individual to withstand the 'slings and arrows of outrageous fortune'. Resilience grows in children who feel secure enough to rise to the challenges that life presents. Some children seem to be more resilient than others from the outset, but even the most resilient infants and children may be overwhelmed if too many risk factors are present. Rutter et al. (2009) identified some of the positive features that can provide extra resilience and protection for all children, regardless of background and economic circumstances. They listed:

- easy temperament
- secure attachment
- affectionate relationships
- good communication skills
- problem solving approach
- sense of humour
- religious faith or sense of belonging
- positive attitude
- capacity to reflect
- wide support network
- supervision and firm reasonable boundaries
- higher intelligence
- lack of severe disharmony in family
- family support for education.

Time to reflect

Do risk factors necessarily determine outcomes for children?
Look at Rutter's resilience factors. Are there any practical steps that early years professionals could take to improve resilience in individual children?

Sleep hygiene

Children need lots of sleep! Sleep deprivation can affect physical growth, mental well-being and social relationships. Parents, practitioners and health workers need to be aware of the effects of sleep (the right kind at the right time) on developing children and to make provision for them to get good-quality rest. Our bodies are linked to the circadian rhythms of our geographical location on the earth – we perceive the length of daylight hours through light sensors in the retina, which tie us into the seasonal rhythms of light and dark (Kreitzman et al., 2004).

Sleep is very important for a child's wellbeing. There's no set amount of sleep that all children of a particular age need, but the following are the required hours of sleep, based on age, recommended by the Millpond Children's Sleep Clinic (NHS Choices, 2015).

Age	
1 week ■ daytime, 8 hours ■ night time, 8 hours, 30 minutes	**3 years** ■ daytime: 0 to 45 minutes ■ night time: 11 hours, 30 minutes to 12 hours
4 weeks ■ daytime, 6 to 7 hours ■ night time: 8 to 9 hours	**4 years** ■ night time: 11 hours, 30 minutes
3 months ■ daytime: 4 to 5 hours ■ night time: 10 to 11 hours	**5 years** ■ night time: 11 hours
6 months ■ daytime: 3 hours ■ night time: 11 hours	**6 years** ■ night time: 10 hours, 45 minutes
9 months ■ daytime: 2 hours, 30 minutes ■ night time: 11 hours	**7 years** ■ night time: 10 hours, 30 minutes
12 months ■ daytime: 2 hours, 30 minutes ■ night time: 11 hours	**8 years** ■ night time: 10 hours, 15 minutes
2 years ■ daytime: 1 hour, 30 minutes ■ night time: 11 hours, 30 minutes	

Adults also need good sleep habits to function well. Typically adults sleep for seven to nine hours. Less than seven hours impairs concentration and energy levels and may be linked to depression, diabetes and obesity.

With electric lights, television, computer technology and mobile devices, it is easy for adults and children to lose the circadian link and to operate on a 24-hour cycle that plays havoc with sleep patterns and hormone balance. Sleep disruption is believed to be implicated in conditions such as diabetes, obesity, ADHD and depression so it is important that children and their parents understand the need for regular patterns of sleep and wakefulness to stay healthy and maintain good social relations and emotional well-being.

Time to reflect

How would you broach the subject of sleep deprivation with a family whose lifestyle seems irregular and chaotic?
How could you help them to monitor and improve their sleep quota?
What steps might they be encouraged to take to improve bedtime routines?

Physical play and exercise

Half of all seven-year-olds in the United Kingdom are not exercising enough to stay healthy and are inactive for between six and seven hours every day (Griffiths et al., 2013). Girls are more inactive than boys – only one in four girls achieves the minimum recommended activity levels, compared to two out of three boys. In densely populated areas with high volumes of traffic, children are less likely to play outside or to walk to school and may spend recreation time indoors. This lifestyle has consequences beyond their physical health; it prevents them from learning the social skills to keep themselves safe and may fuel their own sense of fearfulness about the world beyond home.

In the report *Start Active, Stay Active: a report on physical activity for health from the four home counties' Chief Medical Officers* (DOH, 2011), it is recommended that physical activity should be encouraged from birth. For the youngest children this means 'tummy time' on the floor and lots of activities for reaching and grasping, pulling and pushing; time spent in infant carriers and seats, or time spent sitting in front of televisions should be reduced to a minimum. Movement increases motor skills, improves cognitive development, contributes to a healthy weight and enhances bone and muscle development. For older toddlers, the recommendation is for three hours of challenging active play each day to improve cardiovascular function and muscle coordination. Most UK children currently spend around two hours a day in energetic play, so achieving the guideline means ensuring an extra hour of physical activity per day for most children. For school-age children, the recommendation is that in addition to moderate intensity activities which cause them to breathe harder and get warmer, they should have at least one hour of vigorous exercise like running, playing team games, hopping, skipping or climbing on playground equipment. In addition to the physical benefits, these activities are generally sociable, and they improve children's social and emotional skills and their resilience by encouraging cooperation and providing opportunities to persevere in the face of challenge.

Figure 13.2 It is vital that practitioners find ways to involve all children in challenging play – be they able or disabled, 'good at sport' or not – and to make exercise purposeful and pleasurable.
Source: ISTOCK

As a society, we have a duty to boost physical activity among children by providing safe play areas and parks and affordable activities at sports centres for all children who may otherwise be confined in cramped accommodations.

In schools and early years settings, access to outside play and large play equipment and space for ball games, dance and playground activities is essential to improve the short- and long-term health of children. Introducing children early to the pleasures of taking part in physical activity, to overcoming challenges and to the satisfaction of competing in team games means that they are more likely to lead active, healthy lives. Bad experiences of physical activity, particularly school physical education (PE) and sports can put them off for life – so it is incumbent upon practitioners to find ways of involving all children in challenging physical play, no matter whether they are able or disabled or whether they are 'good at sport', and to make exercise purposeful and pleasurable.

Time to reflect

What kinds of activity might you introduce at a summer play scheme to enable all children, regardless of physical aptitude, to feel challenged *and* successful?
Would you encourage children in the three to eight age range to compete with one another?
How could you support reluctant children in joining in with exercise and physical activity?
Do you need to think about gender and culture when providing physical activities?

Diet and nutrition

While billions of children around the world suffer ill-health brought on by food shortages and lack of nutritional variety in their diet, children in richer countries suffer ill-health from an over-abundance of food – particularly sugar, salt and fat – in their diet. In urbanised societies, obesity, stress and overwork are key factors in lowering health, while in poorer countries poor nutrition, sanitation and clean water supplies are major factors. In developing nations, obesity is concentrated among the wealthy; in developed nations it is concentrated among the poorest. Childhood and adult obesity levels are currently causing alarm because of the implications for the health of individuals and costs of treatment to taxpayers. Some argue that child obesity is the responsibility of parents; others argue that it is a public health issue that can be addressed only through the determined regulation of the food industry (Lobstein et al., 2004).

Focus on *Health and the food industry: the bliss factor*

As nations grow richer, their populations abandon traditional local fruit and vegetable diets and adopt a Western-style diet high in fat, sugar and salt. Salt, sugar and fat are used by manufacturers to make cheap ingredients palatable, and the result is that around the world non-communicable diseases (NCDs) such as obesity, diabetes and high blood pressure have reached epidemic proportions. Children subjected to this diet are forecast to have shorter lives than their parents. Some health professionals believe that parents are entirely to blame for their children's obesity problems because children eat only what they are given by adults. However, Michael Moss (2013) believes that something called 'the bliss factor' is responsible.

The bliss factor

In the 1970s, researchers discovered that children were particularly keen on foods that were salty or sweet. In tests, twice as many children as adults chose the saltiest or sweetest drinks on offer. Later research on the effects of sweetness in food showed that children didn't just *like* sugar; they were consuming much more of it than previous generations. It was suggested that children were developing a craving for more and more sweetness as a result of the massive amount of sugar being added to processed food.

Sugar is of particular concern. There are three aspects of sugar that make it attractive to children – a *sweet taste* which signals foods that is rich in energy, which fast-growing children need and crave; *rarity value* – sweetness rarely occurs in nature and would have been an exciting, pleasurable and highly valued treat in prehistoric times; *analgesic properties* – sugar dulls pain and misery and makes people feel good.

Food technicians attempted to exploit this predilection for sugar by discovering the 'bliss point' of their products, testing children to find out the optimal sweetness that makes the food most enjoyable for them – the optimal concentration at which the sensory pleasure is greatest – and which dictates what they choose to eat and drink. There are individual differences, but as a group, in every culture around the world, children prefer more intense sweetness than adults.

Understanding the optimal levels of salt, sugar and fat that are most attractive to children allows manufacturers to make products which are 'more-ish' (meaning it has a pleasant taste that makes you want to eat more) and to exploit the emotional and physical biology of the child to sell more of their products. Manufacturers are not just providing food and calories but also habituating children to high levels of salt, fat and sugar in their diets, which will stay with them into adulthood. (Michael Moss (2013) *Salt, Sugar, Fat: How the Food Giants Hooked Us*)

How far do you think childhood obesity is the personal responsibility of parents, and how far do you think food manufacturers are responsible?

What factors, other than food, might contribute to childhood obesity?

It is common to find children offered a biscuit and a sugary drink for mid-morning snack. Is this wise? What alternatives might you offer?

(For further analysis, see Lustig Robert H., Schmidt, L.A. and Brindis, C.D. 'Public Health: The toxic truth about sugar' in *Nature* 482: 27–29, 2 February 2012. This is available on YouTube as well.)

Mental health and well-being

A rising number of children are reported to be presenting with emotional, social and behavioural difficulties (Kinderman & Tait, 2004), and as many as 10 per cent have mental health issues. Various factors are blamed for the perceived rise in children's poorer mental health – family breakdown, lack of boundaries at home, absence of positive role models and low self-esteem. Sometimes the rise is attributed to increased testing in schools, cyber and text bullying, time-poor parents or a lack of free play; at other times rising unemployment, economic uncertainty or the prevalence of toxic brain-altering chemicals in modern environments are blamed.

The list seems endless. More certainly, any physical, psychological or sexual abuse in childhood significantly increases the risk of mental ill-health.

Children who experience *positive* mental health can more easily join in with their peers to share the highs and lows of a typical day. Most children will experience some behavioural problems at some stage in their young lives – tantrums, sleep disruption, night terrors and food fads are very common – and they can usually overcome them quite easily with the support of empathetic adults who can tune into their distress and ease their passage through the underlying difficulty. When children are experiencing *negative* mental health, they exhibit behaviours that interfere with their day-to-day ability to get along with their peers or join in with activities. Their behaviour may be off-putting or unpredictable, even violent, or they may be anxious and withdrawn, fearful or deeply sad. Adults and other children may find it difficult to respond to their outward behaviour, and the resulting negative feedback will further compound the problem.

The Leuven Scale of well-being and involvement, developed by Ferre Laevers at the Centre for Experiential Education in Belgium is widely used in early childhood settings (see Laevers, 2011). The scale provides a set of indicators to measure children's well-being (how cheerful and upbeat they are) and their involvement (how engaged they are in their work or play). Well-being is measured on a five-point scale. Level 1 indicates extremely low: children at this level exhibit clear signs of discomfort; they may look dejected, sad, frightened or angry; they do not respond to the environment; they avoid contact and seem withdrawn; they may behave aggressively to others, or they may self-harm. Level 5 indicates high well-being. Children at this level look happy, smile and express pleasure. They may be lively and full of energy; their actions can be spontaneous and expressive; they may talk to themselves, hum and sing; they seem relaxed; they are open and active in their environment; they appear self-confident and self-assured. Similarly, involvement is also measured on a five-point scale. Level 1 indicates low activity: activity may be simple, repetitive and passive; children may seem absent or listless; there may be an absence of cognitive demand and curiosity. Level 5 denotes sustained intense activity; children show continuous and intense activity; they display high levels of concentration, creativity, energy and persistence. Children identified as being high on both well-being and involvement are more likely to develop good learning skills and make faster progress than are children who score poorly. The scale is used diagnostically to identify children who require extra support and intervention in order to make the most of the opportunities on offer – and to alert parents and professionals when something is going amiss.

In addition to the normal day-to-day difficulties of being a child, there are particular stresses that need to be taken into consideration. For example, children who were born prematurely or who were summer-born babies may need more intensive interaction to help them cope with the different developmental maturity they experience among their peers. Other stresses arise during transition periods, for example in preschool when children have to endure separation from carers at the same time as learning the institutional rules of the setting. This can be difficult because at home they can self-regulate their activities and maintain a balance that suits their own needs: they can choose when to have a drink or snack, when to use the toilet and when to rest, exercise, play and work. In the more formal atmosphere of preschool and even more at school, children may lose their autonomy and experience emotional stress over simple practices – queuing for drinks, asking to go to the toilet, playing and working at set times and not being offered a space or time to rest. Dehydration, fatigue and urinary infections are common in young children in preschool and reception classes, and those can lead to inappropriate behaviour or distress and loss of self-esteem.

Time to reflect

Many children experience deep emotional stress over toileting arrangements – they often refuse to use the school toilets and try to hang on until they get home.
Why do you think this might be?
Should adults be concerned about this?
What arrangements can nurseries and schools make to help allay children's anxieties?

The importance of being heard

Simply listening to children, taking their concerns seriously and trying to see the world from their point of view can go a long way towards alleviating distress and can provide practitioners with important clues about a child's state of mind. Cultivating empathetic listening skills is vital for early childhood practitioners. Children who are certain that they will be listened to in a supportive and non-judgemental way are more likely to disclose anxieties that can then be dealt with before they become insurmountable problems (the books of Vivian Gussin-Paley provide a blue-print for exemplary 'constructive listening' in the early childhood setting – see also Chapters 10 and 12).

As professionals, we often spend too long trying to cover our 'to do list' rather than just basking in the ebb and flow of conversation and enjoying the jokes and playfulness that make up a natural part of the day in the company of young children. Taking time to indulge in 'idle' chat with children (and their parents and our own colleagues) gives an insight into the way they see the world, their likes and dislikes, their fears and strengths and their interests and understandings. Health and well-being improve in relaxed, purposeful environments where the agenda is shared rather than imposed and where children and adults are free to run with ideas in a spirit of joint inquiry.

Nature, health and well-being

There is a growing concern that children are suffering a loss of mental, spiritual, social and physical well-being because they spend too much time indoors and that increasing urbanisation has divorced children from the natural environment. Richard Louv (2005) argues that contemporary children are suffering from what he calls 'nature deficit disorder', brought about by a lack of exposure to the outdoors, which is adversely affecting their health and well-being.

E.O. Wilson (1984) uses the term 'biophilia' or love of nature to describe our urge to connect with nature. He hypothesises that humans are hardwired to crave the natural world and that this begins in early childhood when children demonstrate an innately emotional affiliation to other living organisms. He argues that when we deprive children of this vital connection, we risk exposing them to physical, mental and spiritual stress that can lead to serious health problems. Wilson argues that being outside, feeling sunshine and rain, seeing trees blow in the wind, watching rivers run, hearing birdsong, playing with animals and physically engaging with the environment activates the 'spiritual' side of our understanding and contributes to our sense of being at one with the world and with ourselves.

The *Natural Childhood Report* (Moss, 2013) suggests that in the United Kingdom, the relationship between children and nature is particularly broken, with fewer than one in ten regularly playing out – one of the worst scores in Europe. Spending too long indoors, under artificial light, denies children the fundamental benefits provided by the restorative power of nature, as well as denying them the chance to develop their ecological understanding of the planet and the interconnectedness of life in all its forms.

To counter this trend, the Forest School movement (see Chapter 10) has been growing fast in the United Kingdom as more and more people come to recognise the importance of nature to children. Many preschool settings actively encourage children to play outside with free-flow classrooms that provide unfettered access to outside space, recognising that fresh air, natural surroundings, space and opportunity to run activates children's bodies and minds and feeds their imaginations.

> ### Time to reflect
>
> What can health staff, social workers and educational practitioners do to encourage families to spend time outside?
> How could you enthuse families about the benefits of outdoor play and activities?
> Think about your local children and family services. How proactive are they in promoting nature as a component of physical and mental well-being?

Providing a healthy environment for the world's children, now and in the future, should be a central concern for our leaders across the world. Governments and business leaders have a responsibility to make environments safe and clean by reducing toxins in the air, pollution in ground water and poisons in the ground. Every child deserves to have access to safe, green surroundings under a smog-free sky. And everyone working with young children should make outdoor play and nature study a part of every child's daily health routine – no matter what the weather.

Promoting health and well-being in early childhood settings

We can safely assume that most parents are 'good enough parents' to raise their children in a healthy, caring environment. However, children exposed to parental substance misuse, mental illness, neglect, abuse and domestic violence are more likely to experience problems: they may show poor attachment patterns, poor emotional self-regulation and poor social skills, which will affect their holistic development far into the future (Shonkoff & Phillips, 2000). Some epigenetic research suggests that this is because negative effects in childhood are hardwired into the body at a genetic level – but not everyone thinks the research is so definitive. A recent review of the literature by Michael Rutter (2012) suggests that many questions remain unanswered and that the challenge of how to effectively provide interventions for children who have undergone mental and physical adversity is still huge. Werner (1996) points out that even high-risk children can, and usually do, come through to adulthood relatively intact if they have someone who really cares for them. And that someone could be you.

Early childhood professionals who are themselves healthy and positive and who maintain a good work/life balance can provide just the role model for children who are struggling at home. Practitioners need to keep in mind that every child is unique – *uniquely vulnerable* and *uniquely resilient*. Sensitive, caring practitioners who listen and reflect can make a difference in the health and well-being of all children and families. That's what makes the job so rewarding!

Summary

- Public health and individual health are closely linked.
- Health is located in a social framework, not confined to the bio-medical framework of the body.
- Disease prevention and health promotion are twin prongs of the attack on children's ill-health.
- Educating children about healthy living is likely to have long-term effects on global child health because today's children turn into the adults of tomorrow.
- Good physical, mental, social and emotional health correlates with a social gradient of income.
- Love between child and carer provides the foundation of emotional, physical and social health.
- Fostering individual resilience is an important goal for mental health and well-being.
- Attention to diet, sleep, exercise and an outdoor lifestyle can all contribute to children's health and well-being.
- Respectful listening and respectful responding between adults and children lead to good feelings of mental, emotional and social well-being.
- A childcare workforce that models a healthy lifestyle and exemplifies the benefits of a good work/life balance provides the best chance for promoting health and welfare among children and their families.

Topics for further discussion

1 'The most basic capabilities for human development are to lead long and healthy lives, to be knowledgeable, to have access to the resources needed for a decent standard of living and to be able to participate in the life of the community. Without these, many choices are simply not available, and many opportunities in life remain inaccessible.' (United Nations Development Programme (2001) *Making New Technologies Work for Human Development. Human development report*, p. 9. New York: Oxford University Press.) Are choices equally available to all in our society?

2 Read the following passage from page 986 of chapter 42, titled 'The rearing, management and diseases of infancy and childhood' in *Mrs. Beeton's Household Management* (1861):

> We see elaborate care bestowed on a family of children, everything studied that can tend to their personal comfort – pure air, pure water, regular ablution, a dietary prescribed by art, and every precaution adopted that medical judgement and maternal love can dictate, for the well-being of the parents' hope; and find in despite of all this care and vigilance, disease and death invading the guarded treasure. We turn to the foetor and darkness that, in some obscure court, attend the robust brood who, coated in dirt and with mud and refuse for playthings, live and thrive, and grow into manhood, and, in contrast to the pale face and flabby flesh of the aristocratic child, exhibit strength, vigour, and well-developed frames, and our belief in the potency of the life giving elements of air, light, and cleanliness receives a shock that, at first sight, would appear fatal to the implied benefits of these, in reality, all-sufficient attributes of health and life.

What point is Mrs. Beeton making about health and well-being in this extract?
What is the subtext of her argument?
Is her view romantic or realistic?
How far could her words apply to children today?

3 In 2004, the Children Act was amended so that the definition of *significant harm* included 'the harm that children see or suffer by hearing or seeing the ill-treatment of another – particularly in the home'. Why do you think this addition was made? What role do professionals have in helping to protect the health and well-being of children in homes in which there is domestic violence?

Assignments

1 Look at the latest Office for National Statistics (ONS) figures for infant and perinatal mortality in England and Wales. What *social and biological factors* impact on the life chances of babies born in different sectors of society?
2 Think about the health and wellbeing issues which affect boys and girls around the world. Choose a country from the developing world and compare conditions for children there with conditions in the United Kingdom. What are the major difficulties for health and well-being in each country?
3 Find out all you can about ADHD. What evidence is there to support the idea that ADHD is physiological in origin? What evidence is there to support the idea that ADHD is ecological in origin?
4 Access current guidelines to find out the latest advice on healthy eating for newborns to eight-year-olds.

Further reading

Cowie, H. (2012) *From Birth to Sixteen: Children's health, social, emotional and linguistic development.* Abingdon: Routledge. This provides a wealth of information on research into individual aspects of child health.

Underdown, A. (2007) *Young Children's Health and Well-being.* Maidenhead: Open University Press/McGraw-Hill Education. This provides a clear analysis of issues around the promotion of health in the early years.

Redsell, S. and Hastings, A. (eds) (2010) *Listening to Children and Young People in Healthcare Consultations.* Abingdon: Radcliffe. This provides examples of ways in which child healthcare professionals can engage with young children to help them to manage their own health.

Rudolf M., Lee T. and Levene M. (2011) *Paediatrics and Child Health* (3rd edn). Chichester: Wiley/Blackwell. This provides a comprehensive account of clinical practice in common childhood disorders from birth onwards.

Useful websites

The Spirit of '45 by Ken Loach (2013) provides a sobering account of life before the welfare state in Britain. If you want to know how you and your family would have fared in pre-1945 Britain, feed your details into the website: **www.thespiritof45.com**.

Sugar reduction: the evidence for action (2015) from Public Health England provides a compelling case for the link between obesity in children and sugar intake: **https://www.gov.uk/government/publications/sugar-reduction-from-evidence-into-action.**

Stephen Moss, author of the report *Natural Childhood*, has produced a short video to introduce ideas about childhood and nature: **https://www.nationaltrust.org.uk/documents/read-our-natural-childhood-report.pdf.** and **https://www.youtube.com/watch?v=rBwKrbfhgDU**

References

Aldridge, Kenway, P., MacInnes. T. and Parekh, A. (2012) *Monitoring poverty and social exclusion.* Joseph Rowntree Foundation (JRF). https://www.jrf.org.uk/report/monitoring-poverty-and-social-exclusion-2012. Accessed 30 December 2016

Allen, G. (2011) (The Allen Report) *Early Intervention: The Next Steps. An Independent Report to Her Majesty's Government.*https://www.gov.uk/government/uploads/system/uploads/attachment_data/file/284086/early-intervention-next-steps2.pdf. Accessed 30 December 2016

Brancaccio, M.T. (2000) Educational hyperactivity: the historical emergence of a concept. *Intercultural Education* 11(2): pp. 165–177

Child to Child (CtC). www.child-to-child.org

DfES (2003) *Every Child Matters* (Green Paper). London: HMSO

DoH (1997) *National Framework for Children, Young People and Maternity Services.* London: HMSO

DoH (2004) *National Framework for Children, Young People and Maternity Services.* London: HMSO

DoH (2009) *Healthy Child Programme* (HCP): *pregnancy and the first five years of life* https://www.gov.uk/government/publications/healthy-child-programme-pregnancy-and-the-first-5-years-of-life. Accessed 31 August 2013

DoH (2011) *Start Active, Stay Active: A report on physical activity for health from the four home countries' Chief Medical Officers* (updated 2016). https://www.gov.uk/government/publications/start-active-stay-active-a-report-on-physical-activity-from-the-four-home-countries-chief-medical-officers. Accessed 30 December 2016

Field, F. (2010) *The Foundation Years: preventing poor children becoming poor adults.* HM Government http://webarchive.nationalarchives.gov.uk/20110120090128/http:/poverty review.independent.gov.uk/media/20254/poverty-report.pdf . Accessed 30 December 2016

Furedi, F. (2004) *Therapy Culture: Cultivating Vulnerability in an Uncertain Age.* Routledge: London

Griffiths, L.J., Cortina-Borja, M., Sera, F., Pouliou, T., Geraci, M., Rich, C., Cole, T.J., Law, C., Joshi, H., Ness, A.R., Jebb, S.A. and Dezateux, C. (2013, August) How active are our children? Findings from the Millennium Cohort Study. *British Medical Journal* 3(8). doi:10.1136

Kreitzman, L., Foster, R. and Wolpert, L. (2004) *Rhythms of Life: The biological clocks that control the daily lives of every living thing.* London: Profile Books

Laevers, F. (2011) 'Experiential Education: Making Care and Education More Effective Through Well-being and Involvement', in *Encyclopedia on Early Childhood Development.* http://www.child-encyclopedia.com/sites/default/files/textes-experts/en/857/experiential-education-making-care-and-education-more-effective-through-well-being-and-involvement.pdf. Accessed 30 December 2016

Layard, R. and Dunn, J. (2009) *A Good Childhood: Searching for Values in a Competitive Age.* London: Penguin

Lewis, I. and Lenehan, C. (Forum Co-chairs) (2012) *Report of the Children's and Young People's Health Outcomes Forum.* https://www.gov.uk/government/uploads/system/uploads/attachment_data/file/216852/CYP-report.pdf. Accessed 30 December 2016

Lobstein, T., Baur, L. and Uauy, R. (2004), Obesity in children and young people: a crisis in public health. *Obesity Reviews* 5: 4–85. doi: 10.1111/j.1467–789X.2004.00133.x0

Louv, R. (2005) *Last Child in the Woods: Saving Our Children from Nature-Deficit Disorder* Chapeltown, NC: Algonquin Books

Lustig R.H., Schmidt L.A. and Brindis C.D. (2012) Public Health: The toxic truth about sugar. *Nature* 482: 27–29

Marmot Review (2010) *Fair Society: Healthy Lives.* http://www.instituteofhealthequity.org/projects/fair-society-healthy-lives-the-marmot-review. Accessed 30 December 2016

McGuinness, M., McGuinness, J. and Dyer, J. (2000) Risk and protective factors in children adopted from the former Soviet Union. *Journal of Pediatric Health Care* 14(3, May–June): 109–116

Morison, S.J., Ames, E.W. and Chisholm, K. (1995) (Canadian-Romanian Adoption Study) The development of children adopted from Romanian orphanages. *Merril-Palmer Quarterly* 41: 411–430

Moss, M. (2013) *Salt, Sugar, Fat: How the Food Giants Hooked Us*. New York: Random House.

Moss, S. (2013) *Natural Childhood Report*. https://www.nationaltrust.org.uk/documents/read-our-natural-childhood-report.pdf. Accessed 22 August 2013

NHS Choices (2015) Your health, your choices: How much sleep do kids need? http://www.nhs.uk/Livewell/Childrenssleep/Pages/howmuchsleep.aspx. Accessed 7 August 2016

NICE (National Institute for Health and Clinical Excellence) (2012) *Social and emotional well-being: early years*. https://www.nice.org.uk/guidance/ph40. Accessed 30 December 2016

Perry, B.D. (2002) Childhood experience and the expression of genetic potential: what childhood neglect tells us about nature and nurture. *Brain and Mind* 3: 79–100

Rutter, M. (2012) Achievements and challenges in the biology of environmental effects. in *Proceedings of the National Academy of Sciences of the United States of America*. http://www.pnas.org/content/109/Supplement_2/17149.full.pdf. Accessed 23 June 2016

Rutter, M. and the English and Romanian Adoptees (ERA) Study Team (1998) Developmental catch-up, and deficit, following adoption after severe early deprivation. *Journal of Child Psychology and Psychiatry* 39: 465–476

Rutter, M., Beckett, C., Castle, J., Kreppner, J., Stevens, S. and Sonuga-Burke, E. (2009) *Policy and Practice Implications from the English and Romanian Adoptees (ERA) Study: Forty five Key Questions*. Nuffield Foundation. http://www.nuffieldfoundation.org/english-and-romanian-adoptee-study. Accessed 30 December 2016

Sabates, R. and Dex, S. (2012) *Multiple risk factors in young children's development* (published online, accessed 22 March 2013) CLS Cohort Studies Working paper 2012/1. London Institute of Education, London University

Shonkoff, J.P. and Phillips, D.A. (2000) *From Neurons to Neighbourhood: The Science of Early Childhood Development*. Washington, DC: National Academy Press

Sigerist H.E. (1941) *Medicine and Human Welfare*. New Haven, CT: Yale University Press

S. Tai, P. Kinderman et al. (eds) (2009) *Psychological health and well-being: A new ethos for mental health*. A Report of the Working Group on Psychological Health and Well-Being.

Tickell, C. (2011) *The Early Years: foundations for life, health and learning* (Tickell review). https://www.gov.uk/government/publications/the-early-years-foundations-for-life-health-and-learning-an-independent-report-on-the-early-years-foundation-stage-to-her-majestys-government. Accessed 30 December 2016

UN (2013) *The Rise of the South: Human Progress in a Diverse World*. http://hdr.undp.org/en/2013-report. Accessed 19 March 2013

UNCRC (1989) *United Nations Convention on the Rights of the Child*. http://www.unicef.org.uk/Documents/Publication-pdfs/UNCRC_PRESS200910web.pdf. Accessed 30 December 2016

UNICEF (2007) *Child poverty in perspective: An overview of child well-being in rich countries*. http://www.unicef.org/media/files/ChildPovertyReport.pdf Innocenti research centre report Card 7. Accessed 31 August 2013

Weisner, T. (2002) Ecocultural Understanding of Children's Developmental Pathways. *Human development* 45: 275–281. http://www.tweisner.com/yahoo_site_admin/assets/docs/Weisner_20027_Ecocultural_understanding_of_dev_pathways_A48.220134854.pdf. Accessed 19 March 2013

Werner, E.E. (1996) Vulnerable but invincible: high risk children from birth to adulthood. *European Child and Edolescent Psychiatry* 5: 47–51, Supl. 1

WHO (World Health Organisation) (1948) *Preamble to the Constitution of the World Health Organization as adopted by the International Health Conference*, New York, 19–22 June 1946; signed on 22 July 1946 by the representatives of 61 states (Official Records of the World Health Organization, no. 2, p. 100) and entered into force on 7 April 1948. http://www.who.int/governance/eb/who_constitution_en.pdf. Accessed 10 February 2017

WHO (1986) *Ottawa Charter for Health Promotion*. http://www.who.int/healthpromotion/conferences/previous/ottawa/en/. Accessed 30 December 2016

WHO (2015) *Children: reducing mortality. Fact sheet no. 178*

Wilson, E.O. (1984) *Biophilia*. Cambridge, MA: Harvard University Press

THE CHILDREN'S WORKFORCE: PROFESSIONAL PRACTICE

Professional practice for early childhood

Introduction

Children and young people are our future and there are great rewards in being part of the workforce that inspires the next generation. Early childhood has been the Cinderella among services because looking after young children was once seen as something that came naturally and required no training beyond being kind and 'motherly'. It is now recognised that early childhood is a complex area requiring professional expertise – both academic and practical. This chapter provides an account of the pathways available on the journey from student to early years professional and some of the challenges of working in an environment that combines education, health and social care.

Becoming a professional in early childhood services

If you are reading this chapter, you will probably be taking one of the many courses designed to prepare you for work in children's education, health or social care. What qualities do professionals in early years need? In Unwin and Hogg's book *Social work with children and families* (2012), the authors provide a list of desirable attributes for professionals in children's services. These include being

- aware of self and others
- aware of impact of behaviour on others
- aware of strengths and weaknesses
- clear about motivation for being in the job
- willing to invest in children others might give up on
- empathetic and able to listen without judging
- knowledgeable, open to new ideas, willing to learn from others
- wary of accepting superficial explanations
- able to form good relationships quickly with children and families
- politically aware and committed to social justice
- child centred
- organised, efficient and able to sustainably optimise available resources

- capable of clear analysis
- innovative and creative
- able to achieve a healthy work/life balance.

Time to reflect

Would you want to query anything on Unwin and Hogg's list?
Would you want to add anything?
Why do you think achieving a 'healthy work/life balance' is important for professionals in children's services?

Careers in childcare and education

There are many career opportunities in the children's workforce across the private, public and voluntary sectors:

- education – childcare, educational psychology, playwork, library services, primary and nursery teaching, special needs;
- health – art/drama/music therapy, clinical psychology, health visiting, family support, paediatric medicine and nursing, speech and language therapy;
- legal work – family law, youth justice, child protection;
- social care – advice centres, counselling, family courts, social work, fostering and adoption services;
- playwork – after-school clubs, adventure playgrounds, forest schools, animal therapy, family centres, holiday clubs, hospitals, play development for local authorities.

Qualifications

There are dozens of childcare qualifications available in the United Kingdom, and they can be very confusing (Nutbrown, 2012). To work in a day nursery, preschool or out-of-school club, you need a DBS (Disclosure and Barring Service) certificate to show that you have no criminal convictions and minimum level-2 qualification in early years or playwork. However, the national aspiration is for the entire early years workforce (including childminders) to be qualified to level 3. Much of the research and literature into early childhood supports the case for having a highly qualified, highly trained workforce with articulate and reflective practitioners who can help children lead fulfilling childhoods and enjoy satisfying lives (Schweinhart et al., 2005; OECD, 2006; Sylva et al., 2010; Field, 2010; Marmot, 2010; Tickell, 2011; Allen, 2011; Nutbrown, 2012).

Table 14.1 below shows the qualifications required to work in different childcare roles.

Parents need to have confidence in the knowledge and expertise of the professionals looking after their children and to be able to trust them to deliver high-quality care. Formal academic courses can provide an excellent theoretical foundation in child development, policy and care, but a great deal of learning also takes place in the workplace. Eraut (2008) suggests that

Table 14.1 Childcare qualifications in the United Kingdom

Qualification level and role	Qualification
Level 1 – entry level	Award in an introductory course to childcare (optional)
Level 2 – assistant under supervision	Certificate in an introduction to early years education and care
Level 3/4 – supervisory roles	Diploma for the early years practitioner (early years educator)
Level 5 – supervisory and leading roles	Early Years Foundation Degree Higher National Diploma (HND) in advanced practice with children and families
Levels 6/7 – professional roles in education and social work	BA (Hons) degree (level 6). This is a general degree which leads to professional pathways for level 7 qualifications such as early years teacher status (EYTS) to work with children from birth to five, Qualified Teacher Status (QTS) to work with children over five or professional qualifications in child and family social work recognised by the Health and Social Care Council

workplace learning is too often neglected in favour of theoretical learning, and he argues that formal academic learning is most valuable when it is relevant and well timed and when it matches the skills and practice of learners in a working environment. For this reason, working in a setting while studying can be invaluable; it enables you to apply theories to practical situations and to reflect on the outcomes.

Time to reflect

Discuss the relative contributions of 'learning on the job' and 'learning the theory' for the development of professional practice in early childhood.

Rogoff (2008) identifies three distinct phases on any path to professional practice – *apprenticeship phase* (observing and listening), *guided participation* (trying things out under supervision) and *participatory appropriation* (being self-critical and reflecting on practice). She suggests that a professional is someone who has reached a stage of being able to be *critical* and *reflective* about theory and practice. In early years work, the best practitioners can articulate their vision for children and provide practical and theoretical evidence to back up the decisions they make to improve the service they provide.

Finding the right career in childcare services

Students take up a variety of different roles in health, education, law and social work connected with children's issues. They may be self-employed (like childminders); or they may work in the public sector (such as schools and the NHS), the private sector (such as privately-owned nurseries) or the voluntary sector (such as charities). The following case studies describe some career paths of early years professionals as they look for the right niche in childcare and education services.

Case study: A preschool manager in the voluntary sector

Stella has been working in the same preschool for over 20 years. She started by volunteering one morning a week when her children were small. Over the next decade she gradually increased her hours and her commitment. First, she attended training sessions, and then she took up courses leading to qualifications in playwork, childcare and education. When her own children had finished school, she pursued a foundation degree in Early Childhood Studies before tackling a BA (Hons) at her local university. She says, 'My degree experience has definitely increased my confidence and allowed me to do things I never thought I was capable of doing. A lot of the confidence came from mixing with other students and sharing ideas and experiences.'

Stella is now the manager of her preschool, working with four other staff. Her preschool is run by a voluntary committee with whom she has a good working relationship, and they trust her and her team to apply the principles of the early years foundation stage. Stella says that 'the best part of the role will always be the interaction with the children'. But she also enjoys training and developing the young students who come to her through the CACHE (Council for Awards in Care, Health and Education) programme. She finds the paperwork onerous on top of the record-keeping required for OFSTED but she thinks it is worthwhile and gets great satisfaction from passing on her expertise and seeing the students flourish. She is concerned that university costs may put off potential early years students because salaries in the sector are so low after qualifying. In addition, she fears that the new Statutory Framework for The Early Years Foundation Stage (2014), stipulating the ratios of qualified staff in settings, may make her own preschool unsustainable. She is worried that because numbers in the preschool fluctuate each year, and with it her funding, she may be unable to employ the well-qualified staff required by the regulations.

Stella is very keen to improve the professionalism of her staff. The preschool received an 'outstanding' from OFSTED during the last inspection and she wants to maintain the standard. She believes that staff qualification is one of the strongest predictors of the quality of early childhood education. At the moment, she is releasing one member of staff, Karen, an English graduate, to study part-time to achieve EYTS (Early Years Teacher Status) on the graduate employment-based route funded by the NCTL (National Council for Teaching and Learning). Fortunately, Karen held GCSEs at grade C or above in English, maths and science, a requirement for enrolling in the course. The training is for 12 months, and the employer receives £14,000 to pay for the course fee, salary enhancement, supply cover and further training. The scheme is designed to make Karen a 'change agent' who will improve standards by sharing her skills and mentoring the other staff, as well as modelling effective behaviour to safeguard and support children. When Karen has qualified, she will need to be paid more, but the committee hopes that her expertise will help the setting expand and attract more parents and children to enable them to enhance her salary.

Stella and her staff take advantage of all the free training days on offer in the locality, and the management committee has agreed to pay travel expenses and supply cover out of the budget. This means there is less money for other things, like new computers, but they have decided to prioritise the education of staff as the best guarantee of providing excellence for the children.

Discussion questions

Why is Stella prioritising staff development over upgrading equipment?

What does Stella's own career trajectory tell us about the changing attitudes to early childhood care and education?

Case study: A letter from a PGCE student

'I am currently close to finishing my early years PGCE (Postgraduate Certificate in Education). I decided to go down the QTS (Qualified Teacher Status) route rather than EYTS (Early Years Teacher Status) because I think it will give me more employment options (and, hopefully, more money!). I applied for a SCITT (School Centred Initial Teacher Training) placement so that I could learn and earn at the same time, but I didn't get onto the scheme because it was so over-subscribed. However, I'm relieved that I didn't, because I think I would have found writing assignments *and* teaching *and* looking after my family much too stressful.

So far, I have had placements in a reception class and in a foundation stage unit, and my final one will be in a mixed Year 1 and 2 class. This year has made me realise how valuable my ECS degree has been as a stepping stone into teaching. It helped widen my understanding of theories of child development and also reinforced my belief in children's receiving positive learning experiences from a young age. The degree enabled me to develop crucial study skills, which have been a great benefit for PGCE assignments – especially the work I did for my dissertation on using stories in schools. This year I'm focusing on literacy and the changes in the National Curriculum – and the problems the changes are making for early years teachers. It's hard work doing placements and assignments at the same time, but it will be worth it in the end'.

Discussion questions

How far is work/life balance a factor in this student's decision to follow a college-based route to QTS?

Why has she opted for QTS rather than EYTS?

If you were a course tutor, how would you outline the relative strengths of the SCITT and PGCE routes to a teaching career?

Case study: From teaching assistant to art therapist

After completing her BA (Hons) in Early Childhood Studies, Natalie contemplated a career as a primary school teacher. She took a post as a teaching assistant for a year to see if teaching was right for her. The job provided her with practical experience and showed her the realities of working alongside other professionals in a large city primary school. The pay wasn't great, but it helped that she could live with her parents.

She had opportunities to lead lessons with the whole class and to support group work with children with IEPs (individual educational plans). She also attended team meetings and was involved in the whole process of planning, teaching and reviewing. The school sent her on several training courses and invited her to help with a music, art and dance festival put on by older children in the school.

In her second term, she was given a special responsibility: teaching phonics to one child who was struggling to read. She found this very satisfying because she built a close personal relationship with the boy and found all sorts of innovative ways of keeping him engaged. He had a particular, if bizarre, interest in vacuum cleaners, so they based a lot of work around the Henry vacuum cleaner (the one with a face and a bowler hat). Much to her delight, and his, he made good progress and even presented his science work on vacuums to the class during a show-and-tell session.

Although she enjoyed all the challenges of primary teaching, Natalie discovered that she enjoyed working on a one-to-one basis best. She is now working as an assistant in a children's ward at the local hospital, where she helps children with school-work and organises art and craft sessions. Her long-term plan is to get a master's degree in art therapy so that she can work with individual children in a variety of settings, such as schools, homes and clinics.

Discussion questions

What were the benefits of being a teaching assistant for Natalie?

How far could she be described as an apprentice teacher?

Is apprenticeship a useful model for learning?

Case study: Family support adviser for Barnardo's

After leaving school, James spent a year working in an orphanage in Romania. He was shocked by the conditions he found but could understand the pressures staff were under to cater for so many children with such different needs and disabilities. Basic food and hygiene was all they had time to provide. He was disturbed by the evident slow development of many of the children.

He signed up for a course in child development when he got back to England. All the other students were female, so he felt slightly out of place. But they made him feel welcome, and he went on to do a foundation degree in Early Childhood Studies. During his course, he volunteered with Barnardo's. He found himself working on a summer play scheme on a large social housing estate. With a team of playworkers and social services personnel based at the Sure Start Centre, he helped with sports and arts activities and also took his turn in the advice centre, helping parents to access services. He became aware of the difficulties facing the families he worked with, which included poor housing, drugs, mental ill-health, poverty and low aspirations.

He decided that he would like to become a social worker. He applied to turn his foundation degree into a BA (Hons) in childhood studies so that he would be in a position to apply for a post-graduate course in social work. After he graduated, a job came up at Barnardo's, and the manager encouraged him to apply. For two years he worked as a family support adviser, working on a one-to-one basis with parents and children to help improve their chances of a successful future. He finds this work very fulfilling because he likes helping people and solving problems. He is currently studying part-time in a two-year social work course that will qualify him to become registered under the Health and Social Care Council as a social worker. He has recently been involved in providing evidence in the family courts in several custody cases for children in his care, and he hopes that one day he can work in the Children and Family Court Advisory and Support Service (CAFCASS), where he can use his advocacy skills to help get the best outcomes for children who are at risk of failing in society.

Discussion questions

The routes into a career in early childhood services are many and varied. What was your journey?

What further training might James want to access to strengthen his chances of working with CAFCASS?

As you can see, courses in childcare and education offer all sorts of possibilities.

Becoming a reflective professional

One characteristic of being an effective early childhood professional is the ability to *reflect critically* on the practices put in place for children and to make informed interventions to bring about changes and improvements. Reflective thinking is characterised by a questioning or critical attitude towards what you read (information), what you do (action) and how you do it (behaviour). Peters (1991) summarises the process of reflective thinking with the acronym DATA – Describing, Analysing, Theorising and Acting. In early childhood settings, reflective practice helps professionals to make qualitative changes intended to improve outcomes for children (Pence & Pacini-Ketchabaw, 2010). A reflective approach can make the workplace a more rewarding place for children and adults alike because it challenges people to dare to do things differently.

Figure 14.1 Many students are now asked to keep a reflective log at some stage of their professional programme.
Source: Author's own.

Reflective practice is now embedded in many professional programmes, and most students are asked to keep a reflective log at some stage, using one of the models of reflective practice available (Lewin, 1948; Schon, 1983; Kolb, 1984; Peters, 1991; Lindon, 2005). Typically, a reflective log *describes* a significant event or *critical incident* observed in practice, *analyses* the situation more widely, *theorises* possible reasons for the behaviour observed and proposes a course of *action* designed to bring about change; the action is then put into practice and evaluated. If the changes made are unsatisfactory, the process begins again.

One of the most frequently cited models of reflective practice is Kolb's *experiential learning cycle*, which breaks the reflective process down into simple stages:

1 concrete experience (the situation or critical incident under examination);
2 reflective observation (pinpointing and listing the significant aspects of the incident or situation);
3 abstract conceptualisation (teasing out possible meanings or theories underlying the incident);
4 active experimentation (using trial and error to try to change and improve the situation);
5 evaluating impact (assessing outcomes and being prepared to start the process again).

The Early Years Foundation Stage (2014) emphasises the importance of observation, assessment and planning (OAP) in providing activities which start with the individual child. Kolb's experiential learning cycle offers a blueprint for *systematically* describing and examining a problem in order to plan the most helpful way forward. The case study below shows how OAP works in practice.

Case study: Reflective practice in action

Brenda, a playgroup worker, became increasingly frustrated by Daniel's behaviour because he persistently filled a bag with toys from different areas of the room and carried them outside to the sandpit. Despite asking him not to do it and explaining that it took her ten minutes to put everything back in the right place at the end of the day, he continued to do it. On one particularly hectic day, she told him he was naughty, took the bag away and put it on a high shelf out of reach. Daniel was upset and burst into tears. Brenda told him that he couldn't always have his own way and he should find some other game to play.

Karen, a student on her first work placement was shadowing Brenda. She had been observing Daniel for her child study. She did not like to see him upset. Later that morning, she asked him gently why he liked packing the bag and taking it out to the sandpit. He told her that he was going on holiday, so he needed sun cream (the bricks), a toothbrush (the paintbrush), a sun hat (from the dressing-up box) and so on. She was struck by his sense of purpose and decided to describe the incident in her reflective log.

What puzzled her most was that he had repeated the same game at every session she had observed; she could see the link between the sandpit and a holiday at the seaside but was mystified by the repetitive behaviour. She showed her reflective log to her tutor, who directed her towards Piaget's work on *schema theory* and suggested she read *Understanding Schemas in Young Children. Again! Again!* (Louis, Beswick & Featherstone, 2013). She found that Piaget defined a schema as a 'cohesive repeatable action sequence possessing component actions that are tightly inter-connected and governed by a core of meaning' while Athey (2003) described a schema as a pattern of repeated actions which later develop into a coherent concept. She discovered that children have an irresistible urge to repeat certain actions during new phases of learning as they codify and organise new experiences. She read more widely and found that this particular child was probably compelled to repeat his behaviour because he was in the process of perceiving and organising concepts related to space and time. Daniel was learning that it takes time and planning to move from one place to another, and his understanding of the link between time and distance was reinforced by each repetition of the game. In terms of the EYFS curriculum, he was learning about maths and geography.

On her next placement day, she took in a box containing some towels, empty toothpaste boxes, sun cream bottles, some sunhats and a snorkel. She also took along a wheeled 'elephant' suitcase borrowed from a friend. She watched with great interest to see what effect this would have on Daniel. Daniel was excited: he put on a sun hat and then packed the suitcase and wheeled it outside to the sandpit.

Brenda was delighted, 'That's distracted him! He won't take everything else out to the sandpit now.'

Karen said she wasn't really distracting him; she was trying to understand what was driving him. She explained what she had learned about schemas, and Brenda was intrigued. Together they decided to set up a holiday area in one corner to see what would happen. Over the next few weeks, several other children joined in, and the holidays became more and more elaborate. Children shared their experiences of holidays, travel and transport and generated lots of new vocabulary and new thinking about far and near and the length of journeys and places to go. They counted how many paces they needed to get from the classroom to the sandpit. One parent brought in a globe, and the children asked lots of questions about distance and the time it would take to travel from one part of the world to another. One day, Daniel drew a picture showing his journey from home to preschool. He explained it to the group, and soon everyone was drawing pictures of their own journey.

The setting supervisor was impressed by all this activity and asked Karen to make a poster presentation on schemas to staff and parents at the next open evening. Karen later continued her investigation of schemas for her final research dissertation.

Discussion questions

What *changes* resulted from the student's investigation into this critical incident? For Daniel? For Brenda? For other adults? For the student?

How did Karen organise her *systematic* reflection?

How does this reflective process satisfy the EYFS requirement for OAP?

Such careful listening and observation, together with reading, research and a reflective mindset, offer the best route towards fulfilling the EYFS mantra of 'starting with the child'.

Working in a professional team

Most early childhood work involves working in teams – even childminders who work alone are encouraged to belong to networks where they can find support and share ideas and practices. You may find yourself working primarily in education, social work or health care, where teams share a common professional language and purpose. At other times you may find yourself in a multidisciplinary team, where jargon and acronyms and different professional perspectives make communication more difficult.

Successful teams

A successful team is a collection of individuals working towards a common purpose in a spirit of camaraderie. Successful early years teams are motivated by a common desire to provide a high quality of service that puts the needs of the child at the centre of their work (Jones & Pound, 2008). But teams have to be nurtured, maintained and developed over time, adapting to and incorporating the diverse skills and knowledge of the individuals in them. Handy (1990, in Read and Rees, 2003: p. 33) suggests that teams grow through four stages: *forming, storming, norming and performing*. In the forming stage, the team establishes a group identity and a shared philosophy. This is followed by a period of challenge (storming), when individuals begin to assert their particular viewpoint. As things settle around a common ground (norming), the team works more harmoniously. The final stage comes when the team has matured and can implement the core vision effectively (performing). People find their jobs more fulfilling when they can work from their strengths and when their different areas of expertise, skills and talents are recognised. Teams are most effective when roles and responsibilities are clear and when there is open communication that takes into account the identities and cultures of the individuals involved (Floyd & Morrison, 2013).

Moss (1994) argues that in early years services, children and their families should be considered part of the team. He writes that adults should be approachable and non-judgemental in their relations with children and should strive to establish a democratic ethos where everyone's view is respected. He suggests that a democratic approach is more likely to foster qualities of responsibility, perseverance, creative problem solving and self-awareness in adults and children alike because in a collaborative atmosphere, people are more likely to develop the confidence and trust to ask questions, share ideas and tackle new challenges. The EYFS (2014) emphasises the role of the 'key person' and suggests that this key person must be assigned before the child starts attending sessions. Ideally, the key person would begin to build a relationship with the child and family before they come into the setting so that a child can manage the transition from home with a degree of trust and confidence based on a degree of familiarity. This idea of partnership between professional and family is reinforced by the recent rollout of the Foundation Years document 'What to expect when? A Parents' Guide' (4children, 2015), which has been designed to sit alongside the EYFS to help parents support children's learning at home.

Dealing with conflict

Negative comments should be discouraged at all times. Negativity is contagious and makes individuals demoralised; it stymies collaboration; it invites a 'can't do' attitude that can easily permeate the whole organisation. Difficulties and antagonisms grow out of confusion, anxiety and fear of the unknown. Establishing a good working relationship among team members involves adapting to and accommodating the personalities, talents and attitudes of colleagues while enforcing zero tolerance for any expressions of disrespect towards others.

Sometimes disagreement is healthy and provides a springboard for new thinking that allows the organisation to move forward and to improve practice. On the other hand, unacknowledged disagreement can corrode trust between individuals and may divide teams into warring factions. Open communication and a clear understanding of roles and responsibilities can avoid many disagreements – knowing how your actions fit into the picture of the whole organisation reduces the opportunities for stress and conflict for children and adults alike. The key to managing conflict is listening – trying to see things from everyone's point of view in a non-judgemental way, setting out the areas of disagreement in a clear way and negotiating around it.

Honest and open dialogue should be encouraged but sometimes resolution is hard to reach and it may be politic to agree to disagree and to put the item back on the agenda for discussion at a later date!

Dealing with complacency

Too much agreement can be counterproductive too – it can lead to stagnation and doing things because this is the way they have always been done. Rigid role structures can make work boring and unsatisfying and may lead to team members being typecast so that their opportunities for widening their expertise and taking on new challenges are limited. Staff members who are routinely assigned to the same old roles may lose confidence in their abilities and retreat further into what is familiar and consequently become increasingly resistant to change. Complacency can lead to apathy, and people may opt for a quiet life and view change with suspicion, which is not a good basis for maintaining quality in work with young children (Read & Rees, 2003). Entrenched roles can also lead to unhealthy empire building and defensiveness about territory.

Regular reviews and appraisals for individuals can counteract complacency by enabling people to express their aspirations for career development; reviews also provide opportunities for managers to value their employees' contributions and to suggest ways of extending experience and training. The goal is to ensure that all team members feel a sense of shared pride in the work they do with children so that they feel comfortable enough to risk suggesting innovations and to participate in all spheres of activity – from chairing meetings to hands-on work with children. Sharing roles and tasks allows everyone to see the rewards and difficulties and promotes a more democratic ethos where everyone can feel valued and can value the contributions of others in a collegial atmosphere that can brings benefits to the organisation and the children.

Multi-agency teams

There will be occasions when you will work with professionals from other disciplines, perhaps when a child has special needs or when a family is in crisis. You may find yourself in a team comprising professionals from education, social work, health authorities and youth justice. Multi-agency teamwork should ideally rest on the core principles of social pedagogy – respect for children, knowledge of child development and a commitment to democratic principles and inclusion (Dunhill et al., 2009).

Some commonly identified obstacles to effective multi-agency working are as follows:

- poor communication
- inadequate record-keeping
- failure to monitor and report back
- failure to share information
- professional defensiveness
- poor understanding of the role of other agencies
- status anxieties and fears around relinquishing power and authority
- failure to share and accept responsibility
- tendency to sit on difficult decisions
- competing demands for limited resources
- entrenched professional beliefs
- use of jargon that is unfamiliar to other professionals
- inadequate time for reflection and discussion
- failure to access the views of all 'stakeholders' (including children)
- failure to adequately consider gender, class, race, income and education.

When these obstacles go unrecognised or unaddressed, the quality of service deteriorates, and children may suffer as a consequence. In the wake of Lord Laming's report (2003) into failed multidisciplinary collaboration in the Victoria Climbié case, all agencies are now required to use the Common Assessment Framework (CAF) based on the *Every Child Matters: Change for Children* (2004) agenda (promoting children's health, safety, enjoyment and achievement, democratic participation and economic well-being) with the aim of reducing the possibilities for error.

Sharing information across multi-agency teams – the Common Assessment Framework

The Common Assessment Framework is a process for gathering and recording information about children for whom there is concern (perhaps because there is a suspicion that they are being neglected or are suffering physical or mental abuse). It is part of a referral process to support agencies that are initiated by a professional who has noticed that a particular child may have additional needs or be at risk – it could be a teacher, a health professional, a police officer called in to a domestic incident or a social worker alerted by a neighbour. The CAF provides a core assessment to identify children's additional needs at the earliest opportunity so that interventions can begin as soon as possible. It is used for children where there are concerns about growth and development, additional educational requirements or family issues (such as parent/carer needs or families in difficulties). It is an assessment and planning document designed for professionals from all disciplines to share assessments, reports and referrals in a common language to make communication between agencies (and parents and children) clearer. Parents and children give their consent for the assessment to take place and have the right to read and query any report before signing it as a true account. The CAF is an important social document of our times because it represents a desire to democratise relations between children and adults, professional people and laypeople by giving equal weight to all voices in the referral process.

The CAF consists of

- a pre-assessment checklist to determine whether there is cause to make a core assessment;
- a standard form to record the core assessment from whichever professional service is involved;
- a delivery plan to record the action required and a process by which it can be monitored and reviewed.

In most cases, the professionals raising concerns will be able to directly access some form of intervention. For example, a health visitor might refer a child to the GP or a paediatric service; a preschool teacher might consult an educational psychologist; or a social worker might be able to direct the family to benefits agencies or support groups. But where the needs are complex or where there are acute concerns about the child's safety and well-being, a multi-agency meeting will be convened – in the United Kingdom, this is organised under the auspices of the local authority Children, Learning and Young People's (CLYP) Directorate. All the services involved with the child and family, called the Team Around the Child or TAC, will be asked to supply reports, written in accordance with CAF guidelines. The TAC then meets face to face, and a lead professional is appointed to draw up a package of support for the child and to review and monitor progress. The aim is to identify needs early, to coordinate services and to provide an integrated programme of intervention as rapidly as possible. The CAF is designed to streamline the intervention process, to ensure that all professionals are informed and to coordinate their efforts so that no child slips through the support net. However, Munro (2011) argues that the shared language and shared categories of core assessment risks homogenising evaluations and promoting an unhealthy consensus between professionals rather than stimulating debate between them to the detriment of the children in their care.

Time to reflect

Critics argue that an unforeseen consequence of the CAF is that it encourages professionals to focus on documentation, procedures and processes at the expense of the needs of the children. Why might this be so?

Others suggest that the CAF absolves professionals from a direct responsibility to act once they have written up and shared their case notes. How might this happen?

The EYFS (2014) puts schools and settings at the centre of multi-professional networks to coordinate support services for children. What implications might this have for professionals in the education and care sector?

The professional's role in safeguarding children at risk

A primary responsibility of every childcare professional's work, no matter which service they represent, or at what level, is to safeguard and protect children, especially those who may be at risk of ill-treatment and neglect. Health visitors are the first point of contact between families and children's services in the early months of life, and they can direct parents towards available services such as portage (help for children with disabilities), speech and language services, parent support agencies in mental health, employment and financial advice, health programmes, parenting classes, care and education in the local area and many other services provided in the volunteer and charity sector.

Children are most vulnerable to abuse and neglect in the preschool years. Half of all child abuse and neglect cases involve children under five (NSPCC, 2013), during the period of time after the health visitor has stopped visiting and before the time children are formally enrolled in school. During this period, some children are beyond the radar of children's agencies – but even children who are visible and 'in the system' can still be overlooked because most adults have a natural tendency to assume that parents and carers will always protect young children, and so may miss signs of maltreatment.

Signs that children may be at risk

When any form of physical or psychological harm is suspected, professionals should look out for subtle signs *in the child* to decide whether there is a genuine cause for concern. In the early stages, staff can carry out some simple observational checks immediately and with a minimum of intervention. They might ask themselves the following questions:

- Does the child smell unwashed? Do her clothes smell musty? Do other children avoid sitting close to her?
- Is the child unkempt, pale and listless, or perhaps unnecessarily hostile and aggressive? Is he underweight or overweight? Does he gobble his food and ask for more? Does he take food from other children?
- Are there any obvious outward signs of abrasion or bruising?
- When the child speaks, is her voice cracked, feeble or unnecessarily loud? Does she ever disclose disturbing information? Does she behave inappropriately with other children?
- When an adult approaches, does the child stiffen or recoil? Is he unusually rough, or unusually withdrawn? Is he inexplicably clingy with members of staff? Does he routinely reject kindness and offers of help and sympathy?
- What kind of relationship does the child have with the parent/carer? Is the child avoidant or clingy? Is there any evidence of rejection or scapegoating? Is the parent/carer responsive? Are there any changes or difficulties in the family circumstances? If there are siblings, do they show similar symptoms?

Time to reflect

Discuss these signs of risk with colleagues. Would they necessarily provide evidence of neglect or abuse, or could there be alternative explanations?

If you suspect abuse of some kind, raise your concerns with your manager or designated safeguarding officer. Your manager may then ask you to keep a written dated record of your concerns over the next weeks. It is important at this stage to listen to the child, allowing him or her to explain, alone and in confidence, whether anything is troubling them. Reassure them that you are on their side, but do not probe or be intrusive. Your manager may take soundings from other members of staff and may discreetly open a dialogue with parents/carers. If the evidence is strong enough, then the next step is for the manager to refer the matter to health professionals, social services or police. Guidelines for professionals can be found in *What to do if you are worried a child is being abused: Advice for practitioners* (HM Government, 2015 at https://www.gov.uk/government/publications/what-to-do-if-youre-worried-a-child-is-being-abused—2).

When safeguarding fails

When safeguarding and child protection fails catastrophically and death or serious injury ensues, a *serious case review* is called where independent investigators sift through the case notes of the various agencies involved in order to establish where things went wrong and what can be learnt for the future.

Case study: A serious case review

Read the following summary of the serious case review into the death of Daniel Pelka and reflect on the documentation, processes and procedures of the professionals involved in his case.

Daniel Pelka died in Coventry at the age of four at the hands of his mother and her partner. The mother spoke mainly Polish, and her immigrant status meant she could not access social support. Daniel was starved and beaten for months before he died and 26 separate incidents required police involvement at the family home between March 2006 and December 2010. His parents were jailed for 30 years each after being found guilty of his murder.

Here are some of the critical incidents listed in the serious case review:

- **22 January 2009 –** A health visitor makes a referral about Daniel's family to the CLYP after a domestic abuse incident between a woman and her partner. A social worker visits the home to carry out an assessment. No further action is taken because the mother seems capable of protecting the children from her partner.

- **5 July 2010 –** A health visitor goes to the family home to find Daniel has a bruise to the side of his head, with the explanation given that he 'fell over'. Communication is difficult because the mother speaks little English.

- **8 August 2010 –** Police are called to a domestic abuse incident involving knives after an altercation between the couple. The mother has suffered a small cut and reports a strangulation attempt. No reference is made by police about checking the welfare of Daniel and his siblings, aged three and five respectively. The partner is arrested and released without charge.

- **27 December 2010 –** A neighbour calls the police; both adults are intoxicated and fighting in the presence of the children. The police record shows the children were 'none the wiser' and did not witness the incident. No referral is made to CLYP.

- **6 January 2011 –** Daniel is taken to an Accident and Emergency centre by his parents, where a fracture is found on his left arm, along with multiple bruising to the arm, left shoulder

▶

and lower stomach. Daniel is noted to be interacting well with his mother and her partner.

- **7 January 2011 –** Concerns about the history
of domestic abuse incidents at the family
home prompt a meeting and it is decided an
'in-depth assessment' will be undertaken.
CLYP agree to complete a Core Assessment
and to feed back to all professionals.
- **November 2011 –** The school informs Daniel's mother that he is taking food from other
children's lunchboxes and regularly takes
four or five pieces of fruit from the 'fruit corner'. Teachers note that his lunchbox contains the bare minimum.
- **January 2012 –** The deputy head teacher
becomes concerned that Daniel is not growing and organises a meeting with his mother,
who says that Daniel has been raiding the
fridge and getting diarrhoea as a result, so
she is restricting his diet until his stomach
upset is better.
- **December 2011–February 2012 –** Daniel is
seen on various occasions with injuries.
Because of a lack of appropriate recording

within the school, it is unclear what injuries
were seen and when. None of these injuries
are referred to CLYP or the police.

- **3 March 2012 –** At just after 03:00 BST a telephone call is made to the ambulance service, and Daniel is admitted to hospital at
03:28, having suffered head injuries and car-
diac arrest, from which he could not be
resuscitated.

Discussion questions

Could any one of the professionals involved have
predicted Daniel's death based on the information they had?

The mother's first language was Polish. How
might this have affected professionals' understanding of the situation?

From the evidence, do you think Daniel was
consulted?

A Core Assessment was carried out in January
2011 and fed back to the school, the GP, social
services and the police. Why do you think it failed
to be acted upon?

Improving safeguarding

There is currently concern that 'troubled' families are targeted by a dizzying kaleidoscope of
different professionals in the name of multi-agency collaboration (Munro, 2011). It appears
that current safeguarding procedures are geared towards crisis intervention so that when decisions are taken, they are too late, slowed down by bureaucracy, form filling, red tape and a lack
of clear lines of accountability. The resulting stress on professionals in the field brings with it an
alarming and continuous turnover of staff.

The NSPCC (2013) suggests that too often multi-professional teams are cumbersome and
slow to respond and that a more helpful model would be to supply a dedicated social worker,
fully up to speed on the particular family and familiar with the community, to act as a bridge
between the family and other support systems. They suggest four ways of improving protection
for vulnerable children:

1 an expert social worker in every local authority to advise on child neglect cases;
2 improved tools and training to help professionals recognise, provide evidence for and act
decisively on child neglect;
3 a public health campaign so that everyone can spot tell-tale signs of neglect in children;
4 targeted support for vulnerable families and better community support for vulnerable children
with a history of neglect.

Featherstone et al. (2014) agree with these proposals and suggest embedding social workers with direct links to children's services in their local patch, where they can work with individual families within a known community. These child-centred professionals would also address wider issues like social exclusion, bullying, drug abuse, domestic violence and the role of new partners in step-families. In this localised model, risk factors for particular families would be known and could be monitored before crises arise and damage is done.

Time to reflect

In July 2015 the UK government extended the remit for schools, nurseries and childminders to promote British values as part of the Prevent duty strategy aimed at safeguarding children from radicalisation and preventing terrorism. The four key features are

1 the rule of law
2 mutual respect and tolerance
3 democratic values
4 individual liberty.

Can you envisage any difficulties arising in relations between families and settings?

Lifelong learning

Lifelong learning and continuing professional development (CPD) is an important part of being a professional. Regardless of age or seniority, there is always more to learn, and professional development is a mark of commitment over the trajectory of working life. Professionals take control of their own learning by engaging in ongoing reflection and action in the work they do, and this development includes formal activities like courses, conferences and workshops, as well as self-directed activities such as reading journals and keeping up to date with developments in the field through news items and government websites. It should be an empowering and exciting part of working practice, something that stimulates and inspires professionals to achieve their aspirations to offer the best possible service for children.

As a professional you will find yourself with a good deal of responsibility for making important decisions, and it is essential that you maintain a high level of expertise. Throughout your career, you should take every opportunity to share insights with people from other organisations in order to enrich and enhance your own workplace practices for the benefit of the children in your care.

The journey from newly qualified practitioner to reflective professional never ends!

Summary

- For all early childhood professionals, children's well-being is paramount.
- Early childhood professionals need both academic skills and practical skills.

- There are careers in children's services in education, social work, health and youth justice.
- Early career induction is a multi-layered process of apprenticeship in the workplace, theoretical learning and reflective practice.
- Systematic reflection is an important skill to acquire, and there are a variety of models to guide you through the process.
- Listening to the views of children and their families is a key part of creating a democratic ethos where everyone can feel valued.
- Most work with children is based on teams. Teams generally share a common language and set of attitudes which promote collaboration and a shared vision.
- Multidisciplinary teams have members from various professional backgrounds who do not necessarily share a common language, perspective or status.
- The Common Assessment Framework helps teams to standardise communication across different professions and keeps the child at the centre of discussion.
- Safeguarding is a primary aim of all professionals working with children and requires good record-keeping, careful monitoring, clear channels for information exchange and deep reflection on the part of individuals.
- Child protection is difficult to achieve. Communication between agencies, clear lines of responsibility and a system for making sure that actions are followed up are key factors in effective safeguarding.
- Some argue that deploying multi-agency safeguarding teams may be less effective than designating a named social worker to work intensively with troubled families in a limited local patch.
- Continuing professional development is an important part of a career in children's services.

Topics for further discussion

1 How important are parent–professional partnerships in the work of children's agencies?
2 How could you ensure that children feel part of the team working alongside them?
3 Should multi-agency work focus on improving services for all children in a particular neighbourhood, or should resources be targeted at 'troubled families'?
4 What are the key features of successful professional partnerships in multi-agency teams?
5 Why is reflective practice important for professional development?

Assignments

1 In this chapter, we have used Kolb's reflective learning cycle. Find out about different models of reflective learning. What differences in approach are represented?
2 Using one of the available reflective learning models, choose a significant incident from your work with children or from team interactions and go through the process of reflecting on and analysing it. Decide what you want to change and draw up a plan of action. How could you implement and test out your plan?

Further reading

Gillies, V. (2014) 'Troubling families: parenting and the politics of early intervention', in S. Wagg and J. Pitcher (eds) *Thatcher's Grandchildren?* (pp. 204–224). London: Palgrave Macmillan

Elfer, P., Goldschmeid, E. and Selleck, D.Y. (2012) *Key Persons in the Early years: Building Relationships for Quality Provision in Early Years Settings and Primary Schools.* London: Routledge

Useful websites

www.eippee.eu/cms/Default.aspx, the Evidence Informed Policy and Practice in Education in Europe, provides the latest information on training, careers, policy priorities, quality assurance, professional practice and pedagogy with links to what is happening in Europe and elsewhere in terms of professional development in children's services.

www.nspcc.org.uk provides a wealth of information on careers and professional development in children's services, as well as a variety of reports and commentaries on issues like poverty, child protection and policy changes.

References

Allen, G. (2011) 'Early Intervention: The Next Steps' (*The Allen Report*). London: The Cabinet Office

Children Act (2004).http://www.legislation.gov.uk/ukpga/2004/31/pdfs/ukpga_20040031_en.pdf

DfE (2013) *Working Together to Safeguard Children.* London: HMSO

DfES (2003) *Every Child Matters* (Green paper). London: HMSO

DfES (2004) *Every Child Matters: Change for Children.* London: HMSO. http://webarchive.nationalarchives.gov.uk/20130401151715/https://www.education.gov.uk/publications/standard/publicationdetail/page1/dfes/1081/2004. Accessed 3 December 2013

Dunhill, A., Elliot, B. and Shaw, A. (2009) *Effective Communication and engagement with children and Young People, their families and Carers.* Exeter: Learning Matters

Elfer, P., Goldschmeid, E. and Selleck, D.Y. (2012) *Key Persons in the Early years: Building Relationships for Quality Provision in Early Years Settings and Primary Schools.* London: Routledge

Eraut, M. (2008) 'Learning from other people in the workforce', in K. Hall, P. Murphy and J. Soler (eds) *Pedagogy in Practice* (pp. 40–57). London: Open University/Sage

Featherstone, B., White, S. and Morris, K. (2014) *Re-imagining Child Protection: Towards Humane Social Work.* Bristol: Policy Press

Field, F. (2010) 'The Foundation Years: Preventing Poor Children Becoming Poor Adults' *The Field Report.* London: The Cabinet Office

Floyd, A. and Morrison, M. (2013) Exploring identities and cultures in inter-professional education and collaborative professional practice. *Studies in Continuing Education* 36(1): 38–53

Gillies, V. (2014) 'Troubling families: parenting and the politics of early intervention', in S. Wagg and J. Pitcher (eds) *Thatcher's Grandchildren*. London: Palgrave Macmillan

HM Government (2015) *What to do if you are worried a child is being abused: Advice for practitioners*. https://www.gov.uk/government/publications/what-to-do-if-youre-worried-a-child-is-being-abused—2. Accessed 30 December 2016

Jones, C. and Pound, L. (2008) *Leadership and Management in the Early Years: From Principles to Practice*. Maidenhead: Open University Press

Kolb, D. (1984) *Experiential learning: Experience as the Source of Learning and Development*. Englewood Cliffs, NJ: Prentice Hall

Laming, H. (2003) *The Victoria Climbié Inquiry: report of an inquiry by Lord Laming*. London: HMSO

Lewin, K. (1948) Action Research and Minority Problems. *Journal of Social Issues* 2(4): 34–46

Lindon, J. (2005) *Understanding Child Development*. London: Hodder Arnold

Louis, S., Beswick, C. and Featherstone, S. (2013) *Understanding Schemas in Young Children: Again! Again!* London: Bloomsbury

Marmot, M., Allen, J., Goldblatt, P., Boyce, T., McNeish, D., Grady, M. and Geddes, I. (2010) Fair society, healthy lives. *Marmot Review*. London: UCL Institute for Health Equity Accessed 30 December 2016

Moss, P. and Pence, A. (1994) *Valuing Quality in Early Childhood Services*. London: Paul Chapman Publishers

Munro, E. (2011) *The Munro Review of Child protection: Final Report – A Child Centred System*. Norwich: The Stationery Office. https://www.gov.uk/government/publications/munro-review-of-child-protection-final-report-a-child-centred-system. Accessed 30 December 2016

NSPCC (2013) *Neglect and Serious case reviews: A report from the University of East Anglia commissioned by NSPCC*. Authors Marion Brandon, Sue Bailey, Pippa Belderson and Birgit Larrson. University of East Anglia/NSPCC

Nutbrown, C. (2012) 'Foundations for Quality', in *The Nutbrown Review*. Cheshire: Department for Education. https://www.gov.uk/government/uploads/system/uploads/attachment_data/file/175463/Nutbrown-Review.pdf. Accessed 30 December 2016

OECD (2006) *Starting Strong II: Early Childhood and Care*. http://www.oecd.org/education/school/37417240.pdf. Accessed 30 December 2016

Pence, A. and Pacini-Ketchabaw, V. (2010) 'Investigating Quality project: opening possibilities in early childhood care and education policies and practices in Canada', in N. Yelland (ed.) *Contemporary Perspectives on Early Childhood Education* (pp. 121–139). Maidenhead: Open University/McGraw-Hill Education

Peters, J. (1991) 'Strategies for Reflective Practice', in R. Brockett (ed.) *Professional Development for Educators of Adults. New Directions for Adult and Continuing Education*, No. 51. San Francisco, CA: Jossey-Bass

Read, M. and Rees, M. (2003) 'Working in teams in early years settings', in J. Devereux and L. Miller (eds) *Working with Children in Early Years Settings* (pp. 29–39). London:David Fulton

Rogoff, B. (2008) 'Observing Socio-cultural Activity on Three Planes: Participatory Appropriation, Guided Participation, and Apprenticeship', in K. Hall, P. Murphy and J. Soler (eds) *Pedagogy in Practice* (pp. 58–74). London: Open University/Sage

Schön, D. (1983) *The Reflective Practitioner*. San Francisco, CA: Jossey-Bass

Schweinhart, L., Weikart, D. and Toderan, R. (1993) *High Quality Preschool Programs Found to Improve Adult Status*. Ypsilante, MI: High/Scope Foundation

Sylva, K., Melhuish, E., Sammons, P., Siraj-Blatchford, I. and Taggart, B. (eds) (2010) *Early Childhood matters: Evidence from the Effective Pre-school and Primary Education Project*. London: Routledge

Tickell, C. (2011) 'The Early Years: Foundations for Life, Health and Learning', in *The Tickell Review*. https://www.gov.uk/government/publications/the-early-years-foundations-for-life-health-and-learning-an-independent-report-on-the-early-years-foundation-stage-to-her-majestys-government. Accessed 30 December 2016

UNCRC (1989) *United Nations Convention on the Rights of the Child*. New York: United Nations

Unwin, P. and Hogg, R. (2012) *Effective Social Work with Children and Families*. London: Sage

Taking the lead in early years professional practice

15

Introduction

Fashions in leadership come and go, and in the past leadership styles were often based on models deriving from the spheres of politics, business and the military, with their emphasis on orders, discipline and hierarchy. For many, these models sit uneasily with the principles of equality and shared responsibility that underpin work in the early years and can make it difficult to implement concepts like 'listening to the voice of the child', 'consulting parents' and 'collaborating in multidisciplinary teams'.

Research shows that effective leadership in early years has a powerful influence on the quality of care and ultimately affects children's life chances quality (Siraj-Blatchford & Manni, 2006; Moyles, 2006). In the past, many early years professionals had leadership thrust upon them; they found themselves 'leading' not by choice but through circumstance, stepping into the role because no one else was available and with little or no formal training in leadership. More recently, leadership has become an important area in children's studies at undergraduate and postgraduate levels, and leadership courses provided by the National College for Teaching and Leadership (NCTL) have been developed to address the theory and practice of leadership for practitioners in multi-agency environments for children's services.

Calls for leadership training in children's services came in the wake of Lord Laming's report into the death of Victoria Climbié (2003) and the Audit Commission's 2003 inquiry into public governance (Leeson, 2015). Both reports identified failures in leadership in children's services and highlighted poor communication between agencies and inadequate supervision of frontline staff by managers; both called for investment in leadership training. The *Every Child Matters* (DfES, 2003) agenda and the Children Act 2004 established the principles of providing integrated services in welfare, education, health and youth justice through the deployment of multidisciplinary teams in schools and children's centres. This called for a new kind of leadership, one which stressed communicating across different professional disciplines with different perspectives.

In this chapter, we will look at some models of leadership and discuss whether some are more suitable for leadership in early years professional practice than others.

Defining leadership

Leadership has always fascinated people. What makes one person lead and another follow in their footsteps? Why are some leaders more effective than others? Is there a fool-proof recipe for good leadership? Do you need charisma to lead? Do leaders lead from the front, or are they shadowy figures pulling the strings? Can anyone lead when necessity forces them? These are some of the questions associated with trying to establish what defines leadership and who is most suited to the task of leading.

Effective leadership is about successfully persuading other people to share a particular vision or ideology and managing conditions to make sure that the vision is realised in practice. Leaders, for better or for worse, are considered to have a profound impact on the shape and direction of the organisations they lead, and there is a whole industry from psychometric test designers to organisational analysts devoted to identifying the personal qualities and management structures that make leadership work.

Time to reflect

In your groups consider the following pieces of advice on becoming an effective leader:

- 'It is better to be feared than loved' (Machiavelli, 1469–1527, *The Prince*).
- 'Give every man thy ear, but few thy voice' (Shakespeare, *Hamlet*, Act 1, Scene 3).
- 'To handle yourself, use your head; to handle others, use your heart' (Eleanor Roosevelt, 1884–1962).
- 'Trust others so that they trust you' (Barack Obama, in his eulogy to Nelson Mandela, 10 December 2013).

What are the implications of each statement?
What do *you* think makes an effective leader?
Could any of this advice be useful for leaders in an early years setting?

Leaders vs managers

It can sometimes be difficult to distinguish between leadership and management, because immediate calls on 'management' skills can quickly bury 'leadership' under a heap of urgent practical matters. Even the brightest visions can dim at unexpected moments during encounters with young children.

Management is about systems – organising resources, time, personnel, budgets, meetings and structures. Managers manage functions, processes and people on a day-to-day basis to maintain the smooth running of the organisation.

Leadership is more than management (although good leaders need to be good managers); it is a larger role of overseeing and implementing a strategy and maintaining shared core values; it is about keeping abreast of new research and sharing insights with the team. Effective early years leadership is about developing a vision and team culture that is in the best interests of children; it is about setting goals and objectives and monitoring progress; it is about disseminating achievements to parents, staff and the wider community; it is about modelling principles and showing direction (Siraj-Blatchford & Manni, 2006). Above all, early years leadership is about facilitating the development of *others*: children, parents and staff. Early years leadership seems most effective when it is people-centred and inclusive, when it grows out of dialogue, connection and community and where leaders act *with* others rather than asserting power *over* them (Jones & Pound, 2008).

From team member to team leader

Various writers (Katz, 1995; Moyles, 2006; Rodd, 2013) have discussed the ways in which early years' specialists progress from the hands-on care of young children to become professional leaders who can command the confidence of colleagues and parents. The journey begins when new practitioners first lead individuals or small groups of children within the larger framework of a team; at this stage, leading is about making decisions intuitively and responding pragmatically to the immediate situation, for example deciding how to intervene when a child is upset; how to manage a restless child during a group story-reading session; or how best to reassure a parent attending a clinic for their child's two-year-old integrated review and health check. Through experience, reflection and analysis, their expertise gradually grows until they develop a firm philosophy about children, care and education and are ready to take on more challenging leadership roles with adults.

Rodd (2013) suggests that practitioners displaying leadership potential demonstrate well-thought-out sets of principles about early years that they can articulate with confidence to inspire the people around them. She writes that effective leaders know themselves, are knowledgeable and up to date and display a confidence that reassures parents, staff and children that the organisation is in good hands.

She suggests that the following are the most useful and relevant skills that a leader requires in early years practice:

- good communication
- ability to forge and maintain relationships
- expertise in conflict resolution
- decision-making abilities
- problem-solving strategies
- a commitment to collaborative leadership and teamwork
- ability to supervise, monitor and appraise
- a commitment to mentoring and coaching
- ability to manage change.

Theories of leadership

Leadership theories range from psychological explanations (that *inner drives* and *personal attributes* make leaders) to *sociocultural* explanations (that *society*, *language* and *culture* produce different kinds of leaders for different times). The following are some popular theories about effective leadership:

- According to *trait* theory, leaders have innate personality traits that suit them for leadership. They can be identified through psychometric testing because they are natural-born leaders.
- According to *behavioural* theories, leaders learn particular *behaviours* that make them effective. Their management style may be authoritarian, consultative or participative.
- According to *transformational* theories, leaders are visionaries and ideologues who *inspire* their followers.
- According to *relational* theories, leaders who are skilful in personal relationships inspire trust and loyalty and a willingness to cooperate. Emotional intelligence is the key attribute of an effective leader.
- According to *contingency* theories, effective leaders adapt their style to match each situation where changing *contexts* and *contingencies* alter the style of leadership required.
- According to *transactional* theories, effective leaders possess good management skills based on clear aims, tight job descriptions, regular performance appraisals and a system of praise and sanctions that keeps everyone on track.
- According to *collaborative* theories, leaders consult on the overall vision and the strategies adopted to implement it. They canvass opinion before making decisions. Collaborative leaders rely on *cooperation* and *dialogue* to get things done.
- According to *distributive* theories, effective leaders *delegate* and share out management roles and mainly concern themselves with overall strategy.
- According to *nudge* theories, effective leaders 'nudge' their teams by subtle suggestion as they try to shift attitudes and change cultures.

None of these categories is exclusive, and individuals may show a mix of approaches. Perhaps the most effective leaders adapt their behaviour pragmatically to provide the best fit for the people, setting and resources under their care.

Time to reflect

Look through the list of leadership theories. Think about a situation in which you have been led. Which leadership theories do you think your leader was working with? Which ones might you want to adopt yourself?

Leadership styles

Associated with leadership theories are different leadership styles that reflect the underlying beliefs of the person leading the team. Exactly where leaders choose to position themselves along the continuum between authoritarian and consultative will depend on the team, the parents, the children, the context and their own personal disposition – striking a balance is not always easy!

Authoritarian leaders generally have a clear vision about aims and objectives and expect everyone to work towards it. They tend to issue orders, establish a clear hierarchy and generally maintain formality in interpersonal relations. The advantage of this kind of leadership is that everyone in the team knows what is expected of them, there is no pressure to be involved in decision making, and there are clear channels of command that make it easy to access support. A disadvantage is that it can stifle initiative and fail to capitalise on individual expertise. A further disadvantage is that it relies too heavily on one person, so things are likely to disintegrate in their absence. Authoritarian leaders are less likely to listen to or consult with others, which means that concepts that are germane to early years like 'children's voice' or 'parental participation' or 'team collaboration' are overlooked. However, younger, less experienced staff may appreciate an authoritarian approach, where clear guidelines and directions reduce the possibility of error and misunderstanding. On the other hand, more experienced staff may prefer a less authoritarian approach, where they can exercise autonomy in making decisions based on their own professional judgement. At the extreme, authoritarian leaders can become autocratic, reserving the right to make every decision themselves and leaving team members fearful and frustrated.

Consultative leaders generally have a more collaborative style; they listen to children, parents and colleagues, and in a spirit of inclusion and equality, they encourage everyone to actively participate in decisions that affect them. The advantage of this kind of leadership is that it gives everyone a sense of personal involvement and is more likely to lead to higher morale and more positive attitudes. A disadvantage is that it can lead to staff 'burn-out' because it requires such a high level of commitment from everyone. In early childhood situations, the demands are immediate and intense, and some team members, especially young and inexperienced staff, may find the extra demands of consultation and participation more than they can manage. Also, busy parents may find it hard to take part in consultation and might prefer to leave decisions to the 'experts'. Another disadvantage is that consultation is time consuming and can hold up the processes of change and innovation. However, skilful consultative leaders tread a fine line between encouraging individuals to work in their own style while ensuring that the overall strategy for delivering a consistent quality of service is not compromised.

Laissez-faire leaders accept that 'anything goes'; they stand back and leave their teams to sort out problems themselves. Although this may sound attractive and democratic, leaders who fail to provide guidance and direction may also be inclined to accept poor quality performance and behaviour (Rodd, 2013). When there are few guidelines about the standards expected, intolerance and prejudice can flourish, and conflicts and resentments can arise. *Laissez-faire* leaders can leave organisations feeling uneasy and rudderless and subject to discontent. When leaders fail to communicate high expectations among staff, children and families, the right of every individual to enjoy a high quality of service is inevitably compromised.

Emotionally intelligent leaders have good 'people skills'. Goleman (1996) argues that emotional intelligence (insight into one's own and other people's behaviour) is a defining feature of effective leadership; he writes that the most effective leaders display *soft skills* of negotiation, empathy and respect. Moyles (2001) argues that early years work is different from most professions because it requires a particularly high level of emotional intelligence since young children respond primarily from feelings and emotion. Emotionally intelligent leaders are able to collaborate with a diverse range of people because their sensitivity helps them to open up dialogue and to listen constructively to other points of view. Moreover, evidence from neuroscience suggests that early emotional experiences have a role in configuring the brain and may have long-term effects on children's development such that it is essential that those caring for young children have high levels of emotional intelligence (Shonkoff & Phillips, 2000). In addition, professional encounters with parents, staff and children can be emotionally charged, for example when children and parents suffer separation anxiety and fear when first attending a nursery or in the face of a hospital stay, so it is essential that leaders are emotionally intelligent and can impress upon others the importance of emotional sensitivity.

Authentic leaders are principled and knowledgeable and earn the respect and trust of colleagues (Jones & Pound, 2008). Rodd (2013) suggests that in early childhood settings, authentic leadership involves a collaborative approach where everyone shares a belief in certain principles:

- *Children's rights*: children have a voice and their interests are paramount.
- *Democracy*: children, parents and professionals are *empowered*, not oppressed; *listened to*, not lectured; *consulted*, not directed; and encouraged to be *active* participants, not passive recipients.
- *Equality and inclusion*: the active alleviation of disadvantage is accepted as a matter of social justice.

Authentic leaders act with high moral character; they are fair, open and honest and have the confidence to accommodate change and innovation without feeling threatened or criticised, and they lead in a spirit of optimism which encourages others to be confident and hopeful.

Time to reflect

In groups, discuss leadership styles you have encountered in an early years context.
How would you characterise the style?
What qualities made the style more, or less, effective?
Why do you think the idea of an 'authentic leader' has come to dominate early childhood discussions of leadership?

Leadership in early years practice

The early childhood sector has a largely female workforce. However, although women are well represented as leaders in middle management of early years' services, they are still underrepresented as leaders at the higher levels of early childhood policy and government (Rodd, 2013).

Empowering women to take up positions of responsibility and to work in leadership roles is part of a more general and global democratic journey towards equality and justice. In 'modernising' societies, early childhood leadership can be the first step towards a wider emancipation of women and can lead to changing attitudes towards their legitimate roles in the wider society.

Focus on *Empowering female leaders in Bangladesh*

A study by Jill Sperandio (2011) of women's employment in early childhood services in Bangladesh shows how women in traditional societies are taking their first steps towards emancipation and leadership through work with young children. Sperandio describes how, in Bangladesh, many women live under *purdah* – an Islamic custom which confines women to the domestic sphere, denies them schooling and prevents them leaving the house without a male escort.

However, as ideas about the importance of early education and care for the future prosperity and health of the nation have spread, there has been a shift in attitudes and a call for female workers to provide services for young children. Sperandio found that some women are now permitted to work outside the home in the 'acceptable' area of formal education for young children. She argues that this opens up opportunities for female leadership and may provide a first step in the gradual transformation of the women themselves and ultimately of their wider community in the future.

Why has early childhood been a traditional starting point for women entering the professions?

Why might having women in positions of leadership in early years have long-term social repercussions?

In Western societies, can you identify any barriers to the elevation of women to the most powerful leadership positions in early childhood services?

Leading a multidisciplinary team

During the last decade, there has been a significant growth in the number of social care and related professionals working in multidisciplinary settings. Early years professionals working in schools, hospitals, children's centres, Child and Adolescent Mental Health Services (CAMHS) and the Children and Family Court Advisory and Support Services (CAFCASS) often find themselves leading joint meetings for a range of professionals. There may be conflicts over territory, status or philosophical outlooks that need to be managed sensitively and monitored closely to avoid things unravelling.

The National Professional Development Framework for Directors of Children's Services (DCSF, 2008: p. 11) suggests the following generic guidance for leaders of multi-professional teams:

- knowing the legislative framework and understanding strategic, commissioning and policy development;
- building a shared value base and a culture of responsiveness;

- listening, building alliances and challenging others;
- promoting awareness of the child's right/need to be safe and ensuring that practice contributes to the wider ECM agenda;
- focusing on improving service performance and quality.

Leaders working with multi-professional teams rather than single professions may find themselves in a complex organisational structure where different members report to different senior managers with different supervisory and funding arrangements (Anning et al., 2010). The members of the team may have a range of qualifications, values and professional backgrounds. The leader will have to gain respect from the full range of professionals whose own status and identity will be underpinned by different models of practice and ways of working. Effective leaders try to find common ground and build on the similarities among the group rather than focusing on differences. Success depends on clear communication, assertive leadership and the promotion of a supportive culture.

Leading a multidisciplinary team is most effective when the leader

- keeps the service users (children and families) at the centre of every discussion;
- accepts that different disciplines offer different skills, roles and values;
- speaks the different languages of the professions and uses this skill to cross disciplinary boundaries;
- adopts an 'incomplete' leadership style where leadership tasks are delegated and distributed;
- remains fluid and flexible in the face of competing points of view.

The shared aim of all partnership working is to improve services for children. Although leading a multidisciplinary team can be extremely taxing because of challenges around status, different professional perspectives and different professional languages, it can also be extremely rewarding. Working across different organisations, meeting people from different professional cultures and learning to see children's services from different perspectives offer exciting prospects for developing different ways of leading.

Meeting the challenge of leading

What do leaders have to do in practice in the day-to-day business of leading? How do they establish a vision and ensure that everyone buys into it? How do they sustain the vision in the short and long term?

Sharing a vision

Early years leaders work within a clear set of aims and objectives laid down by government (Children Act, 1989; Children Act, 2004; Child Care Act, 2006), which encapsulates the national aspiration for providing a good quality service for children and families. Leaders and their teams translate these national aspirations into a local vision that observes the early years childcare ethics of respect, inclusion, confidentiality and protection from harm (Siraj-Blatchford

& Manni, 2006; Jones & Pound, 2008). Most organisations will have a vision statement; vision statements should be authentic, short and memorable; they should encapsulate a collective belief about values and expectations that can be shared by everyone. The 'Five Outcomes' of the *Every Child Matters* agenda represents a vision statement – safety, health, enjoyment, economic security and positive contribution (SHEEP) but it is one that I personally find incredibly difficult to retain!

Creating an early years ethos

Respect, trust, empathy and tolerance are the basic requirements for anyone working alongside young children. The leader has a duty to set the tone for all the staff and to model the kind of behaviour expected. Cheerful, smiling adults with a sense of fun and purpose signal that parents can feel confident about how their children will be cared for. Cordial relations between staff, an orderly but relaxed atmosphere and a calm sense of joint endeavour where time is made to talk to parents as well as children make for a welcoming atmosphere. Leading by example and supporting other people's efforts to improve standards and the quality of service can inspire confidence and loyalty in children, parents and staff.

Planning

Having established an early years vision and ethos, the next task is to come up with plans and practical goals and targets that will achieve the vision statement. *Plans are useless; planning is essential* said President Eisenhower; in other words, events can overwhelm the best laid plans, but as long as there *is* a plan and leaders know their long-term aims, they can address the deficits and adjust the details.

One way of deciding what should appear in the plan is to apply a 'SWOT' analysis. SWOT stands for **s**trengths, **w**eaknesses, **o**pportunities and **t**hreats. Involving the whole team in a SWOT analysis has the benefit of widening the discussion and incorporating different perspectives rather than relying on the partial knowledge of one individual. It is a neutral and non-threatening way of uncovering lapses and difficulties and has the advantage of keeping everyone informed of the wider picture of a quality-controlled development of the particular early years service that they are providing.

From the SWOT analysis, leaders can put a skeleton plan in place to keep everyone on track. The plan should

- determine short and long-term goals
- set out steps to achieve those goals
- establish priorities
- include a monitoring process to track progress
- provide a timetable of meetings and deadlines
- be available and accessible to everyone.

It is useful to provide everyone with a short summary plan, written in plain English, outlining the goals and targets necessary to achieve the vision. Goals and targets should be

SMART – specific, measurable, achievable, relevant and time-limited (Hunsaker & Hunsaker, 2009) with a clear timetable for review, to assess how well they are being met.

There will inevitably be some drift as people get overtaken by events, but there are various ways of tracking where and why drift is happening, for instance reporting back at meetings, carrying out management reviews or carrying out peer-to-peer observations. When slippage occurs or things get overlooked, it is the leader's job to rejig the original plan by adjusting the timetable for implementation, reordering lines of communication or shifting people's roles and responsibilities in order to ensure that the core vision of quality and excellence is maintained.

Case study: leading a team, changing practice

Katy is the new leader in a preschool nursery. Katy has a background in sports science and an early years teaching qualification and is passionate about fresh air and exercise. She finds herself in a very hierarchical setting where the same people have been doing the same jobs for many years. Everyone is very set in their ways and reluctant to change. The setting has recently received a poor Ofsted report. The inspectors are concerned that children are unnecessarily regimented and that they have few opportunities to play outside. They note the lack of formal qualifications of most staff. They are also concerned that an 'us and them' culture has been allowed to develop between preschool staff and the management committee. The committee wants to make changes to encourage more outdoor activities and has raised funds for a kitchen garden plot and large outdoor play apparatus, both of which have been installed but are rarely used.

Katy calls a meeting to find out what people on her new staff think. They explain that it is too difficult to police children outside because they might run into the neighbouring car park and recreation ground; they are worried about accidents; they think children get too excited and uncontrollable when they play outside ; they are afraid the children will get dirty and that parents will be unhappy; they say there is too much curriculum pressure on literacy and numeracy to spare time for outside play; they say it takes too long to help children into boots and coats; when it rains, climbing frames and play equipment get slippery and dangerous; when it is sunny, the children have too little shade and are at risk of sunburn; in addition, they point out that there is no direct access to the outside play area without going through the toddler room, which presents safety problems.

Katy notes all their objections on a flip chart and then asks whether they think outside activities are important for children during nursery school time. The reaction is mixed – a couple of the most vociferous staff say that nursery time is for 'work' and that outside activities are the responsibility of parents.

Katy realises that the staff feel safer supervising indoor activities and are reluctant to change because they feel comfortable doing things the way they have always done them. She wants to take their concerns seriously but she also wants to respond to the concerns of the management committee and the Ofsted inspectors. She is convinced that introducing more outside activities will improve the quality of care and learning for the children and will consequently improve Ofsted ratings and the reputation of the nursery in the community.

Discussion questions

How can she lead her team to make the change?

What sensitivities should she be aware of?

Produce a SWOT analysis for the setting.

Draw up a SMART plan designed to shift the culture from indoors to outdoors (be creative and think beyond the immediate nursery setting).

The 'incomplete' leader; the art of delegating

One of the characteristics of early years services is the complexity of roles and responsibilities involved – no one person can do it all. Ancona et al. (2007) wrote the article 'In praise of the incomplete leader' to explore the ways in which leaders in complex organisations learn to delegate effectively.

Incomplete leaders trust others to take on duties in order to make the leadership role sustainable. When duties are shared, then the role of leader becomes less dependent on one person, and the organisation can continue even when the leader is absent. Delegated tasks should be seen as an opportunity for career advancement for colleagues (not an occasion to dump less desirable work on a junior) and a useful way of empowering employees by providing them with continuing professional development. However, there is an art to delegating effectively: a delegated task needs to be clearly defined; it should have a suitable timeline for completion; and it should have the level of responsibility and accountability clearly explained with a procedure for support and reporting back to the team and leader. Delegated tasks should be given only to someone competent – offering a task to someone who might fail is bad for the team, bad for the individual and ultimately bad for the quality of service.

Rodd (2013) warns that women who take on leadership roles need to guard against a tendency towards *perfectionism*, which leads them to take on too much because they won't trust anyone else to do a task well enough; this in turn gives rise to *unreasonable feelings of insecurity* about their own performance and the judgement of others. She points out that women leading early years settings often have to contend with low pay and a general under-valuing of childcare work, which makes it difficult for them to see themselves as high-status individuals with authentic leadership qualities. This then makes it even more difficult to delegate confidently.

Being an assertive leader

One way of combating the tendency to take on too much as a leader (or as a team member) is to develop an assertive mindset (Rodd; 2013). Assertiveness is not bossiness; it is a way of calmly saying 'no' to unreasonable demands and being clear about tasks, roles and boundaries.

Assertiveness should not be confused with aggression. Assertion is a matter-of-fact statement that expresses an opinion, belief, desire, or positive/negative response in ways that do not undermine other people. It 'conveys personal confidence and respect for self and others' (Rodd, 2013: p. 81). Non-assertive leaders are paradoxically the ones who use aggression, either passively or directly to get their way: at one moment, they can sound like the wronged victim, and ask, 'Why is it always me that ends up doing this?'; at the next moment, they can sound confrontational when they ask, 'Who was responsible for this? Why hasn't it been done?' An assertive leader, on the other hand, has a clear vision of what is required and the part everyone has to play; an assertive leader might reasonably say without rancour or emotion, 'I think we agreed a rota for this task. I can see everyone is busy now, but can you just check if it is your turn when you have a moment?' In this way, no one loses face and no one gets upset.

Rodd suggests that learning appropriate self-assertion is one of the most important skills for early childhood leaders and their teams to acquire. It is useful for setting limits with children, communicating requests to other adults, expressing opinions directly and honestly without raising antagonism or undermining the other person's self-esteem.

Focus on *Being assertive – using 'I' messages*

Assertive leaders use 'I' messages to get things done. They maintain a reasonable tone and avoid emotionally charged language. Straightforward 'I' messages are preferable to 'you' messages. 'You' messages can sound accusatory and can make the person addressed feel defensive, blamed or guilty. 'We' and 'they' messages can sound sarcastic and shaming.

Consider what reactions the below messages might provoke in the recipient.

'You've forgotten to do the register again, Chloe. We'll be in trouble if there's a fire.'

'Chloe, the office is on the phone. They want your register.'

'Have we done our register yet, Chloe?'

'Hi, Chloe. I see you haven't had time to do the register yet. I'll come back and pick it up in five minutes.'

Which message would you use? Or can you come up with a better one?

Managing conflict

Passion is a necessary accompaniment to early years work (Moyles, 2011), but emotional incontinence is not. Leaders have a responsibility to create a climate of calm and reassurance where negative expressions of emotion are considered inappropriate.

Negative behaviour among children, staff and parents requires immediate and assertive handling. For example, you may have to intervene when a child snatches a toy from another; you may be faced with an irate parent complaining about paint on a child's new trainers; or you may have to deal with a member of staff who has shown impatience and irritation towards a child. It may be enough just to talk generally about values like respect, trust, equality and inclusion, but if the negative behaviour persists, then the leader should listen without judging before offering an opportunity to talk things through calmly and privately at an agreed time. Sometimes, even after reflection and negotiation, a stalemate is reached and mediation through an outside agency is required; this is more likely to happen if the negativity is directed at the leader. But outside mediation can be expensive, so it is better avoided if possible.

Dealing with conflict requires a level-headed, measured and thoughtful approach. But in a crisis it is tempting to fall back on stock phrases rather than to pay attention to the underlying implications of what is actually being said. In conflict situations, leaders should avoid certain actions:

■ Giving advice – *If I were you, I would... What you should do is...*
■ Expressing an opinion – *I think you've got hold of the wrong end of the stick; it seems to me that what you're saying is... I think you are over-reacting.*

- Pouring oil on troubled waters – *We've all been there, don't worry... Never mind, I'm sure it will sort itself out; you just need a break, so let me make you a cup of tea.*
- Interrogating – *Is there something else that you are worried about? Have you had time for lunch?*
- Dismissing – *I really haven't got time now; it will all blow over; he'll grow out of it, trust me.*

These kinds of responses may be intended as supportive or sympathetic, but each of them has the effect of closing down dialogue because they can easily seem patronising, judgemental or hostile to the person on the receiving end.

Communication is the key to conflict resolution – whether the conflict is between combatants in war zones or combatants in the sandpit. There are ways of facilitating communication with body messages such as positive body language, eye contact, calm tone of voice, supportive gesture or touch – before any words are even spoken.

Words should be chosen carefully – this is where assertive 'I' statements (see Focus on/ Being assertive – using 'I' messages), together with positive attitudes, can help defuse tension by demonstrating genuine concern. Leaders can modify their language to show

- Empathy – '*I can see this is a cause for concern. Do you want to tell me about it?*'
- Positivity – '*I saw how you dealt with Emilia earlier on. She's certainly settling in well. Now, let's find a corner to have our chat.*'
- Understanding – '*I see what you mean; that sounds like a tough call...*'
- Interest – '*That's a useful point. How do you think we might move forward on it?*'
- Enthusiasm for further dialogue – '*Shall we set a time to talk about this a bit more?*'
- Confidentiality – '*Is this just between us? Or would you like me to have a word with someone?*'
- Hope for reconciliation – '*Would you like me to find out a bit more about what's going on? Shall we raise the issue in the next team meeting?*'

The success of this approach depends on authenticity (honesty and openness, genuine warmth and sincerity) and an observation of ethics (respect and confidentiality).

Work/life balance

Making time for rest, exercise and fun can mitigate some of the effects of stress, and leaders need to monitor work/life balance for themselves, their staff and children. Everyone needs to get off the family/work treadmill from time to time in order to relax and play – it makes them feel better and they become nicer people to work with.

Short-term stress can be invigorating, a sign of eagerness to do a job well and can even be beneficial in overcoming short-term challenges (Rodd, 2013). But long-term stress prevents people from doing their jobs properly and needs to be addressed as quickly as possible. Stress may be self-induced (fear of failure, perhaps) and mentoring within the team may be sufficient; it may be due to personal circumstance (exhaustion, grief or anxiety) where reduced workload or time off may help. Stress can also be related to the way the workplace is organised: the team member may be in the wrong role, have insufficient training or have poor work practices. In this case the leader needs to be assertive – taking the person aside to get their view of the situation, and then if necessary making changes by moving people into other roles or supporting an individual to complete a particular task that may be overwhelming them.

Leaders are particularly vulnerable to stress because they have the ultimate responsibility for their staff, parents and children and sometimes have to make difficult decisions with hard-to-predict consequences. Stressed leaders risk losing their confidence and this can lead to them losing the confidence of others. When this happens, leaders need to stand back and ask themselves some questions:

- Why am I stressed? Am I exhausted? Are there tasks I could share at home? Are there tasks I could delegate at work? When did I last have time off?
- Why am I finding it difficult to make decisions? Am I afraid of worse consequences if I act? Am I using inactivity as a shield? Is the situation out of control? What is the worst thing that could happen?

Possible ways of dealing with work-related stress may include

- making a list of tasks that need decisions
- prioritising the list
- discussing the list with a trusted colleague and deciding on a strategy together
- setting out the stepping stones for moving forward
- delegating some of the tasks
- monitoring progress and ticking off a checklist of completed tasks

The best way to avert stress is to watch out for and anticipate change. Effective leaders talk to colleagues, listen to the concerns of children and parents, follow the news, attend courses, go to conferences and generally keep abreast of the changing local and national climates. In this way, they get a broader view which keeps the workplace in perspective and stops them being caught off guard by apparently sudden shifts in opinion and policy.

Case study: managing stress

The chair of governors, visiting a large infant school just before an Ofsted inspection, found the head teacher tidying the library shelves. 'If I don't do it, nobody will!' she declared. The chair of governors is legally responsible for the good management of the school. She also approves the appointment of the head teacher and is her 'line manager'. When she enquired about preparations for Ofsted, she was told, 'Everything's under control!'

On her next visit, a scheduled meeting to go through the paperwork for the inspection, she found the head teacher sitting at her desk in tears. The chair expressed concern. Through her tears, the head teacher said in a relentlessly cheery tone, 'Don't worry, I often have a little cry. It's just me! Just ask my staff or the children – they know how emotional I get, they don't take any notice, they're used to it now! It's because I'm so passionate about the job...'

Discussion questions

Should the chair of governors ignore the head teacher's distress and just get on with the job in hand? Or should she probe a bit further?

What responsibilities and obligations does she have as leader of the school community?

What ethical issues are involved?

If you were the chair of governors, what would you say next?

The future

The focus on leadership in early childhood is a major concern for Ofsted inspections in the United Kingdom (Ofsted, 2013; Ofsted, 2015). Interest has grown out of research showing that effective leaders can make a significant impact on the quality of early childhood services. But progress in settings has been slow (Leeson, 2015), and we have yet to realise the recommendation from Laming (2009) that there should be regular training in effective leadership for leaders and managers of frontline services, although some specially tailored courses designed to prepare and train people for professional leadership roles are now in place under the aegis of the NCTL. It is to be hoped that as more and more able and effective early childhood leaders emerge, their professionalism will enhance the status of the sector in the minds of the public and of government.

Early childhood leaders do not have to be charismatic, but they do need to be good listeners who are committed to the core principles of inclusivity – for staff, parents and children. Listening leaders learn from those around them and understand that everyone, themselves included, is a lifelong learner who needs opportunities to develop and extend their skills and thinking if they are to make the best of their talents. Leaders come and go, and the most effective pay attention to the legacy they leave behind; they think about the future and make plans to hand over a robust and healthy organisation to their successors. The most valuable resource in any organisation is the workforce, and forward-thinking leaders offer well-designed training programmes, continuing professional development and a structure that encourages people to fill a variety of roles so that they can emerge as leaders in the future.

Summary

- Traditional hierarchical models of leadership seem unsuited to spheres like early childhood services where the emphasis is on cooperation and partnership with children and families.
- Early childhood education and care has traditionally offered women acceptable employment outside the home and has provided opportunities for developing leadership skills. There are many ways of theorising about leadership, from *autocratic* to *laissez-faire*, but a broadly consultative style which takes account of the views of children, parents and other professionals is favoured by most early childhood commentators.
- Leadership in children's services is about creating the right ethos where children and families can flourish.
- Effective leaders are 'authentic' and 'ethical'; they display confidence and conviction in their understanding of early childhood theory and practice and operate with values based on openness, honesty and respect for others.
- Effective leaders need to be emotionally literate or empathetic; that is, they need to have the capacity, without judging, to step into another person's shoes to understand the world as that other person sees.
- People in leadership roles, particularly women, need to guard against a tendency towards perfectionism and self-deprecation.

■ Effective leaders delegate and trust colleagues to carry out tasks with a minimum of interference.

■ Assertive leaders behave in a measured, reasonable way and focus on maintaining respect, trust and professionalism in the workplace.

■ Stress can interfere with the smooth running of services, and leaders need to ensure that they and their staff, and the children in their care, understand the importance of rest and recreation.

■ Building a good team, based on professional ethics, partnership with others, and continuing professional development, contributes to successful leadership.

■ Professional training for leadership in the early years is now in place. This helps to build the status and value of the early years sector in the minds of the public and society at large.

Leaders do not go on forever, and they should plan for succession and sustainability by ensuring that they train, develop and support emergent leaders in their organisations.

Topics for further discussion

1 How can leaders foster relationships with children, parents and staff that will encourage participation and consultation?

2 Think about women in leadership roles. Do they face different challenges than those faced by men?

3 Think about managers and leaders. How do their roles differ?

Assignments

1 Read and summarise the article 'In praise of the incomplete leader' (Ancona, D., Malone, T.W., Orlikowski, W. J. and Senge, P.M. (2007) *Harvard Business Review* 85(2, February): 92–100.. What does it tell you about leadership?

2 Find out about NPQICL (National Professional Qualification in Integrated Centre Leadership). What contribution does it make to improving children's services?

3 Sheryl Sandberg is a leading executive at Facebook. Watch her funny, clever, thought-provoking video at https://www.ted.com/talks/sheryl_sandberg_why_we_have_too_few_women_leaders. What is her explanation of the underrepresentation of women at the top levels of leadership?

Further reading

Leeson, C. (2015) 'Leadership in early childhood settings', in R. Parker-Rees and C. Leeson (eds) *Early Childhood Studies* (4th edn) (p. 172–188). London: Sage

Rodd, J. (2013) *Leadership in Early Childhood: The Pathway to Professionalism* (4th edn). Maidenhead: Open University Press/McGraw-Hill

Harvard Business Review (2011), *On Leadership*, Harvard Business School Press, Boston. This provides the ten best leadership articles from recent issues of *Harvard Business Review*.

Useful websites

Sign up for email alerts from the government Foundation Years website at http://www.foundationyears.org.uk to keep abreast of all the changes that leaders need to know about.

References

Ancona, D., Malone, T.W., Orlikowski, W.J. and Senge, P.M. (2007) In praise of the incomplete leader. *Harvard Business Review* 85(2, February): 92–100

Anning, A., Cottrell, D., Frost, N., Green, J. and Robinson, M. (2010) *Developing Multiprofessional Teamwork for Integrated Children's Services* (2nd edn). Maidenhead: Open University Press

DCFS (2008) *National Development Framework for Directors of Children's Services*. London: HMSO

DfES (2003) *Every Child Matters* (Green Paper). London: HMSO

Goleman, D. (1996) *Emotional Intelligence*. London: Bloomsbury

Hunsaker, P.L. and Hunsaker, J.S. (2009) *Managing People*. New York: DK Publishing

Jones, C. and Pound, L. (2008) *Leadership and Management in the Early Years: From Principles to Practice*. Maidenhead: Open University Press

Katz, L. (1995) 'The nature of professions: where is early childhood education?' in L. Katz (ed.) *Talks with Teachers: A Collection*. Ablex: Norwood. http://ecap.crc.uiuc.edu/pubs/katz-dev-stages/index.html. Accessed 30 December 2016

Laming, H. (2003) *The Victoria Climbié Inquiry: Report of an inquiry by Lord Laming*. London: HMSO

Laming, H. (2009) *The Protection of Children in England: A Progress Report*. London: HMSO

Leeson, C. (2015) 'Leadership in early childhood settings', in R. Parker-Rees and C. Leeson (eds) *Early Childhood Studies* (4th edn) (pp. 172–188). London: Sage

Moyles, J. (2001) Passion, Paradox and Professionalism in Early Years Education. *Early Years* 21(2): pp. 81–95. Abingdon: Routledge

Moyles, J. (2006) *Effective Leadership and Management in the Early Years*. Maidenhead: Open University Press

Ofsted (2013) *Getting it right first time: Achieving and maintaining high quality early years provision*. https://www.gov.uk/government/publications/achieving-and-maintaining-high-quality-early-years-provision-getting-it-right-first-time. Accessed 30 December 2016

Ofsted (2015) *Early Years: The Report of Her Majesty's Chief Inspector of Education, Children's Services and Skills 2015*. https://www.gov.uk/government/uploads/system/uploads/attachment_data/file/445730/Early_years_report_2015.pdf. Accessed 30 December 2016

Rodd, J. (2013) *Leadership in Early Childhood: The Pathway to Professionalism* (4th edn). Maidenhead: Open University Press/McGraw-Hill

Shonkoff, J.P. and Phillips, D.A. (eds) (National Research Council and Institute of Medicine) (2000) *From Neurons to Neighborhoods: The Science of Early Development*. Washington, DC: National Academy Press

Siraj-Blatchford, I. and Manni, L. (2006) *Effective Leadership in the Early Years Sector (ELEYS) study*. London: Institute of Education, University of London

Sperandio, J. (2011) Context and the gendered status of teachers: women's empowerment through leadership of non-formal schooling in rural Bangladesh. *Gender and Education* 23(2, March): 121–135. Abingdon: Routledge

RESEARCH IN EARLY CHILDHOOD: SEEING CHILDREN DIFFERENTLY

VI

Understanding young children through observation and assessment

16

Introduction

The Early Years Foundation Stage (EYFS) framework requires all early years settings to observe and assess children's progress regularly and to share the information with parents. Observation means noticing what children say, what they understand and what they can do, while assessment involves reflecting on the information gathered – thinking about the child's development and then planning activities and support to help them move forward.

Observing children is fun and full of surprises! Watching them at play or at work or talking to them about what they are doing helps to

- evaluate their strengths and needs
- assess the suitability of the activities and resources you are providing
- plan tailor-made provision for the future
- monitor progress and development.

Good observational records form the basis for providing the right help and support in all childcare services – education, social care, youth justice and health. Over time the records can be used to monitor longer-term trajectories or to alert practitioners to unexpected changes that may indicate cause for concern.

Most courses in Early Childhood Studies require students to produce *child observations* or a longer *child study* to practise and hone their skills of observation. No matter which branch of children's services you specialise in, you will need at some point to write an observation or assessment of a child – it may be a summary of his or her developmental progress, an assessment designed to measure specific competencies or perhaps an assessment for the family courts. Whatever its purpose, writing a child assessment based on observations requires respect, sensitivity and careful reflection – especially as the power of definition lies disproportionately in the hands of the adult and may have long-term consequences for the child.

This chapter explores some of the complexities and potential pitfalls involved in observing children and then producing a reflective report for others to read.

Background

Child observation has a long history in early childhood literature (see Willan, 2009; Podmore & Luff, 2012). For example, Stanley Hall in the American child study movement, Arnold Gessel in his 'laboratory' schools and Jean Piaget at *La Maison des Petites* used close observation to measure and compare children's abilities and characteristics at particular ages to produce their descriptions of developmental 'norms' of physical and intellectual development. Other observers used more general observations to study children. For example, Charles Darwin kept an observational journal of his son's development; Margaret McMillan encouraged her trainee teachers and nurses to make daily observations of the children in their care; Susan Isaacs developed a naturalistic observation schedule for her assistants to use in the Malting House School; Esther Bick pioneered the psychoanalytic observation of infants from birth to two years to investigate infant anxiety and the impact of maternal anxiety on development; Lorenzo Malaguzzi in Reggio Emilia schools used the observation of the 'hundred languages' of children to make portfolios showing the unique development of individual children over time; and Margaret Carr in New Zealand used observation to track individual development to produce a 'learning story' for each child to show their particular and unique progress over the course of their time in Te Whāriki nurseries (see Chapter 10). All these different observational processes feed into the current Foundation Stage Profile assessments developed for children in UK settings.

Observation is an important part of the day-to-day routine for anyone working with children. Children come to settings with different sets of experience, knowledge and abilities, and practitioners need to take these into account in order to provide suitable play, learning or therapeutic opportunities.

Here, a classroom assistant describes how she uses observation in her work with reception children: 'I don't follow them round with a clipboard! I just watch at a distance and maybe jot something down. I watch and listen and think about what they're doing. Later on, I try to draw it all together and think about what stands out and what they're doing differently from last week or last month. Of course, I have to think about learning goals, but mostly I'm just trying to understand each child better and getting to know them without making judgements.'

Here, a nursery teacher describes how she notices different things during trips outside the classroom: 'Every Thursday we go to Forest School. You notice a lot about their physical development just by the way they climb into the minibus! But when we get there, they have all sorts of challenges like stepping stones across the stream and fallen tree trunks and trees they can climb. You can make all your observations about balance and coordination without them even noticing. And in that environment we often see all sorts of social sharing and helping behaviour that we don't see in nursery. And we can observe how they deal emotionally with new challenges – like who is timid or bold or impulsive… All the Early Learning Goals in one! I like observing at Forest School; you see the kids solving problems in their own ways, and it makes you understand their characters better. And I get loads of photos to put in the portfolios for evidence.'

Observation, assessment and the Early Years Foundation Stage

Children's development is a dynamic and largely spontaneous process. Throughout the nursery and reception stage, practitioners will listen to, observe and notice what children are interested in so that they can provide enriching activities to extend children's play, language and confidence. Some of these observations will be recorded and shared with the children and their parents – they may be in the form of photographs, children's work or short accounts of significant moments – and will form the basis of support to match children's current interests, needs and enthusiasms. Parents can also contribute their own observations through learning diaries or home journals. All these records are kept in a 'portfolio'; it is a requirement that these can be easily accessed by children and parents to provide a visible record of development. At the end of the EYFS (the end of reception year in primary school), all the information is pulled together in the Early Years Foundation Stage Profile, which sums up everything that is known about the child across all areas of learning from nursery to reception, including the progress check for two-year-olds and the teacher assessments of progress towards the early learning goals at the end of the year when they turn five. The EYFS Profile provides a baseline for measuring progress through Key Stage 1 (ages five to seven), when practitioner observations will be supplemented by national progress tests, measuring each child against the norm for their age group, such as the phonics screening assessment (aged five) and the standard attainment tests (SATs) at ages six and seven.

Many schools continue to use portfolios throughout the primary years because they offer a useful link between home and school, showing parents, children and practitioners the progress made from year to year. The portfolios follow the child from teacher to teacher as they progress through the school and are often brought out at parents' evenings to be shared with children and their parents. Many schools ask parents to fill in a learning journal to record or comment on significant learning moments. In my experience, some parents find this a trial because it takes up time in their busy day or because they are anxious about their spelling – but others really enjoy it.

One parent said, 'I really like sharing the learning diary. We always look through it at the weekend and read his teacher's comments and add our own. We only put in positive things, and it makes him feel we're all working together as a team'. Her son agreed: 'When I look in it, it reminds me of good things. I like the pictures – look, this is me and Simon and David when we made a submarine and all got inside! Then we did these pictures of submarines and talked about sonar. ... Look, I did my S for submarine backwards when I was little. I don't do it like that now. ... Then we did a project about bats because they have sonar too.'

Portfolios need not be dry records of attainment; they can be a celebration of personal events and milestones that preserve positive memories of a younger self as a touchstone for the present.

Attitudes and values in observation

Observing children is not a neutral process. We may *think* we are being objective when we reflect on what we observe, but we must not forget that we are seeing through the prism of our own subjective beliefs. Our attitudes and values depend on our culturally shared thought frameworks or *paradigms* (Kuhn, 1970). These paradigms influence the way we study children and how we interpret our observations (Rogoff, 2003). It is important to be aware of the cultural dimensions of our language and thinking while we observe and again when we write up reports. Using professional jargon or stereotypes related to gender, race, ability or social class can obscure what is really going on and can lead us to label individuals or to generalise about whole groups, which may in turn lead us to jump to inappropriate conclusions. Reflecting carefully on our observations, especially when we do it collaboratively with other professionals, can help us to become aware of our own values and attitudes and our own habitual assumptions.

Observations and assessments frequently result in written reports for parents, colleagues or a wider audience of inter-agency partners and can acquire an authoritative status which can have long-term consequences for children's lives. Observations should be based only on *evidence not opinion*, and language should be objective. For example, you might write objectively that 'Jane smiled' but not that 'Jane was happy', because the latter is your own interpretation of what her smile meant. Similarly, 'labels', such as those describing a child as 'naughty', 'good' or 'clever for her age' imply a value judgement based on the observer's own expectations of what is 'normal' or 'standard'. Generalisations should be avoided; for instance, writing that 'Emma was well behaved, like most girls' or 'Peter raced around like a typical boy' tell us more about the observer than the child!

Time to reflect

With due regard to protecting your own privacy and the confidentiality of others, discuss with colleagues an incident from your childhood where opinion rather than evidence left you feeling unfairly labelled.

How did the 'labelling' betray the prejudices or stereotyped thinking of the person making the judgement?

Was there an opportunity for you (or your parents) to challenge the judgement made about you?

Why is it important to avoid 'judgemental' language in observation and assessment?

The Common Core of Skills and Knowledge

The Common Core of Skills and Knowledge (CWDC, 2010) puts observation and assessment at the centre of work with children. This document advises that all childcare professionals across the sector should be able to

- observe a child or young person's behaviour, understand its context, and notice unexpected changes;
- recognise signs that a child or young person may be engaged in unusual, uncharacteristic, risky or harmful behaviour, including in the online world;
- listen carefully and respond to concerns expressed about developmental or behavioural changes;
- record observations appropriately, and ensure that they are based on evidence, not opinion;
- evaluate the situation, taking into consideration the individual, their situation and development issues;
- be able to recognise the signs of possible developmental delay and/or regression in the behaviour of children and young people;
- support children and young people with developmental difficulties or disabilities;
- make considered decisions on whether concerns can also be addressed by providing, or signposting, additional sources of information or advice;
- know when to take individual action and when to refer to managers, supervisors or other relevant professionals, where further support is needed;
- judge when it is appropriate to intervene early to stop problems developing.

Time to reflect

Think about your own work with children.

How frequently are you involved in informally observing the children in your care?
When and why do you use more formal observations?
How do you keep a record of what you have noticed?
How do you use your observational records?

Context and observation

Children arrive in early years settings with a full set of beliefs and values that they have learned through observing and imitating their own family, culture and distinctive language patterns that frame the way they see the world (Rogoff, 2003). When observers are tuned in to the subtleties of the contextual factors impacting on a child, their observations are likely to be fairer, richer and more reliable.

Bronfenbrenner's (1979) work on sociocultural contexts places an emphasis on observing children in the round, taking into account environment, family and social worlds in the health, welfare and learning potential of each individual. His theory puts each child at the centre of a series of *nested* contexts (see Chapter 8). At the centre is the *micro*-system of the family, which is surrounded by the *meso*-system of home and school. This is surrounded by the *exo*-system of work and community, which is in turn surrounded by the *macro*-system of larger social and political structures. All of these interconnecting contexts affect children to a degree and influence the way they perform in any situation.

Case study: Observing children in context

A health worker is called in by teachers when Karl, a previously balanced and gregarious six-year-old boy, becomes withdrawn and displays increasingly hostile behaviour towards other children at school. Karl is the child of migrant workers from the Czech Republic. His teachers say that he often has bruises and scratches; sometimes he smells and is shunned by other children. His assessment records show that his attainment scores are falling, and there is concern that he is underweight for his age. Teachers suspect ill-treatment at home.

The health worker interviews the boy in the presence of his classroom assistant in the head teacher's office. She makes notes on a laptop during the consultation. She notes that Karl is pale and tense and refuses to answer most of her questions.

The health worker visits Karl and his parents at home. The third-floor flat is run-down but scrupulously clean and tidy. Karl is in his room playing with Lego and refuses to join them. His mother explains in faltering English that she and her partner both work: She does night shifts in a toothbrush factory, and her husband works as a daytime delivery driver. They receive housing benefit, but because of recent cuts, it is no longer enough to cover the rent. They are under pressure to downsize from their present three-bedroom flat to one with only two bedrooms where Karl will have to share a room with his eight-year-old brother. There is a history of conflict between the two boys, which explains the bruises and scratches. Karl's mother says he is anxious about having to share a room – she whispers that he has begun bed-wetting and his brother teases him about it.

Discussion questions

In your groups, produce a diagram showing how context impacts on Karl.

How might these contextual factors affect the health worker's assessment?

Should she press Karl to speak up for himself? Should she speak to his brother?

How will she report back to the school? What recommendations might she make?

Children's voices and participation

Observation is not simply a matter of watching children as if we are dispassionate outsiders. Graue and Walsh (1998) remind us that we are part of the context we are observing because our age, status and power contribute to an 'observer effect' (sometimes called Hawthorne effect or viewing effect) where the person being observed modifies some aspect of their behaviour in response to knowing that they are being watched or observed. We need to be aware of this and to ask ourselves, How does my presence influence what I see? Am I hearing this person's genuine and authentic voice?

Brostrom (2012) argues that children should be active participants in any observations or assessments made about them because they are the best authorities on their own lives. This idea of including the voice of the child is easier said than done – adults have more power than children, and children are more likely to defer to them or to say what they think the adult wants to hear. So it requires skill on the part of the adult to make the child feel that their opinions are genuinely respected (Hart, 1992; Moss, 2013).

Although participation is an important element in working with children, we also need to remember that children are not miniature adults – they have fragilities and vulnerabilities which need to be recognised if we want to avoid overloading them with too much responsibility (Schiller & Einarsdottir, 2009; Dockett et al., 2012).

Case study: Listening to children

Figure 16.1 'Carpet time' became a source of tension in this school!
Source: PHOTODISC

Key Stage 1 teachers in a primary school all used 'carpet time' as part of their teaching day. When they set up each new activity, they brought all the children together on the carpet to introduce the topic and to explore the themes they wanted to get across. Carpet time was integral to the teachers' beliefs about collabora-tive learning and teacher–pupil dialogue; they thought it was a cosy, intimate way of engaging more closely with their classes. Sometimes the children would sit cross-legged for up to 15 minutes in the introductory session before going off to their tables to do their work. At the end of the activity, they would reconvene on the carpet to recap on the themes and to share difficulties and insights. But all too often during carpet time, children fidgeted, talked or lost concentration and sometimes had to be reprimanded. Occasionally, the fidgeting turned into surreptitious kicking or pinching. Sometimes, one or two children (generally boys and usually the same ones each time) had to stay in at break because they had been disruptive.

Certain children became labelled as 'difficult'. It was easy for the team to believe that it was these difficult children who were causing the problems. They shared their stories about disruptive behaviour but acknowledged that the sanctions like keeping children in at break were not working. In fact, the sanctions only compounded the problems because the miscreants were unhappy and became hostile and uncooperative for the rest of the day.

The team reminded themselves that children are collaborators in the learning process. They realised it would be better to investigate the reasons for the 'bad' behaviour rather than to apportion blame. They decided that they would take turns observing carpet time in other classrooms and then discuss what was happening. The teachers noted that 'bad' behaviour increased with length of carpet time – too much teacher talk and too little pupil participation seemed to lead to more instances of fidgety behaviour. Another part of the observation involved asking children what they thought of carpet time. The teachers were surprised to find that many children found carpet time uncomfortable. Some children complained that they got too hot; others said the floor was hard and hurt their bottoms; and others said it was cramped and made their legs ache because they had to hold themselves tightly to avoid bumping others. Some children pointed out that the teacher was allowed to sit in a comfortable chair, so why couldn't they? The teachers discussed the results and decided to ask the children what could be done. The children said carpet time was 'too long', and they wanted more time to do their own work; they also wanted to rearrange their classrooms so that everyone could face forward and remain on their chairs without having to sit on the carpet at all. The teachers liked carpet time, but they decided to try out the children's suggestions for a limited period. Several worried that they might have less control when the children were spread out and feared it might lead to more distractions and disruptions. But this did not happen. On reflection, the teachers believed that the new arrangement worked well because the children felt a sense of 'ownership'. The 'difficult' children said they felt more grown-up sitting on chairs because carpet time was 'babyish'; other children said they liked having more time for their own work: 'When we had carpet time, we always had to wait for the slow coaches to come!'

Discussion questions

What we see depends on what we look for. How did teachers' attitudes shape their initial analysis of the problem?

What part did reflection play in shifting the emphasis from individual to context?

How did respecting the children's opinions help the adults to identify solutions?

Observation, assessment and planning cycle

The purpose of observation is to provide evidence to inform our assessment of children's well-being and progress to enable us to make the best plans for each child. The cycle starts with observation: looking, listening, noting and *describing* what is happening. Observers in early education and care tend to combine *qualitative* observations (notes of conversations or significant behaviours, collections of children's work and photographs) and quantitative observations (checklists and charts of progress and competencies) to record and keep track of children's development (Sylva et al., 1980; Sylva et al., 2004) (the distinction between quantitative and qualitative research is discussed in more detail in Chapter 17). Qualitative observations can be done at any time, in any situation; quantitative assessments are more likely to be linked to age points and nationally standardised milestones. Some commentators (Fawcett, 2009; Luff, 2012) argue that the EYFS requirements for *both* quantitative and qualitative assessments are contradictory because measuring competencies against 'milestones' and 'norms' runs counter to the idea that each child develops in his own unique way; but I would argue that qualitative and quantitative assessments are complementary and bring into focus more information for professionals to use in individual development planning.

The observation, assessment and planning cycle is a staple of early childhood practice (DfE/Early Education, 2015: p. 3) and serves to monitor children's developmental progress and to provide suitable support activities to help them practise and consolidate their skills.

Sometimes the cycle goes by the name of action research (see MacNaughton & Hughes, 2009), and the case study below offers a real-life example showing the process in practice. It shows how a student teacher used the observation-assessment-planning format to work with a 'reluctant reader' as part of her training in observation and reflection.

Case study: Observation, assessment and planning

Name of child: Tim
Age: 7.0 years
Date: 15 February 2016
Time: 9.30–9.45 a.m.

Investigation of a 'reluctant reader'

Context: Tim is falling behind in his reading. He is in Red group with Pavel, Nihal and Sotiri, his best friends from preschool. Pavel, Nihal and Sotiri have been at school for one term longer than Tim has because the school operates on a 'staggered intake' policy, accepting only those children in the term of their fifth birthday. Tim's mother is informed that Tim is being reassigned to a reading group more suited to his capabilities. She has a meeting with the teacher. She is convinced that Tim can read well for his age because she has overheard him reading to his younger sister. But she admits that she has given up reading practice at home because it provokes tantrums.

Aim: The class teacher asked a student on work placement to observe Tim as he reads with his reading group to assess whether he should stay in Red group.

Objectives: to identify words that Tim finds difficult; to observe his relationship with his peers during reading.

Record of observation

Red Reading Group in the book corner – Tim (7.0) Pavel (7.5), Nihal (7.8) and Sotiri (7. 9). I asked Tim to choose the book for today. P said, 'Tim can't read'. N and S laughed; Tim went red. P read first, then N and S. When it was T's turn, he twisted his hands into his sleeves and looked down at the floor. P, N and S exchanged kicks under the table and smirked. T read in a very quiet voice, hesitating before every word. P, N and S laughed when he read 'filed' for 'field'.

Assessment

Tim made one error – *filed* for *field*. This could have been an over-reliance on phonics or nervousness. He twisted his hands together before his turn to read; he read slowly and almost in a whisper, as if he was scared to make a mistake. P, N and S displayed negative body language and comments.

▶

Tim is almost six months younger than the other boys in his group. He *can* read, but fear of failure in front of his peers may be affecting him.

Planning

The teacher and student reflected on the observation and assessment. Tim made only one reading error. Perhaps he is being undermined in his current group because his friends evidently think he is a poor reader. Is his confidence being damaged? Will it be dented even more if he is put into another group?

They decided his reading should be assessed again in a less threatening situation with a younger reading partner.

Further observation

Tim seemed confident helping the younger child, who was a beginner reader, and he offered words and encouragement when she got stuck. It was clear from his interventions and support that he could read at an appropriate level in this less threatening environment. When he read aloud to the child, he was clear and fluent and read in a normal voice, at a normal volume.

Further assessment

Tim reached the benchmark appropriate for his age and should remain in Red Group.

Further planning

Reading a play 'in the round' might help integrate Tim as a reader in Red Group, especially if he is given a small part. He will benefit from following the script as the others read so that he will hear their errors and corrections and realise that mistakes are part of the process of learning to read. Try easy reader *A Journey to the Centre of the Earth* and assign parts to T, P, N and S.

Final observation and assessment

Over the weeks, Tim has read with increasing confidence and pleasure as he and the other boys got into the play. The negative body language in the group subsided. Tim established himself as 'a good reader'. Recommend that Tim should stay in Red Group.

Discussion question

In your groups, reflect on the use of the observation, assessment and planning cycle.

Writing an observational child study

Most child observations will take place informally as you work alongside children. But sometimes more formal approaches are required, for example in a research report or child study when you need to demonstrate that your observations and assessment are evidence based and rigorous enough to stand up to the scrutiny of others in the field (Graue & Walsh, 1998; Aubrey et al., 2000; Fawcett, 2009). In this case you will need to show your competence in observation and reflection and your ability to integrate professional understanding with practice. You might choose to be a 'covert' observer, unobtrusive, observing at a distance without the child being aware; or you might choose to be a 'participant' observer, talking to the child, working alongside, listening and immersing yourself in their world (Bell, 2005; Cohen et al., 2011; Roberts-Holmes, 2011). The approach you choose will depend on what you want to find out.

Being an observer

Before you start planning your observation, step into the child's shoes and ask yourself some questions:

- Would I like to be observed?
- Would I like the chance to back out if I feel uncomfortable?
- Would I want to read what was written about me?

These questions foreground the notion of respect for the child and make it more likely that you will see him or her as a multifaceted individual, or 'rich child' (Moss, 2013), rather than as a laboratory specimen!

Access

Before you can do any observations with children, you need a DBS (Disclosure and Barring Service) check from the local police authority confirming your suitability to work with children. You will usually be sent a form and asked to provide this before your course starts. Your first task is to seek permission to carry out your observation. This is generally done formally by letter to the head of the organisation or family, with a brief summary of the purpose of the observation and enclosing a letter from your course tutor showing that you are a bona fide student.

Ethics – do no harm

A commitment to ethical practice should underpin any child study or research (Mortari & Harcourt, 2012). This includes the following principles:

- *Informed consent*: In order to get consent for your observations (from children, parents and manager), you will need to provide a written summary of the aims and methods of your study so that consent is truly *informed*.
- *Protection from harm*: Think about and discuss with colleagues any potentially sensitive areas, and be ready to change tack if necessary.
- *Right to respect*: Value your participants; listen to what they say; be kind and courteous; and respect their points of view.
- *Right to withdraw*: Even though people have consented to participate, you need to make it clear that they can withdraw at any time.
- *Confidentiality and anonymity*: Keep data anonymous. Do not let others see your notes. If children disclose something troubling, do not ask any further questions, but report it to the supervisor.
- *Openness and honesty*: Answer any questions about your study clearly and honestly, and offer parents, children and staff the chance to look at any time at what you are recording.
- *Data protection*: Ensure that all data are secure and that no unauthorised person can access them in electronic or paper form.
- *Sharing findings*: Student reports are available only to the tutor, workplace supervisor, parents and children involved. If you want to publish more widely, you need permission from your participants at the outset.

Generally, early childhood researchers follow the ethical guidelines set out in the *Ethical Code for Early Childhood Researchers* (EECERA, 2014) which is tailored to their requirements (see also Chapter 17).

Time to reflect

A student posts a picture of himself and the child he is studying on Facebook with the caption, 'Hi, this is me and Liam at Wood Green primary. He's helping me with my child study. Today I've been observing him working with his special needs teacher on his dinosaur project. He's doing great! He already knows more about Diplodocus than I do!'

Discuss the moral questions raised by this posting.

Were any ethical commitments breached?

What advice would you give to students about using social media during work or placements?

Some ideas for a child study

The document *Development Matters in the Early Years Foundation Stage* (EYFS, 2015) or *The Foundation Years – What to expect, when?* (2015) can provide an excellent starting point for a child study. They offer clear accounts of development from infancy to the end of the foundation stage under the following headings:

- personal, social and emotional development
- communication and language
- physical development
- literacy
- mathematics
- understanding the world.

Under each heading the document offers suggestions about *what to observe, ways to analyse* your observations and *ways to plan* suitable support. The document provides a wealth of topics to take as your starting point. Here are some specific examples from my own students' observations carried out in each of the development categories listed above:

- *Personal, social and emotional development* – patterns of separation at drop-off and pick-up times; incidence of tantrums in a two-year-old with hearing difficulties; seven-year-olds negotiating rules and turn-taking in a playground game of conkers.
- *Communication and language* – early babble; children's jokes at reception age; building vocabulary with four-year-olds inspired by an apple-pressing day; helping an EAL pupil to write a story in Year 2.
- *Physical development* – head control in babies; agility in toddlers; laterality in four-year-olds; fine motor skills in six-year-olds; ball skills in seven-year-olds.
- *Literacy* – mark making in the baby room; emergent writing; rhyming games; sequencing story elements; phonics in reception class; book choices for children under eight.

- *Mathematics* – language of weight and size in the sandbox, matching shapes at age three, sharing and the mathematical concept of division with a six-year-old.
- *Understanding the world* – children talking about their pictures of Divali celebrations; seven-year-old children's responses to the story of the Good Samaritan; discussion between four-year-olds about their visit to the recycling centre.

The possibilities are endless and fascinating!

Methods of observation

The following methods are commonly used in child observation studies. The list is not exhaustive, and you might come up with different ways that better suit your purpose. The following summary draws on Bell (2005).

Narrative record

Journals, diaries, notebooks and narrative records provide field notes where the observer records everything she sees and hears, together with contextual information. It is a naturalistic account of what seems most significant at the time. Sometimes it can throw up 'critical incidents' or stand-out events that require reflection or further investigation.

Target observations

Observations targeted at a single child attempt to capture every detail of a child's actions during a particular activity. Various codes are used as shorthand to keep up with the fast flowing events of children's play and conversation. Sylva et al., 1980 devised a grid and 'shorthand' system: for example, LMM (large muscle movements), PRE (pretend), MAN (manipulating objects), GWR (games with rules) and so on. The intention was to provide a reliable and objective code which could be applied in a variety of settings and reliably compared at a later date. You might want to devise your own fit-for-purpose coding system.

Time and event sampling

Time sampling and event sampling are used to track a particular action or behaviour: for example, you might be concerned about a child who seems solitary and decide to find out how long and how often he plays alone. A time sample approach might be used, for instance, to observe the child for five minutes at half-hour intervals over a morning session. Alternatively, you might adopt an event sampling approach, recording each time the child withdraws from his companions. You might want to record how long the behaviour lasted, what triggered it, whether any child invited him to play, any conversation that took place and whether any staff intervened to help him integrate.

Checklists

Checklists are simple lists of behaviours and competencies which can be ticked off to give a picture of a child's health, well-being or development on a particular day. Sometimes the checklists are calibrated according to age-related norms or 'milestones' (what can be expected of an average child of the same age) such as '40–60 months – beginning to negotiate and solve problems without aggression, e.g. when someone has taken their toy' (Early Education/ DfES, 2015: p. 14). Checklist observations are useful in health, social care and education situations to provide a quick guide to a child's progress relative to children of a similar age.

Rating scales

Rating scales measure the intensity or frequency of behaviours, usually on a scale from one to five: from very high, through medium, to very low. There are many rating scales available for early childhood observations: for example, you might use a rating scale to measure a child's concentration level by using the Leuven well-being and involvement scale (Laevers, 1994); or, if you have received appropriate training, you might use the Early Childhood Environmental Rating Scale (ECERS) to measure the quality of resources and opportunities available in a pre-school. On another occasion you might design your own rating scale for a particular purpose – for example, to assess the stress response of a child undergoing a new medical procedure, such as self-administered insulin injections, in which case you might score a child on a one-to-five scale – from very resistant, through medium, to very compliant – to help you determine the level of ongoing support the child might need.

Video- and audio-recording

It is notoriously difficult to get good data from video- and audio-recordings. The actual equipment makes people behave differently, it is often hard to hear or see clearly what is going on, and somehow everything interesting always seems to happen just out of range! There are often difficult access and permission issues around use of recording equipment too, especially now that it is so easy to duplicate things electronically, with an increased risk that data can fall into the wrong hands. But with careful planning and by letting the children get used to the equipment, results can be eye-opening and great fun, and recordings have the added advantage of being available for multiple viewings and analysis at a later date (with permission, of course).

Time to reflect

What methods would you use to observe the following?

- a child's relationships with his peers
- a child's freedom to access outdoor and indoor play
- a behaviour problem
- language development
- concentration levels
- mother–child interaction
- children's perceptions of the play-value of a new piece of outdoor equipment

Analysing and reflecting on your observations

Once the observation is complete, the next task is to analyse the data and to reflect on its significance. Try to be objective (beware of making assumptions, judgements or sweeping generalisations), and base your analysis only on the evidence you have recorded. As a student, you will be expected to provide an analysis which demonstrates that you can discuss all aspects of child development and behaviour in relation to theories you have learned during your course. Focus on what was expected and what was unexpected, what was consistent or inconsistent. At this point you need to think about 'validity'; that is, you have to ask yourself whether your analysis would stand up to scrutiny if another person looked at your observation record. Is your analysis credible? Does it ring true? Do any of your judgements betray your own personal bias?

You can test the validity of your assessment by comparing your findings to other people's research. Does it differ from, or support, their findings? You might also check whether or not your participants recognise themselves in your analysis; you might ask parents, colleagues or practitioners to act as a critical friend to gauge the level of agreement or disagreement that exists around your interpretation. This multifaceted approach, which brings together multiple data sources, different theories or different perspectives to test the credibility or validity of your interpretations, is called 'triangulation'(Aubrey et al., 2000; McMurray et al., 2004; Mukherji & Albon, 2010) and will give you more confidence in the validity of your analysis.

And finally, observation and assessment is not just about watching children from a distance; it requires you to engage respectfully with children, to listen to what they say and to reflect on your interpretations and assessments. It demands that you know yourself and understand that you are seeing the world through your own cultural values and beliefs. Informed observation is the bedrock of your professional work with children and offers the best chance of enhancing their individual learning and development. It is also good fun and enriches the relationships between adults and children.

Summary

- Observation and assessment provide the foundation for Early Childhood Studies.
- Observations should be as objective as possible, and assessments should be based on evidence, not opinion.
- Avoid value judgements, generalisations, hasty conclusions and labels based on prejudices around gender, race, culture, ability or class.
- Always work ethically by respecting the child, ensuring good relations and keeping data anonymous and secure.
- Choose an observational method that fits your purpose.
- Be systematic and rigorous, and record only what you actually see and hear; write up any observations immediately to make sure your record is accurate.
- When appropriate, involve the children in dialogue, and let them participate in your observations.

■ Be prepared to share your observation reports with parents, children and other practitioners.

■ Use your observations in planning your practice for the benefit of the child.

Topics for further discussion

1 Observation involves more than just looking. What else feeds into the process?

2 Think about how you use observation in your work. Do you tend to rely on developmental checklists, or do you use observations as a way of getting to know children's interest and capabilities? Do you share your observations with parents or colleagues?

3 How do your own values and beliefs influence the observation process?

Assignments

1 Find out about the ECERS and School-Age Child Environment Scales (SACERS) training programmes. Think about a setting you know well. How could training in the use of ECERS/SACERS help assess the quality of provision?

2 Choose a research article on listening to children. What is the underlying research perspective? Did the researcher's perspective influence the direction of the study? How was the study conducted? How were children involved in the study? What were the findings? What were the conclusions? Did you learn anything useful from the study that you might want to incorporate into your own practice?

Further reading

Podmore, V.N. and Luff, P. (2012) *Observation: Origins and Approaches in Early Childhood.* Maidenhead: Open University Press/McGraw-Hill Education

You will find lots of creative ideas and novel approaches to studying children in *Listening to Young Children: The Mosaic Approach* by Alison Clark and Peter Moss (2001: National Children's Bureau and Joseph Rowntree Foundation).

A special issue of the *International Journal of Early Years Education* (Vol. 20, no. 3, September 2012) is devoted to children's participation in the research process and researchers reflect on the challenges of including children as colleagues and co-researchers.

Useful websites

Material to support observation and assessment in the EYFS is available at **www.foundationyears. org.uk/**

Resources to support practice in listening to young children, including the *Listening to young children* series, is available from the National Children's Bureau at **www.ncb.org.uk/resources-publications/resources/listening-way-life-why-how-we-listen-young-children**

References

Aubrey, C., David, T., Godfrey, R. and Thompson, L. (2000) *Early Childhood Educational Research: Issues in Methodology and Ethics*. London: Routledge/Falmer

Bell, J. (2005) *Doing Your Research Project: A guide for First-Time Researchers in Education and Social Science* (4th edn). Buckingham: Open University Press

Bronfenbrenner, U. (1979) *The Ecology of Human Development*. Cambridge, MA: Harvard University Press

Brostrom, S. (2012) Children's Participation in Research. *International Journal of Early Years Education* 20(3, September): 257–269

Cohen, L., Manion, L. and Morrison, K. (2011) *Research Methods in Education* (7th edn). Abingdon: Routledge

CWDC (Children's Workforce Development Council) (2010) *The Common Core of Skills and Knowledge* paragraphs 2.4–2.13. www.yor-ok.org.uk/YorOK-Workforce/Common%20 core%20of%20skills%20and%20knowledge%20for%20the%20childrens%20workforce.pdf. Accessed 30 December 2016

DfE (Department for Education)/Early Education (2015) *Development Matters in the Early Years Foundation Stage*. (EYFS) Early Education: The British Association for Early Childhood Education: https://www.gov.gg/CHttpHandler.ashx?id=104249&p=0

Dockett, S., Einarsdottir, J. and Perry, B. (2012) Young children's decisions about research participation: opting out. *IJEYE International Journal of Early Years Education* 20(3 September): 244–256

Early Education/DfE (2015) *Development Matters in the Early Years Foundation Stage (EYFS)*: The British Association for Early Childhood Education, p. 3. https://www.gov.gg/ CHttpHandler.ashx?id=104249&p=0. Accessed 30 December 2016

ECERS (Early Childhood Environment Rating Scales) (2012) *Mapping the Environment Rating Scales to the Early Years Foundation Stage Framework*. http://www.ecersuk.org/11. html. Accessed 30 December 2016

EECERA (European Early Childhood Education Research Association) (2014) *Ethical Code for Early Childhood Researchers: version 1.2 (May 2015)*. http://www.eecera.org/custom/ uploads/2016/07/EECERA-Ethical-Code.pdf. Accessed 30 December 2016

Fawcett, M. (2009) *Learning through Child Observation* (2nd revised edn). London: Jessica Kingsley

Graue, M.E. and Walsh, D.J. (1998) *Studying Children in Context: Theories, Methods and Ethics*. Thousand Oaks, CA: Sage

Hart, R. (1992) *Children's Participation from Tokenism to Citizenship*. Florence: UNICEF Innocenti Research Centre

Kuhn, T.S. (1970) *The Structure of Scientific Revolution* (2nd edn). Chicago, IL: University of Chicago Press

Laevers, F. (Red.) (1994) The Leuven Involvement Scale for Young Children. Manual and video. Experiential Education Series, No 1. Leuven: Centre for Experiential Education.

Luff, P. (2012) 'Challenging Assessment', in T. Papatheodorou and J. Moyles (eds) *Cross Cultural Perspectives on Early Childhood* (pp. 140–150). London: Sage

MacNaughton, G. and Hughes, P. (2009) *Doing Action Research in Early Childhood Studies: a step by step guide*. Maidenhead: Open University Press/McGraw-Hill Education

McMurray, A.J., Pace, R. W. and Scott, D. (2004) *Research: A Commonsense Approach*. Southbank, Victoria: Thompson

Mortari, L. and Harcourt, D. (2012) 'Living' ethical dilemmas for researchers when researching with children. *International Journal of Early Years Education* 20(3, September): 234–243

Moss, P. (2013) *Early Childhood and Compulsory Education: Reconceptualising the Relationship*. Abingdon: Routledge

Mukherji, P. and Albon, D. (2010) *Research methods in Early Childhood: An Introductory Guide*. London: Sage

Podmore, V.N. and Luff, P. (2012) *Observation: Origins and Approaches in Early Childhood*. Maidenhead: Open University Press/McGraw-Hill Education

Roberts-Holmes, G. (2011) *Doing Your Early Years Project: A Step-By-Step Guide* (2nd edn). London: Paul Chapman

Rogoff, B. (2003) *The Cultural Nature of Human Development*. Oxford: Oxford University Press

Schiller, W. and Einarsdottir, J. (2009) Special Issue: Listening to young children's voices in research – changing perspectives/changing relationships. *Early Child Development and Care* 179(2): 125–130. Abingdon: Routledge

Sylva. K., Melhuish, E., Sammons, P., Siraj-Blatchford, I. and Taggart, B. (2004) *The Effective Provision of Preschool Education (EPPE) Project*. Final Report. London: DfES

Sylva, K., Roy, C. and Painter, M. (1980) *Childwatching at Playgroup and Nursery School*. Oxford: Basil Blackwell

Willan, J. (2009) Revisiting Susan Isaacs – a modern educator for the twenty-first century. *International Journal of Early Years Education* 17(2): 151–165

Doing early childhood research

Introduction

Most early childhood courses will have a research element, usually in the form of a final year dissertation. Research skills are important not just for writing a dissertation but also for reading and assessing journal articles, for critically analysing policy documents and for producing reports as part of your professional work with children.

Doing research for the first time is quite a challenge, but it can be exciting and fulfilling. Even with limited time and resources, you can do interesting and original work, exploring children's worlds and producing evidence about how children experience their lives in the changing contexts of childcare policies and practice. There are many excellent books available about how to conduct research projects in the social sciences, including several written specifically with early childhood in mind. This chapter aims to provide a brief introduction to research skills to give you the confidence to get started on choosing your topic, doing your literature search and designing your study. It gives some pointers on how to present results and analyse findings and how to present the final draft of a report or dissertation.

What do we mean by research?

In a sense we are all researchers. We all (adults and children alike) gather information and make observations and build theories as part of our day-to-day interactions as we construct the world view that determines how we behave and what we do. The distinction between this implicit research and the more explicit research we need for our professional lives is one of degree.

A research project provides an opportunity to explore in more detail a topic that has caught your interest or one that will increase your professional expertise. It may be a problem that needs solving in your workplace, an orthodoxy that you want to challenge or a topic that has intrigued or puzzled you during your studies. You could use libraries or online resources to pursue your research through other people's writings, or you could conduct your own original piece of empirical research, collecting your own data directly from people and situations. It is this empirical research that is the subject of this chapter.

Research approaches

Different research approaches, sometimes referred to as research paradigms, will determine how you design your study and ask your questions. Some studies start with a theory that can be tested: positivist paradigm. Others start with collecting data from which a theory can be built: interpretivist paradigm.

A positivist paradigm, familiar from science lessons, will lead you to search for causes and effects by making objective observations of people in carefully controlled conditions, testing out a theory by deduction to see if it stands up to scrutiny. For instance, you would use a positivist approach if you wanted to test the claim that transparent coloured overlays can help dyslexic children to improve their reading skills. In this case you would stand back and measure the efficacy of the overlays for each child before deciding whether or not the theory was correct.

An interpretivist approach, more familiar in social and educational research, will lead you to ask questions about meanings and processes by finding out what people think and how they react. By using the patterns you find in the responses you collect, you will gradually build a theory about why things are the way they are. For instance, you would use an interpretivist approach if you wanted to know why parents chose to send their children to one particular school rather than another. In this case you would collect your data from a wide group of respondents and then look for patterns which would lead you to formulate a theory by induction to explain the parents' decisions.

Many studies make use of both approaches, combining the quantitative methods associated with positivism with the qualitative methods associated with interpretivism to provide a richer mix of data to work on (Bryman, 2008). For example, you might want to find out if a preschool follows a play-based and child-led approach as required by the EYFS framework. You might begin with a focus group to find out what practitioners in the study understand by play-based and child-led activities and whether they believe that they provide it. You might follow this up with a study of a day in the setting, observing and timing how long children spent in teacher-directed play or child-initiated free play, measuring time given over to teacher instruction and noting how often children had opportunities to influence the direction of activities to suit their own interests. You would use an interpretivist paradigm to analyse the focus group discussion, drawing out the main themes to understand how the group defined teacher-led and child-led play and the relative importance they gave to each. But you would use a positivist paradigm when you came to analyse the data you collected from measuring and charting the instances of each type of play you observed. You would then be in a position to say how closely the practitioners' beliefs about what they were providing matched the reality of the children's daily experience.

Your decisions about your research approach will depend on the topic you choose and what investigative procedure seems most fit for purpose.

Finding a topic

The first challenge in producing a research dissertation is to choose an interesting topic that you feel passionate about – it will need to be something that can sustain your involvement over quite a few months.

There are a number of things you can do to help the process along:

- Look at dissertations written by previous students. What topics did they choose? How do they relate to your interests?
- Use the Internet to look at recent issues of the major Early Childhood Studies journals (*Childhood, Child Development, Paediatrics and Child Health, International Journal of Early Childhood Education*, for example). Skim the contents pages and abstracts to get a sense of what is topical at the moment.
- Think about the major debates and issues you have covered in lectures.

Once you have identified the broad area that you would like to investigate, the next step is to find out what other people are saying about it. You might start by talking to friends and colleagues, watching TV programmes, listening to radio coverage and reading newspapers and magazines. Or you might go straight to the Internet or the library bookshelves and journals. You will gradually build a portfolio of ideas and opinions and information, a list of sources, a list of names and organisations that have something to say on the topic. Quite quickly, you will know what the major debates are, who tends to take which positions, who the key thinkers and researchers are and who are the mavericks and iconoclasts dissenting on the sidelines.

Discovering your research question

Research often involves investigating a *claim* and trying to discover whether there is any truth in it. For example, we often hear claims that children are becoming less sociable because they spend hours in front of computers every day, or claims that children in the twenty-first century have less freedom to roam than their parents did. These are big questions, but they can be scaled down to manageable proportions by being specific, focusing on a particular time or place. Through your reading and discussion, you will gradually refine your own viewpoint until you have reached the point where you can formulate a 'research question' that can be investigated within the limits of your resources. For instance, you might start off by asking yourself, '*Are children really spending all their time on computers instead of with friends?*' And then you refine the question into '*How did six- and seven-year-olds in Class 2 spend their free time during the second week of February?*'

Again you might ask, 'Are children really more confined to their homes nowadays?' And then, more specifically, you ask 'What evidence is there that children in Castle Green have less freedom to roam than their parents had? What do parents and children in Castle Green after-school club think about the boundaries set for them in childhood? Are there any generational differences?'

To help you refine your research question, ask yourself the following questions:

- What do I want to investigate? (Can I summarise it in a sentence or two?)
- How am I going to do it? (Where, when and how am I going to investigate it?)
- Why is it important, valuable and topical? (How does it relate to the contemporary early childhood context?)

Essentially, what is required to turn your ruminations into a research project is a focus that takes you beyond the descriptive into the analytical. So although you may start by describing *what* is happening in your locality, you will end by exploring *why* it is happening and how your evidence corroborates or refutes the research findings of other people working in the same field.

Once you have a rough draft of your research question, ask yourself about the practicalities:

- Is my research question manageable?
- Do I have the time, the contacts, the money and a suitable group or setting where I can carry out the research?
- What sources of information are available in this area?

Be as ambitious as you like, but be aware that you need to find a match between your skills and your aspirations, your resources and the time available to complete your study. For instance, if you wanted to do a comparative study of how parents are involved in their children's education in Sure Start, Reggio Emilia and Te Whaariki, you might find it easy to find documentary sources but rather more difficult to gather 'live' empirical data from practitioners. However, if you are an Italian speaker with contacts in New Zealand, you might manage to gather teachers' and children's views through email questionnaires and online discussion groups to form the basis of a very interesting and up-to-date piece of research!

Reviewing the literature

As your focus becomes clearer, keywords and common terms will begin to emerge. You can then begin a systematic review of the literature relating specifically to your topic by accessing a wide range of relevant journal articles simply by typing in those keywords. For instance, if your research question centred on media reports about obesity in young children, you might have started by typing 'childhood obesity' into Google and quickly come across millions of hits, not to mention problems with accountability, verification and accuracy on many of the websites that came up. By using your specific keywords, in this case perhaps 'preschool and obesity and health guidelines and parental attitudes', and turning your attention to specialist databases like Google Scholar – or those provided by government organisations, hosted on university web pages, or accessed through search engines like BIDS (Bath Information and Data Services at www.bids.ac.uk) – you will be taken directly to relevant, peer-reviewed, scholarly articles which include your keywords.

Start your search by skimming abstracts or reviews of recent articles and books, and then check their references for the most frequently cited authors to give you a feel for the 'big names' in the field. List the strands of thinking represented by the various writers you discover. Critically review the research as you read, and monitor your own response – what do you tend to agree with? Is the evidence strong? What strikes you as odd, weak or challenging? As you read, you may want to refine the focus of your investigation so that it concentrates on a particular aspect of the research question you first thought of. This is not a change of mind; it is a focusing of mind, a familiar part of the process of research.

It is essential that you keep track of what you are reading. You could save time by using Endnote, or similar referencing software, which follows the conventions of the Harvard citation system for social studies research (like the references in this book) and guides you through recording the information you need to build a bibliography. If you don't want to use referencing software, use a card index or notebook. But be systematic, and always write the whole reference down. Look at the references in this chapter and other chapters for examples of what information you will need – and don't forget to note the page number for direct quotations. There is nothing more frustrating than copying down a relevant quote without the page number only to find, when you come to write up, that the book you used has been borrowed by someone else or you can't access the relevant page on the Internet!

When you read an article in a research journal, record the following information:

- the full reference (author, date, title of article or chapter, page numbers, title of journal or book, place of publication, publisher or URL address for electronic sources);
- the research question being asked;
- the paradigm or research approach (positivist/interpretivist/a mixture of both);
- values and ethics (Has the researcher tried to be open and honest in relation to the data? Did the research follow the principle of 'do no harm' and lead to benefits for participants?);
- participants (Who were they? Were they representative? How big was the sample or target group?);
- the research methods;
- the findings;
- validity (Did the study measure what it set out to measure?);
- reliability (Would the study yield similar results if it was repeated under similar circumstances?);
- the full references of any promising books or articles listed in the reference section;
- useful quotes, with page numbers.

These detailed notes may seem tiresome at first, but they will save hours of work when you come to write up your study.

Identifying your participants (sampling)

Once your literature review is well under way and your final research question has emerged, you will need to give some thought to *sampling*. Sampling is a method of obtaining representative observations from a group. You will need to decide who will participate in your research and how representative they are of the population as a whole. If it is possible to include the whole population relevant to your question, then you don't need to worry about sampling. But if, as is more likely, you can survey only a *proportion* of the population you are interested in, then you have to make a selection from among the whole group of possible participants.

Large-scale surveys, for instance, of the kind you encounter in customer satisfaction questionnaires, may use *random* sampling, where everyone in the target group has an equal chance of being selected; or *stratified* sampling, where a *selection* is made, based on preordained criteria such as post-code, age, gender or occupation. With large-scale sampling, researchers can be confident that the sample is *representative* and that any findings can be safely generalised to a larger population. Unless you use online questionnaires, it is unlikely that you will be able to afford the cost of conducting a survey of this magnitude or have the time and resources to analyse it.

For your dissertation, you will probably opt for something more limited and small scale. Sampling for small-scale research is more likely to be based on convenience or opportunity. *Convenience/opportunity sampling* is just what it says: a sample based on who is accessible and what is available. For example, you might use your local Cub or Brownie group as your sample and then select just seven-year-olds as your respondents. While you may learn a lot about these particular seven-year-old Cubs or Brownies, you won't be able to generalise from your findings, because the sample is not representative of the *whole* population of seven-year-old Cubs or Brownies. However, it can still tell you a good deal about the experience of being a seven-year-old Cub or Brownie in your locality. Sometimes your opportunity sample turns into a *snowball* sample, where you start with one or two participants and then, using their recommendations or contacts, you gradually increase the size of your sample and the number of respondents as your study progresses.

Time to reflect

'Convenience' is likely to be the constraining factor in choosing a target group for a small-scale research project. Discuss your research topics and brainstorm the possibilities for recruiting a suitable convenience sample:

- Which target groups might be available in your area?
- Which organisations or individuals might provide useful contacts?
- When might be the best time to access them (term-time, holidays, evenings)?
- What limitations might your convenience sample put on the general value of your findings for the wider population?

Negotiating access

How do you gain access to the information you need for your study? People are very busy, and they may find it difficult to accommodate you when and how you want, so you may need delicate diplomacy skills to ease your passage.

Bryman (2012) suggests that the following strategies can help:

- Use friends, contacts, colleagues to get an introduction.
- Locate someone in the target organisation who can act as your 'champion'.
- Be clear about what you want to do and prepare an outline of your study in plain English (avoid jargon) to include in a letter of request.
- Be aware of any sensitivities that might arise in relation to your topic.

■ Get formal written permission from the top.

■ Be prepared to modify your plans in response to any feedback or advice.

■ Offer something in return, for example a copy of your research report and some voluntary work perhaps, so that people don't feel exploited.

Always show a positive interest in the people and organisations you approach and, wherever possible, indicate your willingness to be flexible to fit in with their schedule and customary practice.

Ethics (see also Chapter 16)

Once you have identified the people you want to study, you will need to think about the ethical issues involved in human research (Christensen & James, 2008). There are published guidelines spelling out the issues that researchers need to consider to ensure that the subjects in a study are protected – the specific guide for research with young children is EECERA's Ethical Code for Early Childhood Researchers (2014). At all points, you need to act with integrity, by offering guarantees about your own conduct and ensuring that your participants know what rights they have if they consent to take part.

Time to reflect

A student wants to conduct interviews with children and physiotherapists about new physiotherapy practices in the children's ward of his local hospital where his mother works as a nurse. He wants to use his smartphone to record evidence as he talks to the participants during treatment sessions.

■ What ethical issues should he be aware of?
■ What modifications might he need to make to his plan?
■ How should he go about getting permission from the hospital/the parents/the children?

Before you make contact with the people who will 'host' your research fieldwork, such as a head teacher, hospital manager or social service manager, you need to design a consent form. At the very least, it should contain the following:

1 the name, address, telephone number of the person and/or organisation from whom you are seeking consent;

2 your our own contact details and the body supervising your research;

3 an outline of the purpose of the study, stating how and why the research is being undertaken and what will happen to the information collected;

4 specific safeguards which guarantee that
   ■ participation is voluntary,
   ■ participants have a right to withdraw at any stage if they wish,

■ any information gathered in the course of the study will be anonymous and confidential and will be kept safe,

■ the report will be available on request after the study is complete;

5 a sign-off space where the participant signs and dates an acknowledgement that they have read the form and agree to its conditions;

6 a second copy of the signed and dated consent form for the respondent to keep on file.

Once you have permission 'from the top', you will also need permission from individual participants (and parents if necessary – although they may already have agreed to delegate this permission to the manager of the service). You should provide suitably adapted versions of the consent form, tailored to the age and abilities of your participants. You may need to be creative if your participants are at a pre-reading stage (a smiley face or an X in lieu of a signature) and you may need to come up with a child-friendly way of letting them withdraw during the study without their losing face.

Time to reflect

How would you design a consent form suitable for use with six-year-old children with severe learning disabilities? How would you ensure that they were fully informed? How would you ensure that they understood that they could withdraw at any time?

Research designs

You will need to choose a research design that best suits the purpose of your research question (Fraser et al., 2004; Christensen & James, 2008; MacNaughton & Hughes, 2009; Roberts-Holmes, 2011). It is likely that, for an undergraduate dissertation, you will choose a small-scale design, perhaps a case study focusing on a particular event, issue or practice; an ethnographic study where you work closely alongside your participants; a piece of action research where you try to change and improve professional practice; or perhaps a mixture of all three. Within this design you might use a combination of qualitative and quantitative methods to gather your data.

Quantitative research uses numerical data and relies on statistical procedures for analysis. It generally involves large samples and is narrow in focus, such as the process of drawing up 'league tables' of test results from schools. The researcher maintains a distance from the participants in order to be objective. The aim is to collect hard, reliable data from which to draw conclusions that can be generalised to a wider population. It is often positivist in intention, starting from a theory or hypothesis which it tests through a structured series of controlled observations to 'prove/verify' or 'disprove/falsify' the original research question. Quantitative research tends to deal in generalities and surface features without exploring the deeper complexities of individual circumstances (Bryman, 2012); for instance, in the example above researchers used raw scores to collate their league tables without exploring whether the school was in a wealthy or deprived area, whether it had a disproportionate number of special needs children or whether it had a rapid turnover of staff.

By contrast, qualitative research is more often associated with small-scale research, where theories and hypotheses *emerge* from the data collecting process and are arrived at by *induction*. It is grounded in the particularities of the context in which it is set, for instance in the detail of a particular group of children or a particular local service, and uses *triangulation* (corroboration through several different evidence sources) to test its credibility. Because the samples are generally small, qualitative research is less likely to be generalisable to the whole population. Qualitative research investigates processes and meanings and generally involves canvassing attitudes and opinions in order to understand the world through the eyes of the participants being studied. The researcher generally builds up a relationship with participants by working closely alongside them and gathering data through conversation, observation and interview. Qualitative data is therefore often richer and more deeply contextualised than quantitative data (Bryman, 2012).

In practice, most research in Early Childhood Studies combines both qualitative and quantitative data. As a student you are most likely to use qualitative methods in your fieldwork and to rely on quantitative research from other people to provide a wider context for your conclusions. This combination of qualitative and quantitative data enables you to look at a particular phenomenon from a number of different viewpoints and to produce a more accurate understanding than would otherwise be possible. It also allows you to check the validity of your own conclusions by considering how far they complement or contradict findings from other research. This 'triangulation' of information from different sources helps to test the findings of your own study as you construct a credible narrative from your data.

Research methods – collecting data

The key point about collecting data is that it needs to be systematic – whichever methods you choose for your research, you must plan meticulously and keep careful records. The research methods you use will be determined by the topic you want to investigate. Whichever methods you use, you should choose an approach that fits the purpose (Denscombe, 2014). Let the topic lead your design, and whenever possible carry out a pilot study first before you do the study 'for real' to check that your design works and provides the information you want – you may be surprised at how many unexpected hurdles come between theory and practice in research projects.

There are many ways of collecting data (see the 'Further reading' section at the end of this chapter) and you can even invent your own. For example, one of my students watched a three-year-old spontaneously interviewing her friend, using a hairbrush for a microphone, and was surprised at how fluent and perceptive she was. This gave her the idea of getting children to be co-researchers in her study on how children support each other's learning during play. She gave each pair of children a microphone and observed them asking each other about their play. She kept detailed notes of their dialogues and was surprised at the sophistication of the questions

Figure 17.1 Patricia (age six) making her contribution.
Source: Author's own.

they asked and the responses they gave. She was also very amused to see that, by age three, they had clearly absorbed the techniques of television interviewers.

Below is a selection of some common methods for collecting data – you may want to use several methods to allow you to cross-reference or triangulate your findings within your own study to provide added validity.

Observations

You may want to make observations as part of your data gathering (see Chapter 16) – for example, to study a physical setting, a group, an individual or an event. You need to think about how you will position yourself to make your observation, both physically and meta-phorically, depending on how involved you want to be with what you are observing. There are degrees of participation in observational approaches: At one end of the scale is the detached observer behind a two-way mirror; at the other end is the participant observer chatting to the children, being involved in what they are doing and making notes or record-ings alongside (Podmore & Luff, 2012). You may want to be somewhere in between. The tools for observation can be as simple as pencil and paper, but more sophisticated recording technology may enable you (with permission) to make a permanent record that you can return to repeatedly as your study progresses.

Interviews

Interviews depend for their success on achieving a rapport between interviewer and interviewee – quick-fire questions without any personal dimension are unlikely to yield any more than a postal questionnaire would. Face-to-face interviews and focus group interviews are usually more successful at getting people talking than telephone interviews. A comfort-able seat, a cup of tea and some small talk all help to put you and your adult interviewees at ease – if you are doing an interview by telephone these will have to be metaphorical. If you are interviewing children, a familiar room, a drink and some fruit might be appropriate. It may also help to introduce a toy or interesting object to get the conversation started. An interview requires much the same thoughtful preparation as a questionnaire (see below), but unlike a questionnaire it has the advantage of allowing the interviewer to ask for further clarification, to pursue an interesting line of thought or to probe into motives and feelings.

There are several types of interviews with various ways to carry them out:

- *Structured interviews* are really verbally administered questionnaires, useful for collect-ing specific information which can be quickly categorised but not at all useful for probing.
- *Semi-structured interviews* are based on written questions or topics for discussion. They allow for a good deal of exploration but minimise the risk of straying away from the central purpose of the investigation. The interviewer can note down responses briefly and write up fuller notes immediately after the interview. It is useful to make a tape recording of the interview to check against your field notes. Transcribing recordings is a slow process, and it may be better to transcribe verbatim only those parts of the tape that illustrate the argument most succinctly and those parts that do *not* fit with your expectations.
- *Unstructured interviews* are usually not scripted and generally lead to wide-ranging discus-sion, much like a conversation. They are rather difficult to control but are very good if you want to analyse people's perspectives to try to find out what they consider to be the impor-tant aspects of the topic under discussion. They can also be useful as preparatory interviews when you are trying to get a sense of the area you want to investigate.

At the end of each question or topic during semi-structured and non-structured inter-views, it is a good idea to check with your interviewee that you have correctly identified the main gist of the argument. You should keep all your field notes and recordings to allow for an independent check on the validity of your interpretations – as long as they are anonymous and you have permission from participants, you can include them in your appendices.

Questionnaires

Questionnaires are easy to send out and difficult to get back! They can also be expensive if posted. They are also difficult to get right. If you are sure that a questionnaire will answer your purposes better than any other method, you will need to think very hard about designing the questions.

There are many ways of asking questions, and the answers you get will depend partly on the way you frame the question (Bell, 2005; Cohen et al., 2011). As you write your questions, try to imagine the sort of answers you might get and how you will deal with the information they elicit.

- You could ask an *open-ended question*, such as 'How do you feel about the present management structure?' and then group your responses under headings.
- You could ask people to tick items in a *list of alternatives*, such as 'Which of the following apply to you?' and then summarise the number of responses in a chart or graph.
- You could provide a list of *categories*, such as 'Circle one of the following to show which best describes your job: professional, managerial, skilled, semi-skilled or manual.'
- You may want respondents to indicate a *rank order of preference*, such as 'Put the following in order of importance ...', or to use a *rating scale*, such as 'On a five point scale, rate how useful you found the management training session on child protection'. Both *rank order* and *rating scale* questions express mathematical relationships and require careful use.

As you write your questions, try them out on colleagues so that you cover as many eventualities as you can to iron out any difficulties in the design. Most importantly, ensure that your final draft questionnaire gets a thorough try-out before you use it for real. You will be surprised at how differently people can read the same straightforward question!

> **Focus on** *Writing questions for questionnaires*
>
> There are many pitfalls in writing questions for questionnaires. The following list might help you avoid some of them.
>
> *Ambiguity* – where respondents don't know exactly what you mean. For example, 'How many places do you have at your nursery?' The nursery may have 25 places in the morning, 25 in the afternoon, and different children attending full or part-time throughout the week. Do you want to know about full-time *and* part-time places or full-time equivalents? Or do you want to know how many different children attend each week?
>
> *Loose wording* – where *you* don't know exactly what you mean. For example, 'Are the recent government policies on young children helpful?' Helpful for whom? Which policies do you mean?

Insensitivity – where you fail to take account of your respondents' possible circumstances. For example, you ask someone over 50, 'Would you agree that the quality of the workforce is improving as more young people with better qualifications join?'

Double questions – where you expect people to answer both halves of the question in the same way. For example, 'Are you a regular visitor to nurseries and reception classes?' They could be a visitor to only one of these.

Hypothetical questions – where you ask an 'if' question that is likely to elicit a meaningless answer. For example, 'If you had a child in your class suffering from separation anxiety, what would you do?' They might do any one of a hundred things, depending on the child and the particular circumstances.

Leading questions – where you imply within the question the answer you expect to get. Sometimes these questions contain assumptions – where you think you know all the possible answers but in reality you don't. For example, 'Do you agree or disagree with the proposition that teenage mothers are irresponsible?' Some may be; others may not. Sometimes they contain presumptions, where you think that there is only one way of looking at something but there are many. For example, 'How far do you think poor results in your school are due to the number of children from single-parent households?' There may be no connection at all.

Overlapping categories – where you offer overlapping alternatives that can be misinterpreted. For example 'How many children do you look after aged birth to two, aged two to five, aged five to eight?' A child aged two and a half could go into either of the first two categories; a child of five and a half could go into either of the second two categories.

(Adapted from Bell, 2005: pp. 136–153)

Action research using logs and reflective diaries

Action research involves identifying a problem and making changes to improve practice. We saw this working in the case study around the 'reluctant reader' in Chapter 16. Action research is a cyclical process in which initial findings generate possibilities for change which are then acted upon and evaluated as a prelude to further investigation and monitoring (Denscombe, 2014). The beauty of using action research as the basis for your dissertation is that it can lead to the satisfaction of making a real difference. Logs and reflective diaries are often used as a data source in action research where practitioners want to observe the effect of changes in their work practices or to follow their own development or learning curve over a period of time.

One of my students had a son whose stammer was preventing him building good relations with teachers and classmates. She used her research project to find out all she could about the different theories and therapies associated with stammering. She also conducted interviews with a range of specialists. As her study progressed, she shared her new knowledge with her son. She kept a reflective log, charting her discussions with her son and reflecting on the changes in their relationship to each other and to the 'problem' of his stammer. By the end of the study, they both emerged with a new understanding of each other and new insights into the history of the treatment of stammering.

Analysing and interpreting data

As you collect your data – your questionnaires, your interviews, field notes, recordings, children's work, accounts or stories – try to see what is emerging. Be systematic; your purpose at this stage is to discover patterns and themes in the data. Begin your analysis by looking at surface features: sample size, number of responses, common concerns, opposing points of view and intriguing and unexpected outcomes. This will give you a sense of how to organise and categorise the data you have collected.

Raw quantitative data collected perhaps from checklists, question responses, coded observations, scores and test results are initially relatively easy to arrange by category. But numbers and statistics can be difficult to handle, particularly when the sample is small. Genuine patterns can be found only in large samples – think of comparing the average height of three people against the average height of 1000 people. You need to look with a critical eye at any figures you produce. In particular, you need to distinguish between *correlation* (a link between two or more factors that may be just chance) and *causation* (proof that one factor is linked to another by *cause* and effect). Many things can be linked or *correlated* by chance without being in any way causally related. For example, we might find that Key Stage 1 maths results in a school show that boys are lagging behind girls. Does this mean girls are better than boys at maths? Or could it be explained by random chance? Does it mean that this *particular* cohort of girls is better at maths than this particular cohort of boys? What might the result be if the test was replicated with another year group? It is tempting to make claims for quantitative data which are unsupported by deeper analysis.

Qualitative data, on the other hand, is bulky and difficult to manage. It is worth spending time at the outset to find a sorting system that works best for you. You might use grids for interview responses, highlighter pens for transcripts, line numbering for interview data, time indications for recordings, charts to map the ebb and flow of dialogue and/or piles and heaps of children's drawings arranged around themes – anything that imposes order on chaos! Quantitative data can be made more manageable by summarising, coding, clustering like with like and listing any inconsistencies or unexpected results in separate categories. Gradually, themes will emerge that enable you to make a tentative interpretation that you can then compare with published sources to explore whether your results corroborate or contradict the findings of other people in the field.

Checklist for analysing and interpreting your findings

- *Sample size*: How many people did you ask to take part?
- *Achieved sample*: How many people actually took part?
- *Response rates*: How many people answered each question?
- *Patterns*: What are the most frequent and least frequent features?
- *Similarities and differences*: Are there any differences or similarities? Are they related to any variables relevant to your research question – age, gender, ethnicity, attitude, likes and dislikes?
- *Clusters*: Can you usefully group responses together under a category?

- *Themes*: Are there common or contrasting themes running through the data?
- *Data that doesn't fit*: Are there maverick responses? Remember that negative data is still data and worthy of comment, because what is not there, or doesn't fit, can be revealing.
- *Dominant perspectives*: Is there any evidence to show that your respondents subscribe to particular views that might account for their responses? Are there any counter-examples to help define the limits of your developing theory?
- *Testing propositions*: Can you test the strength of evidence for your proposition/hypothesis/ research question by collecting quotes, examples or figures that illustrate or fail to illustrate it? (Remember that your job is to provide a *fair* summary of your findings, not to sell your proposition or to talk it up to confirm it.)
- *Checking your interpretations*: Can you check your interpretations with other viewpoints? Remember that social scientists test evidence through triangulation –interrogating their data from at least two other viewpoints or through three techniques of investigation.

The credibility or validity of your interpretations depends on your honesty in accurately representing the data you have collected. Your analysis will seem more authentic if you can illustrate your interpretations with strong evidence from your raw data – graphs and charts, verbatim quotations, detailed descriptions of events as they were recorded in the field, photographs, children's drawings and so on – to give a sense of the real voices of the children and adults you have studied.

Drawing conclusions and making recommendations

Your interpretation will rest on your understanding of the underlying patterns revealed through your analysis. Small-scale research studies are unlikely to produce conclusions that can be applied more widely to society at large; the purpose is more often to cast light on a quite specific situation, event, child or relationship. Students producing quantitative data in their investigations are sometimes tempted to make grand claims for their research with liberal sprinklings of percentages and pie charts to show their findings. By all means, present your data in the form of a table or graph, but be very clear to point out if the numbers involved are small and the effects that you are describing are specific to your study. Your conclusions should relate to the title and purpose of your study and should arise out of the evidence presented in your findings. They should set your research into the wider context of your reading by cross-referencing with your literature review and analysis. Any recommendations you make need to be feasible and appropriate.

Writing up

Writing up can be fun; it is very satisfying to bring all that work and information neatly together in a spiral binding. But it can also be lonely and demoralising because it takes such a long time. Keep talking to friends and colleagues; understand that you will be your own fiercest critic; and share your anxieties with other people who know how hard it is to write reports. Try reading Stephen King's *On Writing* (2000) if you get stuck. It is entertaining, and you will see that the same principles apply to all writing, whether you are producing horror books or research dissertations.

Here are a few tips that may help the process along:

- Write a plan, but don't expect to stick to it slavishly.
- Don't procrastinate; just keep writing – at least you will have something to work on as the deadline approaches.
- Use simple words to convey complex ideas in a straightforward way.
- Keep paragraphs short.
- Use plenty of subheadings.
- Use bullets, diagrams and other devices for clarity.
- Expect to rewrite and reorder, and rewrite and reorder again (we all do it).
- Read and reread each draft, taking out flowery prose and unnecessary words (Stephen King says that a second draft is equivalent to a first draft minus 10 per cent).
- Make sure you have referenced work fully and correctly, including page numbers for direct quotes (check your own institution's referencing guidelines – they all differ slightly).
- Take breaks and have little treats to keep morale up!

Once you are satisfied that everything is present and correct, you are finally ready to write an abstract. Bring everything together in a few succinct sentences, summarising what you wanted to find out, how you went about it and what you discovered. And then breathe a sigh of relief!

Plagiarism and pitfalls

Honesty is the key to writing a decent research report: honesty with the participants, honesty with the data and honesty with oneself. The two major crimes of research are fabricating evidence and plagiarising the words of others. Fabricating evidence means making up data or making claims that do not stand up to scrutiny. Plagiarising means using other people's ideas or words without acknowledging the source – whether that source is a book, the Internet or any other medium. Both these misdemeanours can, and do, result in failed degrees and ruined reputations.

And finally...

Don't worry if your research hasn't added to the great store of human knowledge – it is more important that you acted with integrity and wrote up your report with due regard for the difficulties and rewards that you encountered along the way. Lots of research is inconclusive, and many published research reports end with the words 'more research is needed...' As long as you have collected your evidence fairly and explored it thoroughly with due regard for the strengths and weaknesses of your methods and interpretations, you should have nothing to fear. Good luck!

Checklist for writing up a research report

The following checklist was given to Early Childhood Studies undergraduates for an 8000-word dissertation.

- *Title page*: a title that captures the spirit of your research question, name/identity number, date and institution.
- *Acknowledgements*: a courtesy page to thank all the participants and the other people who have provided support during the project.
- *Abstract*: a one-page summary, in italics, of your research topic, your methods and the main findings.
- *Contents*: main section headings with page numbers.
- *Introduction*: 500–1000 words explaining what sparked your interest in your investigation, why it is topical and why it is important.
- *Literature review*: 1000–2000 words describing the main arguments around the topic and the evidence for each.
- *Methodology*: 1000–2000 words explaining *why* you chose the methodological approach and outlining strengths and limitations for exploring your research question.
- *Findings*: use as many words as it takes to present the results of your investigations. You might include charts and summaries of questionnaire responses, verbatim illustrative quotes from observations, interviews, documentary evidence, logs and reflective diaries.
- *Discussion/analysis*: 2000–3000 words explaining what your findings show and how they relate to previous studies covered in the literature review.
- *Conclusions*: 500–1000 words showing the implications of your study for further thinking and the recommendations that you would make in light of your findings.
- *References*: a list of sources *directly referred to* in your report.
- *Appendices*: these should be numbered; include your ethics protocol, permissions, any letters sent out to participants, raw scores and results, transcripts, copies of questionnaires or interview schedules, documentary evidence, logs, reflective diaries.

Summary

- Your research project should be a systematic enquiry which tries to make explicit the factors underlying the topic you are investigating; it should go beyond the descriptive and provide analysis related to your reading.
- Choose a topic that will maintain your interest over a sustained period and that will extend your professional practice.
- Let your research question gradually emerge as you read about your topic; refine it to fit with your time and resources.
- Use your literature review to discover the major positions around your topic.
- Keep a fully referenced record of your sources, including page numbers of direct quotations.
- Identify a target group or sample that is manageable and accessible.
- Seek permission from the top when you negotiate access.
- Be ethically circumspect and sensitive; get consent from all participants.

■ Choose research methods that fit your purpose, and use more than one method or source to allow for triangulation of data to give your findings credibility.

■ Analyse data by looking for patterns, differences and similarities. Check whether your data supports or contradicts the published findings from other studies referred to in your literature review.

■ Don't make grandiose claims for your findings – keep them in perspective.

■ Be honest – plagiarism and fabrication of data may have uncomfortable repercussions.

■ Keep writing – it takes longer than you think!

Topics for further discussion

1 Think about recent TV and newspaper reports concerned with children. What topics are trending? Which might be suitable for a small-scale research study?

2 In your setting, you notice that girls are spending less time on computers than boys. How could you find out why?

3 You have noticed that playground helpers are reluctant to let children play out of sight in the den at the far side of the play area. The den is generally an underused and dead space. You think that children can benefit from playing in the den. How could you design an action research programme to allay adult fears and to make the den a usable space?

Assignments

1 Choose an article related to your research question. What is the underlying research paradigm? Is it positivist or interpretive or a mixture of both? What methods did the researchers use to collect their data? Did the researchers adequately address any relevant ethical questions? How was the data analysed? Did you find the conclusions convincing?

2 Think about a work practice that puzzles, pleases or annoys you. It could be something from your workplace or from your place of study. How could you explore it using action research to change the practice? How can you make sure that your investigation is practical, brings about change, involves everyone concerned and is monitored on a cyclical basis?

3 Find out more about research with children. What is the current thinking about the ethics of children's involvement in the research process? Think about the power relations between researcher and researched. How do researchers adapt their methods to make children's participation authentic?

Further reading

Bell, J. (2005) *Doing Your Research Project: A Guide For First-Time Researchers in Education and Social* Science (4th edn). Buckingham: Open University Press. This is straightforward and much loved by students.

Bryman, A. (2012) *Social Research Methods.* Oxford: Oxford University Press. This provides a comprehensive overview of all kinds of research in the social sciences.

MacNaughton, G. and Hughes, P. (2009) *Doing Action Research in Early Childhood Studies: a step by step guide*. Maidenhead: Open University Press/McGraw-Hill Education. This focuses specifically on research that can bring about change for young children.

Christensen, P. and James, A. (eds) (2008) *Research with Children: Perspectives and Practices* (2nd edn). Abingdon: Routledge.

Roberts-Holmes, G. (2011) *Doing Your Early Years Research Project: A Step-By-Step Guide* (2nd edn). London: Paul Chapman. Highly recommended by many of my previous students.

Useful websites

An American organisation, Child Trends, has an easy to use data bank that can be searched by keyword, author or date to let you access international sources of 'big data' in the social sciences. It also has a blog, *Trend Lines*, which lets you see what is currently 'trending' in childhood research at **www.childtrends.org**.

References

Bell, J. (2005) *Doing Your Research Project: A Guide For First-Time Researchers in Education and Social Science* (4th edn) (pp. 136–153). Buckingham: Open University Press

British Psychological Society (1997) *Code of Conduct, Ethical Principles and Guidelines. Leicester: British Psychological Society*

Bryman, A. (2008) *Social Research Methods* (3rd edn). Oxford: Oxford University Press

Bryman, A. (2012) *Social Research Methods* (4th edn). Oxford: Oxford University Press

Christensen, P. and James, A. (eds) (2008) *Research with Children: Perspectives and Practices* (2nd edn). Abingdon: Routledge

Cohen, L., Manion, L. and Morrison, K. (2011) Research Methods in Education (7th edn). Abingdon: Routledge

Denscombe, M. (2014) *The Good Research Guide for Small-Scale Social Research Projects* (5th edn). Maidenhead and New York: Open University Press

EECERA (European Early Childhood Education Research Association) (2014) *Ethical Code for Early Childhood Researchers: version 1.0.* www.becera.org.uk/docs/EECERA_Ethical_Code.pdf. Accessed 30 December 2016

Fraser, S., Lewis, V., Ding, S., Kellett, M. and Robinson, C. (eds) (2004) *Doing Research with Children and Young People*. London: Sage

King, S. (2000) *On Writing: A memoir of the craft*. London: Hodder and Stoughton

MacNaughton, G. and Hughes, P. (2009) *Doing Action Research in Early Childhood Studies: a step by step guide*. Maidenhead: Open University Press/McGraw-Hill Education

Podmore, V.N. and Luff, P. (2012) *Observation: Origins and Approaches in Early Childhood*. Maidenhead: Open University Press/McGraw-Hill Education

Roberts-Holmes, G. (2011) *Doing Your Early Years Research Project: A Step-By-Step Guide* (2nd edn). London: Paul Chapman

Index